'The world of disasters is changing, creating deep challenges for practitioners and academics alike. A truly interdisciplinary group of disaster researchers have joined perspectives from as far afield as theology and economics, history and anthropology, risk and law. This intriguing book puts Copenhagen on the map as a new center for disaster research. Warmly recommended!'

– Arjen Boin, Professor of Public Institutions and Governance,
Leiden University, The Netherlands

'With an explicitly multidisciplinary approach, this excellent new book on disasters brings together the fields of anthropology, law, communication, theology, and politics into a single place. Combining detailed case studies of catastrophes with illuminating theory, this internationally-focused volume will be of service to researchers and graduate students alike.'

– Daniel P. Aldrich, Professor of Political Science,
Northeastern University, USA

'Congratulations to the authors and editors for bringing together so many topics in relation to disasters – topics which require more interaction and cross-over. This book breaks through disciplinary boundaries, demonstrating the need to work together and providing an inspiration to do so.'

– Dr. Ilan Kelman, Institute for Risk and Disaster Reduction,
University College London, UK

'This timely and wide-ranging volume provides an excellent overview of disaster and accident research from a multidisciplinary perspective. The authors demonstrate a thorough understanding of the theoretical and empirical literature and illustrate their points through the use of case studies. Recommended for everyone who wants to know about where the field of disaster research has been and where it is going.'

– Kathleen Tierney, Professor of Sociology and Director of the Natural
Hazards Center, University of Colorado Boulder, USA

T0331270

Disaster Research

Given the tendency of books on disasters to predominantly focus on strong geophysical or descriptive perspectives and in-depth accounts of particular catastrophes, *Disaster Research* provides a much-needed multidisciplinary perspective of the area.

This book is structured thematically around key approaches to disaster research from a range of different, but often complementary academic disciplines. Each chapter presents distinct approaches to disaster research anchored in a particular discipline; ranging from the law of disasters and disaster historiography to disaster politics and anthropology of disaster. The methodological and theoretical contributions underlining a specific approach to disasters are discussed and illustrative empirical cases are examined that support and further inform the proposed approach to disaster research.

The book thus provides unique insights into fourteen state-of-the-art disciplinary approaches to the understanding of disasters. The theoretical discussions as well as the diverse range of disaster cases should be of interest to both postgraduate and undergraduate students, as well as academics, researchers and policy-makers.

Rasmus Dahlberg is PhD Fellow and Co-Founder of Copenhagen Center for Disaster Research, University of Copenhagen, Denmark.

Olivier Rubin is Associate Professor of Disasters and Global Politics, Department of Society and Globalization, Roskilde University, Denmark.

Morten Thanning Vendelø is Associate Professor and Co-Founder of Copenhagen Center for Disaster Research, Copenhagen Business School, Denmark.

Routledge Humanitarian Studies Series

Series editors: Alex de Waal and Dorothea Hilhorst

Editorial Board: Mihir Bhatt, Dennis Dijkzeul, Wendy Fenton, Kirsten Johnson, Julia Streets, Peter Walker

The Routledge Humanitarian Studies series in collaboration with the International Humanitarian Studies Association (IHSA) takes a comprehensive approach to the growing field of expertise that is humanitarian studies. This field is concerned with humanitarian crises caused by natural disaster, conflict or political instability and deals with the study of how humanitarian crises evolve, how they affect people and their institutions and societies, and the responses they trigger.

We invite book proposals that address, amongst other topics, questions of aid delivery, institutional aspects of service provision, the dynamics of rebel wars, state building after war, the international architecture of peacekeeping, the ways in which ordinary people continue to make a living throughout crises and the effect of crises on gender relations.

This interdisciplinary series draws on and is relevant to a range of disciplines, including development studies, international relations, international law, anthropology, peace and conflict studies, public health and migration studies.

Disaster, Conflict and Society in Crises
Everyday politics of crisis response
Edited by Dorothea Hilhorst

Human Security and Natural Disasters
Edited by Christopher Hobson, Paul Bacon and Robin Cameron

Human Security and Japan's Triple Disaster
Responding to the 2011 earthquake, tsunami and Fukushima nuclear crisis
Edited by Paul Bacon and Christopher Hobson

The Paradoxes of Aid Work
Passionate professionals
Silke Roth

Disaster Research
Multidisciplinary and international perspectives
Edited by Rasmus Dahlberg, Olivier Rubin and Morten Thanning Vendelø

Disaster Research

Multidisciplinary and international perspectives

Edited by
Rasmus Dahlberg,
Olivier Rubin and
Morten Thanning Vendelø

Routledge
Taylor & Francis Group

LONDON AND NEW YORK

First published 2016 by Routledge

2 Park Square, Milton Park, Abingdon, Oxon OX14 4RN
711 Third Avenue, New York, NY 10017, USA

Routledge is an imprint of the Taylor & Francis Group, an informa business

First issued in paperback 2017

British Library Cataloguing-in-Publication Data
A catalogue record for this book is available from the British Library

Library of Congress Cataloging-in-Publication Data
Disaster research : multidisciplinary and international perspectives /
edited by Rasmus Dahlberg, Oliver Rubin and Morten Thanning Vendelø
    pages cm
    1. Disasters – Research. 2. Disaster relief – Research. 3. Disasters –
    Psychological aspects. I. Dahlberg, Rasmus, editor. II. Rubin, Oliver,
    editor. III. Vendelø, Morten Thanning, 1976– editor.
    HV553.D5677 2016
    363.34072–dc23   2015011525

ISBN: 978-1-138-85066-8 (hbk)
ISBN: 978-1-138-05161-4 (pbk)

Typeset in Baskerville
by HWA Text and Data Management, London

Contents

Contributors

Kristoffer Albris is a PhD fellow at the Department of Anthropology, University of Copenhagen. He has previously done fieldwork in Fiji on the relations between development expertise and disaster risk reduction. His current doctoral research focuses on civic responses to floods in Dresden, Germany. He is part of the interdisciplinary research programme Changing Disasters at the University of Copenhagen.

Nina Blom Andersen is an associate professor at Roskilde University at the Communication Program. She has been involved in research concerning disasters, emergence management and social crisis since 2004. Her current research focuses on how people engage in questions of disaster prevention and how they involve themselves and interact with authorities and the media when disasters occur. She is the coordinator of the Research Network of Disaster, Conflict and Social Crisis under the European Sociological Association.

Peter Berliner is a professor of community psychology at the University of Aarhus, Denmark; Professor of Social Work, Ilisimatusarfik (Greenland University); Founder of the University of Copenhagen Centre for Multi-Ethnic Traumatic Stress Research and Practice and co-founder of the Master of Disaster Management programme, University of Copenhagen and Lund University. He has more than thirty years' experience with practical interventions and research in zones of conflicts and disasters – with the UN, the Red Cross, Save the Children, the Rehabilitation Centre for Torture Survivors (RCT) and in locally planned and implemented community programmes of social resilience.

Erik Bækkeskov is an assistant professor in the Section for Health Services Research at the University of Copenhagen's Department of Public Health. He holds a PhD in political science from the University of California, Berkeley. His research explores the intersection of crisis management, public health and politics, and decision-making in public administration.

Maurizio Catino is a professor in the Department of Sociology and Social Research at the University of Milan-Bicocca, Italy, and visiting scholar in the Department of Sociology at New York University. He studies sociology of organization with a primary focus on the dark side of organizations: human error and organizational accidents, organizational myopia and organized crime. He has published several articles on learning from organizational errors and the problem of blame culture, medical error and defensive medicine, the logics of inquiry in case of disasters, and mafia organizations.

Rasmus Dahlberg is a PhD fellow at the Copenhagen Center for Disaster Research and with the Danish Emergency Management Agency. His MA is in history, and he has lectured and written extensively on resilience, safety culture, human factors and technological disasters in the 20th century. He investigates unpredictability, uncertainty and resilience in emergency and risk thinking at the incident and national level as well as extreme emerging threats to safety in the Arctic.

Alessia Bianco Dolino holds a PhD in Applied Sociology and Methodology of Social Science, obtained at the University of Milan-Bicocca. Her research interests include high reliability organizations, organizational accidents, risk management and risk regulation.

Peter Elsass is a professor of Clinical Psychology at the University of Copenhagen. He holds a DMSc in neuropsychology, has been affiliated with the Rehabilitation Center for Torture Survivors in Copenhagen and has done research concerning the process and outcome of psychotherapeutic treatment as well as coordinated mental health activities in Kosovo for WHO. His research includes studies in neuropsychology, cultural psychology and clinical psychology.

Peter Fisker is a PhD fellow at the University of Copenhagen, enrolled under the cross-faculty programme Changing Disasters. He has a background as a consultant working for the World Bank and holds a master's degree in economics. His current research focuses on the broader impacts of disasters on socioeconomic development, including studies of the global cost of earthquakes and droughts as well as case studies on adaptation strategies and disaster response coordination.

Niels H. Gregersen is a professor of systematic theology at the University of Copenhagen and a co-founder of the Changing Disasters programme. His primary research fields are contemporary theology and science and religion. He has published widely on the intersection of science and religion, complexity and nature and theology.

Henrik Hansen is a professor at the Department of Economics, University of Copenhagen. His research interests are within development economics and applied econometrics. Starting as a time-series econometrician he has gradually moved into development economics focusing on issues of economic growth, foreign aid and poverty. Present research interests include the long-run impact of disasters on economic development. He is a member of the Development Economics Research Group and active in the Copenhagen Center for Disaster Research.

Silja Henderson holds an MSc in psychology and a PhD in disaster psychology. Silja has had an interest in psychological trauma, cross-cultural issues and vulnerable groups throughout her academic life. She has volunteered in Bolivia, worked on research projects to enhance community well-being in Greenland and the familial well-being of traumatized refugees in Denmark, and analysed qualitative and quantitative data from the International Red Cross's psychosocial interventions in South-East Asia after the 2004 tsunami, with the purpose of establishing evidence and recommendations for post-disaster mental health and psychosocial interventions.

Isak Winkel Holm is a professor of comparative literature at the University of Copenhagen and a co-founder of the excellence research project Changing Disasters, University of Copenhagen. His research fields cover disaster imagination, literary theory, Greek tragedy, Franz Kafka and Søren Kierkegaard.

Lynn Horton is an associate professor of sociology and director of the MA in International Studies programme at Chapman University. Her areas of research interest include Latin America and the Caribbean, gender, social movements and qualitative research methods.

Peer Illner is a PhD fellow at the Copenhagen Center for Disaster Research and a member of the Changing Disasters programme. He holds an MA in Visual Culture from Goldsmiths College, University of London. His research focuses on the projective dimension of disaster studies and the way that disasters open up vistas of the future, and publishes widely on issues connecting disasters with politics and aesthetics.

Kristian Cedervall Lauta is an Assistant Professor at the Faculty of Law, University of Copenhagen. He co-heads the interdisciplinary research project Changing Disasters, and is among the founding members of the Copenhagen Center for Disaster Research. His research regards the intersection between law and disasters, and his latest book *Disaster Law* (2014) sets out to explain how, and why, a field of disaster law has emerged.

John Rand is a professor at the Department of Economics, University of Copenhagen. His main research areas are within development economics, in particular understanding the importance of enterprise dynamics for guiding industrial policy. Recently, his research has also focused on the economic impacts of large-scale natural disasters with a special attention to the mechanisms through which rare events influence established institutional settings in the longer run. He is a member of the Development Economics Research Group and the Copenhagen Center for Disaster Research.

Olivier Rubin is an associate professor of disasters and global politics. He has specialized in investigating the political dimensions of natural disasters and famine and is currently affiliated with Roskilde University at the Department of Society and Globalization. Rubin is not choosy when it comes to types of disasters, and his publications include analyses of climate-induced flooding in Vietnam, famines in India and Africa, disaster adaptation in Latin America, global flu pandemic responses and even zombie plagues. His present primary regional interests are in South-East and South Asia.

Birgitte Refslund Sørensen is an associate professor at the Department of Anthropology, University of Copenhagen. She has conducted extensive field research in Sri Lanka, focusing primarily on processes of displacement, resettlement and social reconstruction in relation to infrastructure development and armed conflict, as well as on the politics of humanitarian interventions. Her current research concerns Danish soldiers' homecoming, social reintegration and non-military careers, including in the security, offshore and disaster sectors.

Morten Thanning Vendelø, PhD, is an associate professor at the Department of Organization, Copenhagen Business School, a member of the school's board of directors, and a co-founder of the Copenhagen Center for Disaster Research (COPE). His research interests include breakdown and recreation of meaning in organizations, crowd safety management, improvisation and learning in organizations, and sensemaking and sensegiving in organizations. His research is published in books and journals such as *Creativity and Innovation Management, International Studies of Management and Organization* and *Management Learning*.

Foreword

Unbeknownst to us at the time, the seed for this volume was actually planted some years ago when we, together with a number of other scholars, were asked to contribute with 'multidisciplinary perspectives' to the Master of Disaster Management program at the University of Copenhagen. There we encountered the often chaotic, at times wearisome, but always extremely rewarding process of multidisciplinary teaching. We gained tremendously from this activity. Above all, it broadened our academic horizons and nurtured a profound appreciation for other disciplinary contributions to the field of disaster research. Back then, we searched in vain for an academic book that provides a multidisciplinary overview of disaster research. At that time, however, as obvious as it might seem in retrospect, we did not come up with the idea to compile such book ourselves. We were all three too stuck in our own disciplinary worlds at different universities.

That changed with the establishment of COPE (Copenhagen Center for Disaster Research) in December 2012. COPE is run as a joint venture between the University of Copenhagen and the Copenhagen Business School, and hosts international disaster researchers and projects from all disciplines. It proved to be a great facilitator for collaboration between scholars approaching disasters from very different angles. A number of the contributors to this volume have been associated with COPE in its first years, and many of the ideas and perspectives presented in the chapters have been discussed at COPE workshops and seminars. The book was conceived at one such seminar two years ago, where a historian, an organizational theorist and a political scientist met up at the subsequent social venue – a crammed bar in the centre of Copenhagen – and started discussing how to best convey to a larger audience the great benefits of multidisciplinary approaches to disaster research. The rest, of course, is history, but only because the Routledge Humanitarian Studies series has courteously agreed to publish the manuscript. We wish to thank the two anonymous reviewers for some constructive and encouraging remarks to the manuscript. Our excellent editor Khanam Virjee provided the best advice of all: that we should allow the book to stand as an edited research monograph rather than turning it into a textbook. And our editorial assistant, Margaret Farrelly, generously gave us, above anything else, her patience.

We also wish to thank colleagues, visiting scholars and students associated with COPE for fruitful discussions of drafts and ideas during the work on this volume. Rasmus Dahlberg especially thanks Suhella Tulsiani and Peter Kjær Mackie Jensen, Department of Public Health, University of Copenhagen, and Per Grau Møller, Department of History at the University of Southern Denmark, for useful comments to his chapter. Morten Thanning Vendelø would like to thank Claus Rerup, Ivey Business School, University of Western Ontario, for inspiring comments to his chapter. Olivier Rubin wishes to thank a great number of colleagues at the Department of Society and Globalization, Roskilde University, for their many constructive comments and suggestions. While too numerous to mention by name, allow me to extent my heartfelt appreciation collectively. Our student assistant Helene von Ahnen A.S. Haugaard contributed with editorial assistance and many valuable comments.

Money does not make the world go round but it is definitely nice to have in research. Olivier Rubin would like to thank the Danish Research Council for providing the funds that allowed for the luxury of putting everything else aside for a full six months while authoring and compiling this book. Rasmus Dahlberg thanks the Danish Emergency Management Agency and the Institute for Sustainability Studies at the University of Iceland for funding and hosting him during the editorial process.

Rasmus Dahlberg, Olivier Rubin and Morten Thanning Vendelø
Copenhagen, March 2015

1 Disaster research

An introduction

Rasmus Dahlberg, Olivier Rubin and Morten Thanning Vendelø

It was all of a sudden – a single devastating blast;
then the sound as of the crashing of a thousand chandeliers.
Men and women cowered under the shower of debris and glass.
There was one awful moment when hearts sank,
and breaths were held.

(Samuel Henry Prince, *Catastrophe and Social Change*, 1920)

Introduction

Disasters can be frightening, devastating phenomena that change the lives of persons, the status of societies, and the fates of nations in mere hours, minutes, or even seconds. Sometimes catastrophic change is slow and almost invisible, but just as lethal and costly, if not more so, as sudden disastrous events. As individuals and as communities we try to avoid disasters if possible – and at the same time we prepare for the inevitable. We strive for robustness and resilience and attempt to avoid vulnerability and weakness. Furthermore, we continuously try to improve our knowledge and understanding of disasters in order to 'build back better'.

Disasters, however, are also fascinating phenomena that for millennia have prompted scholars, clergy and thinkers to contemplate their causes and effects. In the ancient world they asked if volcanic eruptions or earthquakes were signs of the gods' wrath, or perhaps caused by unfortunate constellations of the stars. They speculated if future disasters could be mitigated by offerings, or if it required more prayers, less indulgence, or more donations in the temple. Emperor Nero claimed it was a sign of divine favour, when the theatre he was performing in during the AD 64 Campania earthquake collapsed immediately *after* the audience had left (Jashemski and Meyer 2002: 35). More recently, scholars have looked into how the scientific revolution in the 16th, 17th and 18th centuries changed the interpretations of disastrous events, as well as if the great Lisbon earthquake of 1755 really was the first 'modern disaster', as framed by Kant, Voltaire and Rousseau in a new scientific and secular discourse (Dynes 2000). Others again have focused on how inventions of the 20th century, such as nuclear weapons and atomic energy, challenged the classic understanding of disasters as having natural causes (Sagan 1995). Presently, attention is being paid to what the capsizing of the

Costa Concordia or the triple disaster at the Fukushima Daiichi nuclear plant might tell us about perceptions of risk and safety, and about the Italian and Japanese legal systems.

Definitions of *disasters, accidents* and *catastrophes* are plentiful and diverse. Ask a firefighter what she thinks a disaster is, and she'll probably tell you that it is an incident that cannot be managed with the available resources. Ask a sociologist and he might say it is a breakdown of meaning among society's entities. Ask an engineer and she will think of new ways to build more resilient structures. Disaster and catastrophe are contested concepts that most people will have some kind of notion of, but closer examination often reveals these terms to be subject to political struggle regarding the right to add content to them, and interpret their meaning. We will not engage in the semantic exercise of how to define disasters as this issue has been addressed by others, for example, Perry (2007) who provides an excellent overview. Instead, we suggest that the many understandings attached to disasters by a society inform us more about that particular society itself, than about the disaster – if the two can be separated at all. Following this argument, disaster research can be said to represent a broad collection of scientific approaches to understanding the functions of contemporary and historical societies, and how they change over time, by looking at them through the lens of disasters. The subtitle of this volume indicates that we advocate for such a multi-disciplinary approach to the study of disasters, acknowledging that they constitute hybrid phenomena which need to be examined through a multitude of analytical perspectives.

We hope the present volume will contribute to the field by offering an array of approaches and perspectives to disaster research. While we have strived to cover a broad spectrum of disciplines, it has never been our aim to provide an exhaustive overview of approaches to disaster research. Our own expertise lies within the social sciences, and therefore, we have opted not to venture too far outside this field.

In this introduction we provide a brief overview of disaster research historiography as well as a contextualization of this volume in the current trends of the field of disaster research. We then outline the structure of this volume and provide summaries of each of its chapters. While the multi-disciplinary character of the volume may impel our readers to engage in a selective reading of the chapters based on their specific interests, we strongly urge them to keep an open mind and to seize the opportunity to be inspired by analytical approaches and discussions from less familiar disciplines. In the epilogue we offer a brief discussion of what the contributions in this volume tell us about the present state of the field of disaster research.

Disaster research in the literature

Modern disaster research was born in the early hours of 6 December 1917 in Halifax, Nova Scotia, shortly after two ships collided in the Narrows connecting the Upper Halifax Harbor with the Bedford Basin. One of the ships was loaded with massive amounts of explosives, ammunition and fuel, and the blast from the collision sent lethal heat and shock waves through the city of Halifax. Nearly 2,000 people died from the explosion, perhaps as many as 1,600 in the initial blast. 9,000 of Halifax's inhabitants were injured, while about 6,000 found themselves homeless after the explosion had destroyed or damaged more than 10,000 homes (Howell and Ruffman 1994; Kitz 2008). The Halifax explosion of 1917 was the most powerful man-made release of energy in history, prior to the detonation of the first atomic bombs in 1945. The explosion impacted the city and its inhabitants enormously – and it also sparked an academic and structured approach to disaster research that came to influence especially sociology in the 20th century. Less than a year and a half after the disaster, Samuel Henry Prince, a priest and assistant rector at St Paul's Church in Halifax, enrolled at the department of sociology at Columbia University to write a PhD on 'Catastrophe and social change', based partly on his own experiences from that dreadful morning. Prince's main interest was the 'fluidity' or 'flux' of crisis and catastrophe, as it brought about social change which could be investigated scientifically. His doctoral thesis became the first scientific piece of work to focus on the sociological effects of disaster, and – even if parts of his empirical evidence today seem questionable and his theories are outdated – he is still quoted and regarded as 'the founding father' of disaster sociology (Scanlon 1988; Quarantelli 1998). Prince described phenomena such as emergent organizations in times of crisis long before it was common practice, but his contribution to the field of disaster research has become somewhat forgotten over time (Scanlon 1988). More lasting impact was achieved by Lowell J. Carr, with his paper 'Disaster and the sequence-pattern concept of social change' (1932), in which he divided catastrophes into three discrete periods: (i) the *preliminary or prodromal period* during which the 'forces which are to cause the ultimate collapse are getting under way'; (ii) the *dislocation and disorganization phase* where the 'catastrophe is known by its works'; (iii) the *readjustment and reorganization phase* characterized by a 'badly shaken' community fighting its way back (1932: 209).

Carr's sequence pattern constitutes an early precursor to the emergency management cycle model encompassing mitigation, preparedness, response and recovery. This model did not surface until the National Governor's Association report in 1979 (Neal 1997; Baird 2010), but this clear-cut integrated approach to disaster management has since gained support from both emergency managers and disaster researchers worldwide, while many of the contributors to this volume also apply it as a fundamental framework for understanding disasters and emergencies.

Another important contribution of Carr's 1932 paper is his notion that it is 'the collapse of the cultural protections that constitutes the disaster' – a radical position for his time, which feeds into the still ongoing discussion of natural vs. man-made disasters (Bankoff 2010). Some scholars (Evans and Reid 2014) go even further and conceptualize a new paradigm: the *Anthropocene*, in which Man is Man's greatest enemy.

Building on the works of Prince and others, Carr divided disasters into (at least) four different types: (i) *instantaneous-diffused* with sudden impact on a large community (like the Halifax explosion); (ii) *instantaneous-focalized* with sudden impact on an isolated part of a community (e.g. an explosion at a school); (iii*)* *progressive-diffused* with slow onset that influence a large community (like floods and hurricanes); (iv) *progressive-focalized* with slow onset influencing an isolated community (e.g. the sinking of the *Titanic*) (1932: 208).

While Carr's division between instantaneous (fast) and progressive (slow) disasters was instrumental for defining disaster throughout a large part of the 20th century, it has been almost completely abandoned by contemporary disaster researchers, acknowledging that '[a]ll disasters are slow-onset' (Kelman 2014) in the sense that they are social (not environmental) phenomena, with multiple, complex causes, requiring a broad outlook and a focus on vulnerability rather than trigger mechanisms and immediate consequences.

Carr also emphasized the need to identify 'initiating events' based on observations of empirical data, not philosophical speculations about 'so-called necessary sequences'. His call for a focus on an initiating event was made even more explicit by the sociologist Charles Fritz who provided what became a classic definition of disaster in 1961:

> an event, concentrated in time and space, in which a society or a relatively self-sufficient subdivision of a society, undergoes severe danger and incurs such losses to its members and physical appurtenances that the social structure is disrupted and the fulfillment of all or some of the essential functions of society is prevented.
>
> (Fritz 1961: 655)

Around the time of Fritz's writing, disaster research was closely linked to the Cold War, and the threat of a nuclear war between what were then the two superpowers of the world – a kind of catastrophe where the *triggering event* may be intentional, but where the consequences could very well have resembled those of the Halifax explosion. Fritz's notion of an 'agent' external to the society under investigation also resonated with the Cold War context. The leading research environment, the Disaster Research Center (DRC), was founded at Ohio State University in 1963 by Enrico L. Quarantelli, Russell Dynes and others, who during the second half of the 20th century rose to become the heirs of Prince, Carr and Fritz. DRC moved to the University of Delaware in 1985 where it is still located. The Natural Hazards Center, founded in 1976 at the University of Colorado in Boulder, has also been an important epicentre of disaster research. Both centres subscribe to an interdisciplinary approach to the topic, although traditionally with a strong sociological bias.

A number of scholars have reviewed the disaster research literature, most recently Lindell (2013), and therefore, we limit our review to a short presentation of a selected set of important works published in the field of disaster research. Modifying Carr's sequence-pattern concept of social change, Powell (1954) described no fewer than eight disaster phases (*pre-disaster, warning, threat, impact, inventory, rescue, remedy* and *recovery*) – a number later brought down to seven by Stoddard (1968). Inspired by Fritz's definition of disasters, Barton (1969) reviewed empirical studies of social organizations under stress, and laid a solid theoretical foundation for understanding and developing emergency social systems, while Dynes (1970) presented a number of theoretical tools within disaster research and emergency management that are still relevant. A comprehensive encyclopedic overview of disaster sociology, a quarter of a century after Fritz's seminal article, was provided by Drabek (1986). Around the turn of the millennium, disaster research became very focused on the concept of human and social *vulnerability* to natural hazards (Blaikie *et al.* 2004), a perspective that from 2005 onwards was challenged and to a certain degree replaced by *resilience* (Chandler 2014; Tierney 2014; Walker and Cooper 2011), even if the applicability of this concept to social systems is still debated and somewhat contested (Davidson 2010). Finally, over the last decade, the *Handbook of Disaster Research* (Rodríquez *et al.* 2006) has been considered the primary source of information and direction for emergency and disaster students, researchers and managers.

Disaster and emergency research has, since Prince observed the aftermath of the Halifax explosion in 1917, however evolved along two different, but related paths: (1) an academic tradition dominated by North American disaster sociologists (see e.g. Rodríguez *et al.* 2007) who discuss and develop theoretical understandings of concepts such as disaster, risk, vulnerability, etc.; and (2) a practical, empirically based tradition (see e.g. Drabek and Hoetmer 1991; Farazmand 2001; Coppola 2011) focusing on lessons learned from specific events, aimed at developing and refining tools, technologies and methods to mitigate future disasters.

The approach pursued in this volume is mostly in line with the academic tradition described above. Yet, it includes a much larger variety of academic perspectives than would ever be found in a volume published by North American disaster sociologists, and simultaneously it completely neglects lengthy academic discussions of concepts such as risk, disasters, vulnerability and resilience. Our aim has been to present a collection of relevant and useful theoretical frameworks, from a variety of different disciplines, as well as to provide examples of how these frameworks have been or can be applied to empirical cases.

The structure of this volume

This volume is structured thematically around key approaches to disaster research from different, but often complementary, academic disciplines. The aim is to present state-of-the-art approaches to disaster research, each anchored in the individual authors' disciplinary background. Hence, it has been a challenge to settle on an order of chapters in the volume, as no single discipline should carry more weight than the others, and no discipline naturally precedes others in a multidisciplinary disaster analysis. Still, there is no way around presenting the chapters in a sequential order. As a guiding principle, therefore, we have exploited the fortunate fact that the authors have chosen rather different styles and foci for their chapters. Although the individual chapters follow an overall structural template, the chapters also display enough variety to allow for some categorization; something which to a great extent is caused by the paradigmatic traditions and discourses inherent in each discipline. The chapter on law, for instance, is concise, with ample use of endnotes, while the chapter on theology uses a more argumentative style. Other chapters impartially present a genealogy of disaster approaches, while some engage in more opinionated discussions. Others again present a particular disaster as a pivotal point for theoretical discussions, while others draw more ad hoc on several examples of disasters. After considering different solutions to our 'grouping problem', we decided to group the chapters together in four parts of very unequal size.

Part I consists of two chapters that discuss the advantages of introducing history and theology in disaster research. These two disciplines are not usually associated with contemporary disaster research, but the authors make a convincing case for including these disciplinary perspectives in disaster research. The purpose of the chapters is not to break down particular approaches within the disciplines, but more fundamentally to argue for the relevance of the disciplines. In that way, these two chapters transcend the juxtaposing of different analytical approaches, to make room for a disciplinary refutation of the 'modern' in perspectives on disasters.

In Chapter 2, Dahlberg discusses historical approaches to disaster analysis. Rather than providing a genealogy of the multitude of subdisciplines of history and their potential contribution to disaster research, Dahlberg prudently focuses on how selected historians have approached past disasters. Many see the 1755 Lisbon earthquake as the turning point between perceiving disasters as a divine force to applying a more naturalistic/scientific perspective on disasters. Historical research, however, indicates that this view is somewhat simplistic; the analysis of the Friuli 1348 earthquake reveals contemporary perceptions and narratives that cannot simply be reduced to a 'wrath of God' view. The main message of the chapter is that historical disaster research needs to extend beyond both 'reconstructive seismology' (focusing on estimating the physical destruction and magnitude of past disasters) as well as 'local history' (reciting eyewitness account of past disaster events), to include a broader scope of socioeconomic dimensions of disasters. While history can contribute with important geophysical and climatological reference points for present disasters, *socially rooted* studies should be at the heart of historical disaster research. A social scope enables the researcher to analyse disasters as a source of change; to uncover ancient perceptions of disasters; to engage in a discussion of the narratives and myths surrounding disasters; and to provide a history of disaster mentalities. All are factors that can inform contemporary disaster understandings. In short, disasters allow historians access to people's lives without the usual smokescreen of keeping up appearances. The eruption of Mount Vesuvius in AD 79, for instance, froze people's everyday lives in metres of ashes and dust. The more modern 1906 earthquake in San Francisco also provided unexpected access to people's private lives. Dahlberg points to both conceptual history (tracing the history of key disaster-related concepts through different historical periods) and counterfactual history (asking what could have been in the absence of the disaster or to avoid it) as fruitful approaches to be pursued in historical disaster research.

In Chapter 3, Gregersen argues for an important added value of theological reflections in relation to sociological disaster studies. Rather than dismissing perceptions of the divine in disasters as nothing more than pre-modern superstition, theological reflections could foster a wider view on the natural roots of disasters, as well as a long-term view on socioeconomic processes. In short, theology can improve our understanding of the complexity of religious responses to disasters. Religious people are important as agents of recovery (many of the first and closest responders are faith-based organizations) as well as victims of disasters (84 per cent of the world population describe themselves as religiously affiliated). Systematic theology allows researchers to reflect upon the semantic dimension of disasters as it relates to religious traditions. Gregersen charts out territory for integrating theology in disaster studies, both in terms of assessing the impacts of religious agents and in the form of internalizing the understanding of religious agents. Although the particularistic 'act of God' view of disaster surely can be identified in many religious traditions, it is relatively rare and often rivalled by other expressions of the divine. Specifically, the chapter discusses the use of deluge stories and liturgies across different religious traditions. A theological understanding of disasters, therefore, needs to transcend this 'act of God' view to focus on how to limit the suffering from disasters, and to provide answers to the existential questions that will inevitably surface in the wake of disasters. Rather than trying to decipher the divine *intentions* with disasters, one should turn to the analysis of the divine *presence* even in the depth of suffering. Gregersen refers to the latter approach as *theodicy from below* or, in the terms of disaster research, *a theology of resilience*. The task of theology is not to explain away the pain and suffering of disasters (as the will of God), but to help disaster victims move on by emphasizing the divine presence.

Part II includes seven chapters (Chapters 4–10). These chapters provide more of a genealogy of approaches to disaster research from the perspectives of seven different disciplines: culture, anthropology, politics, law, conflict, communications and gender. The aim of the chapters is to introduce and discuss disaster-relevant approaches or emphases within the disciplines. Some approaches – for example, *voter retrospection* in the chapter on politics, or *doctrinal analysis* in the chapter on law – are well-established subfields within the disciplines; whereas other approaches, such as the *emergency regime approach* in the chapter on culture, are developed specifically to inform disaster research. The chapters differ with regard to how much attention they devote to the empirical cases. Some chapters draw on extensive analyses of particular disasters. For example, the 2010 Haiti earthquake is much used in the gender chapter, and the 2004 fireworks disaster in Denmark is fundamental to the communication chapter. Other chapters mainly draw on disasters as examples; the anthropological chapter, for instance, draws on a diverse range of disasters, such as the 2004 Indian Ocean tsunami, the 2008 Sichuan earthquake, 1998 Hurricane Mitch, the 1986 Chernobyl nuclear accident and the 1984 Bhopal chemical disaster. Despite these differences, the chapters share a focus on clearly identifying different state-of-the-art approaches and/or key research findings from their individual discipline that can inform disaster research.

In Chapter 4, Illner and Holm explore a cultural approach to disaster analysis. The cultural approach perceives disasters as shaped by the cultural practices which create a common sensibility to disasters, and determine their perception. Cultural studies of disaster contribute to disaster research by exploring the manifold aesthetic practices through which we produce a common sense of disasters. *Aesthetics* in cultural studies refers to the common sensibility through which we perceive disasters. In this sense, cultural studies views culture as a repertoire of practices, images, narratives, genres and styles that determine what can be experienced as reality. Using Hurricane Katrina as their empirical foundation, Illner and Holm discuss five important theoretical approaches which have been applied in cultural studies of disasters: (i) a *trauma approach* that understands cultural practices as a means to inscribe traumatic events within individual or collective memory in order to avoid forgetting and aid the therapeutic process of coping with the destructive mental and material effects of disaster; (ii) a *vulnerability approach* that looks at disasters at the level of the community and describes aesthetic practices as a negative. Cultural practices contribute to the social production of disasters by functioning as blinders that prevent social actors from becoming aware of their own risk production, thereby aggravating disasters; (iii) a *state of exception approach* that sees disasters as an event that can be separated from a normal, everyday rule, and views disaster at the level of the state by exploring the underlying structures of social and political life; (iv) a *cultural history* (or apocalypse) *approach* that views disaster on the level of the world, exploring how we make sense of the world by telling stories about its end and by projecting neat patterns on to human life; and (v) an *emergency regime approach* that views disaster at the level of social practice, and understands disasters at the centre of contemporary society, as the emergency regime isolates, stigmatizes and pathologizes certain parts of the population. The relation between culture and disaster is conceptualized as a configuration – an image of social life in the language of disaster. The use of the 'tipping point' metaphor as an explanation for Hurricane Katrina is an example of a configuration of such epidemiologic imagery.

In Chapter 5, Sørensen and Albris apply the anthropological perspective to disasters. Anthropology is concerned with how human beings inhabit and make sense of their worlds at the intersection of society, culture and the environment. In this perspective, disasters are not just events which strike and affect societies, only to thereafter disappear as recovery progresses. Instead, disasters are both the result of previous conditions *and* the new conditions that they bring about. The anthropological discipline is well suited to detect the perpetual presence of disaster as it reveals itself in political practices, social organization, landscapes, bodies, language, rituals, material culture and memory. Sørensen and Albris introduce four main anthropology perspectives on disasters. (i) *Meaning-making*: the question is not what a disaster objectively is, but how it is experienced, made meaningful and acted upon by different people. Ethnography can go beyond the loss of material livelihoods to describe senses of self, community and dignity. (ii) *Politics*: political anthropology focuses on the formal and informal institutions and practices that negotiate the control, production, distribution and use of resources, as well as their associated ideas and values. Humanitarian relief, for instance, is not a neutral intervention but inevitably repositions disaster-affected people in different political, social and cultural contexts. (iii) *Time*: anthropology can provide useful insights into how the rhythms of particular disasters intersect with the seasonal and everyday rhythms of communities and households. Disasters are analysed as processes rather than singular or sequential events, in order to capture the temporal rhythms of disasters and cultural notions of time that influence understandings of and responses to disasters. (iv) *Space:* although disasters can only be experienced locally, contextualizing local scenes of disasters in a global field allows anthropologists to better comprehend the dynamics and power relations at play in disaster situations, and their aftermath. Sørensen and Albris contest that the resilience concept should be seen in this light: while resilience builds on the notion of clearly demarcated social systems, communities cannot be reduced to easily identifiable static systems, but are formed by the disaster and reconstruction processes. For the purpose of illustrating this, Sørensen and Albris provide an example of how two communities in Honduras after the 1998 hurricane Mitch, experienced very different recovery trajectories, despite not being geographically or socially delimited entities prior to the disaster. Rather, the capacities of these communities were shaped by the politically charged relationships between the disaster survivors, the NGOs, donors and the local authorities.

In Chapter 6, Rubin provides insights into how the discipline of political studies can contribute to disaster research. Politics is here understood narrowly as being concerned with the nexus between voting behaviour and political behaviour. The chapter dispels the idea that disasters have a strong influence on politics; even the greatest disasters do not appear to have played any major role in overthrowing political leaders and/or systems. Indeed, the empirical evidence points to political systems as being quite resilient to natural disasters. The impact of disasters on politics is more subtle, as disasters can act as a catalyst that either accelerates or derails existing processes, but disastrous events are not sufficiently strong to directly create these processes. Quantitative studies indicate that voters are retrospective with regards to disasters, and that they punish governments electorally for both presiding over disasters, as well as for failing to respond to them. Hence, pluralistic institutions appear to increase government incentives to provide disaster relief. Rubin points out, however, that most natural disasters occur in poor countries with no or few functioning democratic institutions. Even mature democracies are not necessarily compelled to pursue effective disaster management policies, as they can draw on many other viable political strategies that can annul most electoral damage, and can perhaps do so more cheaply than disaster relief and reconstruction. Rubin focuses particularly on *blame avoidance strategies* pursued by both democratic and non-democratic governments. The chapter recommends, therefore, an open-ended context-specific analytical perspective, where focus should be less on the natural disaster itself and more on how it is framed in the political arena where different myths, narratives and symbols compete for dominance. Rubin shows how these symbols, images and narratives played a role for voting behaviour in Sweden (in the wake of the 2004 tsunami) and in the US (after 2005 Hurricane Katrina).

In Chapter 7, Lauta discusses both the portfolio of disaster law as well as academic approaches to disaster law. According to Lauta, law is central to the socialization of disasters; it is the instrument through which disaster management can be integrated into every institution of a given community. Consequently, law is one of the main instruments to recalibrate and reinstitutionalize societies in the different phases of disaster management. Law plays an important role in creating incentives to undertake adequate insurance, to enforce building standards and to update emergency plans. It distributes responsibility (who does what), delegates competences (what can they do), limits discretionary margins (how far can they go) and enforces basic rights (limiting what can be done), which are all essential features of modern disaster responses. Today, almost all countries have implemented specific disaster regulations that designate responsibilities and competences, and establish linkages to the other regulations. Law also constitutes the platform from which criminal as well as economic liability can be addressed. Lauta lists five different methodological approaches to disaster law. (i) A *doctrinal approach* is the most prevalent approach to disaster law, and aims to fill gaps or clarify contradictions in present law as well as to comment on new developments in case law and its implications to legal doctrine. (ii) A *critical approach* aims to analyse and criticize present law through non-legal standards such as social justice, scientific inputs or economic rationales. The approach focuses on distributive aspects (risk, response or compensation) of disasters. (iii) A *theoretical approach* aims to describe and understand the foundations of law through legal theoretical discussions of the fundamental concepts applied or the concrete legal decisions. It addresses the foundations of emergency responses and in particular the law's ability to accommodate crisis. (iv) An *interdisciplinary approach* aims to integrate different interdisciplinary aspects of disasters such as sociological studies of legal reform, philosophical and anthropological considerations about legal responsibility or economic considerations. (v) A *risk approach* aims to analyse how law deals with major risks in general. The approach is policy-oriented, with strong emphasis on regulatory design, and integration of scientific knowledge. Lauta uses the substantial juridification of the 2005 Hurricane Katrina, which spawned more than one million legal claims, to demonstrate the practical application of some of these legal approaches.

In Chapter 8, Rubin explores the link between natural disasters and violent conflict, and identifies two contrasting perspectives. One of these stresses the conflict potential of natural disasters, while the other emphasizes the scope for increased cooperation. Regardless of perspective, the majority of studies reviewed do not find any deterministic relationship between natural disasters and violent conflict. Some studies suggest that natural disasters in combination with the wrong socioeconomic factors – like any other significant exogenous shock – can destabilize societies and increase the risk of conflict. Yet, with the right mix of socioeconomic factors, natural disaster can also promote conflict resolution. The studies emphasizing the conflict potential of natural disasters point first and foremost to the chaotic conditions that follow in the wake of natural disasters. Chaos can be exploited by rebel groups to challenge the authority of governments, which might already have suffered due to an inadequate disaster response. However, a number of recent studies have questioned the empirical foundation for expecting natural disasters to increase the risk of violent conflicts. This has led to an interest in investigating the beneficial dynamics of natural disasters through the *disaster diplomacy approach*. A natural disaster might provide the conflicting fractions with the opportunity to resolve their disputes and work together to meet the challenges inflicted on the area. Such rapprochement processes could be furthered by an increase in international awareness following a natural disaster. Rubin's empirical case of the 2004 Indian Ocean tsunami displays both conflict and rapprochement dynamics. The tsunami exacerbated the ongoing conflict between the Tamil Tigers and the government in Sri Lanka, whereas it accelerated peace negations in Indonesia between the government and the Free Aceh Movement. Thus, Rubin argues that it might be fruitful to look at natural disasters as a potential tool for mobilization where the conflict potential relies on the prevailing discourses, narratives and symbols that emerge in the wake of the natural disaster. The pure framing of disasters, therefore, adds an additional and more complex dimension to conflict analysis. In terms of future research, one of the great unknowns, highlighted by Rubin, is the extent to which social groups and societies are increasingly blamed for climate-related disasters due to their explicit link to greenhouse gas emissions and/or environmental degradation.

In Chapter 9, Andersen explores the phenomenon of communication processes during disasters. She distinguishes between two overarching fields of communication research, one which understands communication as an *intentional activity*, and one which understands it as a *constitutive practice*. When approached as an intentional activity, disaster communication has the purpose of establishing cause-and-effect to improve disaster management. This view is typically pursued by institutions and authorities involved in the practicalities of disaster planning and management. Three subcategories can be identified within this type of functionalist research. (i) *Transmission and information processing* deals with questions of identifying and characterizing the source and channels of communication; in particular, attention is on how to effectively convey a message to a large group of people in stressful situations. (ii) *Risk communication* focuses on understanding people's perceptions of risk; here the purpose is to make people react in an appropriate way through motivation and influence on attitudes. (iii) *Crisis communication* aims at persuading an audience about the sender's credibility and accountability in order to prevent crises of legitimacy in the response and recovery phase of a disaster. When approached as a *constitutive practice*, disaster communication processes are understood as an integrated part of everyday practices and not as an intentional activity. The aim here is to analyse communication processes at the collective level (rather than at the individual level), and focus is on how influential discourses are produced and reproduced in a hegemonic sense. Andersen identifies two subcategories within this type of critical research: (i) *life-world and meaning-making*, concerned with everyday discursive constructions of key social groups, and how these constructions are often amplified post-disaster, and (ii) *media and ideology research* that deals with the symbolic, hegemonic, ideological and powerful influence that the media have on society – in particular during disasters. Andersen draws on the lethal firework warehouse explosion in the suburbs of a Danish town in 2004 as empirical underpinning of the five different analytical approaches to communication processes. Future research, according to Andersen, should investigate potential bridges between the two different fields of communication research.

In Chapter 10, Horton describes how disaster research can benefit from a gender perspective that employs gender as the central organizing concept for analysing disaster impacts. Gender is often included as a cross-cutting theme in development and disaster research. However, disaster research may gain substantially from applying a fully fledged gender perspective. Due to gender mainstreaming, relief policies often fail to adequately consider specific historical contexts, regional geopolitics and culturally specific gender relations. A gender analysis of disasters, on the contrary, offers a theoretical window into invisible and naturalized social structures, processes and identities, as they are destabilized and reconfigured. This is necessary because disasters bring physical dislocation, deepen existing gender inequalities and disrupt gender roles, norms and ideologies. Gender socialization implies that women's risk behaviour during disaster is often linked to caretaking responsibilities, cultural constructs of appropriate behaviour and limitations on mobility. Accordingly, the 2004 Indian Ocean tsunami showed highly skewed gender mortality rates, in part because many women had never been taught how to swim and had more limited mobility. Horton applies *intersectionality* as a way to analyse the multiple axes of subordination in an intertwined manner, rather than merely adding up various forms of gender disadvantages. Horton's analysis of the 2010 Haiti earthquake illuminates how long-term patterns of intersecting gender, class and race-based vulnerabilities were intensified after the earthquake. Women's gender identities intersected with their class and racial identities to generate increased vulnerability where poor women were found to be the most likely to still live in emergency camps years after the earthquake. They had to live with a lack of privacy and dignity, as well as a greatly enhanced risk of gender-based violence and sexual assault. Many female earthquake victims were stigmatized (as promiscuous and/or prostitutes), which contributed to justifying inadequate state responses and contested women's claims to housing, land and other post-disaster services. Gendered intersectionality can also provide possible pathways forward. Placing women's voices at the forefront facilitates the use of disasters as opportunities for gender transgressions, individual and collective empowerment, and transformative structural and institutional changes towards gender equity. Horton identifies important future work to be done in the areas of bridging women's immediate post-disaster gender needs and promoting long-term strategic projects of gender equity.

Part III includes three chapters rooted in organization theory (Chapters 11–13). The three chapters share the organizational point of departure, but apply very different perspectives in their analyses. The first chapter outlines different organizational approaches to the study of accidents in much the same way as the chapters above. In contrast, the two other chapters demonstrate how an organizational perspective can inform disaster research, but from two different levels of analysis: one of the chapters applies a concrete and detailed analytical perspective to one particular small-scale accident (boat-capsizing), while the other applies a global analytical perspective to shed light on the transboundary disaster of pandemics.

In Chapter 11, Dolino and Catino discuss organizational accidents. The authors offer a critical review of three key contributions on organizational accident genesis and identify the core practical implications of those contributions. The three approaches all go beyond a reductive conception of accident genesis, which focuses on human or technological triggers to consider intrinsic limits of organizational and systemic factors. First, (i) *the normal accident theory* focuses on the structural-organizational properties of organizations as crucial in explaining accidents. Systems, in particular organizations with complex interactions and tightly coupled connections, are constantly exposed to possible breakdowns as individual parts may malfunction, setting off chain reactions. Thus, accidents are unavoidable properties of highly complex systems, and the human element in accidents is not analytically relevant. The 1979 Three Mile Island accident is explained by the complex structural and systemic characteristics of the production of nuclear energy. Single component failures (valve and light malfunctions) within this complex system generated chain reactions that were extremely difficult to understand and avoid by the operators. Second, (ii) *organizational accident theory* frames accidents as the outcome of everyday organizational decision-making processes. While accidents are man-made, they follow from the interaction of social, organizational and technological processes. Thus, accidents are explained by organizational factors inducing errors and violations, rather than the errors and violations in and of themselves. According to the organizational accident theory, the 2001 accident in Linate Airport, Italy, where two planes collided leading to 118 fatalities, evolved from the fact that pilots and ground controllers operated in an organizational system equipped with weak defences, which resulted in various error traps. Finally, (iii) *epistemic accident theory* looks at the intrinsic limits of the engineering knowledge from a constructivist perspective. Engineering knowledge cannot prevent organizational accidents; in fact, accidents are a result of unavoidable knowledge gaps and miscalculations. Epistemic accidents are not predictable or avoidable *ex ante* as the complexity of the real world cannot be fully reproduced or simulated. An accident genesis cannot be determined solely as a maintenance failure, but should also be linked to the failure of the technology paradigm itself. As a promising venue for future organizations accident research, Dolino and Catino point to the *Resilience Engineering approach* that emphasizes lessons learned from all the daily non-accidents.

In Chapter 12, Vendelø presents the sensemaking perspective, using the Præstø Fjord incident as the case. This perspective is useful when investigating organizational accidents in complex, unpredictable settings. One teacher died, and thirteen pupils and another teacher from a boarding school came close to perishing, when a dragon boat capsized in freezing cold water. Vendelø looks into the sense-making that allowed a rather innocent organizational activity to evolve and become dangerous, and examines why no attempts were made to stop the organizational activity of dragon boat sailing as it unfolded. The focus of the sense-making perspective is on how individuals and groups of individuals create order out of ambiguous and uncertain situations in organizations. Vendelø presents Weick's constructivist theory according to which reality is an ongoing accomplishment, emerging from efforts to create order and make retrospective sense of what is going on. The three key concepts in sense-making are: (i) *cues*, (ii) *relations* and (iii) *frames*. Order is constructed by interpreting an experience or a sudden change (the cue) and the relation between this cue and a broader paradigm or shared understanding (the frame). When the two teachers and thirteen pupils ventured out on Præstø Fjord in the school's dragon boat in February 2011 to beat a time record set by another team, the activity was not perceived as dangerous because sense-making in the organization was guided by a common frame, stating that if the experienced outdoor teacher organized an activity, it would be safely guided. A number of cues (strong wind, wave height, etc.) were too weak to challenge the sense-making of the teacher, who only decided to turn around and head back towards shore when it was too late. Fear of being sanctioned prevented the pupils from voicing their concern, and Vendelø shows that, due to the specific organizational practices at the boarding school, it would have required very powerful doubting and dissent to change the sense-making of the teacher in charge of the activity. With regard to directions for future research, Vendelø suggests that it should focus on the role of emotions and embodied experiences as elements of sense-making, as well as on inter-organizational and adaptive sense-making.

In Chapter 13, Bækkeskov investigates the particular characteristics of global pandemics, as a distinct type of disaster with growing importance. Lately, pandemics have taken the forms of various influenzas, as well as outbreaks of the Ebola virus. The most essential trait of these pandemics is that they are transboundary crises, characterized by interdependence among key actors at different levels: the severity of the challenge in a country depends on what others have done to stop their own domestic spread. Thus, multiple supranational and subnational jurisdictions need to be mobilized, and many different organizations need to be activated and coordinated to ensure an effective global response. Bækkeskov illustrates how global responses to pandemics tend not to be completely uniform across national boundaries, yet the response is also decidedly non-chaotic and uncoordinated. The responses to the 2009 flu pandemic, for instance, displayed substantial variations in the *degrees* of responses (e.g. vaccination policies varied significantly between otherwise similar countries), but it also showed a remarkable consensus across countries on the kinds of interventions that were used. Bækkeskov uses insights from public administration and political science to analyse how different organizing principles (hierarchy, markets and networks) combine to form a global response to pandemics. While *hierarchy* is the classical solution to coordination problems between actors, the international character of pandemics makes coordination difficult to resolve through hierarchy alone. This is especially true in the case of supranational organizations such as the WHO and EU, who only have limited legal authority with respect to national governments. *Markets* offer an alternative way to coordinate activities between actors. Concretely, pandemic responses appear to depend much on the action of private companies/ organizations such as drug companies, logistics providers, and private caregivers and facilities. Finally, *networks* offer a third mechanism for coordinating pandemic response activities. Networks can be constituted by transnational interactions by health professionals and agencies on specific issues and topics. Bækkeskov makes the case for including the impact of rules and norms in an organizational analysis of pandemic responses, as the current international push for uniformity is bound to confront existing national rules and norms.

Part IV consists of the last two chapters, which provide important insights into disaster research rooted in disciplinary approaches focusing on specific disaster relief instruments. The financial chapter discusses the pros and cons of three new insurance instruments, while the chapter on mental health highlights the importance of participatory and community-based recovery interventions to enhance the likelihood of psychological recovery for the surviving victims.

In Chapter 14, Fisker, Hansen and Rand analyse how to improve disaster insurance. No individual or company wishes to carry the economic burden of catastrophic events on their own, so there is a natural request to share the cost and spread the risk through insurances. Rather than outlining a particular disciplinary approach to disaster research, the authors discuss actual instruments and outline the pros and cons of three new insurance instruments all centred on market-based risk transfer mechanisms. Two factors in particular spur the demand for these instruments: the first relates to the fact that, while governments usually act as insurer of disasters by means of public financing, large-scale disasters pose a problem for governments in developing countries with limited funds available; the second relates to the quality of existing catastrophe models that are used to price insurances according to the expected risk. Historically, these models have consistently underestimated the actual losses of disasters. The basic idea behind market-based insurance is to limit the transaction costs of claims investigations, and speed up disbursements using measurable predefined triggers, such as earthquake intensity or rainfall. The three instruments are: (i) *government-supported catastrophe insurance programmes*, where external actors (the IMF and the World Bank) provide support to facilitate the creation of government-supported catastrophe insurance programmes; (ii) *index-based crop and livestock insurance*, where governments who wish to insure against large-scale natural hazards do so based on an index describing the observable and measurable features, such as the magnitude of an earthquake, wind-speed of a hurricane, or measured rainfall in relation to droughts and floods. Index insurance overcomes classical insurance problems by having low transaction costs, less adverse selection and reduced moral hazard. This instrument is widely used in India where it is linked to weather patterns, and in Mongolia where it is linked to the number of surviving livestock; and (iii) *catastrophe bonds*, that pay out on the occurrence of a specified event. Bonds make it possible to distribute the covariate risk related to natural hazards across time and space, and the instrument is gaining popularity among governments of countries which are highly exposed to disasters and economically vulnerable, for example, Mexico and Malawi.

Finally, in Chapter 15, Henderson, Berliner and Elsass emphasize the importance of factoring in mental health concerns in disaster interventions. The field of mental health has been surrounded with much controversy due to the complex nature of the topic. In the chapter, the authors focus on theoretical and research-based implications for interventions. Post-Traumatic Stress Disorder (PTSD) has been studied thoroughly in disaster settings, and quantitative studies have found that very high percentages of people exposed to natural disasters show signs of PTSD. The authors emphasize the importance of intervening when it comes to children and adolescents, as their psychological development may otherwise be affected severely. The Inter-Agency Standing Committee's 'pyramid-of-care' is presented as a tool for specifying the levels of care that can be addressed after a disaster. Drawing on their own research, the authors describe how chronic stress constituted a better prediction of post-traumatic symptoms in 404 adults exposed to the 2004 Indian Ocean tsunami in Sri Lanka than the particular threat to life experienced during the tsunami. Also, the widely accepted Sphere standards for humanitarian intervention are discussed in relationship to community-based approaches to disaster mental health. Ultimately, the authors' suggestion for a 'people-centred humanitarian response' leads to a number of directions for future research on the topic, for example, reducing the gap between research and practice by undertaking more research on psychosocial interventions, such as child-friendly spaces, counselling and promotion of community support.

In the epilogue we offer a brief discussion of what these fourteen disciplinary chapters contribute to the present state of the field of disaster research. We also discuss the notion of multi-disciplinarity with regard to disaster research and present examples of contemporary attempts to tear down the walls between established traditions and disciplines. Finally, we suggest a very broad view of the way ahead for multi-disciplinary disaster research.

References

Baird, M.E. (2010) The 'Phases' of Emergency Management. Background paper prepared for the Intermodal Freight Transportation Institute (ITFI).

Bankoff, G. (2010) No such things as 'natural disasters': Why we had to invent them. *Harvard International Review*, 24 Aug.

Barton, A.H. (1969) *Communities in Disaster: A Sociological Analysis of Collective Stress Situations*. New York: Doubleday.

Blaikie, P., Cannon, T., Davis, I., and Wisner, B. (2004) *At Risk: Natural Hazards, Vulnerability and Disasters*. 2nd edn, London: Routledge.

Calhoun, C. (2004) A world of emergencies: Fear, intervention, and the limits of cosmopolitan order. *Canadian Review of Sociology and Anthropology*, 41(4), 373–95.

Carr, J.L. (1932) Disaster and the sequence-pattern concept of social change. *American Journal of Sociology*, 38 (2), 207–18.

Chandler, D. (2014) *Resilience: The Governance of Complexity*. London: Routledge.

Coppola, D. (2011) *Introduction to International Disaster Management*. Oxford: Butterworth Heinemann.

Davidson, D.J. (2010) The applicability of the concept of resilience to social systems: Some sources of optimism and nagging doubts. *Society and Natural Resources*, 23(12), 1135–49.

Drabek, T.E. (1986) *Human Systems Responses to Disaster: An Inventory of Sociological Findings*. New York: Springer.

Drabek, T.E., and Hoetmer, G.J. (eds) (1991) *Emergency Management: Principles and Practice for Local Government*. Washington, DC: International City Management Association.

Dynes, R.R. (1970) *Organized Behavior in Disaster*. Lexington, KY: Heath Lexington Books.

Dynes, R.R. (2000) The dialogue between Voltaire and Rousseau on the Lisbon Earthquake: The emergence of a social science view. *International Journal of Mass Emergencies and Disasters*, 18(1), 97–115.

Evans, B., and Reid, J. (2014) *Resilient Life: The Art of Living Dangerously*. Cambridge: Polity Press.

Farazmand, A. (2001) *Handbook of Crisis and Emergency Management*. London: CRC Press.

Fritz, C.E. (1961) Disasters. In R.K. Merton and R.A. Nisbet (eds), *Contemporary Social Problems*. New York: Harcourt, Brace & World, 641–94.

Howell, C., and Ruffman, A. (1994) *Ground Zero: A Reassessment of the 1917 Explosion in Halifax Harbour*. Halifax: Nimbus.

Jashemski, W.F., and Myer, F.G. (2002) *The Natural History of Pompeii*. Cambridge: Cambridge University Press.

Kelman, I. (2014) Vulnerability, resilience, disasters, and health. Presentation given at COPE, 20 Oct., slide 7.

Kitz, J. (2008) *Shattered City: The Halifax Explosion and the Road to Recovery*. 3rd edn, Halifax: Nimbus.

Lindell, M.K. (2013) Disaster studies. *Current Sociological Review*, 61(5–6), 797–825.

Neal, D.M. (1997) Reconsidering the phases of disaster. *International Journal of Mass Emergencies and Disasters*, 15(2), 239–64.

Perry, R.W. (2007) What is a disaster? In H. Rodríguez, E.L. Quarantelli and R.R. Dynes (eds.) *Handbook of Disaster Research*. New York, NY: Springer, 1–15.

Powell, J.W. (1954) *An Introduction to the Natural History of Disaster*. Baltimore, MD: University of Maryland Disaster Research Project.

Prince, S.H. (1920) *Catastrophe and Social Change*. New York: Longmans, Green & Co.

Quarantelli, E.L. (1978) *Disasters: Theory and Research*. Beverly Hills, CA: Sage.

Quarantelli, E.L. (ed.) (1998) *What is a Disaster? A Dozen Perspectives on the Question*. London: Routledge.

Rodríguez, H., Quarantelli, E.L., and Dynes, R.R. (2007) *Handbook of Disaster Research*. New York: Springer.

Sagan, S. (1995) *The Limits of Safety. Organizations, Accidents, and Nuclear Weapons*. Princeton, NJ: Princeton University Press.

Scanlon, J. (1988) Disaster's little known pioneer: Canada's Samuel Henry Prince. *International Journal of Mass Emergencies and Disasters*, 6(3), 213–32.

Stoddard, E.R. (1968) *Conceptual Models of Human Behavior in Disasters*. El Paso, TX: Texas Western Press.

Tierney, K. (2014) *The Social Roots of Risk: Producing Disasters, Promoting Resilience*. Stanford, CA: Stanford University Press.

Walker, J., and Cooper, M. (2011) Genealogies of resilience: From systems ecology to the political economy or crisis adaptation. *Security Dialogue*, 42(2), 143–160.

Part I

Broad perspectives

2 Cracks in the past

Historical approaches to disaster research

Rasmus Dahlberg

Introduction

History is a thing of the past – or is it? Since the earliest stages of its development, the historical discipline has found itself split between history as object (the past) and history as contemporary understandings of the past (historiography). This division is fundamentally complementary in that the one cannot be without the other; history is where the past and present meet. Total reconstruction of the past is not possible because of the present's partial blindness due to lacunae in source material and bias of the interpreter. Rather, the historian creates a narrative based on (and not contradicting) the credible pieces of evidence that exist, using theories about the past that are necessarily grounded in present perceptions. In this chapter I argue that catastrophic events are particularly relevant and interesting to the historian, because sudden disruptions of physical and social structures typically create a lot of data to be subjected to analysis later. Disasters may thus be seen as cracks in otherwise impenetrable areas of the past.

This chapter introduces historical disaster research through a three-tier approach: first, the study of history as a scientific field is demarcated through a brief history of the discipline (from antiquity to the present), in order to provide the reader with a basic understanding of the discourses that have characterized its development; second, historical disaster research is shown to have grown out of a multi-disciplinary approach, combining elements from seismology, geography and traditional history; third, a number of examples of how disasters can be analysed from a historical angle are presented, using the 1348 Friuli and the 1906 San Francisco earthquakes as cases. Furthermore, finally, implications for future historical disaster research are suggested.

I have limited my study to works of historians focusing directly on specific past disasters, thus excluding the multitude of papers and books that investigate the entire history of collapsing societies (such as Diamond 2005), biographies of persons involved in catastrophic events or histories of modern technologically produced disasters. My aim is merely to provide the reader with an understanding of how selected historians have approached disasters in the past, as objects for study.

'Wie es eigentlich gewesen'

The Ancient Greek scholars Herodotus and Thucydides laid the foundations for the study of history. While Herodotus was the first to use criticism of sources in a systematic way, Thucydides, in his *History of the Peloponnesian War* (approx. 400 BC), emphasized cause-and-effect and chronology as structuring principles. Thucydides also described human decisions and actions, instead of interventions from the gods, thereby directing later historians' attention towards causality. In the fourteenth century, the Arab historian Ibn Khaldun introduced a scientific method to the study of history by rejecting uncritical acceptance of historical data, but it was not until the 1800s that a modern and truly secular approach to history emerged, most notably through the works of the German philosopher Hegel and his framework of absolute idealism, which explained the progress of history as a dynamic between contradictions that eventually are elevated to a higher unity ('Aufhebung').

More than anyone else, the German historian Leopold von Ranke has been credited with professionalizing history. His *History of the Latin and Teutonic Peoples from 1494 to 1514*, first published in 1824, was based on a variety of historical sources such as eyewitness accounts, official documents and diaries, which the author analysed thoroughly. It was, however, a single sentence that elevated Ranke's book to fame and came to define the discipline of historical research for at least the next century: 'To history has been assigned the office of judging the past, of instructing the present for the benefit of future ages. To such high offices this work does not aspire: it wants only to show what actually/essentially[1] happened' (Ranke, in Stroud 1987).

Ranke's phrase 'wie es eigentlich gewesen' was taken by the generations of historians that followed as a *leitmotif* in their attempts to write objective histories of what 'actually' or 'essentially' happened in the past. Like most other disciplines of the time, the founding fathers of history were inspired by the great achievements of natural science during the Scientific Revolution. In the 19th century, history tried to mimic the hard sciences by developing laboratory-like methods for evaluating the credibility of sources. A common approach would be to thoroughly examine the origin of written sources and ask questions like: 'When, why and by whom was this source produced?' 'What were the intentions behind producing it?' After such scrutiny, the historian would be able to utilize the source in constructing his narrative, either as a credible description of events witnessed by the creator, or – if the source did not meet the historian's criteria – as a piece of evidence providing information on the creator himself and the creation of the source.

To Ranke the historian should always keep an eye on the universal, while taking pleasure in the particular at the same time. Still, history as a scientific discipline often finds itself caught somewhere between the faculties of social science and the arts. There is, inarguably, both a nomothetic and an ideographic aspect to the study of history: most historians look for uniqueness ('Einmahligkeit') and patterns/structures at the same time. As an extreme example of the latter, Carl G. Hempel argued for 'general laws of history' with limited success in the middle of the 20th century (Hempel 1942). Much more triumphant was the French structuralism of the Annales school represented by Fernand Braudel, Marc Bloch, Lucien Febvre and Emmanuel La Durie; they preferred to explain the social history of especially Europe in the Middle Ages through the long-term development of mentalities ('l'historie la longue durée') over short-term events ('l'historie d'événementielle').

History took a *linguistic turn* at the end of the 20th century, becoming highly influenced by discourse analysis, textual analysis and anthropology. Micro-histories such as Carlo Ginzburg's seminal study of a literate and heretic Italian miller of the 16th century (Ginzburg 1980 [1976]) marked an interest in the oddities of the past, of the individuals who stood out from the masses. This represented a very different approach to the study of history than what had been practised by Marxist historians earlier in the century, with their focus on historical materialism, dialectics and the masses. It was to this historiographical battlefield that disasters were introduced as specific objects for investigation in the last quarter of the 20th century.

The emergence of disaster history

Disasters and catastrophes (used hereafter synonymously) are intrinsically interesting topics for the historian to study, as they may represent cracks in otherwise impenetrable blocks of past experiences. 'All disasters have a temporal dimension and may be understood as the result of complex, historically induced causal connections', as two leading disaster historians have noted (Juneja and Mauelshagen 2007: 6). The Mount Vesuvius volcanic eruption in AD 79 – perhaps more than any other catastrophic natural event in recorded history – allowed historians and archaeologists many centuries later to peek into the daily life of a Roman city, by burying Herculaneum and Pompeii in ash. Pliny the Younger wrote his eyewitness account of the disaster to his friend Tacitus twenty-five years later, providing historians of antiquity with valuable knowledge about both normal and extraordinary times under Pax Romana. The excavations of the two buried cities, beginning in the 18th century, function as a window to the past, still enjoyed by hundreds of thousands of visitors each year (Özgenel 2008).

If *catastrophe* etymologically is the 'reversal of the expected' (from the Ancient Greek *katastrophé*: 'overturn'), the event itself also could tell us something about what was and wasn't expected in a past society. Disaster understood as sudden disruption of societal order also potentially reveals valuable insights into meanings, hierarchies, structures and causalities otherwise hidden. The 1755 Great Lisbon earthquake sparked a 'debate over modernity' between Rousseau and Voltaire, and inspired other great thinkers like Kant to write books and treatises that introduced scientific approaches to disasters (Dynes 2000). Acknowledging that all disasters unfold in a historical context with past, present and future dimensions, and that history to a certain degree could be seen as driven by disasters – especially technological developments as well as policy and legislation – also constitutes the historian's argument for studying them.

Dedicated historical disaster research is, however, a rather recent contribution to the study of history as a whole. Before 1990, 'most historians assigned (natural) disasters to the domain of fate, as exceptional incidents within the course of human history – something destructive that might interrupt social normalcy and which could not be grasped through recourse to socio-cultural concepts of historical change' (Juneja and Mauelshagen 2007: 6).

As late as in 1998, French medieval historian Jacques Berlioz in a collection of essays on catastrophe in the Middle Ages (Berlioz 1998) proposed a new 'total history', including the study of 'natural catastrophes' as well as geography, culture and social aspects of them. Berlioz argued that historians, traditionally, had preferred studying humans rather than nature, and that this accounted for the lack of historical inquiries into disasters. The term *natural catastrophe* requires special attention: while disaster sociologists have discussed for decades what constitutes the subject itself (Quarantelli 1998), whether historians choose to use the prefix 'natural' or prefer to leave it out 'seems to depend on their perspectives and familiarity with recent debates in the social sciences' (Juneja and Mauelshagen 2007: 14).

Environmental historian Greg Bankoff of the University of Hull stated in early 2015 on his website that 'disasters are set to become a major new field of historical studies, receiving increasing popular and governmental attention that corresponds to their escalating magnitude and frequency'. Bankoff himself has been one of the most prominent academics promoting the notion that 'natural disasters' do not exist: instead, he advocates for a necessary distinction between hazards (which may be natural, such as earthquakes, volcanic eruptions, etc.) and disasters that follow when more or less vulnerable man-made socioeconomic/technical systems are affected (Bankoff 2002, 2010). Bankoff argues that vulnerability reminds us that, even if natural hazards may be physical processes, disasters are 'quintessentially historical ones, that is they are the outcome of processes that change over time and whose geneses lie in the past' (Bankoff 2007: 110).

While disaster history emerged through the 1990s, particularly focusing around Berlioz and others at the University of Grenoble, the most important recent contribution has its origins in Germany: Gerrit Jasper Schenk and Franz Mauelshagen created the network 'Historical disaster research with a view to contemporary cultural study' (Historische Erforschung von Katastrophen in kulturvergleichender Perspektiv) in 2005, funded by the German Research Foundation (2005–9). This network brought together German and foreign historians with a common interest in disasters through a number of meetings and publications, including research anthologies and special journal issues (cf. Schenk and Engels 2007; Schenk 2009; Janku *et al.* 2012; Schenk *et al.* 2014). The ontological position of this German tradition within disaster history acknowledges the US sociological tradition (Quarantelli 1998) without fully accepting it. The editors state in the introduction to a recent publication that, 'while these only too real events [recent earthquakes and tsunamis] make it sound cynical to speak of disasters as purely "socially constructed," they are never entirely "natural" either' (Schenk *et al.* 2012: 2).

Schenk's network took a highly interdisciplinary approach to disaster history. The participants focused 'on the historical exploration of disasters with a natural core' (Schenk and Engels 2007: 19) as opposed to previous quantitative studies by historians of epidemics and similar fields. Schenk identified a turn away from positivist (number of victims, amount of damage, risk probability or the geological, climatic and biological causes of disasters, etc.) to 'more constructivist issues like the perception and interpretation of dangers, risks and disasters, cultural dealings with them and their long-term effects' (Schenk and Engels 2007: 13).

The Friuli earthquake in 1348

Earthquakes offer a particularly interesting pool of data to the disaster historian, as they represent the kind of disastrous events that have been catalogued over the longest period of time, beginning with the publication of Marcello Bonito's *Terre tremante* in 1691 (Rohr 2003: 139). Much of these data, however, are 'ridden with serious mistakes, gaps and inaccuracies' (Schenk and Engels 2007: 11). If credible data can be found, however, archaeological, seismological and historical evidence in the form of written and graphical accounts can – even centuries after the ground ceased to shake – be triangulated to construct informed narratives that fall either into the category of what Rohr calls 'historical reconstructive seismology' (focusing entirely on magnitude estimations and damage classification) or 'local history' (mere accounts of past events that do not live up to scientific criteria for evidence, methods and theory) (Rohr 2003: 130).

An important contribution to the development of a historical approach to disaster studies was a paper published by the German historian Arno Borst (1925– 2007) in *Historische Zeitschrift* in 1981. In his paper, Borst – one of Germany's then most influential historians of the Middle Ages – stated that a motivation for collecting historical data on disasters traditionally has been the need for evidence-based risk assessments in the industrialized societies. Based on knowledge about the frequency and distribution of magnitude of earthquakes in a specific area, risk experts claimed to be able to calculate the risk of future events, and on this basis place chemical factories, nuclear power plants, etc. in locations less exposed to natural hazards (Schenk 2007: 11). Borst, however, comments that, after an earthquake in Italy the year before he published his article, experts claimed that it was the first time that such a vast area in Italy had been struck. But the recorded seismological data only went back to 1805, so no one considered the earthquake that struck on Christmas morning 1222, causing severe shaking tremors in all of northern Italy, totally destroying the town of Brescia. Information on this was recorded in medieval chronicles, but nevertheless remained unknown to modern seismologists (Borst 1981: 530). History thus serves as an important reference, especially with regard to low-frequency extreme events such as earthquakes.

Arno Borst selected for his own study the 6.9 Friuli earthquake, which occurred in 1348 in the Alps, in the area that is today the border region between Austria and Italy. This disaster almost coincided with another catastrophe of natural origin: the plague, which hit the same area just weeks after the earthquake. At about 4:00 p.m. on 25 January 1348, the ground began to shake in and around the Austrian town of Villach. The movements caused by the earthquake, whose epicentre later was shown to have been located in the Italian Friuli South Alpine region, were felt more than 600 kilometres away, in cities such as Prague and Naples. An unusually large number of sources mentioning the earthquake and its consequences are known to this day. They were created by contemporary eyewitnesses and chroniclers, and written down and copied by monks, clerics, traders and scholars all over Europe in the decades following the incident.

One of the eyewitnesses was Heinrich Sterner, a wealthy merchant from Regensburg who happened to be passing through Villach at exactly the right (or wrong) moment. 'The city of Villach, the castle wall, the monastery, the churches and all the walls and towers with as many as eleven battlements fell to the ground', wrote Sterner (trans. Borst 1981: 534). Accounts like this may seem very subjective and of limited value when compared to the vast amounts of quantitative seismological data gathered by modern seismologists – but to a historian, exactly these kinds of qualitative data from contemporary sources are of great importance.

Borst was actually able to estimate the duration of the initial shaking caused by the earthquake using an eyewitness account by Johannes von Parma who was 'Domherr' (canon or prebendary) in Trient. He experienced the earthquake just as he was preparing for vespers (evening prayers) in the cathedral on the evening of 25 January 1348: first came a short trembling and soon thereafter a much longer and powerful shaking of the ground, '[a]nd this earthquake lasted for as long as I would use for the thoughtful recitation of three Lord's Prayers and three Hail Marys' (trans. Borst 1981: 536).

In his seminal paper, Borst also argued that a historical interpretation and appreciation of the 1348 earthquake could not be limited to the 1340s and 1350s. He found traces of 'literary aftershocks' as late as the 16th century, when for instance Paracelsus, a doctor who lived for a period of time in Villach, published a chronicle of the Kärnten area in 1538 that included a theory of the earthquake (Borst 1981: 557). Borst emphasized the long-term effects of disasters in history, when he noted that the most important result of the Friuli earthquake was that a natural event at the foot of the Alps as slowly as possible 'entered the historical consciousness of Europe' (trans. Borst 1981: 558). This was most important, as Borst identified a European reluctance to include disasters in the study of history. While he pioneered a scientific approach to historical disaster research, Borst failed to synthesize his new-found knowledge on the people who experienced the 1348 earthquake into a structured system. Historian Christian Rohr attributes this to Borst's background as a classical medieval historian, which prevented him from accessing recent progress and discoveries within seismology. As Rohr puts it, Borst's greatest achievement was to inspire others to investigate the 1348 earthquake in more detail from new angles (Rohr 2003: 130).

A historical geographical approach

Christa Hammerl of the Institute of Meteorology and Geophysics at Vienna University was one of the scholars whom Borst inspired. In 1992 she wrote her

PhD dissertation on the same topic studied by Borst, and has since published several articles about the 1348 earthquake (Hammerl 1994). Her objective was to reconstruct the event using both historical sources and modern seismological methods, combined into an approach that falls under the disciplinary umbrella *historical geography*.

Hammerl combed through archives and publications for sources on the Friuli earthquake and found 110 written accounts of the earthquake between the more than 200 contemporary sources she investigated in all. She mapped the origins of these sources and created a typology, listing whether it was a monk (Benedictine, Cistercian, Dominican, etc.), a priest or canon, or perhaps a merchant who created it.

The novelty of Hammerl's approach lay not in her combination of a geographical quantitative and a historical qualitative approach (this had been done before), but rather in the questions she asks like: 'Why did the news of this earthquake spread so far?' Hammerl goes into a deeper analysis of each historical source to determine its origin and on the basis of this to estimate its credibility – thus working like any professional historian. The fact that the earthquake was reported, she pointed out, should not lead to the conclusion that the earthquake was truly felt in that locality (Hammerl 1994). Her study shows how previous studies all state the German town of Lübeck, 1,000 kilometres away, as the 'northernmost boundary of the felt area'. This is, however, erroneous according to Hammerl, who hypothesizes that news of the Friuli earthquake spread rapidly throughout Europe, primarily through the Benedictine and Cistercian orders. Most of the sources have their origin in places with monasteries, and due to the fact that traveling monks were the heralds of the Middle Ages, a mere mentioning of the earthquake in a local chronicle or annal should not be accepted as proof that the earthquake was actually felt in this particular location. A prerequisite for quantifying the data from the qualitative sources is to understand the contemporary network mechanisms that produced them in the first place.

By applying historical methods in her source analysis, Hammerl actually moves the epicentre of the 25 January 1348 earthquake about 100 kilometres to the south-southwest – from Villach in Austria to Udine in Italy's Friuli region. By questioning centuries-old sources from a new perspective, she thus gained valuable new insights into the natural phenomenon that triggered the disaster.

A history of mentalities

A decade after Christa Hammerl did her work on the Friuli earthquake, historian Christian Rohr from the University of Salzburg, Austria, also turned his attention to the 1348 event. He revisited the same sources that Borst and Hammerl had used, but with a somewhat different aim. Rohr wanted to examine the mentalities of people in the Late Middle Ages, following the tradition of *Annales* historians.

To Rohr, studying the mentalities of the past meant (re)constructing not the event (the earthquake), but the contemporary perceptions of the event, in order to understand how people made sense of and described it. For this purpose, a disaster was most useful, as it 'is the nature of numerous narrative sources, especially those produced in the Middle Ages, to find only the unusual worth reporting' (Rohr 2003: 128). He defined mentalities as 'horizons of experience and the sum of all the factors determining the possibilities (and also the impossibilities) of thinking in a given society or in parts of it' (Rohr 2003: 128). When defining *disaster*, Rohr – not surprisingly – included people's helplessness in explaining the event as a parameter.

Rohr built upon a three-step model for how humans perceive nature: (1) myths and supernatural creatures are introduced to excuse human weaknesses; (2) man perceives nature as wild and unpredictable, but copes with it using technology; and (3) nature's aesthetics are discovered for man to enjoy. In his paper on the 1348 earthquake, Rohr hypothesized that step 2 dominated the mentalities during and after the Friuli event, and emphasized that 'natural disasters were not necessarily perceived as the wrath of God, but rather were often seen as being tremendous events which, nevertheless, constituted an exceptional and unexpected part of everyday life' (Rohr 2003: 128). Rohr doesn't explicitly mention the Great Lisbon earthquake of 1755, which is usually seen as a turning point in the shift from a divine to a more natural interpretation of catastrophe causality, but his hypothesis is nonetheless a well-disguised provocation from a modest Austrian medieval historian.

Building on Borst and Hammerl, Rohr characterized the available sources using classic historical methodology: the value of the abundance of annals and chronicles was countered by the fact that they were seldom written by eyewitnesses. Also, more importantly, the 'reports became distorted, or embroidered, not least because of the different horizons of expectations' (Rohr 2003: 132). Accounts were in other words filtered through the mentalities of people and institutions relaying the narratives.

In his paper, Rohr addresses yet another issue which Borst and Hammerl had discussed: the proximity of the Friuli earthquake to the Black Plague that struck many of the same areas just weeks later. Separating causalities is a well-known challenge to historians, and there is little doubt that many of the sources containing information about the earthquake mix up the consequences of the seismic event with the epidemic. To a disaster historian trying to determine the exact number of casualties of the earthquake, such confusion would be highly problematic – but not so much to a historian of disaster mentalities such as Rohr. That the earthquake happened to be followed by an epidemic is actually an advantage to him, as it probably played an important role in boosting the overall number of written sources about this 'compound catastrophe' of the Middle Ages (Rohr 2003: 133–4).

An example of how Rohr investigates the mentalities surrounding the earthquake concerns banking – a then fairly new enterprise emerging in Renaissance Italy in the 14th century. Giovanni Villani of Florence, and his brother Matteo, were in Udine close to the epicentre during the earthquake: 'According to them the bankers of Udine were frightened by such tremendous miracles and as a sign of remorse they forgave the interest of their debtors for eight days' (Rohr 2003: 134).

This and other examples in Rohr's study raise the question of representation: is it possible to conclude anything of value about the mentalities in more general terms from such an account? As with the micro-historical approach developed by Ginzburg and others in the decades leading up to Rohr's study, it's about zooming in on the detail instead of trying to fathom the entire painting at a glance. Exactly the fact that Vallini found it worth mentioning in his narrative, that the bankers of Udine perceived the earthquake 'as a *memento mori*, as a sign to turn back', as Rohr puts it, provides the disaster historian valuable information about the mentalities in play.

Rohr's study of the 1348 earthquake serves as a recipe for how to approach disaster research from the historical discipline, in the tradition of history of mentalities. Exactly because disasters are unexpected, overwhelming events that force people and organizations out of their comfort zones and destroy everyday patterns and structures, they leave a lot of traces in the form of written or visual accounts – allowing the historian to conduct an autopsy that would otherwise not have been possible.

Disaster history and the city

Historically, disasters have been understood as 'catalysts for urban construction, institutional, social and political change that, amongst other things, also triggered productive and creative responses like the professionalization of fire brigades or innovation in law and urban planning, but also promoted social segregation' (Schenk and Engels 2007: 17). Likewise, Greg Bankoff *et al.* (2012) analysed how the constant risk of fire throughout history has left lasting imprints on almost every dimension of urban society. Histories of cities struck by catastrophe thus form another aspect of disaster history with great potential.

Kevin Rozario, also a historian, has investigated how the 1906 San Francisco earthquake has been framed in terms of 'creative destruction', as formulated by the economist Joseph Schumpeter (Rozario 2001; Schumpeter 2010 [1942]). This idea of capitalist systems re-energizing themselves through destructive processes, which actually originated with Karl Marx as 'annihilation' ('Vernichtung'), seems almost too obvious for the disaster historian to apply; as theory it could perhaps even provide a framework for understanding how (capitalist) societies in the long run benefit from catastrophe. Schumpeter himself, however, never related the concept to disasters of natural or man-made origin when he published his book on capitalism, socialism and democracy in 1942. In his analysis, the disruptive force came in the shape of innovative entrepreneurs who entered a market with novel technologies or ideas, which simply wreaked havoc upon the established businesses.

It is extremely difficult to talk about 'winners and losers' in a disaster, due to challenges in micro- as well as macro-economic analysis of catastrophic change, as well as the moral implications (Scanlon 1988). The application of 'creative destruction' as a conceptual approach to historical disaster research is mostly a (powerful) metaphor. One thinker who actually did view disasters as a necessary and even beneficial part of capitalist systems was John Stuart Mill. As Rozario notes, Mill 'expected disasters to produce long-term benefits by obliterating old stock and encouraging manufacturers to introduce new efficiencies into their production processes, adopting better technologies and building more efficient plants' (Rozario 2001: 77).

An example of such a benefit is a business that profited tremendously from the flux that followed the 1906 San Francisco earthquake and fire. The Bank of Italy was founded just two years before by Amadeo Pietro Giannini, the son of Italian immigrants. When the earthquake struck in the early hours of 18 April, Giannini moved quickly. With the help of another Italian immigrant he hid the contents of his bank's vault under layers of garbage and simple drove the money out of the devastated city to his home in San Mateo. While many of the other banks in San Francisco lost their buildings as well as their holdings to the flames, Giannini was able to reopen his business very quickly using a plank across two barrels as substitute for a real bank counter. This head-start on his competitors, combined with the Italian banker's firm faith in a handshake, resulted in a huge number of loans to small-business owners and citizens from the middle class who were then able to rebuild their shops and homes. Giannini later merged his Bank of Italy with a Los Angeles bank, and under his chairmanship the new financial institution grew to unprecedented size. Its name was Bank of America, today one of the world's biggest companies (see Kurzman 2001 for a colourful recollection of Giannini's story).

Businessmen like Gianinni were not the only ones to see a window of opportunity open as the earth trembled beneath San Francisco. A progressive movement consisting of wealthy and influential industrialists and professionals had in the years leading up to 1906 formulated a vision for improving the city's architecture and infrastructures with a blend of 'artistic form and efficient function' (Rozario 2001: 84). Public transport and service should be the finest in the country, and wide boulevards and spacious parks would benefit its citizens' physical as well as mental well-being. As Rozario notes, the progressives in San Francisco wanted for their city what the Parisians got half a century before when Georges-Eugène 'Baron' Haussmann under the auspice of Emperor Napoleon III (who himself looked to another great catastrophe, the Great Fire of London in 1666 for inspiration) tore down the old city and built a new one, thus propelling Paris into the 20th century well ahead of time (Rozario 2001: 84–5). But even though the progressives moved quickly, and tried to seize the moment to put their great 'Burnham Plan' for rebuilding San Francisco into practice, they failed miserably, mainly due to conflict within the movement and widespread opposition among local businessmen towards the 'monumentalism' of the vision of the architect Daniel Burnham (who had built the 'White City' for Chicago's World's Fair in 1893) for their city (Rozario 2001: 87). In the end, San Francisco was rebuilt within five years with insurance money paid to those who could agree to reconstruct rather than revolutionize.

Another interesting take on the 1906 earthquake in San Francisco is Andrea Rees Davies's *Saving San Francisco*, a social history of the disaster. Rees Davies is a trained historian with an unusual background: before she became an academic she worked as a firefighter in San Francisco, and as such she gained entrance to people's private lives: 'I walked into the lives that people really lived, not the versions that they put on display for relatives, friends, or neighbors. After all, there is no time to tidy up after dialing 911' (Rees Davies 2012: 1). This personal experience inspired her approach to historical disaster research.

Using the earthquake and the fire that followed as a lens, she investigates the political and social changes brought about by the disaster, to challenge what she terms the 'long-lived myth' that the catastrophe in 1906 erased social differences as it levelled the city. Just as she as a first responder walked into people's 'real lives' and got to see and hear things that would otherwise have remained private, Rees Davies draws upon the unexpectedness and outspokenness of the disaster to tell its secrets. She shows, convincingly, that the 1906 earthquake didn't create the opportunities for positive social change that was claimed afterwards – it merely exposed existing social inequalities and, in many cases, reinforced them: 'In the drive to restore the city's losses, the new San Francisco reconstructed the social divisions it claimed to eschew' (Rees Davis 2012: 142).

Ted Steinberg, professor of history and law, argues that the 1906 San Francisco earthquake was followed by decades of what he calls 'seismic denial'. Even though the disaster was described in hundreds of books and articles, it was never properly represented as a historical event – merely as an archetype produced by popular media that never questioned the political leaders' interests in framing the core of the disaster as a fire, rather than an earthquake (Steinberg 2001: 103).

Future research: concepts and counterfactualism

The German historian Reinhardt Koselleck pioneered what has become known as 'Begriffsgeschichte' ('Conceptual History') in the late 20th century. This specific branch of history traces the history of concepts such as 'crisis' or 'democracy' through time, often from antiquity to the modern. The source material for such studies would be dictionaries, encyclopedias, lexica, policy documents, legislation, etc. What interested Koselleck and his fellow conceptual historians was how the content of the concepts under investigation changed, reflecting the shifting paradigms of thought, power hierarchies and cultural dimensions. Of specific interest to the disaster historian is Koselleck's entry on *Krise* ('Crisis') in *Basic Concepts of History* (*Geschichtliches Grundbegriffe*), which is as close to a conceptual history of 'Disaster/Catastrophe' as he got (Koselleck and Richter 2006). Even though important contributions have been provided by disaster scholars such as Enrico Quarantelli, Wolf Dombrowsky and Russel Dynes, and, most recently, Gerrit Schenk and his network, it is still left to a future professional historian to write a complete conceptual history of this important concept.

Another branch of the historical discipline, which might prove helpful to the disaster historian, is *counterfactualism*. This somewhat contested approach asks 'what might have been' and typically focuses on defining moments in history and alternative outcomes, mirroring possible contingencies as an antidote to determinism (Black 2008). While not a genre in and of itself, but rather a mode of argumentation, counterfactualism offers a kind of 'retrospective disaster risk reduction' opportunity: is it possible to rewind history and play it differently with slightly altered settings?

What was, for instance, the role of Captain Smith on the *Titanic's* maiden voyage in 1912? Is it plausible that history would have unfolded in a different way if he had been replaced by Captain Haddock of the sister ship *Olympic*? Perhaps not. But that would be the same as to say that he did not play any role at all in the tragedy. Another counterfactual take on disaster history could be to analyse the role of specific catastrophic events by speculating on their absence. How might the European Enlightenment have evolved if not for the 1755 Lisbon earthquake and the intellectual discussion it fuelled? What role did that disaster play in the secularization of Europe's societies and communities?

Counterfactual reasoning, as controversial as it may be, often provides the historian with a useful intellectual playroom where new insights and old prejudices and assumptions may be brought out and exercised in the open. It is always about *what happened* – but this Rankean version of history is mirrored in contingencies and alternatives serving as antidotes to determinism (Dahlberg 2004). And, if nothing else, historical counterfactualism gives us the opportunity to avoid a disaster or two in retrospect.

Note

1 There is some controversy as to the correct English translation of Ranke's famous expression. Due to the lacking 'ist' at the end of the original sentence in German, it can be both 'actually' and 'essentially' (Stroud 1987).

References

Bankoff, G. (2002) *Cultures of Disaster: Society and Natural Hazard in the Philippines*. London: Routledge.

Bankoff, G. (2007) Comparing vulnerabilities: Toward charting an historical trajectory of disasters. *Historical Social Research*, 3(32), 103–14.

Bankoff, G. (2010) No such things as 'natural disasters': Why we had to invent them. *Harvard International Review*, 24 Aug.

Bankoff, G., Lütken, U., and Sand, J. (2012) *Flammable Cities: Urban Conflagration and the Making of the Modern World*. Madison, WI: University of Wisconsin Press.

Berlioz, J. (1998) *Castastrophes naturelles et calamites au moyen âge*. Florence: Edizioni del Galluzzo.

Black, J. (2008) *What If? Counterfactualism and the Problem of History*. London: Social Affairs Unit.

Borst, A. (1981) Das Erdbeben von 1348: Ein historischer Beitrag zur Katastrophenforschung. *Historische Zeitschrift*, 233, 530–69.

Dahlberg, R. (2004) 'Roads Not Taken', in P.H. Hansen and J. Nevers (eds), *Historiefagets teoretiske udfordring*. Odense: University of Southern Denmark Press, 207–29.

Diamond, J. (2005) *Collapse. How Societies Choose to Fail or Succeed*. New York: Viking Press.

Dynes, R. (2000) The dialogue between Voltaire and Rousseau on the Lisbon Earthquake: The emergence of a social science view. *International Journal of Mass Emergencies and Disasters*, 18(1), 97–115.

Ginzburg, C. (1980) *The Cheese and the Worms: The Cosmos of a Sixteenth-Century Miller*. London: Routledge & Kegan Paul.

Hammerl, C. (1994) The earthquake of January 25th, 1348: Discussion of sources. In P. Albini and A. Moroni (eds), *1994 Materials of CEC Project Review of Historical Seismicity in Europe*, vol. 2. Milan: CNR.

Hempel, C.G. (1942) The function of general laws in history. *Journal of Philosophy*, 39(2), 35–48.

Janku, A., Schenk, G.J., and Mauelshagen, F. (eds) (2012) *Historical Disasters in Context: Science, Religion, and Politics*. London: Routledge.

Juneja, M., and Mauelshagen, F. (2007) Disasters and pre-industrial societies. Historiographic trends and comparative perspectives. *Medieval History Journal*, 10(1–2), 1–31.

Koselleck, R., and Richter, M. (2006) Crisis. *Journal of the History of Ideas*, 67(2), 357–400.

Kurzman, D. (2001) *Disaster! The Great San Francisco Earthquake and Fire of 1906*. New York: HarperCollins.

Özgenel, L. (2008) A tale of two cities: In search for ancient Pompeii and Herculaneum. *METU JFA*, 1(25/1), 1–25.

Quarantelli, E.L. (1998) *What is a Disaster? A Dozen Perspectives on the Question*. London: Routledge.

Rees Davies, A. (2012) *Saving San Francisco: Relief and Recovery After the 1906 Disaster*. Philadelphia, PA: Temple University Press.

Richer, M. (2001) Preface to the translation of the introduction and prefaces to Reinhardt Koselleck's 'Geschichtliches Gundbegriffe'. *Contributions to the History of Concepts*, 6(1), 1–37.

Rohr, C. (2003) Man and natural disaster in the late Middle Ages: The earthquake in Carenthia and Northern Italy on 25 January 1348 and its perception. *Environment and History*, 9(2), 127–49.

Rozario, K. (2001) What comes down must go up: Why disasters have been good for American capitalism. In S. Biel (ed.), *American Disasters*. New York: New York University Press, 72–102.

Scanlon, J. (1988) Winners and losers: Some thoughts about the political economy of disaster. *Journal of Mass Emergencies and Disasters*, 6(1), 47–63.

Schenk, G.J. (ed.) (2009) *Katastrophen: Vom Untergang Pompejis bis zum Klimawandel*. Ostfildern: Thorbecke.

Schenk, G.J., and Engels, J.I. (2007) Historical disaster research: Concepts, methods and case studies (special issue). *Historical Social Research*, 121(32/3).

Schenk, G.J., Juneja, M., Wieczorek, A., and Lind, Ch. (2014) *Mensch. Natur. Katastrophe. Von Atlantis bis Heute*. Regensburg: Schnell & Steiner.

Schumpeter, J. (2010) *Capitalism, Socialism and Democracy*. London: Routledge.

Steinberg, T. (2001) Smoke and mirrors. The San Francisco Earthquake and seismic denial. In S. Biel (ed.), *American Disasters*. New York: New York University Press, 103–26.

Stroud, R.S. (1987) 'Wie es eigentlich gewesen' and Thucydides 2.48.3. *Hermes*, 115(3), 379–82.

3 Theology and disaster studies

From 'acts of God' to divine presence

Niels H. Gregersen

Introduction

Since the early 1950s, disaster research has emerged as an academic field firmly based in the social sciences. Whether or not disasters happen as a result of natural hazards, technological accidents or intentional acts of violence, social scientists have taken the lead in framing the field from its beginnings and up to today. A recent review article states without further ado: 'Disaster studies address the social and behavioral aspects of sudden onset collective stress situations typically referred to as mass emergencies or disaster' (Lindell 2013: 797).

I take this to be a fair description of the field as hitherto developed. Accordingly, other disciplinary approaches to disaster studies will be asked about their particular input to understanding the disaster cycle of prevention, preparedness, short-term response and long-term reconstruction. In this chapter, I lay out what I think is the added value of theological reflections in relation to sociological disaster studies, while also pointing to some structural limitations in current disaster research. For even though sociology is rightly regarded as the queen of disaster studies, any discipline has its blind spots. So, what is *basis* and what is *bias* in prevailing paradigms of disaster research?

I begin this chapter by pointing out some disciplinary limitations of sociological disaster research. The subsequent section points to obvious areas of shared interest between disaster studies and theology. Then, I discuss the potential value of bringing academic theology into future disaster research, both as an added value and as a structural expansion of research areas. I here argue that disaster researchers would benefit from having a better understanding of the importance of religious communities, both as victims and as agents of recovery, while listening to their interpretative frameworks. How do people of faith understand disasters from religiously informed perspectives? What I hope to show is that the *pragmatic* repertoires of religious disaster response are linked to more comprehensive *semantic* repertoires of religion, that is, to the potentials of faith-based interpretations of reality. Religious responses to disasters tend to have a wider scope than often acknowledged, involving both a psychological preparedness for 'passive' endurance and 'active' sources for helping victims in overcoming disaster-related traumas. What theology might bring into the interdisciplinary field is a better understanding of the complexity of religious responses to disasters – from the small-scale local traditions to overarching religious patterns of meaning. A religious semantics may thus nurture a variety of attitudes simultaneously, attitudes such as (1) seeing disasters as imbued with potential meaning, (2) motivating people for overcoming post-disaster effects, and (3) understanding human social existence as entangled with natural conditions, leading to personal tragedies and commonly experienced disasters.

In the final section, I move into the domain of philosophically reflected second-order theologies as exemplified in the tradition of theodicy. How are religious beliefs in the love and might of God compatible with experiences of threatened and devastated life conditions? While criticizing the Enlightenment view that we live in 'the best possible world', epitomized in Leibniz's *Theodicy* of 1710, I argue that theodicies may continue to play more humble roles in contemporary theological reflections on disasters, provided that they acknowledge that chaos and cosmos, creativity and destructivity, inevitably go together in the package deal of creation. From this perspective, the theodicy-expectation of living a smooth life beyond dangers and risks may be part of the problem rather than of its solution. Theodicies are thus not able to provide answers to the kind of unanswerable questions that we as human beings continue to ask: 'Why me?' 'Why us?'

How can such questions be addressed theologically without falling into a religious narcissism? In a more normative vein informed by the resources of Christian theology, I propose that the constructive task of theology is not to explain away the experience of damage and evil within cleverly contrived theodicies, but to help disaster victims to move on. Rather than seeing disasters as particularistic 'acts of God' (like adverse miracles), I propose to see disasters as situations in which people of faith both experience and appeal to a sensed divine presence – in, with, and under the disastrous happenings themselves. But lived religion is also involved in the processes of recovery and reconstruction following upon experiences of disaster. In this context I refer to some recent proposals for a theology of trauma – a theology developed for victims rather than evil-doers.

Blind spots of disaster studies?

In a highly self-reflective study on the social and historical factors affecting the early development of disaster research, Quarantelli (1987) points to the extent to which the external funding conditions influenced academic disaster research since its beginning in the 1950s. The major programmes of disaster research (located at the Universities of Chicago, Ohio and Delaware) were all funded by the US military system in order to investigate social and psychological effects of a possible use of nuclear and chemical weapons. Quarantelli speaks of a 'wartime orientation' of early disaster studies, which lasted well into the 1960s. The sponsors wanted to know, for example, whether victims tend to act selfishly or pro-socially, and how to handle post-disaster situations. This background, as Quarantelli points out, may be responsible for choosing major earthquakes, volcanoes or tornadoes as 'the prototype of a disaster', rather than the more 'diffuse emergencies' related to recurrent disasters with long-term effects such as 'famines or droughts or epidemics, and even large scale riverine flooding' (Quarantelli 1987: 301).

Another institutional background for the development of disaster studies, also highlighted by Quarantelli, is the predominant role of sociologists in the field: 'disaster is primarily a social phenomenon and is thus identifiable in social terms'; more precisely, 'most of the disaster research by sociologists has been of an organizational nature' (Quarantelli and Dynes 1977: 24, 30). This already applied to the so-called *dominant paradigm* of disaster research, reigning from the 1950s to the 1970s. While gradually bracketing the issues pertaining to post-atomic catastrophe, disasters were defined as events with wide-ranging damaging effects on societies, to be counteracted by technological and organizational interventions. This view was eminently captured by Fritz in his famous definition, according to which a disaster is 'an event concentrated in time and space, in which a society or one of its subdivisions undergoes physical harm and social disruption, such that all or some essential functions of the society or subdivision are impaired' (Fritz 1961: 655).

Around 1980, the so-called *vulnerability paradigm* emerged. In several regards, its advantages are obvious. By emphasizing the vulnerability of societies, the focus shifts from singular outbreaks of catastrophe to cycles of recurrent emergencies such as drought, famine and epidemics, including the long-term process of climate change with its 'dispersed causes and effects' (Gardiner 2011). The vulnerability paradigm points to natural hazards as amplifiers of already existing 'normal' conditions; disasters are not just rare, extreme and sudden outbreaks. Moreover, vulnerabilities are not equally shared in terms of economic and social resources – some are more vulnerable than others. Finally, the vulnerability paradigm rightly points out that a society remains responsible for the effects of disasters, even if they emerge 'naturally'.

Gradually, the vulnerability paradigm also opens up to the importance of cultural factors such as social capital. As argued by Nix-Stevenson,

> I contend that social capital is a key factor in moving toward a culture of disaster prevention and risk reduction and that social capital can generate both the conditions necessary for mutual support and care and the mechanisms required for communities and groups to exert effective pressure to influence public policy.
>
> (Nix-Stevenson 2013: 1)

With the inclusion of cultural factors, also the role of faith communities comes into view. Social resilience has many layers, from national and international agencies to individual and community-based capacities. The questions here are, 'Who cares?' 'Who is prepared to care for whom?'

Thus, also the vulnerability paradigm may have its limitations, and perhaps we are currently on the move towards a *resilience paradigm* (Dahlberg *et al.* 2015). Resilience has many levels, from social capacities to ecological and geophysical systems (Nix-Stevenson 2013: 8). These 'spatial' aspects of natural systems should be addressed by the natural sciences. Similarly, the focus on social capital, including the religious sense of meaning and vocation, may lead us to take a broader view on the cultural traditions that shape mentality and capacity-building over time. Social capital is not something that is only there to be utilized; it takes the work of generations to nurture the repertoire of attitudes important for coping with disaster effects.

Provided that theology is a second-order reflection of living faith traditions, theological reflections tend to keep alive a *wide-scope view* of the natural roots of disasters while also taking a *longer view* on sociocultural processes. This longer historical view is at odds with the attitude of a secular supersessionism expressed by some sociologists, who see religion as tied up with a 'premodern' fatalistic attitude, whereas sociologists take themselves to be more 'modern' or managerial in attitude, if not even 'postmodern' in analytical orientation. In earlier work I have questioned the simplistic tripartite scheme of premodern 'fate', modern 'control' and postmodern 'constructivism' in the risk theories of Ulrich Beck and Anthony Giddens (Gregersen 2006). A similar scheme seems at work within sociological disaster research, where one finds the idea that an 'act of God' perspective is successively replaced by an 'act of Nature' perspective, which is finally superseded by an 'acts of Men and Women' approach (Quarantelli, cited by Merli 2010: 106). Nonetheless, in face of disasters we are, as it were, placed in a premodern situation in which major events are falling upon us. In brief, by taking a longer historical view and a wider view of the human entanglement with cosmic forces, theological reflection presupposes that we simultaneously live in a premodern, modern and postmodern mentality – not the one without the other.

Shared areas of interdisciplinary contact: the pragmatics of faith traditions

Liverpool geologist Chester has rightly called for a much-needed dialogue between theology and disaster studies (Chester 1998, 2005). Let me here point to two obvious areas of contact.

First, religious communities tend to be committed *agents of recovery*. Alongside governmental institutions (police and fire departments, local or national emergency agencies, and the army), religious communities serve as non-governmental organizations (NGOs) capable of empathizing, offering help in first phases of emergencies, and coping with long-term disaster effects. Many NGOs are faith-based organizations (FBOs).

As noted by Smith, 'In the past, studies of community disasters and disaster recovery have tended to ignore the activities of religious organizations' (Smith 1978: 133). Yet Smith was able to show the extent to which the collection and distribution of food, shelter, clothes, money, etc. was in fact organized by religious communities. In Xenia, Ohio, no less than eighty-six local congregations worked in a post-tornado setting in 1974. After Hurricane Katrina, Koenig offered a comprehensive analysis of the North American situation. The book *In the Wake of Disaster* (Koenig 2006) evidenced that in the US alone more than fifty FBOs are continuously involved in disaster response, including one Hindu and one Jewish organization. While the

Lutheran Disaster Response, the Catholic Charities Office, and the Salvation Army are the largest organizations in terms of staff and resources, smaller communities can also play a significant role. For example, the Church of the Brethren responded to Hurricane Agnes in 1972 with no less than 2,203 volunteers assisting 725 affected households in the town area of Wilkes-Barre in Pennsylvania (Koenig 2006: 59).

It would be a task for future research to gain an overview of the different forms of faith-based disaster response worldwide. Usually, FBOs work in tandem with humanitarian organizations such as the Red Cross or Red Crescent. While some religious groups still differentiate between true believers and sinners (Merli 2010), most FBOs follow universalistic humanitarian principles and help victims regardless of class, gender and religion. Thus Actalliance, a worldwide alliance of 140 churches, states unreservedly in its 'Guide on community-based psychosocial support' (accessed October 2014): '*Evangelisation and proselytising during an emergency is inappropriate and cannot be permitted*' (emphasis in original).

Second, religious people are not only agents of recovery, but among the victims of disasters. By 2010, about 84 per cent of the world's population described themselves as religiously affiliated (PewResearch, 18 December 2012). Since human beings can be described as 'self-interpreting animals' (Taylor 1985), it should not come as a surprise that also catastrophic events are interpreted in religious terms. In a recent study using the big data provided by the *World Values Survey* and the *European Values Survey*, Copenhagen economist Bentzen has shown that experiences of disaster may even trigger religiosity. Testing no less than 800 regions of the world, and excluding potential confounders (such as income, education, demography, religious differences and country-dependent factors), it appears that regions located closer to events of disaster turn out to be significantly more religious than other regions (Bentzen 2013: 2). Meanwhile, other studies indicate that people of faith tend to recover better in post-disaster settings than non-religious individuals (see Koenig 2006: 29–42). The jury is still out, however, on how exactly to measure the religious factor in terms of long-term coping, and how to balance negative and positive coping aspects of different forms of religiosity.

Standard academic discourse usually describes disasters in purely scientific terms. However, 'religious explanations of disasters not only persist, but also transcend religious tradition and place' (Chester and Duncan 2010: 87). Investigating material comprising fifty-nine natural hazards occurring between 1902 and 2004, Chester and Duncan showed that only seventeen disasters were not couched in religious terms in non-academic disaster reports. Moreover, inquiry into intentional divine agency seems as widespread in the more recent disasters as in earlier times, sometimes even stronger, although Chester and Duncan (2010: 88–90) also note that religious explanations in terms of a divine judgement appear more frequently in less economically developed societies.

Religious responses to disaster are inherently complex. Even strong religious explanations in terms of divine judgement may well be accompanied with an active involvement in disaster relief efforts (Chester and Duncan 2010: 90; Rokib 2012). In her study of local religious responses to an earthquake in Java, May 2006, anthropologist Judith Schlehe notes,

[T]he Javanese are not any more 'superstitious' or in any categorical sense more inclined to believe in supernatural explanations for disasters than people elsewhere. They know very well that there are scientific, geological reasons behind an earthquake. *Besides* tectonic activity, though, for many Javanese causality is rooted in the spiritual realm as well. They see more dimensions … Thus, people everywhere can and do combine and negotiate manifold co-existing explanations and coping strategies in an enduring entanglement of secular and religious interpretations of natural hazards and disasters.

(Schlehe 2010: 113)

This combinatorial capacity of religious interpretation should not come as a surprise; similar features come up in other examples of crisis-related religion, for example, among cancer-survivors (Johannesen-Henry 2012). Provided that the task of theology is not so much to categorize religious beliefs as to understand their meanings, there is here a natural affinity between theological and anthropological approaches. Just as theologians aim to interpret religious life also through internal perspectives, so anthropologists practise an ethics of 'ethnographic listening':

I advocate an ethics of dialogue and engagement based on a detailed understanding of the ways in which various local figures and communities deal with disasters. This is meant to emphasise the importance of ethnographic listening, a way of focusing attention on people's knowledge and beliefs, imaginations and interpretations. A culture-specific and site-based reading of the discourse on a natural disaster exemplifies that disaster-linked cognitive coping strategies are always unique and contingent formations in response to local culture and politics. Notwithstanding, local culture and politics must be seen in their larger global context.

(Schlehe 2010: 113)

While theologians wish to share an ethics of listening, they would probably add that religious views are not 'always unique and contingent'; even local disaster-responses make use of semantic repertoires stemming from the major religious traditions. The task of anthropologists and theologians may here be said to be complementary to one another: while anthropologists give privilege to local traditions, theologians prioritize the wider traditions. Obviously both aspects should be addressed and coordinated as far as possible.

The question of the meaning of disasters: the semantic dimension of theology

The analysis of the semantic repertoires of the major religions constitutes a third area, in which theology may contribute to disaster research. Religions – ancient and modern – foster myths and metanarratives about the order and disorder of the universe and produce what may be termed 'moral cosmologies' about preferential roads to take in view of impending dangers.

The discipline of 'systematic theology' is exactly to reflect upon the meaning of such large-scale views of reality and on their contemporary uses (and misuses) by people of faith. Also here, the semantics and pragmatics of faith traditions belong together. Just as religious worlds of meaning can be interpreted in various ways (some more illuminative than others), so too can religious practices take a variety of forms (some more helpful than others). In theology, as well as in philosophy, normative questions cannot be eschewed. Accordingly, academic theology has a two-fold representative role in contemporary society: representing religious concerns and commitments to the wider culture, and representing the concerns and commitments of the wider society to religious practitioners.

It goes without saying that experiences of tragedy and disaster are reflected in most developed religions. In the biblical traditions, we have stories of *personal tragedy* (such as Job) and stories of *social fiasco* (such as Jesus). Tragedies are highly individualizing, to the point of creating absolute loneliness. Job stood alone among his so-called friends who continued to argue that he himself was guilty of his losses. Likewise, Jesus was alone among his followers who slept when he wept (in the Garden of Gethsemane), and who fled from the danger of association when he was approaching Calvary. Tragedies, like Shakespeare's *Hamlet*, are stories about being radically alone and not being understood by others. The particular pain of tragedy is that the world around you continues as if nothing has happened. Catastrophes, by contrast, deal with socially shared experiences of horrors – conditions that continue to be threatening, also to the survivors. Religions reflect on disasters no less than on tragedies: the Quran frequently refers to earthquakes; the Hebrew Bible tells about starvation and plagues; the New Testament refers to a world which is going to dissolve from top to bottom. Hereby, the great stories of religion prepare the mindset of religious people for the possibility of the impossible: the onset of catastrophes.

A prominent example is the story of the great deluge, best known in our culture from the Hebrew Bible (Genesis 6–9). This is certainly a story of God's retributive judgement, but the biblical story is followed by God's self-commitment never again to perform such 'acts of God':

> As for me, I am establishing my covenant with you and your descendants after you, and with every living creature that is with you, the birds, the domestic animals, and every animal of the earth with you, as many as came out of the ark … God said, 'This is the sign of the covenant that I make between me and you and every living creature that is with you, for all future generations: I have set my bow in the clouds, and it shall be a sign of the covenant between me and the earth … the waters shall never again become a flood to destroy all flesh.
>
> (Genesis 9: 9–14; NRSV)

From the late 15th century, Europeans began to collect deluge stories among the 'heathens'. Already a Renaissance humanist like Michel de Montagne (1533–92) saw in one of these deluge stories 'vaine shadowes of our religion', which 'witnesse the dignity and divinity therof' (*Essays*, 2: 12; cited by Lang 1985: 605). Later, in *Die Traditionen des Menschengeschlechts oder die Uroffenbarung Gottes unter den Heiden* from 1869, the Catholic priest Heinrich Lüken collected a vast ensemble of deluge stories from Persia, India, China, Africa, North and South American, and the Pacific islands. Lüken's interpretation was apologetic in nature, since he took these stories to reflect 'God's original self-revelation' to all people. At the turn of the 20th century, another interpretation was taken by historians of religion such as Sir James George Frazer (in *Folk-Lore in the Old Testament*, 1918), who rather argued that such stories have emerged from a common structure in the human mind, reflecting a 'primitive mentality' (Lang 1985: 614).

A third interpretation, however, is less ideologically loaded: deluge stories (often accompanied by stories of an ascending rainbow) express widespread human experiences of flooding and recovery. In this view, myths are not produced within the minds of human beings, but emerge in the interaction between self-interpreting animals and their ever-changing socionatural environments. Stories of floods, earthquakes and volcanoes express the awareness that disasters belong to the human condition – now, then and in the future. But religious myths do not merely describe typical states of affairs; they also formulate hopes for a non-repetition of catastrophic events. In Genesis 6–9 this hope is based in God's self-commitment to establish a unilateral pact that narrows the scope of future 'acts of God' while widening the covenant to include all life-forms on earth. In religious texts, hope is expressed in prayers to be able to endure and survive the impact of disasters or in lamentations – cries from the devastated earth to a God who is not only depicted as a 'speaking' God but also as a 'listening' God (Genesis 16: 13; cf. Matthew 6: 6).

In the wake of disasters, old routines cannot just be continued. Something new must happen. Recovery is therefore never a return to *status quo* – it is constructive. Here liturgy plays a central role in religious coping: liturgies combine a religious communication with a bodily coordination among the participants, regardless of their prior faith commitments. Just to mention two recent examples: the Indian Ocean tsunami on 26 December 2004 and the massacre by Anders Breivik of sixty-nine youngsters on the island Utøya outside of Oslo on 22 July 2011. In both cases, liturgies established frameworks for collective bereavement and hope. While expressing loss and bewilderment from a 'present tense'-perspective, the liturgies were also both 'backwards-looking' when dealing with the scars of involuntary remembrance, and 'forwards-looking' in orientating victims and helpers towards the future. New liturgies were made up – such as 'counterfeit funerals' for bodies that could not be found after the 2004 tsunami (Falk 2010). But for most, traditional liturgies were only slightly revised and re-enacted for remembrance and mourning. This was also the case in Norway in 2011. Even in secular Scandinavia, the sacred and the secular appear to be intertwined rather than separated (Wyller *et al.* 2014).

In liturgy, a religious semantics is at work in a redemptive therapy that often brings up ancient patterns of religious sensibility. One example is the renewed sense of a community between living and dead. The conviction that ancestors are present in the midst of the life of their descendants is prominent not only in African, but also in Chinese and Japanese cultures. Even though Buddhism officially denies the existence of persons after death, Buddhist funeral ceremonies in Thailand in 2004 not only separated the living from the dead, but also articulated the spiritual bonds between the departed and the remaining ones (Falk 2010).

Traditionally, within Christianity funerals serve to give thanks for the life of those who have passed away while also delivering the dead into the hands of God. Also here, the separation between the living and the deceased is accompanied by a sense of a coexistence between the living and the dead within the life of God. According to the Apostles' Creed (the baptismal formula in most Christian churches), the church is not spoken of as a member-based religious organization. Theologically, the Church (as an institution) is 'the communion of the saints' (*communio sanctorum*) – a communion of believers from all ages, even going back to the forebears long before Christianity was established (see Hebrews 11: 1–13). The celebration of the Lord's Supper similarly gives liturgical prominence to a co-presence of the deceased under the Eucharistic meal, often explained by reference to the (invisible) half-circle behind the altar which closes the circle with the (visible) half-circle of those partaking in the Eucharistic meal during a service. 'The Kingdom of God', in this view, is here a virtual no less than an actualized reality, expressing God's world-including life. For 'in him we live and move and have our being' (Acts 17: 28), a view of God sometimes referred to by philosopher-theologians as 'panentheism' (Clayton and Peacocke 2004).

There should be no doubt that the major religious traditions differ markedly from one another in terms of practices and beliefs. But even so, there are surprising overlaps across religious traditions. Not everything is written in the plural, since religions address universal problems of the human condition such as life and death, flourishing and destruction, individuality and sociality. Put more formally: any religious semantics says *something* (the meaning) *about something* (the referent) *for somebody* (the religious interpreter) in a specific *context*. The aforementioned reference problems, as well as shared local contexts (such as disasters), explain some of the overlaps between religious traditions, whereas the distinctiveness of religious traditions derive from what religious traditions actually *say* about these issues (their different semantics), and how this is pragmatically lived out by self-interpreting religious communities.

Moreover, religions tend to follow shared trajectories concerning the inherent *logic* in concepts of divinity, or ultimate reality. In monotheistic religions, including Western and most Hindu traditions, one would look in vain for views of divinity according to which God exists only on some days (say, sunny days) and not on other days (say, stormy days). Nor is God spatially constrained to specific geographic areas (say, Palestine). A medieval tract, *The Book of the 24 Philosophers* (§2), formulates the logic as follows: 'God is like an infinite sphere whose center is everywhere, and whose periphery is nowhere'. The logic is as follows: if God *is*, God does not exist like an empirical thing or person in the inventory of the universe. Rather, God is the creative source of all that exists, or may come into existence, in the empirical world. Furthermore, if God is the creative source of *all* reality, divine agency refers to everything that exists – not just to some fatal events designated as 'acts of God'. The latter phrase may be a suitable term for insurance companies and for presidents of the US when declaring an emergency as *force majeure*, for which human actors are not responsible (Steinberg 2000). But from a theological point of view, the particularistic notion of 'acts of God' is a dubious concept.

From 'acts of God' to divine presence: theodicies 'from above' and theodicies 'from below'

Nonetheless, the ascription of disasters to distinctive 'acts of God' is likely to persist. Human beings have a causal instinct to seek answers to the question, 'Why this, not that?', but speaking about a dimension of meaning 'in the midst of things' is not the same as singling out disastrous events as particularly designed by God. The teaching of Jesus is particularly clear on this point:

> At that very time there were some present who told him about the Galileans whose blood Pilate had mingled with their sacrifices. He asked them, 'Do you think that because these Galileans suffered in this way they were worse sinners than all other Galileans? No, I tell you; but unless you repent, you will all perish as they did. Or those eighteen who were killed when the tower of Siloam fell on them – do you think that they were worse offenders than all the others living in Jerusalem? No, I tell you; but unless you repent, you will all perish just as they did.
>
> (Luke 13: 1–5; NRSV)

This is a flat rejection of moralistic 'act of God' theologies. Nonetheless, the Old Testament is full of stories of divine vengeance and education, and Christian thinkers have often followed the Western church father Augustine (354–430) in assuming that evil has two sources: one coming from perverted creatures, the other from God's judgement upon them (*Handbook of Faith, Hope and Love*, 8.23). Reflecting on the earthquake in Lisbon 1755, the otherwise warmhearted preacher-theologian John Wesley (1703–91) speaks of a divine revenge,

> Is there indeed a God that judges the world? And is he now making inquisition for blood? If so, it is not surprising that he should begin there, where so much blood has been pourd on the ground like water! Where so many brave men have murdered, in the most base and cowardly as well as barbarous manner, almost every day, as well as every night, while none regarded or laid it to heart.
>
> (Wesley 1812: 397–8)

For Wesley, the inhabitants of Lisbon received only their fair retribution, given the widespread torture by the Roman Catholic inquisition silently supported by affluent Lisboan citizens. Only few 20th-century Christian theologians would take such position today, but 'act of Allah' theologies continue to be strong in Muslim countries (Schmuck 2000; Merli 2010).

One might think that theistic religions are more prone to such intention-and-agent-based thinking than non-theistic ones. But on 30 December 2004, the prominent Buddhist monk and writer, Thich Nthat Hanh, gave a speech in which he reflected on the relationship between human evil and the Indian Ocean tsunami on 26 December:

> The human species and the planet Earth are one body. I have the feeling that our planet Earth is suffering, and this tsunami is the cry of the Earth as it writhes in pain: a lament, a cry for help, a warning. We have lived together so long without love and compassion for each other. We destroy each other; we abuse our mother Earth. So the Earth has turned back on us, has groaned, has suffered. The Earth is the mother of all species. We make each other suffer and we make our mother suffer. These earthquakes are bells of mindfulness. The pain of one part of humankind is the pain of the whole of humankind. We have to see that and wake up.
>
> (Cited by Falk 2010: 99)

Here Hanh speaks of nature as an intentional agent sending signals of warning and wake-up calls to the human race – a thought pattern consistent with the Buddhist conviction that a self-aware Buddha-body pervades the whole of nature, from bottom to top. *Karma* is operative across the nature–culture distinction. Note, however, that Hanh wisely avoids singling out the victims as sinners in a particular sense. Nonetheless, both theistic and non-theistic religions assume that the full circle of God (respectively the primordial Buddha awareness) is present in the midst of reality everywhere, in suffering as well as in joy.

Already the philosophical tradition of theodicy transcended the particularistic 'act of God' view by focusing on the relation between divine agency and the world as a whole. Leibniz's classic *Theodicy* from 1710 is probably more often referred to in passing than read and digested. And so the picture comes forth that Leibniz's Enlightenment theology was expressing a cosmic optimism, which then paved the way for a cosmic pessimism expressed in Voltaire's novel *Candide* from 1759 (Dynes 2000: 101–2). The picture is more complex, though. For Leibniz did not argue that all that happens is good. In *Theodicy*, §43, he states that one cannot deny that 'there is in the world physical evil (that is, suffering) and moral evil (that is, crime) and even that physical evil is not always distributed here on earth according to the proportion of moral evils, as it seems that justice demands' (Leibniz 1985: 98).

Leibniz took from Augustine the distinction between physical evil (*malum physicum*) and moral evil (*malum morale*). But in §§20–1 he added the category of metaphysical evil (*malum metaphysicum*). Leibniz thus argued that imperfections and variegations are necessary implications of the fact that the world cannot be fully perfect, since God alone is perfect. Put in contemporary terms: the alterity of the world of creation vis-à-vis God (and the concrete differences between always limited creatures) implies some constraints on creaturely existence. 'Metaphysical evil' reflects the goodness that each and any creature is something specific, though inevitably also restricted in capacity (Leibniz 1985: 86–7). In summarizing his argument, Leibniz states that 'the best is not always the one which tends towards avoiding evil, since it is possible that the evil be accompanied by a greater good' (Leibniz 1985: 378). This exemplifies a 'greater good' theodicy. Unfortunately Leibniz goes beyond this view by arguing that 'this universe must be indeed better than every other possible universe' (Leibniz 1985: 378). It is for this exaggerated argument of a 'best-possible world' that Leibniz has rightly been criticized. For couldn't we imagine a world with some fewer imperfections (less life-destructing disasters, for example)? But Leibniz did not describe this world as a perfect utopian world, nor did he ascribe goodness to all experiences in particular. According to Leibniz, the world is good only in the penultimate sense of providing a maximum of variation.

Can a more modest theodicy be made in the light of disaster studies? I think it can. First, the *vulnerability paradigm* of disaster studies shows the extent to which human factors influence the scope and intensity of disaster effects on human populations. Here one is reminded of Shakespeare: 'We make guilty of our disasters, the sun, the moon and stars' (*King Lear*, Act 1, Scene 2). There is, as argued by Chester (2005), ample room for a liberation theology focusing on how to diminish the structural evil that makes some human groups more vulnerable to catastrophes than others. But the vulnerability paradigm also shows the extent to which disasters are not to be treated only as exceptional cases. In a post-Darwinian perspective, disasters belong to the package deal of woes and joys in being a biologically limited creature. For example, we would not have an atmosphere around our globe without life-damaging volcanoes, nor would we have beautiful Iceland (and beautiful Icelanders) without preceding volcanic activities. Wherever we stand in matters of religion, we live and thrive in an ever-changing world where devastating effects go hand-in-hand with the very life-supporting structures that we live by. The expectation of living a smooth life beyond dangers and risks seems out of sync with reality. The more modest alternative is to affirm that our mere being here, and our remaining in existence, is an intrinsic good, while conceding that the world is far from perfect. In this view, a theodicy reminds us of the inevitable limitations of the human condition, but should not claim that we live in the best possible world. After all, no theodicy is able to provide answers to the existential questions that human beings continue to ask, 'Why me?' 'Why us?'

How, then, can such questions be addressed theologically without falling into a religious narcissism, and without falling back to ideas of a God wilfully designing evils? Rather than claiming to decipher divine intentions ad hoc, we might ask about forms of divine presence evident even in the depths of suffering. We hereby move from what a modest theodicy can achieve 'from above', to a more expressive theodicy 'from below', developed with a concern for victims. Speaking in the categories of disaster research we are hereby moving from a theology of vulnerability towards a *theology of resilience*.

As expressed by Jones in *Trauma and Grace,* 'traumatic events are "overwhelming" insofar as they are experienced as inescapable and unmanageable. They outstrip our capacity to respond to and cope with them. Like the wave of a tsunami, they drown you and disable your normal strategies for dealing with difficulties' (Jones 2009: 15). For a theology of trauma the point is not to defend divine justice from a theoretical point of view, but about learning in a practical sense about how to move on in the middle of grief and bewilderment. Classic theological themes such as guilt may still be relevant – 'Could I have done more to save the life of others?' – but the main theological issue to address is that of the victims; how to resist despair and be redeemed from the traumas of involuntary remembrance?

The motif of divine compassion thus becomes central. As argued by theologian Wendy Farley, divine compassion resists structural and personal evil while also resisting the power of suffering to overtake the life of sufferers (Farley 1990: 116). In this view, divine power is not the same as a magic overpowering of natural processes, but the patient power of love, consolation and courage. Farley is here referring to Paul who writes that 'Neither death, nor life … nor anything else in all creation will be able to separate us from the love of God' (Romans 8: 38–9). Divine compassion is not the same as a causal determinative power. The compassion of God means, rather, that the loving (infinite) God stretches over the experienced span between creativity and destruction. For Christians, God is the giver of life (God the creator) who chose to become a victim of life and death (the incarnate God). As the creative source of life, God remains ultimately responsible for the interplay between creativity and chaos in the package deal of creation. As such, God is present even in dark times of destructions – to be cried out to in lament and to be appealed to in prayer. But as compassionate, God is placed on the side of the sufferers, sharing the conditions of living without shelters. In this view, God learns what it means to be traumatized and not being able to find an answer, as when Jesus died on the cross crying, 'My God, my God, why have you forsaken me?' (Matthew 27: 46).

This is the vulnerability motif in Christian theology, for which classic theodicies find no room. But there is also a resilience motif in Christian thinking, based in the faith in God the Spirit as the generative aspect of divine life, ceaselessly at work in reconstructing the battered lives in a fellowship with disaster survivors who retain their wounds and mental scars. The traumatized have to find a way forward without knowing exactly how.

Conclusions

The aim of this chapter has been to chart the territory for mutual engagements between theology and disaster studies. In my analysis, I have moved from a more external view of religion as a set of practices to more internal understandings of religious agents as engaged in a search for meaning in the aftermath of disasters and tragedies. Hereby, I have emphasized the complexity of religious responses to disasters both in terms of practical engagement and self-reflexive capacity. I have also argued that the 'acts of God' perspective, often tacked on to religion by secular observers, is relatively rare today, at least within the Christian tradition. In its place, we find stronger expressions of a divine presence involving a wide spectrum; from accepting the hardships of reality to revolting against their consequences for others as for oneself. What is really interesting is what happens in the midst of this spectrum of religious attitudes and not only at its extreme poles.

For a future theology engaged in disaster studies it seems to me important to privilege the situation of the victims, while protesting against the structural evils at social levels. Theology is not only about individual existential questions, nor just about questions of guilt. A theology of disaster therefore needs to be pro-science in orientation. Theology has the capacity to remind the natural sciences that disasters are not always purely anthropogenic in nature; there are always untamable aspects of natural systems, as evidenced in earthquakes, floods, hurricanes and meteors. At the same time, a theology of disaster should support the preventive and curative measures against disasters offered by organizational sociology and psychology. In the end, there will always be an irreducible societal and personal aspect to living and coping with disasters. Being vulnerable to the point of traumatic experiences and finding ways for reconstruction are the two poles of religious experience. As I have argued above, there are striking parallels between this view of the roles for a future theology of disasters and the tension between the vulnerability paradigm and the resilience paradigm in contemporary disaster research.

Note

Research for this chapter was funded by the Changing Disasters Programme at the University of Copenhagen. The author thanks his colleagues in this programme for very helpful discussions of an earlier draft.

References

Bentzen, J.S. (2013) *The Origins of Religiousness: The Role of Natural Disasters*. Discussion Papers Department of Economics, University of Copenhagen 13/02. Copenhagen: CDR. www.econ.ku.dk/Bentzen (accessed Sept. 2014).

Chester, D.K. (1998) The theodicy of natural disasters. *Scottish Journal of Theology*, 51(4), 485–505.

Chester, D.K. (2005) Theology and disaster studies: The need for a dialogue. *Journal of Volcanology and Geothermal Research*, 146, 319–28.

Chester, D.K., and Duncan, A.M. (2010) Responding to disasters within the Christian tradition, with reference to volcanic eruptions and earthquakes. *Religion*, 40, 85–95.

Clayton, P., and Peacocke, A. (eds) (2004) *In Whom We Live and Move and Have Our Being: Panentheistic Reflections on God's Presence in a Scientific World*. Grand Rapids, MI: Eerdmans, 2004.

Dahlberg, R., Johannessen-Henry, C.T., Raju, E., and Tulsani, S. (2015) Resilience in disaster research: Three versions. *Civil Engineering and Environmental Systems*, 32(1–2), 44–54.

Dynes, R. (2000) The dialogue between Voltaire and Rousseau on the Lisbon earthquake: The emergence of a social science view. *International Journal of Mass Emergencies and Disasters*, 18(1), 97–115.

Falk, M.L. (2010) Recovery and Buddhist practices in the aftermath of the tsunami in Southern Thailand. *Religion*, 40, 96–103.

48 *Niels H. Gregersen*

Farley, W. (1990) *Tragic Vision and Divine Compassion: A Contemporary Theodicy*. Louisville, KY: Westminster John Knox Press.

Fritz, C.E. (1961) Disasters. In R.K. Merton and R.A. Nisbet (eds), *Contemporary Social Problems: An Introduction to the Sociology of Deviant Behavior and Social Disorganization*. New York: Harcourt, Brace & World, 651–94.

Gardiner, S.M. (2011) *A Perfect Moral Storm: The Ethical Tragedy of Climate Change*. Oxford: Oxford University Press.

Gregersen, N.H. (2006) Beyond secular supersessionism: Risk, religion, and technology. *Ecotheology*, 11(2): 137–58.

Johannesen-Henry, C.T. (2012) Polydox eschatology: Relating systematic and everyday theology in a cancer context. *Studia Theologica*, 66(2), 107–29.

Jones, S. (2009) *Trauma and Grace: Theology in a Ruptured World*. Louisville, KY: Westminster John Knox Press.

Koenig, H.G. (2006) *In the Wake of Disaster: Religious Responses to Terrorism and Disaster*. Philadelphia, PA: Templeton Foundation Press.

Lang, B. (1985) Non-semitic deluge stories and the Book of Genesis: A bibliographical and critical survey. *Anthropos*, 80(4–6), 605–16.

Leibniz, G.W. (1985) *Theodicy: Essays on the Goodness of God and Freedom of Man and the Origin of Evil*, trans. E.M. Huggard. Chicago, IL: Open Court.

Lindell, M.K. (2013) Disaster Studies. *Current Sociology Review*, 61(5–6), 797–825.

Merli, C. (2010) Context-bound Islamic theodicies: The tsunami as supernatural retribution vs. natural catastrophe in Southern Thailand. *Religion*, 40, 104–11.

Nix-Stevenson, D. (2013) Human response to natural disaster. *SAGE Open* (July–Sept.), DOI: 10.1177/2158244013489684.

PewResearch Religion & Public Life Project (2012) The global religious landscape, 18 Dec., www.pewforum.org/2012/12/18/global-religious-landscape-exec (accessed Sept. 2014).

Quarantelli, E.L. (1987) Disaster studies: An analysis of the social historical factors affecting the development of research in the area. *International Journal of Mass Emergencies and Disasters*, 3, 285–310.

Quarantelli, E.L., and Dynes, R.R. (1977) Response to social crisis and disaster. *Annual Review of Sociology*, 3, 23–49.

Rokib, M. (2012) The significant role of religious group's response to natural disaster in Indonesia: The case of *Santri Tanggab Bencana* (Santana). *Indonesian Journal of Islam and Muslim Societies*, 2(1), 53–77.

Schlehe, J. (2010) Anthropology of religion: Disasters and the representations of tradition and modernity. *Religion*, 40, 112–20.

Schmuck, H. (2000) 'An act of Allah': Religious explanations for floods in Bangladesh as survival strategy. *International Journal of Mass Emergencies and Disasters*, 1, 85–95.

Smith, M.H. (1978) American religious organizations in disaster: A study of congregational response to disaster. *Mass Emergencies*, 3, 133–42.

Steinberg, T. (2000) *Acts of God: The Unnatural History of Natural Disaster in America*. Oxford: Oxford University Press.

Taylor, C. (1985) Self-interpreting animals. In Philosophical Papers, vol. 1. Human Agency and Language. Cambridge: Cambridge University Press, 45–76.

Wesley, J. (1812) Some serious thought occasioned by the late earthquake at Lisbon (1755). In *Works of the Rev. John Wesley*, vol. 11. London: Conference Office, 397–411.

Wyller, T., Breemer, R. v. d., and Casanova, J. (eds) (2014) *Secular and Sacred? The Scandinavian Case of Religion in Human Rights, Law and Public Space*. Göttingen: Vandenhoeck & Ruprecht.

Part II

Societal and cultural perspectives

4 Making sense of disaster

The cultural studies of disaster

Peer Illner and Isak Winkel Holm

Introduction

We have a sense of disasters long before we have an actual sensation of them. In the last days of August 2005, before Hurricane Katrina hit the coast of Louisiana, newspapers and news networks visualized the possible path of the hurricane through the Gulf of Mexico with computer simulations and speculated on the damage that would be caused by the hit. In the direct aftermath of the hurricane's landfall on 29 August, when aid was painfully slow to arrive, unfounded media reports of looting and killing in the flooded streets of New Orleans caused George W. Bush to mobilize the National Guard, which further delayed relief operations. In the ten years that went by after the destruction of New Orleans, news stories, political speeches, insurance cases, Katrina tourism, novels like Dave Egger's *Zeitoun* (2009), movies such as Bench Zeitlin's *Hushpuppy* (2012), TV documentaries like Spike Lee's *When the Levees Broke* (2006) and cartoons like Josh Neufeld's *A.D.: New Orleans After the Deluge* (2007–8) have continued to make sense of the events in August 2005. The legacy of the most lethal storm to hit the US since 1928 equally lives on through monuments such as the Katrina Memorial Park (2008), and music such as Mos Def's *Dollar Day (Katrina Klap)*.

It is the wager of this chapter that the way we perceive disasters is shaped by the cultural practices of designing computer simulations, editing news stories, documenting damage in insurance cases, as well as by writing novels, making movies and composing music. Such practices create our common sensibility for disasters and, consequently, determine what we see and how we act in a world ravaged by disaster at an ever-increasing rate. We suggest naming those cultural practices 'aesthetic', in the sense developed by German idealism; not as a concept from the realm of fine arts, but, more fundamentally, as a concept for the sensible as such – the *aisthesis* – in this case the common sensibility through which we perceive Hurricane Katrina. When speaking of aesthetics in the following, we therefore do not mean works of art that *represent* an original raw experience of Katrina. Rather, we are talking about how our everyday cultural practices *produce* what presents itself to sense experience in the first place, about how they configure our common regime of the visible and the invisible, the sensible and the imperceptible.

Cultural studies is a discipline committed to the study of the aesthetic in this wider meaning of the term. Hence, cultural studies of disaster contribute to disaster research by exploring the manifold aesthetic practices through which we produce a common sense of disasters. Rather than restricting culture to the sphere of habits and rituals, as in anthropology and ethnography, or analysing culture only in terms of the *habitus* of scientific research, as in science studies, cultural studies suggests viewing culture as a repertoire of practices, images, narratives, genres and styles that determine what can be experienced as reality.

For an Anglo-American reader, cultural studies is likely to connote the Birmingham School of Cultural Studies founded in the 1960s by Richard Hoggart, Stuart Hall and Angela McRobbie, among others. At the University of Birmingham, the Centre for Contemporary Cultural Studies set out to challenge the academic conservatism of the 1950s by collapsing the boundary between 'high' and 'popular' forms of culture, and analysing culture as a battleground of linguistic and symbolic meaning-systems, directly connected to people's identities. For a German or Scandinavian reader, on the other hand, cultural studies is more likely to connote the German tradition of *Kulturwissenschaft*, born in the Weimar Germany of the 1920s (but recognized only much later) through the culture-philosophical writings of German-Jewish thinkers such as Aby Warburg, Georg Simmel and Walter Benjamin. Whereas the traditional German humanities, or *Geisteswissenschaften*, viewed culture idealistically as emerging from the realm of pure spirit, the early *Kulturwissenschaft* argued that culture was always technically conditioned by its various media of expression.

British cultural studies and German *Kulturwissenschaft* have markedly different objects and different theoretical approaches, but both traditions originate from a critique of the 'frontier police' who try to deter researchers from crossing the conventional borders between academic fields (as the art historian Aby Warburg quipped). In both versions of cultural studies, cultural analysts study aesthetic practices in the context of a larger collective sensibility that configures our awareness of the world.

In this chapter, we will honour the cross-disciplinary ambition of both cultural studies and *Kulturwissenschaft*. Rather than listing the various aesthetic disciplines (musicology, art history, museology, visual culture, film studies, literary studies and theatre studies) and their contributions to disaster research, we will move between the borders of university departments in order to give an overview of the most important theoretical approaches used by cultural analysts of disaster, these being: a *trauma* approach, a *vulnerability* approach, a *state of exception* approach and a *cultural history* approach. After discussing these four major approaches and demonstrating their relevance to the case of Hurricane Katrina, we will conclude by sketching a lesser-known theory, which we suggest dubbing an *emergency regime* approach.

Trauma

In *Testimony: Crisis of Witnessing in Literature, Psychoanalysis and History* (1992), literary scholar Shoshana Felman and psychoanalyst Dori Laub ask how it is possible to bear witness to traumatic events. Analysing works of literature, as well as films and video archives, Felman and Laub explore the remembrance of the Second World

War generally, and the Holocaust specifically. Starting from the psychoanalytic assumption that a trauma constitutes a shock so powerful that it is not immediately absorbed by the psyche, the two writers diagnose a problem at the heart of testimony:

> As a relation to events, testimony seems to be composed of bits and pieces of a memory that has been overwhelmed by occurrences that have not settled into understanding or remembrance, acts that cannot be constructed as knowledge nor assimilated into full cognition, events in excess of our frames of reference.
>
> (Felman and Laub 1992: 5)

For Felman and Laub, narrating a traumatic event is difficult because trauma escapes a direct expression in language. Witnessing is the careful reconstruction of inchoate memories into a coherent whole. According to the authors, both literary and psychoanalytic practice constitute narrative acts with a fragile relation to a real event, which can only be grasped retrospectively. Exploring representations of the Second World War in video testimony, in Albert Camus's 1947 novel *The Plague,* and in Claude Lanzmann's landmark documentary *Shoah* (1985), Felman and Laub reconstruct trauma as a crucial problem for the writing of history.

With *Testimony,* Felman and Laub helped establish what is today called trauma studies. When we perceive disaster through the lens of trauma, we focus on the wound (in Greek *trauma*) inflected on to the human psyche by a violent event. The theory of trauma was developed within the field of psychology in the wake of railway accidents of the 19th century and the industrialized warfare of the 20th century (Micale and Lerner 2001; Schivelbusch 1977). While treating veterans returning from the front after the First World War, Freud observed that many soldiers – while not displaying any traumatic symptoms in their everyday lives – vividly relived painful scenes from the war as nightmares during their sleep. Freud concluded that the psyche records traumatic events unconsciously. He believed the shock of the traumatic impact to be so overwhelming that the event itself escaped symbolization. For Freud, trauma only persisted as a trace, manifesting itself in dreams, anxieties and breakdowns later in life. For trauma studies and memory studies today, this view remains the fundamental insight into the psychological processing of trauma.

The trauma framework is active whenever cultural analysts approach disaster as a matter of an individual's or a group's psychic health, impacted by the shock of a sudden and unexpected event. An important issue for trauma scholars is the question of the trauma's representability in memory and in language. If trauma is a senseless shock, a pure hit that cannot be absorbed into the human psyche, then how is it to be narrated and spoken about? While the trauma itself escapes direct representation, witness reports, testimonies and memoires can circle around the fragmented event, providing us with a palliative language to mourn and commemorate lives lost or damaged. Today, trauma is beyond doubt the dominant interpretative model in the cultural studies of disaster. Cultural analysts have explored the role of disaster-induced trauma in, to name only a few examples, the atrocities of the Second World War as witnessed in survivor literature (Caruth 1996; Kilby and Rowland 2013; LaCapra 1994, 1998; Sebald 2004), disasters as represented in literary works in the genre of magical realism (Arva 2011), in visual art (Foster 1996), in photography (Zelizer 1998), and in media and cultural life more generally (Kaplan 2005; Meek 2010).

In the case of Hurricane Katrina, this ongoing process of witnessing is materially traceable in the Katrina National Memorial Park that commemorates the damage wrought on the city by the hurricane. The debate that followed the construction of the memorial also shows the conflicted nature of commemoration and witnessing, where different actors often argue over which personalized or nationalized story of loss becomes the dominant trauma narrative. Commenting on the aesthetic of the Memorial Park that literally adopts the spiral shape of a hurricane, leading visitors and tourists to its metaphorical eye, Lindsay Tuggle has critiqued the 'architectural re-enactment' performed by the memorial, 'that reconstructs aspects of trauma within structural design' (Tuggle 2011: 71). For Tuggle, this mimetic relationship between the memorial and the disaster relegates the process of commemoration to the architecture, thereby liberating the visitors from working through the painful elements of trauma themselves. Furthermore, according to Tuggle, the hurricane shape of the Memorial Park disregards the ways in which Katrina was just as much a social as a natural disaster.

To sum up, the trauma approach views the function of aesthetic practices as a commemoration of disaster. Consequently, the relation between culture and disaster can be conceptualized as a *working-through*. The trauma approach understands cultural practices as a means to inscribe traumatic events within individual or collective memory in order to fight against forgetting, and aid the therapeutic process of coping with the destructive mental and material effects of disaster. The strength of the trauma approach lies in its potential to generate a unique insight into the individual and the collective memory of disaster survivors. In addition, it is a useful heuristic tool to make sense of the many cultural artefacts that surround a disaster event in the weeks, months and years after its occurrence. However, the conceptualization of disaster as a single instant or hit also significantly limits the trauma approach's scope. The focus on the psychic health of the individual human being, caused by an unrepresentable and quasi-religious event, tends to foreclose an analysis of the social and political dimension of disasters.

Vulnerability

In *The Social Roots of Risk: Producing Disasters, Promoting Resilience* (2014), sociologist Kathleen Tierney asserts that the origins of disaster lie not in nature, and not in technology, but rather in the ordinary everyday workings of society itself: 'Put simply, the organizing idea … is that disasters and their impacts are socially produced, and that the forces driving the production of disaster are embedded in the social order itself' (Tierney 2014: 4). Tierney's book is a forceful articulation of the vulnerability approach that dominates contemporary sociological and anthropological disaster research. This methodological framework extends the analytic gaze beyond the immediacy of the disaster onto the everyday workings of society, exploring the social, cultural, political and ecological conditions that play a role in the production of disaster (or exacerbate its severity). New Orleans, for instance, was a highly vulnerable city, due to its bad levees, its location beneath sea level, the eradication of the coastal vegetation outside the city, its poor transportation system, but also as a consequence of its impoverished black population and racially segregated urban structure. All too often, natural disasters are talked about in a vocabulary that effaces their social logic. The zooming-out movement of the vulnerability approach makes it possible to 'denaturalize' disasters, and tease out their underlying political economy (Klinenberg 1999).

Tierney devotes a chapter to the relationship between culture and disaster. When dealing with the hard facts of disaster, culture is important, she explains, 'in that cultural frames such as those involving nature, technology, growth, and progress, along with the perceptions, beliefs, and cultural practices associated with those frames, are strongly implicated in the social production of risk' (2014: 81). According to Tierney, cultural frames constitute our pre-scientific belief systems. As such, she concedes to them a primarily negative role, arguing that they contribute to the social production of disasters by functioning as 'blinders' that prevent social actors from becoming aware of their own risk production. According to Tierney, culture impairs our accurate grasp of disasters by placing 'cognitive limits on people and institutions so that they are blind to worst cases' (2014: 81). If, for Tierney, the roots of both risk and resilience are social, a subset of these roots can be defined as 'cultural' (2014: 68).

Tierney's discussion of the relationship between culture and disaster is characteristic of cultural analysts inspired by the vulnerability approach. In 2007, sociologist Gary R. Webb anticipated that, even if the field of disaster research 'has not fully made a cultural turn, it is moving in that direction', adding that this 'cultural path is worth taking' (Webb 2007: 432ff.). Disaster studies' 'cultural turn' sets out from the concept of vulnerability. Hollywood disaster movies, Webb suggests, 'often perpetuate harmful stereotypes about race, class, and gender' (2007: 435), hereby propagating misperceptions that contribute to disasters. In an early and important work in this research tradition, anthropologists Anthony Oliver-Smith and Susanna Hoffman list 'ideology', 'prejudices', 'mores and many other sociocultural elements' (Hoffman and Oliver-Smith 1999: 25, 22, 29) as examples of 'pre-disaster conditions' (p. 4), which activate or aggravate disasters. The bulk of sociocultural vulnerability studies explore how the news media create 'disaster myths' or 'disaster fictions' that in turn create an inaccurate perception of disaster. Recent analyses have contributed to our understanding of the cultural production of disaster concerning deviant behaviour, such as panic, looting and price gouging (Fischer 1994: 70); the feeding of infants during disasters (Gribble 2013); processes of social change (Russil and Lavin 2011); as well as issues of race and disaster (Dyson 2006).

In a number of articles, Tierney has applied the vulnerability approach to the US media-constructed regime of public visibility during Hurricane Katrina:

> Initial evidence suggests that the media's relentless adherence to disaster myths and to frames emphasizing civil unrest and urban insurgency, along with the strategic response measures these reports justified, had a number of immediate negative consequences. ... Distorted images disseminated by the media and public officials served to justify calls for greater military involvement in disasters.
>
> (Tierney *et al.* 2006: 75)

Even if the disaster images disseminated by the media and public officials turned out to be fictitious, they had important consequences for the facts on the ground. Three days after the collapse of the levees, the Governor of Louisiana and the Mayor of New Orleans suspended lifesaving operations, and ordered emergency responders to concentrate on arresting looters and deterring crime; 63,000 troops from the National Guard were deployed in what came to be perceived as the 'war zone' of downtown New Orleans, many with fresh combat experience from Iraq. Thus, the vocabulary of the distorted media coverage of Katrina was strongly implicated in the social production of the disaster.

In conclusion, according to the vulnerability approach, the function of aesthetic practices is to trigger or exacerbate disaster. In this theoretical perspective, the relation between culture and disaster can be conceptualized as *causation*. Sociologists and anthropologists tend to view the aesthetics of disaster as a kind of 'anaesthesia', a harmful way of being unaware of the social production of disaster. As we shall see in the following sections of this chapter, aesthetic practices also do other things than directly causing disaster by disseminating erroneous beliefs. However, as Tierney's interpretation of Hurricane Katrina shows, there is no doubt that the vulnerability approach opens up a forceful critical perspective on disaster media and disaster fiction.

State of exception

Philosopher Giorgio Agamben's *Homo Sacer: Sovereign Power and Bare Life* can be understood as an extended meditation on the political application of the state of exception. Accordingly, 'in our age, the state of exception comes more and more to the foreground as the fundamental political structure and ultimately begins to become the rule' (Agamben 1998: 20). If we understand disasters as exceptional 'moments of interruption and novelty' that disrupt an otherwise normal state of affairs (Aradau and Munster 2011: 10), then Agamben's continued relevance to disaster studies becomes clear. For Agamben, the state of exception (or state of emergency) concerns the definition of an event that can be separated from a normal, everyday rule. Arguing on a legal scale, Agamben defines the exception as a case that cannot be grasped within the regular legal order and thus necessitates an extraordinary response. In legal theory, this entails a suspension of civil law, including the civil liberties normally granted to citizens in a constitutional democracy. Under the exceptional rule of America's 'War on Terror' for instance, the combatants captured in Afghanistan were neither defined as prisoners of war, nor as ordinary criminals. At Guantanamo, they were treated as outlaws, men outside the law, who were not eligible for a trial and whose bodies could be disposed of without providing any justification for their killing or abuse.

Agamben draws his argument from a long tradition within state law. According to the Roman constitution, the Senate could, in cases of emergency such as invasions or natural disasters, appoint a dictator who would enjoy unconstrained sovereignty for up to six months. The legal concept of the state of exception entered political theory through a controversy between the Nazi jurist Carl Schmitt and the German-Jewish philosopher Walter Benjamin. While Schmitt defended the sovereign use of the state of exception and even defined the sovereign as 'he who decides on the exception' (1985: 5), Benjamin sought to create an emancipatory version of the exception, which would not strengthen, but instead abolish, sovereign rule (Benjamin 1986).

In the years following the attacks on the World Trade Center, the state of exception has come to play a vital role in the attempts to understand a modern social and political life, constantly threatened by disasters. Cultural analysts have, among other things, focused on the state of exception in politics (Lazar 2009), in the theory of democracy (Honig 2009), in the American War on Terror (Butler 2004) as well as in architecture (Aureli 2011) and literature (Martel 2011, 2012; Spanos 2011). A prominent example is *Creaturely Life* (2006), a book by American literary scholar Eric Santner on the German author W.G. Sebald. According to Santner, Sebald's literary works are 'visions of world destruction and ruin (by war, by erosion, by entropy, by natural disaster, by combustion)' (Santner 2006: 178). Using the works of Sebald as a prism, Santner intends to 'open a new way of understanding how human bodies and psyches register the "states of exception" that punctuate the "normal" run of social and political life, … a specifically human way of finding oneself caught in the midst of antagonisms in and of the political field' (p. xix).

Slovenian philosopher Slavoj Žižek has shown how a state of exception approach to Hurricane Katrina can shift the analytical focus onto the way a segment of the population is structurally excluded from social participation. Analysing the political rhetoric and media reports in the aftermath of Katrina, he comments on the impression of social collapse that was generated by the media: 'For a few days, New Orleans apparently regressed to a wild preserve of looting, killing, and rape. It became a city of the dead and dying, a post-apocalyptic zone where those the philosopher Giorgio Agamben calls Homini Sacer – people excluded from the civil order – wander' (Žižek 2008: 93).

According to the state of exception approach, aesthetic practices open a way of understanding the deeper meaning of disaster. Hence, the relation between culture and disaster can be conceptualized as an *exposure* – an uncovering of the dominant political structure through works of art. Similar to the vulnerability approach, the state of exception approach mobilizes a powerful critical potential by extending the analytical gaze beyond the immediacy of the disaster, and onto the underlying structures of social and political life. However, its scope runs even deeper, as it not only highlights differential conditions of vulnerability in the lead-up to disaster, but instead focuses on the production of social inequality at large. On the other hand, the elevation of the state of exception to a general social condition can also make it seem unspecific and inept at analysing specific disaster situations. By relying on a static definition of sovereignty – assumed to be unchanging over time – this approach risks equating disparate cases of political violence, while overlooking their historical specificity.

Cultural history

In *The Sense of an Ending* (1967), literary scholar Frank Kermode explores how we make sense of the world by telling stories about its end. 'Men, like poets, rush "into the middest," in *medias res*, when they are born; they also die in *mediis rebus*, and to make sense of their span they need fictive concords with origins and ends, such as give meaning to lives and to poems' (Kermode 1967: 7). Since the writing of the Bible, the apocalyptic narrative about the end of the world has lived on in Western culture as a pattern that gives meaning to lives and to poems. 'The paradigms of apocalypse continue to lie under our ways of making sense of the world', Kermode claims (1967: 28), and they do so because they can be used to construct a meaningful plot with a beginning, middle and dramatic ending. Inasmuch as we are living in the middle of things, in *mediis rebus*, we experience historical time as senseless chaos and contingency, but the paradigms of apocalypse can help us construct a narrative that organizes chaotic time into a concordant plot. As such, '[a]pocalypse, which resumes the Bible, projects its neat, naive patterns on to history' (Kermode 1967: 14).

Inspired by the German tradition of *Kulturwissenschaft*, Kermode does not approach the apocalyptic texts of the Bible as vessels of theological truth, but rather, as templates for apocalyptic thinking and feeling. The apocalypse provides 'models of the world', 'paradigms', 'patterns' and 'figures' (1967: 4, 6, 9, 27), and the task of cultural history is to explore how these models work. In Kermode's programmatic words, the critical business consists in 'making sense of some of the radical ways of making sense of the world' (p. 29).

The cultural history approach to disaster has pursued this critical business by making sense of the vast repertoire of cultural patterns (concepts, images, narratives, genres and styles) by help of which humans make sense of disaster. Among the cultural patterns thoroughly studied are the apocalypse (Boyer 1992; Bull 1995; Derrida 1982, 1984; Robinson 1985; Wojcik 1997; Zamora 1989); the theodicy (Israel 2011; Kendrick 1957; Lauer and Unger 2008; Löffler 1999; Neiman 2002); the sublime (Adorno 1983; Ray 2005), and the risk calculus (Walter *et al.* 2006). Some works within the cultural history approach focus on specific geographical places such as Los Angeles (Davis 1998), Switzerland (Utz 2013) and Latin America (M.D. Anderson 2011). Other works focus on specific art forms and fictional genres such as disaster movies (Keane 2001; Sontag 1965) and zombie movies (Bishop 2010). Comprehensive accounts of the cultural history of disasters are available in Horn (2014), Schenk and Janku (2012) and Walter (2008).

Anthony Dyer Hoefer offers an example of the cultural history approach applied to Hurricane Katrina. The 'apocalyptic imaginary', Hoefer argues, has played a vital role in the production of the regional identity of the American South, from William Faulkner up to today (Hoefer 2012: 13). Hoefer ends his book with an analysis of how apocalyptic patterns were used by poets, preachers and playwrights to make sense of Katrina: 'In no time in recent years has the landscape of the apocalyptic imaginary come so close to materiality in the South as it did in the Crescent City in late 2005' (2012: 156).

To sum up, according to the cultural history approach, the function of aesthetic practices is to make sense of the world by projecting neat patterns on to human life. Thus, the relation between culture and disaster can be conceptualized as a *schematization*. This approach is markedly different from what we saw in the first two sections of this chapter. Aesthetic practices are not commemorating or working through the unspeakable experience of disastrous event, as in the trauma approach, nor are they causing disasters by preventing social actors from becoming aware of their own risk production, as in the vulnerability approach. Rather, they project cognitive schemes on to our experience of disaster.

To be sure, it is vital to understand the historical depth of the modern disaster imaginary. But by turning towards the vast archive of historical disaster patterns in literature, film, art, philosophy, theology and popular culture, cultural analysts run the risk of blinding themselves to the way these patterns are actually used and misused in specific social practices, as the vulnerability approach convincingly argues. If it is true that the critical business consists in making sense of our ways of making sense of the world, it ought also to consist in exposing what is systematically overlooked when we are busy making sense of disasters.

Emergency regime

In this final section, we will call attention to a subset of cultural history, which combines the latter's historical rigour with an attention to the way in which frames of emergency are used in contemporary modes of government. This *emergency regime* approach, as we suggest calling it, has its roots in Michel Foucault's studies of the connection between the birth of the modern state and the simultaneous containment of elements, deemed threatening to that state. In a number of influential books and lectures, Foucault showed how the key institutions of modernity – the penal system, modern health care, the psychiatry, as well as urban planning and architecture – constituted themselves specifically in order to regulate the dangers of crime, illness and social deviance that were seen as threatening the smooth functioning of the nascent state (Foucault 1995, 2007). Rather than situated outside the social, disaster is in this narrative constitutive of modern society itself, whose *raison d'être* becomes to protect itself from internal and external harm. According to this approach, disaster is at the centre of contemporary society, since the emergency regime isolates, stigmatizes and pathologizes certain parts of the population and the environment that are seen as the bearers of danger.

'Contagion is more than an epidemiological fact', asserts literary scholar Priscilla Wald (2008). In line with Foucault's account, she inquires into the role of culture within the modern emergency regime. For Wald, epidemiological figures, phrases, images and story lines are used to make sense, not only of strictly medical phenomena, but also find application in wider social domains. In her exploration of the epidemiological imaginary, Wald focuses on 'the outbreak narrative', a paradigmatic story of an infection emerging, spreading through the global networks, and finally being contained. Such outbreak narratives not only *represent* specific infections, they also *produce* the way we experience infections in the first place:

> Outbreak narratives … have consequences. As they disseminate information, they affect survival rates and contagion routes. They promote or mitigate the stigmatizing of individuals, groups, populations, locales (regional and global), behaviors, and lifestyles, and they change economies. They also influence how both scientists and the lay public understand the nature and consequence of infection, how they imagine the threat, and why they react so fearfully to some disease outbreaks and not others at least as dangerous and pressing.
>
> (2008: 3)

Outbreak narratives have consequences, and according to Wald, these consequences are not only destructive, as in the kind of harm done by the cultural frames described by the vulnerability approach. Rather, the consequences of the outbreak narratives are productive; they reframe and reconfigure social life by creating and disseminating new models of public life, based on the principles of public health.

According to the emergency regime approach, to sum up, disasters are more than brute *facts*, but also more than cultural *figures* to be studied in canonical works of fiction and theology. Instead, they function as cognitive *frames*, epistemological technologies, embedded in specific social practices and legitimating specific forms of social control. These frames enable us to make sense of social life, understood as a distribution of dangers and threats across the politic body. 'Emergency', in the words of sociologist Craig Calhoun, 'is a way of grasping problematic events, a way of imagining them that emphasizes their apparent unpredictability, abnormality, and brevity and that carries the corollary that response—intervention—is necessary' (2004: 55).

Scholars have studied the emergency regime operative in a variety of practices. Among others, in humanitarian interventions (Fassin 2012; Fassin and Pandolfi 2010), in the campaigns of the New Deal policy-makers during the Great Depression (Dauber 2013), in the management of Palestinian territories by the Israeli Defense Forces (Ophir 2010; Weizman 2011), in contemporary disaster exercises (B. Anderson 2010; Aradau and Munster 2011), and in the 'creative destruction' of American capitalism (Rozario 2007). Approaches like these ask what is legitimated when social life is imagined – framed, verbalized, problematized or constructed – *as* a disaster.

Media researcher Chris Russil and political theorist Chad Lavin have explored the emergency regime at work in the management of Hurricane Katrina. In the legal aftermath of the disaster, FEMA's officials made frequent use of the 'tipping point' metaphor in order to explain why things went wrong. Already a common trope during the US war in Iraq, FEMA's choice of rhetoric was based on Malcolm Gladwell's 2000 *The Tipping Point*, a bestseller in management literature, which suggests social change be explained by means of the terms and tropes of epidemiology. FEMA's use of the tipping point metaphor is an example of the epidemiologic imaginary that explains social phenomena as diverse as fashion trends, crime waves, television programming and poorly managed hurricanes in the language of epidemiology. 'Americans', Russil and Lavin propose, 'have become increasingly prepared to view the world through the lens of infection and contagion' (Russil and Lavin 2010: 66). In this perspective, the epidemic is neither a brute scientific fact, nor a mere cultural figure, but rather a cognitive frame, a cultural 'lens' that configures our awareness of the social world.

Methodologically, the emergency regime approach views the function of aesthetic practices as a way of naming something a disaster. In this case, the relation between culture and disaster can be conceptualized as a *configuration*, a construction of the public image of social life in the language of disaster. The task of the disaster researcher, then, is to unearth the deep-seated cultural notions of victimization, stigmatization, aid, abnormality and heroism that format our everyday experience.

In this chapter, we have introduced five approaches in the contemporary cultural study of disaster. Our ambition has been to show that these five approaches present five very different notions of disasters, as well as of culture (see Table 4.1). They zoom out gradually from the individual human being to the whole world: (1) the trauma approach tends to view disaster on the level of the individual, focusing on the working-through of the rupturing event by a single human being; (2) the vulnerability approach tends to view disaster on the level of the community, describing the social and cultural 'pre-disaster conditions' that activate or aggravate disaster; (3) the state of exception approach views disaster on the level of the state, extending the scope of the exploration to the fundamental political structure of the Western national states; (4) the cultural history approach, in this case exemplified by the cultural history of the apocalypse, views disaster on the level of the world, studying the famous TEOTWAWKI question (about the end of the world as we know it); and (5) the emergency regime approach, finally, views disaster on the level of social practice, as a configuration that manages bodies and populations, and is therefore halfway between the individual and the world.

The emergency regime approach is our own term since, at present, this is not an acknowledged and demarcated approach with a methodological framework of its own. It is constituted rather loosely as a connected group of contributions

Table 4.1 The cultural study of disaster: five approaches

Approach	Inspired by	Function of aesthetic practices	Scope
Trauma approach	Psychology, Psychoanalysis, Memory Studies	Working-through, commemoration	Individual
Vulnerability approach	Sociology, Anthropology	Causation	Community
State of exception approach	Political Theory, State Law	Exposure	State
Cultural history approach	*Kulturwissenschaft*, History of Ideas	Schematization	World
Emergency regime approach	Michel Foucault, Science Studies	Configuration	Social practice

from the fields of cultural studies, sociology, anthropology and political science. Nevertheless, we find this emerging approach highly promising. By taking this approach, cultural analysts do not restrict themselves to describing how the perceptions of disaster have changed since the first religious legends of the flood. Instead, they explore how disasters change the structure of the modern world, from the famous 1755 Lisbon earthquake, through to the increasingly frequent and increasingly violent man-made and natural disasters of today. By making sense of our ways of making sense of disaster, cultural studies gives us access to the way we see and the way we act in a contemporary world threatened by future disasters.

References

Adorno, T.W. (1983) *Negative Dialectics*. New York: Continuum.
Agamben, G. (1998) *Homo Sacer: Sovereign Power and Bare Life*. Stanford, CA: Stanford University Press.
Anderson, B. (2010) Preemption, precaution, preparedness: Anticipatory action and future geographies. *Progress in Human Geography*, 34(6), 777–98.
Anderson, M.D. (2011) *Disaster Writing: The Cultural Politics of Catastrophe in Latin America*. Charlottesville, VA: University of Virginia Press.
Aradau, C., and Munster, R. v. (2011) *Politics of Catastrophe: Genealogies of the Unknown*. London: Routledge.
Arva, E.L. (2011) *The Traumatic Imagination: Histories of Violence in Magical Realist Fiction*. Amherst, NY: Cambria Press.
Aureli, P.V. (2011) *The Possibility of an Absolute Architecture*. Cambridge, MA, and London: MIT Press.
Benjamin, W. (1986) *Illuminations*, ed. H. Arendt. New York: Schocken Books.
Bishop, K.W. (2010) *American Zombie Gothic: The Rise and Fall (and Rise) of the Walking Dead in Popular Culture*. Jefferson, NC: McFarland & Co.

Boyer, P.S. (1992) *When Time Shall Be No More: Prophecy Belief in Modern American Culture.* Cambridge, MA: Belknap Press of Harvard University Press.

Bull, M. (1995) *Apocalypse Theory and the Ends of the World.* Oxford: Blackwell.

Butler, J. (2004) *Precarious Life: The Powers of Mourning and Violence.* New York: Verso.

Calhoun, C. (2004) A world of emergencies: Fear, intervention, and the limits of cosmopolitan order. *Canadian Review of Sociology and Anthropology,* 41(4), 373–95.

Caruth, C. (1996) *Unclaimed Experience: Trauma, Narrative, and History.* Baltimore, MD: Johns Hopkins University Press.

Dauber, M.L. (2013) *The Sympathetic State: Disaster Relief and the Origins of the American Welfare State.* Chicago, IL: University of Chicago Press.

Davis, M. (1998) *Ecology of Fear: Los Angeles and the Imagination of Disaster.* New York: Metropolitan Books.

Derrida, J. (1982) Of an apocalyptic tone recently adopted in philosophy. *Semeia,* 23: 63–97.

Derrida, J. (1984) No apocalypse, not now (full speed ahead, seven missiles, seven missives). *Diacritics,* 14(2), 20–31.

Dyson, M.E. (2006) *Come Hell or High Water: Hurricane Katrina and the Color of Disaster.* New York: Basic Civitas.

Fassin, D. (2012) *Humanitarian Reason: A Moral History of the Present Times.* Berkeley, CA: University of California Press.

Fassin, D., and Pandolfi, M. (2010) *Contemporary States of Emergency: The Politics of Military and Humanitarian Interventions.* New York and Cambridge, MA: Zone Books.

Felman, S., and Laub, D. (1992) *Testimony: Crises of Witnessing in Literature, Psychoanalysis, and History.* New York and London: Routledge.

Fischer, H.W. (1994) *Response to Disaster: Fact versus Fiction and its Perpetuation.* Washington, DC: University Press of America.

Foster, H. (1996) *The Return of the Real: The Avant-garde at the End of the Century.* Cambridge, MA: MIT Press.

Foucault, M. (1995) *Discipline and Punish: The Birth of the Prison.* 2nd edn, New York: Vintage Books.

Foucault, M. (2007) *Security, Territory, Population: Lectures at the College de France, 1977–78.* Basingstoke: Palgrave Macmillan.

Gribble, K.D. (2013) Media messages and the needs of infants and young children after Cyclone Nargis and the WenChuan Earthquake. *Disasters,* 37(1), 80–100.

Hoefer, A.D. (2012) *Apocalypse South: Judgment, Cataclysm, and Resistance in the Regional Imaginary.* Columbus, OH: Ohio State University Press.

Hoffman, S.M., and Oliver-Smith, A. (1999) *The Angry Earth: Disaster in Anthropological Perspective.* New York: Routledge.

Honig, B. (2009) *Emergency Politics: Paradox, Law, Democracy.* Princeton, NJ: Princeton University Press.

Horn, E. (2014) *Zukunft als Katastrophe.* Frankfurt am Main: S. Fischer.

Israel, J. (2011) *Democratic Enlightenment: Philosophy, Revolution, and Human Rights 1750–1790.* New York: Oxford University Press.

Kaplan, E.A. (2005) *Trauma Culture: The Politics of Terror and Loss in Media and Literature.* Piscataway, NJ, and London: Rutgers University Press.

Keane, S. (2001) *Disaster Movies: The Cinema of Catastrophe.* London: Wallflower.

Kendrick, T.D. (1957) *The Lisbon Earthquake.* Philadelphia, PA: Lippincott.

Kermode, F. (1967) *The Sense of an Ending: Studies in the Theory of Fiction.* New York: Oxford University Press.

Kilby, J., and Rowland, A. (2013) *The Bloomsbury Companion to Holocaust Literature.* London and New York: Routledge.

Klinenberg, E. (1999) Denaturalizing disaster: A social autopsy of the 1995 Chicago heat wave. *Theory and Society*, 28(2), 239–95.

LaCapra, D. (1994) *Representing the Holocaust History, Theory, Trauma*. Ithaca, NY, and London: Cornell University Press.

LaCapra, D. (1998) *History and Memory After Auschwitz*. Ithaca, NY: Cornell University Press.

Lauer, G., and Unger, T. (2008) *Das Erdbeben von Lissabon und der Katastrophendiskurs im 18. Jahrhundert*. Göttingen: Wallstein Verlag.

Lazar, N.C. (2009) *States of Emergency in Liberal Democracies*. Cambridge: Cambridge University Press.

Löffler, U. (1999) *Lissabons Fall – Europas Schrecken: Die Deutung des Erdbebens von Lissabon im deutschsprachigen Protestantismus des 18. Jahrhunderts*. Berlin: de Gruyter.

Martel, J.R. (2011) *Textual Conspiracies: Walter Benjamin, Idolatry, and Political Theory*. Ann Arbor, MI: University of Michigan Press.

Martel, J.R. (2012) *Divine Violence: Walter Benjamin and the Eschatology of Sovereignty*. Abingdon, Oxon, and New York: Routledge.

Meek, A. (2010) *Trauma and Media: Theories, Histories, and Images*. New York: Routledge.

Micale, M.S., and Lerner, P.F. (2001) *Traumatic Pasts: History, Psychiatry, and Trauma in the Modern Age, 1870–1930*. Cambridge: Cambridge University Press.

Neiman, S. (2002) *Evil in Modern Thought: An Alternative History of Philosophy*. Princeton, NJ: Princeton University Press.

Ophir, A. (2010) The politics of catastrophization: Emergency and exception. In D. Fassin and M. Pandolfi (eds), *Contemporary States of Emergency: The Politics of Military and Humanitarian Interventions*. New York and Cambridge, MA: Zone Books, 59–88.

Ray, G. (2005) *Terror and the Sublime in Art and Critical Theory: From Auschwitz to Hiroshima to September 11*. New York: Palgrave Macmillan.

Robinson, D. (1985) *American Apocalypses: The Image of the End of the World in American Literature*. Baltimore, MD: Johns Hopkins University Press.

Rozario, K. (2007) *The Culture of Calamity: Disaster and the Making of Modern America*. Chicago, IL: University of Chicago Press.

Russil, C., and Lavin, C. (2010) The ideology of the epidemic. *New Political Science*, 32(1), 65–82.

Russil, C., and Lavin, C. (2011) Tipping point to meta-crisis. Management, media, and Hurricane Katrina. In C. Johnson (ed.), *The Neoliberal Deluge: Hurricane Katrina, Late Capitalism, and the Remaking of New Orleans*. Minneapolis, MN: University of Minnesota Press, 3–31.

Santner, E. (2006) *On Creaturely Life: Rilke, Benjamin, Sebald*. Chicago, IL: University of Chicago Press.

Schenk, G.J., and Janku, A. (2012) *Historical Disasters in Context: Science, Religion, and Politics*. New York: Routledge.

Schivelbusch, W. (1977) *Geschichte der Eisenbahnreise: Zur Industrialisierung von Raum und Zeit im 19. Jahrhundert*. Munich: Hanser.

Schmitt, C. (1985) *Political Theology: Four Chapters on the Concept of Sovereignty*. Cambridge, MA: MIT Press.

Sebald, W.G. (2004) *On the Natural History of Destruction*. New York: Modern Library.

Sontag, S. (1965) *The Imagination of Disaster Against Interpretation*. New York: Picador.

Spanos, W.V. (2011) *The Exceptionalist State and the State of Exception: Herman Melville's Billy Budd, Sailor*. Baltimore, MD: Johns Hopkins University Press.

Tierney, K. (2014) *The Social Roots of Risk: Producing Disasters, Promoting Resilience*. Stanford, CA: Stanford University Press.

Tierney, K., Bevc, C., and Kuligowski, E. (2006) Metaphors matter: Disaster myths, media frames, and their consequences in Hurricane Katrina. *Annals of the American Academy of Political and Social Science,* 604, 57–81.

Tuggle, L. (2011) Encrypting Katrina: Traumatic inscription and the architecture of amnesia. *Invisible Culture,* 16, 65–87.

Utz, P. (2013) *Kultivierung der Katastrophe: Literarische Untergangsszenarien aus der Schweiz.* Munich: Wilhelm Fink.

Wald, P. (2008) *Contagious: Cultures, Carriers, and the Outbreak Narrative.* Durham, NC: Duke University Press.

Walter, F. (2008) *Catastrophes: Une histoire culturelle, XVIe–XXIe siècle.* Paris: Seuil.

Walter, F., Fantini, B., and Delvaux, P. (2006) *Les cultures du risque: XVIe–XXIe siècles.* Geneva: Presses d'Histoire Suisse.

Webb, G.R. (2007) The popular culture of disaster: Exploring a new dimension of disaster research. In H. Rodríguez, E.L. Quarantelli, and R.R. Dynes (eds), *Handbook of Disaster Research.* New York: Springer, 430–40.

Weizman, E. (2011) *The Least of all Possible Evils: Humanitarian Violence from Arendt to Gaza.* London: Verso.

Wojcik, D. (1997) *The End of the World as We Know it: Faith, Fatalism, and Apocalypse in America.* New York: New York University Press.

Zamora, L.P. (1989) *Writing the Apocalypse: Historical Vision in Contemporary U.S. and Latin American Fiction.* New York and Cambridge: Cambridge University Press.

Zelizer, B. (1998) *Remembering to Forget: Holocaust Memory through the Camera's Eye.* Chicago, IL: University of Chicago Press.

Žižek, S. (2008) *Violence: Six Sideways Reflections.* New York: Picador.

5   The social life of disasters

An anthropological approach

Birgitte Refslund Sørensen and Kristoffer Albris

Introduction

Anthropology is concerned with how human beings inhabit and make sense of their worlds at the intersection of society, culture and the environment. Disasters, from this perspective, are not just events that strike and affect societies from the outside, disappearing as recovery progresses. Disasters have a continuous life as part of the history and organization of communities and societies. They are created by the conditions of society, and in turn reshape society. The life of a disaster is in other words inherently social and cultural.

In this chapter, we outline an anthropological approach to disasters. Building on the existing literature and our own research, we show how anthropology's distinct ethnographic and holistic approach may enhance our understanding, not only of the effects of disasters, but of disasters as dynamic social phenomena. We suggest that anthropology contributes to the field of disaster studies in several ways. First, ethnography shows how people do not just lose their material livelihoods in disaster situations. Their senses of self, community, dignity, etc., are also challenged, and issues of morality, justice and security emerge. Second, ethnography demonstrates that disasters not only break down societies. They also offer a gap in time and space in which authorities and people rebuild, reimagine and reinvent society, which make disasters inherently political. Third, anthropology provides an alternative view of how the realities of a disaster are constructed by expanding the analytical delineation of the disaster field beyond the affected area and disaster victims to include all relevant actors and flows. Finally, ethnography addresses how diverse temporal rhythms of disasters and cultural notions of time influence understandings of and responses to disasters.

We do not intend this to be a review of disaster anthropology. Earlier and thorough reviews are available elsewhere (Henry 2005; Oliver-Smith 1996; Oliver-Smith and Hoffmann 1999; Torry 1979). Rather, the aim of this chapter is to introduce and discuss the distinct features that anthropology brings to the interdisciplinary field of disaster studies. We begin by outlining anthropology's ethnographic approach and the historical roots of disaster research in anthropology. While disasters were often marginal in the ethnography of earlier times, there now exists a burgeoning anthropology of disasters, which takes disaster as its basic empirical and theoretical focus. Building on this more recent research, we then move on to discuss four selected issues and perspectives that we consider innovative and fruitful contributions to disaster studies in general. These are (1) people's meaning-making practices, (2) the politics of disaster, and (3) the spatial and (4) temporal aspects of disaster. As these issues demonstrate, the anthropology of disasters is methodologically and theoretically tied to sociocultural anthropology proper, and the many other subfields found within the discipline. We conclude the chapter by addressing anthropological stances towards current important concepts in disaster work such as vulnerability and resilience.

The anthropological trademarks: ethnography, relativism and holism

Before we deal specifically with disaster anthropology, we outline a few key notions of the methodological and epistemological approaches that are vital for situating the discipline's contribution to disaster studies. Anthropology's approach to human societies and cultures rests on the ethnographic method and ideas of relativism and holism, which are distinct in the social sciences.

Since its inception as a modern scientific discipline in the late 19th century, anthropology has sought to understand human societies and cultures in all their forms and varieties. A decisive shift in anthropology came with the invention of ethnographic fieldwork in the early 20th century. The invention of ethnographic fieldwork is often ascribed to Bronislaw Malinowski (1984 [1922]), who conducted several years of fieldwork on the Trobriand Islands, where he lived amongst people in order to acquire first-hand experience of their culture and society. While ethnographic fieldwork typically involves different kinds of methods (interviews, surveys, etc.), its central methodology is participant observation, which implies that the ethnographer participates in the ordinary practices and activities of a community, while remaining sufficiently distant to observe and take notes of everyday life.

The invention of ethnographic fieldwork by European anthropologists coalesced with the establishment of American cultural anthropology, which took a relativist stance towards culture. The idea of cultural relativism disputed the contemporary view that race and biology determine cultural behaviour, thus challenging ethnocentric analysis and judgement of other cultures from the perspective of one's own culture. In the 1980s, anthropologists increasingly problematized the discipline's essentialist understanding of culture, forcefully arguing that any native's point of view would always be positioned and partial and that this too had to be taken into consideration – both methodologically and analytically (Clifford and Marcus 1986). Not only are societies and cultures different from each other, they are also experienced and perceived differently from within depending on individuals' ethnicity, religion, gender, age, class, political conviction, etc.

Ethnographic fieldwork and cultural relativism are intimately linked to the notion of holism, a cornerstone of anthropological inquiry. In general terms, holism suggests that in order to understand a particular culture one has to understand all the elements that it consists of, and their interconnections. For instance, in his famous discussion of gift exchanges and relations of reciprocity, Marcel Mauss (2002[1924]) points out that phenomena like gift exchange relate to all parts of cultural forms and social institutions, and constitute what he terms 'total social phenomena'. A holistic approach to disasters resists any *a priori* definition and delineation of the field. As researchers, we must not and cannot assume how entities are constituted and related in a given context. Methodologically, we must approach our research from the premise that everything is potentially connected.

In this respect, anthropology is well suited to understand variations in how people experience and deal with disasters and emergencies. The empirical, ethnographic approach, we argue, fundamentally alters the way the field of disaster is conceived and delineated, emphasizing its contingent and emergent nature. Anthropology's holistic stance is particularly well suited to capture and appreciate the full breadth of disasters as phenomena. Furthermore, cultural relativism, ethnographic accounts of internal differentiation and positioned interpretations of disaster, we argue, provide a valuable counterpart to 'objective', generalizing and standardized understandings of disaster. This will be a recurrent point throughout the chapter.

A short history of disaster anthropology

Before the Second World War, disasters and hazards were not of specific interest to anthropologists. That is not to say that they did not appear in early ethnographic writings. E.E. Evans-Pritchard's classic work on the Nuer (1940) for instance, included observations about the impact of droughts and floods. Yet anthropologists mostly studied disasters by accident, when they were already present in places where extreme events struck.

The anthropologist Anthony F.C. Wallace was one of the first social scientists to focus specifically on disasters, in his study of the social impact of a tornado in Worcester, Massachusetts. Wallace (1956) attempted to develop and test a theoretical time-space model of the effect of disasters on communities, which sought to understand social life when 'all hell breaks loose' (Oliver-Smith 1996: 320). More ethnographic disaster studies began to appear in the 1970s, as disaster studies more broadly began to take form (Quarantelli 1978). However, as Torry wrote in his review of disaster anthropology, 'anthropological case-study data are too sparse and fragmentary to serve as a scaffold for any theory that goes much beyond the level of gross generalization' (Torry 1979: 519).

As the end of the 20th century approached, disaster anthropology expanded. Anthony Oliver-Smith is perhaps the most important figure during this period. Originally trained as an economic anthropologist, he turned his attention to post-disaster recovery when a cataclysmic earthquake struck the Yungay Valley in Peru in 1970, where he was doing fieldwork (2009: 11). Oliver-Smith's work is enormously important, not least due to his engagement with other disciplines, his theoretical work on disasters (Oliver-Smith 1999), and his contributions to applied anthropology, especially concerning resettlement issues (Oliver-Smith 2005).

As Oliver-Smith's work shows, disasters occur at the intersection of a society's relationship with its environment, and are the results of the preconditions that render some groups more vulnerable than others (Oliver-Smith 1996: 303).

Two edited volumes by Oliver-Smith and Susanna Hoffman published around the turn of the millennium took disaster anthropology into a new phase (Hoffman and Oliver-Smith 2002; Oliver-Smith and Hofman 1999), and in recent years, disaster anthropology has gradually expanded into a mature subdiscipline of anthropology (Henry 2005). This is also reflected in the growing number of monographs based on extensive ethnographic research in disaster contexts (Adams 2013; Falk 2015; Fortun 2011; Fothergill 2004; Gamburd 2014; Petryna 2013; Revet 2007; Thurnheer 2014; Ullberg 2013). Importantly, during this development, disaster anthropologists continue to draw upon other interests in anthropology, such as war, conflict, migration, development, environment, health, politics, identity, ethnicity and globalization.

In the following sections of the chapter, we cover four selected themes that disaster anthropologists have focused on, which support our main point: that disasters are inherently social events and processes, and constitute total social phenomena that weave different spheres of social life together.

The social meaning of disasters

The anthropologist's ambition is to describe and understand how people's being in the world is experienced and made meaningful under the assumption that this inevitably also guides their actions. This, however, sometimes inadvertently portrays people's understandings of the world as entirely coherent and consistent. Meaning, it is important to note, is influenced by culture, but not deducible from it. The establishment of meaning is an active, dynamic social practice made up by differently positioned individuals' ongoing interpretations. These interpretations draw upon both cultural imaginaries and pragmatic situational considerations (Slater 2013). As individuals negotiate their versions of reality and search for social recognition and legitimacy within intersubjective arenas, they are constantly exposed to alternative visions and subjected to contestations. Those challenges to subjective reality turn meaning into something that is always in the making, requiring constant social labour and attention.

From a constructivist, interpretative perspective, disasters can be argued to constitute critical events, which not only destroy the surrounding environment and economic livelihoods of people, but 'bring about a rupture of previous knowledge(s) ... and propose a new truth' (Humphrey 2008: 360). In addition to loss of property, assets and perhaps loved ones, disasters are experienced as a 'violation of taken-for-granted expectations', a 'violation of cultural categories' (Gamburd 2014: 19), which for some people may generate trauma and apathy, but which also sparks a creative process of reconstructing the world anew. The uncertainty produced by disaster concerns not only the re-establishment of viable livelihoods, but also questions of possible future social standings and moral being. From this perspective, the imperative question is not necessarily 'what *is* a disaster' (objectively) but how it is experienced, made meaningful and acted upon by different people. The sociocultural significance of a disaster pertains to how it is incorporated into people's ordinary lives and leaves traces in the social organization and identity of communities.

In the context of disaster, ethnographic research shows that people are not only occupied with making sense of disaster itself. Relief and recovery aid also constitute important new experiences in need of meaning-making, and both involve questions of morality and subjectivity. The social interpretation of disasters is generally concerned with issues of causality and responsibility, which are embedded in larger questions about ethics, justice and morality. Gamburd (2014) demonstrates how, in the wake of the 2004 Indian Ocean tsunami, people negotiated the possible relationship between the tsunami and karmic justice. Some contended that the tsunami itself was a karmic result of all the bad things happening at the beach (e.g. the killing of fish and tourism-related prostitution), while others used the logic of karma to explain particular tsunami deaths as a result of individual immoral behaviour. Yet others defended the fishermen's economic livelihoods as moral, and instead suggested that the disaster was a result of environmental destruction, or, alternatively, the outcome of moving tectonic plates creating an earthquake. To judge these competing interpretations on the basis of the available scientific criteria alone and dismiss religiously framed understandings as irrational would prevent an understanding of how people experienced the tsunami, what they considered to be appropriate responses, and how the tsunami will shape future social relations (Falk 2015). It would also miss the point that Western experts and relief-workers are themselves caught up in social and cultural constructions of reality that affect how they perceive and act in situations of disaster and make disaster policy (Albris 2013; Tierney and Bevc 2007).

While disaster professionals typically conceive of their interventions in terms of neutral solutions to a crisis expressed in a humanitarian ethos of 'doing good', recipients of humanitarian aid are well aware that there is no such thing as a free gift and speculate about the motives of the donors (cf. Mauss 2002). Regardless of their declared good intentions, faith-based organizations may be accused of wanting to trade relief for conversion; governments may be criticized for favouring capital over citizens; politicians may be suspected of favouring their supporters and using relief to buy votes; entrepreneurs may be criticized for profiting from others' suffering; international or national non-governmental organizations may be accused of undermining state power; and foreign philanthropists may be blamed for cultural imperialism and their local counterparts accused of using others' misery, as a means to achieve greatness as a patron (Adams 2013; Fothergill 2004; Gill *et al.* 2013).

Disaster-affected people are often deeply concerned with how humanitarian relief positions them as social, moral beings. Slater (2013) reports how Japanese tsunami victims rejected help from volunteers, because they could not reciprocate the humanitarian gift. While the volunteers framed their assistance in terms of humanitarianism and altruism, their help violated the local population's sense of moral being, as it left them indebted. From an altogether different context, Fothergill

(2004) shows how Caucasian American middle-class women felt humiliated and stigmatized as 'black' and 'poor' when having to queue for assistance at public relief centres wearing tattered clothes. While some victims may reject assistance to preserve moral dignity, others may reconceptualize the exchange to protect their self-esteem. As Fothergill demonstrates, many middle-class flood-victims in her study reinterpreted relief assistance as a right and entitlement they deserved, because all their life they had worked hard, earned an income and paid their taxes. Victimhood was here construed through a more dignifying and empowering notion of citizenship.

These ethnographic examples illustrate the many ways in which a disaster and the subsequent inflow of relief assistance can be interpreted, contested and negotiated. Such considerations reflect the inevitable political nature of disasters, to which we now turn.

The political life of disasters

In recent years, the attention to the political dimensions of disasters has grown. Several factors have contributed to this, including the increase in man-made (e.g. technological) disasters, the occasional entanglement of disasters and armed conflicts, and the shifting modes of relief interventions. While classical political anthropology mainly occupied itself with ethnographic accounts of formal political structures and institutions in small-scale societies, political anthropology today asks the additional question, 'what is the political?' This brings into the purview of political anthropology, the informal institutions and practices that negotiate the control, production, distribution and use of resources, as well as their associated ideas and values. While politics is not reducible to power, power relations play an important role.

Building on a long tradition of critical research into colonialism, development aid, armed conflicts and emergency relief, some anthropologists have focused on understanding humanitarian interventions as a particular mode of power (de Waal 1997; Ferguson 1990; Malkki 1996; Sørensen 2008). What these authors have in common is a critical view of *how* humanitarianism works. According to de Waal, humanitarianism has not only established itself as a self-justifying professional enterprise, but more importantly it has shifted focus from establishing political accountability to improving technical solutions, thus becoming an international political action (de Waal 1997: p. xv). Whether spearheaded by international agencies or national governments, humanitarian discourses of risk, emergency, vulnerability, etc., have been used to legitimize extraordinary political measures against populations, such as forced displacement (Hilhorst *et al.* 2013: 6; Hyndman 2007). In recent years, the number and kinds of actors intervening in disaster situations have multiplied and diversified. Accordingly, competing understandings of humanitarianism have been inserted into the politics of disaster and new means of dealing with disaster-prone or affected populations have arisen. Based on ethnographic research in New Orleans, Tierney and Bevc (2007) and Masco (2013) demonstrated how deployed American troops militarized the disaster, and read New Orleans as a war zone, seeing disaster victims as enemy insurgents. Moreover, Adams (2013) and Gunewardena and Schuller (2008) provide ethnographic examples of what Naomi Klein (2007) termed 'disaster capitalism': the neo-liberal strategies and tactics that corporations and governments employ in disasters for economic benefit. Military and corporate actors, it seems, increasingly exert defining and regulating power over disaster situations.

Moving to the micro-level, other anthropologists have explored how humanitarianism works through its concrete interventions and projects, which become sites of governance. Malkki examined how the universal discourse of victims stripped refugees of their unique identities rooted in particular histories and places, and reduced them to a silenced 'sea of humanity' (1996: 377). Hyndman (2000: pp. xxii, xxviii) likewise addressed this 'politics of representation' that erases local social differences, but also showed how in a camp for displaced people, a 'microphysics of power' was exercised through both coercive and disciplinary means.

The impact of humanitarianism can be felt beyond the confines of particular discourses and projects, as it becomes part of the reworking of existing power constellations. Hilhorst (2013) points out that the perceived legitimate authorities differ between particular actors. Sri Lanka provides a strong example, as the national government and Tamil separatists were contesting power in regions worst hit by the tsunami. Inevitably, humanitarian relief played into the struggle and became heavily politicized. As Sørensen (2008) has shown, humanitarian interventions may not only alter power relations, but also challenge, undermine and replace cultural understandings of authority, as when international relief workers communicate through young male adults, channel valuable resources through women or train local partner organizations to operate according to externally imposed norms and procedures that may alienate them from their traditional constituencies.

Anthropologists' attention to lived experience has resulted in research into how people respond to and cope with crisis and recovery, either through a politics of the everyday (Hilhorst 2013), creative appropriation of policies (Sørensen 2008), or through more pronounced political actions, such as protesting and activism (Brunsma et al. 2007; Fortun 2001; Ullberg 2013). People's overt political responses to disaster have contributed to raising our awareness of the social, man-made dimensions of disasters. Disasters expose the political contract between people and the state, revealing people's experiences of marginalization and disappointed expectations as (political) citizens. In post-tsunami Sri Lanka, the government was severely criticized for corruption and for favouring the interests of the tourist sector over those of the local fishing communities (Gamburd 2014; Gunawardena and Schuller 2008). In New Orleans, the government authorities' delayed and biased response revealed the discriminatory workings of race, class, gender and age in the American social order, and eroded people's trust in the authorities (Brunsma et al. 2007). In the wake of the 2008 earthquake in Sichuan, China, angry parents formed citizen's groups that staged public demonstrations, blaming the authorities for corruption and for disregarding building regulations. In Japan, victims of the nuclear disaster in 2011 held the authorities responsible and accused them of lax monitoring of the nuclear plant and for withholding critical information. In some situations, popular protests have been met with sanctions and further marginalization, while in others they have paved the way for more democratic governance and inclusive citizenship. Disasters may in other words set in motion more general political transformations, for better or for worse (Pelling and Dill 2010).

Disaster scapes: the question of space and place

In spatial terms, disaster studies tend to concentrate its analytical gaze on zones of destruction and reconstruction. Anthropology is no exception, in so far as it is concerned with documenting and understanding the localized social and human impacts of a disaster. However, in the past few decades of a postcolonial globalized world, many anthropologists have questioned the validity of their own customary notion of the ethnographic field as a (remote) bounded community with a smooth correspondence between territory, culture and identity. Instead, focus has been directed at how different phenomena are constituted through linkages and networks, which – despite the fact that they are always, and can only be, experienced locally – are global in character. To conceptualize this new understanding of the field, Arjun Appadurai (1996) coined the notion of 'social imaginaries', subdivided into five different 'scapes' (ethnoscapes, mediascapes, technoscapes, financescapes and ideascapes) to draw attention to different aspects of global disjunctures.

In line with this view, we contend that a methodological and analytical focus on 'disaster scapes' may give a better comprehension of the dynamics and power relations at play in disaster situations and their aftermath. Locating local scenes of disasters in a global field allows us to see and focus on the financial, political, social, and cultural influences of actors like migrants, refugees, tourists, philanthropists, media, private companies, the military, etc.; actors who usually escape our attention because they are not local, and are not perceived as distinctly humanitarian. Disasters are not only global phenomena because nature does not abide by national borders, but because social relations and exchanges have become increasingly globalized. From an ethnographical point of view, the distinction between global and local actors and relations is of less importance, as they are all constitutive of the local field. Put differently, anthropologists do not conceive of, for example, humanitarian aid as an external force that simply acts in and impacts a pre-existing local setting, but rather as a co-producer of that particular setting (Hilhorst 2013).

Spatial considerations do not only concern how we as researchers and practitioners construct the field of our investigations and interventions, but also how people inhabit the world. As pointed out above, the relationship between humans and the environment is a key issue in anthropology. Anthropologists emphasize people's place-making strategies and practices, arguing that the environment is not merely a provider of resources, but part of people's identity and being (Sørensen 1997). People inscribe themselves on the landscape through everyday activities of cultivation, built environments and symbolic markers. Simultaneously, they embody their environment through an orchestration of their daily practices and routines, and through the consumption of the environment's products. It follows that the loss of house, land, assets and personal belongings in a disaster is not only an economic loss, but also a loss of social status or even a loss of identity that may generate psychological suffering. When disaster response and risk reduction include processes of forced resettlement in camps or new environments, this sense of loss and disorientation may inadvertently be reinforced, separating individuals from identity-producing habits, landmarks, religious forces, etc. (Gill *et al.* 2013; McGilvray and Gamburd 2010; Sørensen 1997).

The above perspective finds a micro-level parallel in the distinction between 'shelter'/'house' and 'home'. Humanitarian actors provide shelter and houses to disaster victims as protection against harsh weather conditions or the intrusion of strangers as well as a private space for family life. Numerous examples exist of housing projects that have failed to provide culturally appropriate designs, especially regarding the location of toilets and kitchens, which are symbolically significant as spaces where substances leave and enter bodies, and make individuals particularly vulnerable (Gamburd 2014). And even when shelters are well-designed, considerable social labour is required to transform these into homes, where people can feel 'at home'. Steger (2013) demonstrates how Japanese camp dwellers paid extreme attention to cultural rules and practices of cleanliness associated with a proper home, not only to avoid infection, but also to uphold dignity in the wake of disaster. As Blunt and Varley (2004: 3) argue, a 'home is invested with meaning, emotions, experiences and relationships', which implies that home-making is a long-term social process.

Disaster times: the question of time and change

Anthropologists' concern with space and place is matched by an equally important interest in time and temporalities. Anthropology can provide useful insights into how the rhythms of disaster types (e.g. sudden, slow-onset, seasonal) intersect with the seasonal and everyday rhythms of communities and households. Moreover, ethnography has provided rich evidence of how religious, cultural notions of time (e.g. the Buddhist belief in karma and reincarnation) affect people's experiences of disaster and response strategies (Falk 2015; Gamburd 2014; Merli 2010). Apart from such cultural knowledge, anthropologists are interested in how disasters shape and are shaped by societies over the long term, which places emphasis on analysing disasters as processes rather than singular or sequential events (Fortun 2001; Petryna 2013). This is also especially pertinent in seeking to understand patterns of vulnerability created through long-term historical developments (Oliver-Smith 1992).

Central to any discussion about the relationship between disasters and time is the question of whether and to what extent disasters cause social change or continuity. For Hoffman, two issues require clarification in order to address the issue. First, we need to ask whether changes from disasters are minor or major.

Second, we need to ask whether such changes are lasting or not (Hoffman 1999: 303). A range of other questions follow: for instance, whether such changes are minor shifts in existing patterns or whether they are fundamental breaks with former social practices. Analysing how disasters happen within and change existing political, economic and social contexts is central for disaster research in general (Pelling and Dill 2010). From an anthropological standpoint, however, it is not only a matter of placing disasters in context. It is a matter of tracing how disasters themselves produce new contexts by creating new associations and relations among actors over time. Disasters are both the result of previous conditions and emergent conditions brought about by the event. Anthropological methodology is well suited to detect the perpetual presence of disaster as it reveals itself in political practices, social organization, landscapes, bodies, language, rituals, material culture, memory, etc.

All disasters shape future societies, but technological disasters are exemplary. As Ulrich Beck (1986) noted in his thesis of the 'Risk Society', many societies are becoming increasingly vulnerable to the risks posed by technological developments. Prophetically, Beck published his thesis almost at the same time as the 1986 Chernobyl nuclear accident. Adriana Petryna studied the social, biological and political ramifications of Chernobyl through extensive fieldwork among contaminated individuals, radiation scientists, government bureaucrats and other actors in Ukraine. Her study exemplifies the ethnographic attention to the long-term effects of disasters. As Petryna chillingly notes, the Chernobyl accident damaged 'human immunities, and the genetic structure of cells, contaminating soils and waterways' (Petryna 2013: 1). The disaster's reconfiguration of biological life, Petryna shows, was mirrored by changes at the political level, as human biology became tied to citizen rights, constituting a new and particular 'biological citizenship'. A new disaster vernacular was simultaneously developed, where people affected by the radiation would refer to themselves as 'bio-robots' or the 'living dead' (Petryna 2013: 2–3). Kim Fortun's study of the Indian Bhopal chemical disaster in 1984 similarly shows how this disaster got entangled in political, economic and legal issues over time: 'Bhopal showed no evidence of boundaries of time, space, or concept. Bhopal as I encountered it, was a disaster that entangled the local and the global, the historic and the future, continuity and dramatic change' (Fortun 2001: 1). From the point of view of affected people or those dealing with the ramifications of disasters, there is no stable point of reference in space or time where the event can be said to exist. The task for every individual and group involved in a disaster situation, as both Petryna's and Fortun's studies show, is to negotiate when and where a disaster begins, and where it ends.

While the emphasis on disaster as a prolonged process that entails both formative continuities and changes is of vital importance, we should not neglect people's active engagement with time, which exhibits significant variations across cultures. Anthropologists' general interest in social memory, remembrance and commemoration, we suggest, is of potential relevance here, but so far this perspective has received scant attention. Exemplary of an ethnography which concerns itself with societal memory, Ullberg's study illustrates how memories of urban flooding in Santa Fe, Argentina, are materialized in monuments and documents, as well as enacted in rituals and public demonstrations. Her work reveals memory as being dynamic, involving both active remembering and forgetting, and it demonstrates the political nature of memories as they are 'differently distributed over the various sections of society and scale of public life, which are linked to historical processes of social geography' (Ullberg 2013: 15). Falk (2015) similarly discusses the politics of remembering in her comparison of government-organized official commemorations and community-based initiatives to remember the victims of the tsunami in Thailand. While the government went to great lengths to invite and accommodate the needs of a global population of tsunami victims, and used the event to boost its own image as responsible and efficient internationally, it failed to properly involve and represent certain local groups of survivors.

The question of disasters as catalysts for social change (or continuity) is a difficult issue in itself, but the way disasters affect notions of rights, citizenship and self are inherently complex and emergent. Moreover, disasters affect collective ways of remembering and social memory. These points, and the others we have presented in the above sections, are relevant not just for disaster theory or anthropology. They are relevant for disaster work in general.

The dynamics of disaster: anthropological perspectives

In this section, we address how the anthropological approaches and perspectives discussed so far can be relevant to disaster policy and practice. We argue that anthropology offers a reflexive critical stance on modeling in disaster management, and draws attention to contingency, uncertainty and emergence as significant aspects of two central concepts: vulnerability and resilience.

Above, we dealt with the temporal dimensions of disasters, which also relates to the different phases that disasters go through, usually referred to as the disaster management cycle. The cycle is an ideal type or model, which depicts the phases of a disaster – preparedness, response, recovery and mitigation (the order can vary, and phases can be added). The cyclical model has been useful for disaster studies and management, because it replaced or complemented an older linear model. The cyclical model, however, as pointed out by numerous scholars (cf. Bankoff 2004: 28), is problematic in that the phases cannot be clearly differentiated empirically, and often overlap. From an anthropological perspective, all models of society reduce complexity, and offer simple technocratic solutions to complex problems (Ferguson 1990). However, models like the disaster cycle are also performative: they are models *for*, not models *of* (Geertz 1973: 93–4). In other words, the disaster cycle model is a model *for* managing, rather than a model *of* disasters. This pertains equally to how people make meaning out of disasters, how politics influence people's agency in emergencies and crisis, and how the spatial and temporal dimensions of disasters are experienced differently.

What is most problematic in the disaster cycle model, however, is that it cannot address the deeper ideological, economic and social factors that place people at risk. The central concept here is vulnerability. As Oliver-Smith has argued, a disaster reveals a story about a society's total adaptation strategy 'within its social, economic, modified and built environments' (1999: 25). In Oliver-Smith's view, disasters come about through a process of natural hazard events interacting with a historically produced pattern of vulnerability – which means that a 'disaster begins prior to the appearance of a specific event-focused agent' (1999: 29). Being at risk from disasters implies that certain social, political, economic and ideological forces create and amplify conditions of vulnerability. This view of disasters and risk has been popularized in the form of the Disaster Pressure and Release Model (PAR), developed by Wisner *et al.* (2004). The PAR model resonates with the anthropological attention to disasters, as it depicts how vulnerable and unsafe conditions are shaped by the root causes and dynamic pressures that in turn create society. Disasters happen not because extreme events occur, but because these events interact with a given society's culturally and historically produced patterns of vulnerability (Bankoff *et al.* 2004: 4).

Following the widespread attention to vulnerability, resilience has become immensely popular in social science in recent years. Resilience is defined and used differently by different disciplines, which often leads to some conceptual ambiguities. Originally, resilience implied a system's or material's ability to recover from shock and retain its core functions. However, resilience has gradually taken on a more dynamic meaning, implying not only a 'bounce-back' effect, but also an adaptive capacity on the part of societies and communities in dealing with shock. On the one hand, resilience implies an ability to retain original functions, and on the other, a capacity for positive adaptation. These conflicting notions reveal an ongoing debate about the theoretical and operational value of resilience, which is yet to be settled (Boin *et al.* 2010). From an anthropological point of view, the notion of a social or cultural system, which resilience relies on, is problematic. Societies and cultures do not have clearly marked insides and outsides, and they do not remain constant over time, this poses an analytical and empirical challenge for resilience, as it is fundamentally a systemic concept (Hastrup 2009: 20).

Barrios's (2014) study of post-Hurricane Mitch house reconstruction in southern Honduras deals specifically with community resilience as a problematic concept. Barrios researched two communities, which had seen very different changes in the post-hurricane period. One had experienced bad housing projects, failed and unfinished infrastructural projects and a surge in gang violence. The other community had seen successful house construction projects, and a strengthening of local grassroots movements and residents' initiatives. One community exemplified vulnerability – the other resilience. Yet, as Barrios notes: 'these two communities did not exist as geographically or socially delimited entities prior to the disaster' (Barrios 2014: 338). Rather, the reconstruction processes were shaped by the politically charged relationships between the disaster survivors, the NGOs, donors and the local authorities. As Barrios points out, 'the qualities and capacities of these communities took shape in the midst of these relationships' (2014: 339). As this case illustrates, a community is not a static entity, but comes into being through the disaster event. In addition, the factors that are analysed as part of a resilient response to disasters are formed in the process of recovery, especially by political processes, and are not necessarily the result of some inherent features of a community, regardless of whether resilience is understood as a rebound effect or an adaptive capability.

It is never irrelevant how a concept such as resilience is defined and measured. Thus, the importance of discussing the concepts of resilience and vulnerability is that they, like the disaster management cycle model, will come to serve certain disaster management purposes. Their meanings and definitions can affect the disaster response and recovery, as people will seek to benefit from being labelled either vulnerable or resilient (Benadusi 2013). This needs to be complemented with an attention to the emergent dynamics of disaster situations, and how communities are changed in the course of them. An anthropological attention to vulnerability and resilience ideally takes people's different experiences and perceptions of what constitutes vulnerable conditions or resilient capacities into account (Bankoff *et al.* 2004: 3). The subjective experience of disaster – its social life – is relevant for disaster management in that it can offer wider or alternative perspectives of concepts such as vulnerability and resilience, while being attentive to the emergent and dynamic character of social phenomena.

Conclusion

In this chapter, we have outlined an anthropological approach to disasters. We have argued that ethnography, holism and relativism are fundamental features of anthropology that are not only relevant, but also important for advancing our understanding of disasters. By invoking the idea of the social life of disasters, we have focused on four main perspectives for an anthropology of disasters: meaning-making, politics, time and space.

We have argued that disasters need to be understood in relation to how meaning is produced within them, how the distribution of power and the operations of politics frame them, and how they are experienced differently across multiple understandings of time and space. Disasters are social phenomena, and as such, produce different experiences, which need to be understood, not just in order to process them, but also to manage them.

The approach we have outlined here is representative of certain key features in anthropology in general and in disaster anthropology specifically. Still, our approach is especially shaped by a particular attention to politics and meaning-making. Other anthropological approaches would focus on other themes such as health or environmental adaptation, while some would have a more historical orientation. We believe, however, that the present chapter presents an instructive picture of what disaster anthropology is, and how it can inform the wider field of disaster studies.

References

Adams, V. (2013) *Markets of Sorrow, Labors of Faith: New Orleans in the Wake of Katrina*. Durham, NC: Duke University Press.

Albris, F.K. (2013) Developing manageable futures: An ethnography of expertise, predictions and disaster risks in Fiji. Master's thesis, Copenhagen: University of Copenhagen.

Appadurai, A. (1996) Disjuncture and difference in the global cultural economy. In *Modernity at Large: Cultural Dimensions of Globalization,* Minneapolis, MN: University of Minnesota Press, 27–47.

Bankoff, G. (2004) Time is of the essence: Disasters, vulnerability and history. *International Journal of Mass Emergencies and Disasters,* 22(3), 23–42.

Bankoff, G., Frerks, G., and Hilhorst, D. (eds) (2004) *Mapping Vulnerability: Disasters, Development and People.* London: Earthscan.

Barrios, R.E. (2014) Here, I'm not at ease: Anthropological perspectives on community resilience. *Disasters,* 38(2), 329–50.

Beck, U. (1986) *Risikogesellschaft: Auf dem Weg in eine Andere Moderne.* Frankfurt: Suhrkamp.

Benadusi, M. (2013) The two-faced Janus of disaster management: Still vulnerable, yet already resilient. *South East Asia Research,* 21(3), 419–38.

Blunt, A., and Varley, A. (2004) Geographies of home. *Cultural Geographies,* 11(1), 3–6.

Boin, A., Comfort, L.K., and Demchak, C.C. (2010) The rise of resilience. In L.K. Comfort, A. Boin and C.C. Demchak (eds), *Designing Resilience: Preparing for Extreme Events.* Pittsburgh, PA: University of Pittsburgh Press, 189–220.

Brunsma, D., Overfelt, D., and Picou, J.S. (eds) (2007) *The Sociology of Katrina: Perspectives on a Modern Catastrophe.* Lanham, MD: Rowman & Littlefield Publishers.

Clifford, J., and Marcus, G. (eds) (1986) *Writing Culture: The Poetics and Politics of Ethnography.* Berkeley, CA: University of California Press.

de Waal, A. (1997) *Famine Crimes: Politics and the Disaster Relief Industry in Africa.* Oxford: James Currey.

Evans-Pritchard, E.E. (1940) *The Nuer: A Description of the Modes of Livelihood and Political Institutions of a Nilotic People.* Oxford: Clarendon Press.

Falk, M.L. (2015) *Post-Tsunami Recovery in Thailand: Socio-Cultural Responses.* London: Routledge.

Ferguson, J. (1990) *The Anti-Politics Machine: 'Development,' Depoliticization and Bureaucratic Power in Lesotho.* Minneapolis, MN: University of Minnesota Press.

Fortun, K. (2001) *Advocacy After Bhopal: Environmentalism, Disaster, New Global Orders.* Chicago, IL: University of Chicago Press.

Fothergill, A. (2004) *Heads Above Water: Gender, Class, and Family in the Grand Forks Flood.* Albany, NY: State University of New York Press.

Gamburd, M.R. (2014) *The Golden Wave: Culture and Politics After Sri Lanka's Tsunami Disaster.* Bloomington, IN: Indiana University Press.

Geertz, C. (1973) Religion as a cultural system. In *The Interpretation of Cultures.* New York: Basic Books, 87–125.

Gill, T., Steger, B., and Slater, D. (eds) (2013) *Japan Copes with Calamity: Ethnographies of the Earthquake, Tsunami and Nuclear Disasters of March 2011.* Oxford: Peter Lang.

Gunewardena, N., and Schuller, M. (eds) (2008) *Capitalizing on Catastrophe: Neoliberal Strategies in Disaster Reconstruction.* Lanham, MD: AltaMira Press.

Hastrup, F. (2011) *Weathering the World: Recovery in the Wake of the Tsunami in a Tamil Fishing Village.* Oxford: Berghahn Books.

Hastrup, K. (2009) Waterworlds: Framing the question of social resilience. In K. Hastrup (ed.), *The Question of Resilience: Social Responses to Climate Change*. Copenhagen: Det Kongelige Danske Videnskabers Selskab, 11–30.

Henry, D. (2005) Anthropological contributions to the study of disasters. In D. McEntire and W. Blanchard (eds), *Disciplines, Disasters and Emergency Management: The Convergence and Divergence of Concepts, Issues and Trends. From the Research Literature*. Emittsburg, MD: Federal Emergency Management Agency (FEMA).

Hilhorst, D. (ed.) (2013) *Disaster, Conflict and Society in Crisis: Everyday Politics of Crisis Response*. London: Routledge.

Hoffman, S. (1999) After Atlas shrugs: Cultural change or persistence after a disaster. In A. Oliver-Smith and S. Hoffman (eds), *The Angry Earth: Disaster in Anthropological Perspective*. New York and London: Routledge, 18–34.

Hoffman, S., and Oliver-Smith, A. (eds) (2002) *Catastrophe and Culture: The Anthropology of Disaster*. Oxford: James Currey.

Humphrey, C. (2008) Reassembling individual subjects: Events and decisions in troubled times. *Anthropological Theory*, 8(4), 357–80.

Hyndman, J. (2000) *Managing Displacement: Refugees and the Politics of Humanitarianism*. Minneapolis, MN: University of Minnesota Press.

Hyndman, J. (2007) The securitization of fear in post-tsunami Sri Lanka. *Annals of the Association of American Geographers*, 97(2), 361–72.

Klein, N. (2007) *The Shock Doctrine: The Rise of Disaster Capitalism*. New York: Henry Holt.

Malinowski, B. (1984) [1922] *Argonauts of the Western Pacific: An Account of Native Enterprise and Adventure in the Archipelagoes of Melanesian New Guinea*. Prospect Heights, IL: Waveland Press.

Malkki, L. (1996) Speechless emissaries: Refugees, humanitarianism and dehistorization. *Cultural Anthropology*, 11(3), 377–404.

Masco, J. (2013) Bad weather: The time of planetary crisis. In M. Holbraad and M. A. Pedersen (eds), *Times of Security: Ethnographies of Fear, Protest and the Future*. London: Routledge, 163–97.

Mauss, M. (2002) [1924] *The Gift: The Form and Reason for Exchange in Archaic Societies*. London and New York: Routledge.

McGilvray, D.B., and Gamburd, M.R. (eds) (2010) *Tsunami Recovery in Sri Lanka: Ethnic and Regional Dimensions*. London: Routledge.

Merli, C. (2010) Context-bound Islamic theodicies: The tsunami as supernatural retribution vs. natural catastrophe in Southern Thailand. *Religion*, 40, 104–11.

Oliver-Smith, A. (1992) *The Martyred City: Death and Rebirth in the Peruvian Andes*. Prospect Heights, IL: Waveland.

Oliver-Smith, A. (1996) Anthropological research on hazards and disasters. *Annual Review of Anthropology*, 25, 303–28.

Oliver-Smith, A. (1999) What is a disaster? In A. Oliver-Smith and S. Hoffman (eds), *The Angry Earth: Disaster in Anthropological Perspective*. New York and London: Routledge, 18–34.

Oliver-Smith, A. (2005) Applied anthropology and development: Induced displacement and resettlement. In S. Kedia and J. Willigen (eds), *Applied Anthropology: Domains of Application*. Westport, CT: Praeger, 1–12.

Oliver-Smith, A. (2009) Anthropology and the political economy of disasters. In E. Jones and A. Murphy (eds), *The Political Economy of Hazards and Disasters*. Lanham, MD: Altamira Press, 11–28.

Oliver-Smith, A., and Hoffman, S. (eds) (1999) *The Angry Earth: Disasters in Anthropological Perspective*. New York: Routledge.

Pelling, M., and Dill, K. (2010) Disaster politics: Tipping points for change in the adaptation of sociopolitical regimes. *Progress in Human Geography*, 34(1), 21–37.

Petryna, A. (2013) *Life Exposed: Biological Citizens After Chernobyl*. Princeton, NJ: Princeton University Press.

Quarantelli, E.L. (1978) *Disasters: Theory and Research*. Beverly Hills, CA: Sage.

Revet, S. (2007) *Anthropologie d'une catastrophe: Les coulees de boue de 1999 au Venezuela*. Paris: Presses Sorbonne Nouvelle.

Slater, D. (2013) Urgent ethnography. In T. Gill, B. Steger and D. Slater (eds), *Japan Copes with Calamity: Ethnographies of the Earthquake, Tsunami and Nuclear Disasters of March 2011*. Oxford: Peter Lang, 25–49.

Steger, B. (2013) Solidarity and distinction through practices of cleanliness in tsunami evaluations shelters in Yamada, Iwate Prefecture. In T. Gill, B. Steger and D. Slater (eds), *Japan Copes with Calamity: Ethnographies of the Earthquake, Tsunami and Nuclear Disasters of March 2011*. Oxford: Peter Lang, 53–76.

Sørensen, B. (1997) The experience of displacement: Reconstructing places and identities. In K.F. Olwig and K. Hastrup (eds), *Siting Culture: The Shifting Anthropological Object*. London: Routledge, 142–64.

Sørensen, B. (2008) Humanitarian NGOs and mediations of political order in Sri Lanka. *Critical Asian Studies*, 40(1), 89–112.

Thurnheer, K. (2014) *Life Beyond Survival. Social Forms of Coping After the Tsunami in War-Affected Eastern Sri Lanka*. Bielefeld: Transcript.

Tierney, K., and Bevc, C. (2007) Disaster as war: Militarism and the social construction of disaster in New Orleans. In D.L. Brunsma, D. Overfelt and J.S. Picou (eds), *The Sociology of Katrina: Perspectives on a Modern Catastrophe*. Plymouth: Rowman & Littlefield Publishers, 35–50.

Torry, W.I. (1979) Anthropological studies in hazardous environments: Past trends and new horizons. *Current Anthropology*, 20(3), 517–40.

Ullberg, S. (2013) *Watermarks: Urban Flooding and Memoryscape in Argentina*. Stockholm Studies in Social Anthropology, NS 8. Stockholm: Acta Universitatis Stockholmiensis.

Wallace, A.F.C. (1956) *Tornado in Worcester: An Exploratory Study of Individual and Community Behavior in an Extreme Situation*. Washington, DC: National Academy of Science.

Wisner, B., Blaikie, P., Cannon, T., and Davis, I. (2004) *At Risk: Natural Hazards, People's Vulnerability and Disasters*. London and New York: Routledge.

6 Natural disasters and politics

Olivier Rubin

Introduction

This chapter examines the effect of natural disasters on politics. The focus is primarily on investigating the nexus between voting behaviour and political behaviour. For other perspectives on politics in this volume, the reader can consult Chapter 5 by Sørensen and Albris for insights into humanitarianism in politics and Chapter 4 by Illner and Holm for a discussion of the political application of *state of exception*.

The direct influence of natural disasters on politics is difficult to predict *ex ante*. Any impacts natural disasters have on politics depend to a great extent on the way they are included and handled in the political arena. In other words, the political impacts of disasters are strongly dependent on the political symbols and narratives that emerge in the wake of the disasters. This chapter recommends, therefore, an open-ended context-specific analytical perspective. Rather than having an immediate causal effect, the discourse surrounding natural disasters might trigger certain sentiments and feelings within the population, which – if they take root – could have long-term political consequences. I will start by presenting and assessing the theories and the empirical evidence that focus on the political implications of natural disasters. This is followed by a more detailed discussion of the sociopolitical factors that could influence the political dynamics in the wake of natural disasters. Finally, I conclude the chapter with deliberations of the analytical implications.

Theories of government responsiveness to natural disasters

Political theories based on rational choice predict that governments will go to great lengths to aid natural disaster victims if it can help them stay in power (Flores and Smith 2013; Gasper and Reeves 2011; Morrow *et al.* 2008; Diamond 2008; Boin *et al.* 2008, 2005; Mesquita *et al.* 2003; Sen 2009, 1999). The basic assumption is that political survival is the essence of politics, and states are governed by a tenure-maximizing leadership that relies on a coalition of supporters to remain in power (Morrow *et al.* 2008; Mesquita *et al.* 2003).

Natural disasters pose a risk to governments, because the socioeconomic impacts of disasters could undermine the necessary support from key fractions in society. In democracies, the support of the electorate is of primary concern for governments, due to the inherent opportunity for citizens to oust incumbent governments at the subsequent elections. Voters can punish governments that do not do their utmost to ease the adverse impacts of natural disasters, which is why government responsiveness in times of distress is hypothesized to be stronger (*ceteris paribus*) in more pluralistic political systems (Flores and Smith 2013; Sen 2009, 1999; Boin *et al.* 2005; Kahn 2005). The opposition parties, the electorate and the free media form a trinity that creates the political dynamic impelling governments to act. The media cover the natural disaster, and critically assesses the government's handling of it. The existence of a vibrant opposition presents the voters with a credible ruling alternative; the opposition might even be able to overturn the government directly through parliamentary procedures (a vote of non-confidence, for instance); and it will generally be highly critical of the government's handling of the disaster, and eager to expose any policy mistakes or belated responses. The government, very aware that both the media and the opposition will be critical of its strategy for dealing with the disaster, will therefore respond proactively – and with great force – in an attempt to minimize any electoral damage (Diamond 2008; Boin *et al.* 2005).

Application of theory – empirical evidence of electoral pressure

Empirical evidence overwhelmingly suggests that voters are indeed retrospective and electorally punish governments for inadequate disaster responses. Risk-adverse governments, aware of this, have been found to pursue proactive disaster policies – in particular in competitive political settings and close to elections. However, the empirical evidence also indicates that two important qualifications need to be made in this regard: one is that the government is not always put under pressure by the key political actors. The second qualification relates to the fact that governments do not always react to political pressures in ways that are most beneficial from a humanitarian perspective.

The theory of retrospective voting assumes that voters evaluate the past performance of the incumbent government when deciding their vote. Retrospection can be divided into two separate dynamics (Fiorina 1981): *simple (or blind) retrospection*, referring to the fact that the electorate judges the incumbent government based on each voter's own situation, regardless of whether the government actually influenced the situation; and *mediated retrospection*, when voters judge incumbent governments based on their policies. There has recently been increasing interest in analysing voter and government behaviour during natural disasters. The advantage is that natural hazards (as opposed to fiscal and economic indicators) can generally be treated as an exogenous shock beyond direct government control. It would therefore be rational for voters to pay more attention to government responses to natural hazards than for instance their responses to issues related to business cycles or budget deficits, which are plagued by cross-country multiple inference challenges. In the following, the empirical evidence of blind and mediated retrospection will be discussed.

Blind retrospection and disasters

The theory of blind retrospection dictates that, in situations of natural disasters, voters possess bounded rationality and will therefore not necessarily have the required information to punish governments that react slowly and ineffectively to natural disasters. They will therefore behave 'blindly' with respect to government policies, instead punishing the government for the mere occurrence of natural disasters. There are several reasons for this – that voters are ignorant is not necessarily one of them. A reason is rather that gaining political insights is not cost-free. It requires some effort to immerse yourself in politics, in order for you to assess the government's decisions. Often voters choose to prioritize survival, food, work, friends, family or other hobbies (political dedication is nowhere to be found in Maslow's hierarchy of needs). Empirical research seems to indicate that voting behaviour – even in mature democracies – to a certain extent is affected by the *outcome* of different events rather than on how the governments have *handled* the events. Studies have documented that voters electorally punish government for everything from shark attacks (Achen and Bartels 2004) or the international price of oil (Wolfers 2002) to the defeat of their local football team (Healy *et al.* 2010).

With respect to natural disasters, empirical studies suggest a substantial element of blind retrospection in voting behaviour. Voters electorally punish incumbent governments for merely presiding over a natural hazard, even though the hazard has little to do with the actions of the governments. In their highly cited research paper Achen and Bartels (2004) find that the incumbent government's voter support decreases in US constituencies that experienced an extreme natural hazard prior to the presidential election. Healy and Malhotra (2010) conclude along the same lines in their study, where the effects of tornado damage in US counties are found to decrease the incumbent presidential party's vote share. Cole *et al.* (2012) document in their study that Indian voters also display the same dynamics of blind retrospection, as voters across twenty-eight Indian states appear to electorally punish the incumbent government coalitions for extremes in rainfall.

Mediated retrospection and disasters

While it appears that voters do indeed punish government for presiding over disasters, more detailed studies of the political effects of natural disasters have identified two conflicting phases in retrospective voting behaviour during a natural disaster: initially, the incumbent government starts out at a disadvantage, because – as evidenced above – it will instantly lose voter support during a natural disaster due to blind retrospection. There is also a second phase, however, where the government can regain some of the lost votes by handling the disaster effectively (mediated retrospection).

Many studies indicate that voters also take into account the actions of the government. Healy and Malhotra (2010), for instance, find that tornado damage might actually increase voter share for the president's party in a given country *if* the incumbent president issues a disaster declaration and releases federal funds. The same authors reach a similar conclusion with regards to natural disasters in general: the US counties in which natural hazards are followed by relief aid generate a higher share of votes for the incumbent party (Healy and Malhotra 2009). There is ambiguous empirical evidence as to the share of votes that can be regained by effectively responding to a natural disaster. Cole *et al.*'s (2012) Indian study indicates that even though voters do reward politicians who provide emergency aid to disaster-struck states, the governments can only regain a fraction of what they initially lost for just presiding over the natural hazard. However, other studies indicate that a government could end up gaining more votes than it lost in the first phase. In Bechtel and Hainmueller's (2011) analysis of German voting behaviour after the Elbe flooding in 2002, it appears that the incumbent government was rewarded quite substantially for its effective disaster response with a vote share increase of 7 per cent in the affected areas. One speculative explanation for the difference between the two studies could be that widespread poverty and illiteracy rates in India make voters even more myopic and blindly retrospective compared to German voters. A recent 2014 study by Remmer, however, suggests that mediated retrospection also flourishes in less mature democracies. Remmer analyses democratic accountability in twenty-one Caribbean islands with respect to both economic and natural disaster shocks. Controlling for the governments' general competence and political autonomy, she finds 'no evidence that voters blame incumbents for natural disasters, despite the relative frequency and intensity of such events in the region' (Remmer 2014: 1170). Rather, Caribbean voters appeared to avoid blind retrospection, instead rewarding and punishing politicians for their competence in managing the disaster.

The behaviour of governments

A few studies have documented the consequences of retrospective voting on governments' natural disaster response. Healy and Malhotra's 2009 study of US relief expenditure across counties documents that incumbent governments are more prone to provide disaster relief in politically supportive constituencies. The authors further show that governments are electorally rewarded only for *responding* to natural disasters and not for *preventing* disasters, which leads to perverse political incentives in disaster management. Despite obvious financial cost-benefit advantages in favour of preventive disaster measures ($1 spent on disaster preparedness would reduce future damages within the same election cycle by more than $7) there are few political advantages in implementing preventive measures (Healy and Malhotra 2009). In other words, politicians are not rewarded politically for a well-maintained dam; the lack of a disaster is a non-event most likely to slip under the radar screen of the voters. Should the levee break, however, politicians would suddenly have the voters' full attention, which would allow for political rewards and penalties to come into play.

Reeves (2011) finds that highly competitive states in the US presidential elections receive twice as many disaster declarations from the president, after controlling for the actual impact of the natural disasters. As other studies have also shown, this political behaviour is rooted in an attempt to boost electoral rewards by the retrospective voters. In order for the president to declare a disaster and dispatch federal disaster relief, the governors of the disaster-affected state must first make a formal request. Gasper and Reeves (2011) have analysed the governors' willingness to do just this during the period 1972–2006, and the result is that governors from battleground states appear to have asked above and beyond objective measures of disaster need. Interestingly, term-limited governors (who do not face re-election) have not displayed this behaviour – which is in accordance with the theory of political survival. Sainz-Santamaria and Anderson (2013) have analysed the electoral politics of disaster preparedness across US counties from 1985 to 2008. Their results indicate that higher electoral returns 'incentivize higher spending until the county is safe enough that electoral patterns are irrelevant for the investment' (Sainz-Santamaria and Anderson 2013: 244). Thus, disaster spending peaks in the most competitive counties, where the incumbent is elected with about half the votes.

Note that these empirical studies do not suggest that government policies are uninfluenced by political ideology, altruism or popular demand; all the studies above found that disaster relief was indeed distributed according to need (measured by disaster damages). The argument is rather that pure political considerations *also* play a significant role in voter and government behaviour.

Empirical case: incumbent government benefiting from effective disaster response

The Conservative party leader Edmund Stoiber was headed for a sure election victory in the 2002 German elections: the August voting polls gave his coalition 51 per cent of votes, with the election less than a month away, while the incumbent Social Democrats led by Gerhard Schröder could only muster 44 per cent. Then the worst flooding in contemporary German history took place; several cities along the Elbe River were flooded, 30,000 people had to be evacuated and damages ran into the billions of euros (Bechtel and Hainmueller 2011). One would expect – based on theories of blind retrospection – the flooding to put Schröder's government under increased pressure: it was widespread (affecting a large share of the electorate) and it occurred in the immediate run-up to the election. However, a couple of weeks after the flooding, public opinion had changed drastically in favour of the incumbent government, and at election-day 53 per cent now preferred the incumbent government, while only 43 per cent preferred the opposition (Roberts 2003). This could in part be ascribed to mediated retrospection. Schröder allocated billions of euros in disaster relief to the worst affected areas, while at the same time delaying the promised tax reductions for a year. He also ensured that help was available immediately: 45,000 soldiers were dispatched to the affected areas to provide help, and just two days after the establishment of an emergency aid fund, the first payments were already being made (Bechtel and Hainmueller 2011). A few months after the flood, the majority of the affected households expressed widespread satisfaction with the government relief and reported full recovery rates of between 31 and 60 per cent (Thieken *et al.* 2007).

Discussion of government responsiveness

While the theory of political survival broadly appears adept at explaining some of the behaviour of both voters and governments in the wake of natural disasters, there are several factors that undermine a deterministic (or even probabilistic) relationship between natural disasters and government/voting behaviour. The first qualification to the dynamics described above is the fact that political pressure on the government might not always materialize in the aftermath of a natural hazard. This section will examine three factors that could undermine political pressure to act: (1) voters are myopic and do not exert a political pressure; (2) the media and opposition parties fail to exert political pressure; (3) the political system does not allow for a pluralistic political pressure.

Myopic voters

Some empirical evidence on voting behaviour indicates that voters often fail to punish government for inadequate disaster policies, thereby annulling the political incentives an incumbent government have to act. On a temporal dimension, the importance of election cycles in retrospective voting behaviour is well-established. Achen and Bartels (2004) document that the number of years until the next election reduces the electoral impact of natural hazards. Lenz (2010) documents through both historical data and experimental data that voters' experiences at the end of terms appear to shape their memories of the incumbent government's earlier performance. Cole *et al.*'s (2012) Indian study suggest that voters respond to disaster relief only in the year preceding an election. Bechtel and Hainmueller (2011) examine the durability of voter gratitude for effective disaster policies by drawing on voting behaviour after the Elbe flooding in 2002. The rewards, according to Bechtel and Hainmueller (2011), were substantial – but decline quickly over time. By comparing the changes in vote shares between the affected and unaffected districts, the gain of 7 per cent in the 2002 elections for the affected areas declined to 2 per cent in 2005 and finally to no significant effect in 2009 (Bechtel and Hainmuelle 2011: 859).

Although declining, there is still a high degree of inertia in voter movements. Most voters identify with a specific party and it would take a lot to trigger major shifts in voting patterns (Green-Pedersen and Mortensen 2010). Natural disasters can thus be a shock to society, but natural disasters rarely result in a political shock. Voters also have political interests other than disaster relief, particularly if the natural disaster is limited both in scope and destruction. The majority of natural disasters, barring truly catastrophic events, will strike locally, and the disaster victims often only comprise a small percentage of the overall electorate. The extent to which voters might sympathize with the victims depends on a multitude of factors: are the unaffected voters at risk of being struck by a similar disaster in the future? Do the voters feel secondary economic effects from the disaster? Do they share key socioeconomic characteristics with the victims? And so on.

Opposition and media

It is also questionable whether it will always be in the interest of the media and opposition to put pressure on the government. Rubin (2010) emphasizes that a natural disaster often bears the hallmark of *force majeure*, and an aggressive and insensitive opposition will not necessarily be appreciated by the voters. The opposition may also withhold criticism either because it is partly responsible for failing to prevent the disaster (as a result of parliamentary compromise or because it has been in power when vital decisions were made) or because it is aware that it will one day assume office and is therefore interested in maintaining a truce when it comes to unmanageable and unpredictable disasters. Even if opposition parties did criticize the government for their handling of a natural disaster, the effect of such criticism on voters should not be overestimated. Boin *et al.* (2009) draw on fifteen case studies of crises to list four rather restrictive conditions that need to be met for the opposition to gain from a crisis: (1) the crisis must be perceived to be caused primarily by internal causes (thus making it more likely that the blame will stick to the government); (2) the incumbent government must have been in office for a long time (thus making sharing/reversing blame less likely); (3) the government must already be on the defensive from a critical press; (4) the opposition must be in a position to capitalize on any potential official inquiry (thus exploiting independent experts politically).

   In some instances, therefore, many of the key players could have a shared interest in downplaying the adverse consequences of a disaster. An illustrative (and famous) example of such alliance is the cooperative behaviour of the major political actors following the 1906 San Francisco earthquakes. On 18 April 1906, San Francisco was hit by a number of serious earthquakes. It is estimated that over 3,000 lives were lost and that half the town's population became homeless. What is interesting from a political perspective is that industry and the politicians had a common interest in blaming fires for the destruction, despite the fact that large parts of the business district had collapsed directly from the earthquake. In the first public appearance following the disaster, the governor did not talk about the earthquake as such; instead he emphasized that San Francisco had been destroyed by fires, but that the town would quickly be rebuilt. Seeing that the insurance companies covered fire damage but not earthquake damage, citizens were quick to also claim that their house had burned down rather than collapsed. Even independent media such as the *Los Angeles Times* described southern California immediately following the disaster as the safest place on earth.

Authoritarian regimes

Many of the arguments above of retrospection hold little merit for authoritarian regimes where governments are not subjected to the same potential pressure from opposition parties, the media and the electorate. Most natural disasters occur in low-income countries with no or few functioning democratic institutions (EM-DAT 2014).

There are some advantages with authoritarian regimes with regards to natural disaster responses, which might compensate for the lack of the democratic political pressure. Authoritarian regimes can potentially provide a much quicker and extensive mobilization of resources, as the government does not need to abide by the same political rules as democracies. In democracies, disaster management policies often need to be negotiated in parliament, which can lead to delays and dilutions of disaster relief (Rubin 2010). The democratic government might have to engage in compromises, negotiations, electioneering, lobbyism and political games (as explored further below). Many authoritarian regimes build their legitimacy to a large extent on the perception of a strong government capable of taking care of its own population, and they would be most adamant in trying to quickly neutralize the chaos ensued by a natural disaster. Flores and Smith's (2013) quantitative study (going back to the 1800s) suggests that the political leadership in autocracies might be more vulnerable to disaster *occurrences* but more resilient to disaster *fatalities*, compared to democracies. The danger for leaders in autocracies, the argument goes, is the potential for disasters to concentrate displaced people and enhance the ability of the disenfranchised to organize (Flores and Smith 2013: 843). It should be emphasized that authoritarian regimes have been responsible for some of the worst man-made disasters in modern times, including famine and genocide (Stalin's famine-induced genocide in Ukraine 1932–3; Mao's famine in China 1959–61; Pol Pot's Cambodian genocide 1975–9; Kim Jong-Il's famine in North Korea, 1990s). However, in terms of their management of natural disasters, the empirical evidence does not produce a clear picture suggesting they are substantially worse than democratic governments (Rubin and Rossing 2012; Pelling and Dill 2006). One of the most famous cases of effective disaster management, for instance, has been the hurricane responses of authoritarian Cuba, which have been repeatedly praised by the UN (2004, 2011).

The shock from rapid-onset disasters could be hypothesized to have a destabilizing effect on the authoritarian regimes themselves (and not just their leaders). The empirical evidence, however, indicates that this is rare. In modern times, only two political revolutions can be identified that were partly triggered by natural disasters (Cavallo *et al.* 2010). First, the Iranian revolution in 1979, which replaced an authoritarian monarchy with an authoritarian theocracy, took place in the aftermath of the 1978 earthquake that claimed the lives of 25,000 people. Even though there are few direct links from the earthquake to the revolution, the state's belated and inadequate response to the earthquake might have provided a much-needed window of opportunity for the Islamic revolutionary guard to improve their level of organization and popularity. Second, the 1972 Nicaraguan earthquake, which killed 5,000 people and made 250,000 homeless, may also have paved the way for the 1979 revolution, which replaced the dictatorship with an authoritarian socialist government. Once again, the connection is not direct, but the lack of emergency aid might have undermined the government's legitimacy, paving the way for the ousting of the regime seven years later (Cavallo *et al.* 2010). However, in neither of the above cases did natural disasters lead to fundamental shifts in the political systems; in other words, dictatorships did not transform into blossoming democracies. It is not difficult to pinpoint several natural disasters where it was expected that they would have a profound effect on the authoritarian political system, but where they failed to do so: the major flooding in Pakistan during 2010; Hurricane Nargis hitting Myanmar in 2008; and the famine in North Korea in the 1990s. Instead, the most comprehensive changes to political systems appear to be unrelated to natural disasters: the wave of decolonization in Africa in the 1960s; the democratization of Latin America in the 1980s; the peaceful revolutions in Eastern Europe's authoritarian communist regimes at the end of the 1980s; the collapse of the Soviet Union in 1991; and the revolutions in the Middle East and North Africa in 2011. It is clearly easier for natural disasters to impact political processes and alliances than to lead to major macro-shifts in the political systems. While Carlin *et al.*'s (2014) analysis of the impact of the 2010 earthquake on trust in the local Chilean government suggests that natural disasters could erode legitimacy in such new democracies (at least in the transition phase between emergency and reconstruction), fundamental political changes necessitate that broader socioeconomic factors support such a change. The empirical evidence thus points to the fact that political systems are indeed quite resilient to natural disasters. Natural disasters can therefore act as a catalyst that accelerates (or derails) existing processes, but they are not strong enough to directly create the processes (Omelicheva 2011).

Governments respond adversely to political pressure

Whilst the previous section questioned whether a political pressure would always mount in the wake of natural disaster, in the following we will assume that the government is indeed under a political pressure to act. However, the fact that the opposition, the media and the voters are critical of the government's handling of natural disasters does not necessarily compel the government to implement effective disaster policies. It appears that political pressure on the government does not always lead to a natural disaster being handled in an effective and humanitarian way. A humanitarian disaster is not necessarily a political disaster. And humanitarian assistance is not necessarily good politics (Flores and Smith 2013: 843).

The government can use its resources to place blame for the disaster on other relevant political actors, such as the opposition, authorities, former politicians or companies (McLennan and Handmer 2012; Hood 2002). Besides these blame games, there are other political dynamics that could undermine effective disaster management; including everything from direct lobbying conducted by outside groups, to 'log rolling' and 'vote trading' from factions within the political system. Disaster relief could be further prevented by 'pork barrel politics' or the corresponding 'not in my backyard' attitude, where locally elected politicians place the interests of their home constituents ahead of humanitarian needs (Sainz-Santamaria and Anderson 2013; Rubin 2010). Furthermore, a multi-layer democratic system (through a federal structure and/or extensive decentralization) can dilute accountability, thus fostering political blame games (Birkland and Waterman 2008). The institutions can avoid responsibility by 'passing the buck' and blaming other layers in the state apparatus. This is even more the case if competing political parties are in power at the central and state levels. When the population of Louisiana was asked who was mainly responsible for the lack of emergency aid in New Orleans following Hurricane Katrina in 2005, 35 per cent answered the federal government (the president and agency for disaster management (FEMA)), 33 per cent pointed to the state government (governor) and 18 per cent said the local government (mayor) (Gomez and Wilson 2008). It was clearly hard for the voters to ascertain which democratic institution had the ultimate responsibility. Through an analysis of the 2009 pandemic responses across several Western democracies, Baekkeskov and Rubin (2014) put forward a related but novel argument by including the bureaucratic level in the analysis: strong expert agencies could depoliticize disaster management. The theory of political survival has difficulty accounting for the highly divergent responses to the 2009 pandemic (in terms of vaccine purchases and distribution) in otherwise similar democratic settings. Instead, the different responses could be explained by a bureaucratic logic: public health agencies, following their expert judgements and practice, act as lightning rods for public criticism and insulate the incumbent governments from the usual public scrutiny and accountability, hereby allowing for the observed variations in disaster responses. Thus, creating and empowering autonomous regulatory or advisory agencies can be part of political strategies of blame-avoidance.

Analytical implications and venues for future research

It is clear that the political outcomes of disasters contain a great deal of variation that cannot be fully predicted by the logic of political survival and retrospective voting. A fruitful approach would therefore be to focus less on the natural disaster itself, and focus more on the way it is used (or abused) politically. The causes and consequences of a natural disaster are not crystal clear for voters, not just because of their myopic and blindly retrospective voting behaviour, but because they are communicated in a political arena where different myths, narratives and symbols fight for dominance. As rightly noted by Boin *et al.* (2009: 83) '[i]t is not the events on the ground, but their public perception and interpretation that determine their potential impact on office-holders and policy'. Pelling and Dill (2006: 3) appear to argue along the same lines when they conclude that disasters have important symbolic power, and that sociocultural contexts play a key role in shaping political outcomes. Myths and symbols should not be understood as imaginary or unreal folklore, but instead as sociopolitical narratives that provide meaning and comfort in the wake of a natural disaster (Hart 1993). Dominant actors will have an interest in manipulating emotions and perceptions of the disasters to support their political agenda. Andersen in Chapter 9 refers to this as *crisis communication*.

In earlier times (and still in some religious circles today), natural disasters were believed to be God's punishment for immoral political and religious behaviour. This narrative was put under serious pressure during the Age of Enlightenment where the science behind natural hazards became generally accepted. The prevailing narrative was still, however, one of an exogenous force overwhelming an unprepared society. Today, natural disasters are perceived to be much more endogenous to society: the extent to which natural hazards turn into disasters depends crucially on socioeconomic factors – so citizens expect their government to *act*. Governments should act with regards to concrete relief policies, but they should also be a uniting force in times of chaos: conveying the nation's compassion to the disaster-stricken area, grieving with those who have lost loved ones and instilling hope and optimism for the future. These symbolic functions are integral parts of today's narrative of society's response to natural disasters. Recall how the incumbent German government benefited politically from the 2002 Elbe floods. Partly this can be ascribed to the timely and extensive disaster policies, but it can be ascribed to Schröder's success on a symbolic level: in days following the flood the media reported how he tirelessly visited one affected city after another; his opponent Stoiber, on the other hand, waited a whole week before visiting the affected areas.

The political effects of natural disasters thus depend on which narratives and myths prevail in the public debate. Major natural disasters (and other crises) tend to give rise to conflicting interpretations based on a plurality of political values and interests. The political theory of disasters therefore needs to capture not just the physical impacts of the disaster, but also the struggle over which disaster narratives translate into political and policy implications. In other words, analytical insights into the framing of disasters are warranted (cf. Rubin 2015; Kamradt-Scott and McInnes 2012; Kuttschreuter *et al.* 2011). Keeping in mind the inertia in voting behaviour, an interesting hypothesis is therefore that natural disasters might actually have greater long-term political consequences than immediate short-term political consequence. The natural disaster may awaken feelings, moods and particular narratives that mature and evolve in the aftermath of the disaster, leading to political changes which slowly materialize. An interesting function of symbols and narratives is that they often transcend the different political issues. Perceptions of weakness in handling a given situation run the risk of spilling over into other largely unrelated areas. A retrospective voter might not be able to assess in great detail the government's disaster policies, but the retrospection might be much more rooted in the sentiments, pictures and symbols surrounding the disaster. Much depends on the prevailing discourses that materialize after the natural disasters: who emerge as the heroes and who emerge as the villains? Such retrospection could be referred to as *narrative retrospection* in that it is based less on actual policies and more about perceptions of likability. The following two very brief examples could help illustrate these retrospective dynamics.

More than 500 vacationing Swedes lost their lives in the 2004 Indian Ocean tsunami. The actions and statements of the Swedish Foreign Minister drew heavy criticism and public outrage that transcended the more systemic critique of the administrative and government procedures (Óden *et al.* 2005). Media outlets reported that the Foreign Minister went to the theatre, despite initial reports of more than 100,000 tsunami fatalities; that she did not show up for work in the Ministry until more than thirty hours after the tsunami disaster; that she admitted to having absolutely 'no idea what Phuket was'; and that she was unaware that Thailand was a popular tourist site for Swedes (Rubin 2015). She was persona non grata at the memorial ceremony the subsequent year, and she finally had to resign in 2006, largely due to her inept handling of the tsunami disaster, which had stuck with the voters. All major newspaper outlets referred to her personal – rather than political – tsunami missteps in their legacy features.

Another example is the fact that 2005 Hurricane Katrina did not appear to have any immediate effect on President Bush's approval rating, despite substantial media attention and criticism of the government's disaster management (Gallup 2006). Even when looking at the opinion polls from the state of Louisiana, which was particularly hard hit by the hurricane (the entire state was declared a disaster zone when New Orleans was flooded), it is hard to discern any movements – positive or negative – in Bush's approval ratings in the months following the disaster (SurveyUSA 2005). At the state level, all seven members of Louisiana's House of Representatives were re-elected in 2006, as was the mayor of New Orleans. The greatest recent natural disaster in America thus did not appear to have any measurable short-term political consequences. Still, President Bush admitted in his autobiography that his handling of Hurricane Katrina was probably his biggest mistake as president (Bush 2010). In particular, he emphasized how a photo taken of him peeking out the window of Air Force One hovering high above the destruction in New Orleans came to embody the public's perception of his disaster management efforts. The photograph cemented the narrative from another photograph taken a few years earlier: the 2003 photograph of Bush standing in front of a huge 'mission accomplished' banner on-board aircraft carrier USS *Abraham Lincoln*, proclaiming an end to major combat operations in Iraq. For a large part of the electorate it helped frame a narrative of a president out of touch with the reality on the ground. Like any skilful politician, Bush was well aware of the power of such narratives, and it is interesting that his greatest regret looking back was not that he failed to provide adequate relief to the victims of Hurricane Katrina, but that he failed on a symbolic and iconic level.

Summary

Natural disasters will often initially be a burden for those in power (due to blind retrospection), but can be turned into an electoral advantage if dealt with appropriately (due to mediated retrospection). Ample empirical evidence points to the fact that voters are retrospective, and that their voting behaviour affects government policies in times of distress. Studies also indicate that increased pluralistic competition increases incentives to provide disaster relief. However, it does not necessarily follow that the government will pursue effective disaster policies. Governments have many other viable response-strategies to cope with a potential mounting political pressure in the wake of disasters. So rather than expecting a *humanitarian* response, one should expect a *political* response. The political implications of disasters are to a large extent dependent on the symbols, images and narratives that emerge in the wake of natural disasters, more so than the disaster's actual physical impact. This could be coined *narrative retrospection*, and is likely to be prominent in situations of natural disasters that are often shocking, graphic and chaotic. Context-specific research on the political struggle to dominate the narrative of the natural disaster would appear to be a beneficial academic approach.

References

Achen, C., and Bartels, L. (2004) Blind retrospection: Electoral responses to drought, flu, and shark attacks. Paper at the Annual Meeting of the American Political Science Association, Boston, www.international.ucla.edu/media/files/PERG.Achen.pdf (accessed 28 February 2015).

Baekkeskov, E., and Rubin, O. (2014) Why pandemic response is unique: Powerful experts and hands-off political leaders. *Disaster Prevention and Management*, 23(1), 81–93.

Bechtel, M., and Hainmueller, J. (2011) How lasting is voter gratitude? An analysis of the short- and long-term electoral returns to beneficial policy. *American Journal of Political Science*, 55(4), 851–67.

Birkland, T., and Waterman, S. (2008) Is federalism the reason for policy failure in Hurricane Katrina. *Journal of Federalism*, 38(4), 692–714.

Boin, A., Hart, P., and McConnell, A. (2009) Crisis exploitation: Political and policy impacts of framing contests. *Journal of European Public Policy*, 16(1), 81–106.

Boin, A., McConnell, A., and Hart, P. (2008) *Governing After Crisis: The Politics of Investigation, Accountability and Learning*. Cambridge: Cambridge University Press.

Boin, A., Hart, P., Stern, E., and Sundelius, B. (2005) *The Politics of Crisis Management: Public Leadership under Pressure*. Cambridge: Cambridge University Press.

Bush, G. (2010) *Decision Points*. New York: Crown.

Carlin, R., Love, G., and Zechmeister, E. (2014) Natural disaster and democratic legitimacy: The public opinion consequences of Chile's 2010 earthquake and tsunami. *Political Research Quarterly*, 67(1), 3–15.

Cavallo, E., Galiani, S., Noy, I., and Pantano, J. (2010) *Catastrophic Natural Disasters and Economic Growth*. Washington DC: Inter-American Development Bank. Department of Research and Chief Economist, http://idbdocs.iadb.org/wsdocs/getdocument.aspx?docnum=35220118 (accessed 28 February 2015).

Cole, S., Healy, A., and Werker, E. (2012) Do voters demand responsive governments? Evidence from Indian disaster relief. *Journal of Development Economics*, 97: 167–81.

Diamond, L. (2008) *The Spirit of Democracy: The Struggle to Build Free Societies throughout the World*. New York: Times Books.

EM-DAT (2014) Emergency Database, www.emdat.be/database (accessed 28 February 2015).

Fiorina, M. (1981) *Retrospective Voting in American National Elections*. New Haven, CT: Yale University Press.

Flores, A., and Smith, A. (2013) Leader survival and natural disasters. *British Journal of Political Science*, 43(4), 821–43.

Gallup (2006) Job-approval survey, www.pollingreport.com/BushJob1.htm (accessed 28 February 2015).

Gasper, J., and Reeves, A. (2011) Make it rain: Retrospection and the attentive electorate in the context of natural disasters. *American Journal of Political Science*, 55(2), 340–55.

Gasper, J., and Reeves, A. (2011) Governors as opportunists: Evidence from disaster declaration requests. Working paper for the American Political Science Association 2010 Annual Meeting, 27 Aug., www.andrew.cmu.edu/user/gasper/WorkingPapers/govreqs.pdf (accessed 28 February 2015).

Gomez, B., and Wilson, J. (2008) Political sophistication and attributions of blame in the wake of Hurricane Katrina. *Journal of Federalism*, 38(4), 633–50.

Green-Pedersen, C., and Mortensen P. (2010) Who sets the agenda and who responds to it in the Danish parliament? A new model of issue competition and agenda-setting. *European Journal of Political Research*, 49: 257–81.

Hart, P. (1993) Symbols, rituals and power: The lost dimensions of crisis management. *Journal of Contingencies and Crisis Management*, 1(1), 36–50.

Healy, A., and Malhotra, N. (2009) Myopic voters and natural disaster policy. *American Political Science Review*, 103: 387–406.

Healy, A., and Malhotra, N. (2010) Random events, economic losses, and retrospective voting: Implications for democratic competence. *Quarterly Journal of Political Science*, 5(2), 193–208.

Healy, A., Malhotra, N., and Mo, C. (2010) Irrelevant events affect voters' evaluations of government performance. *Proceedings of the National Academy of Sciences*, 107(29), 12804–9.

Hood, C. (2002) The risk game and the blame game. *Government and Opposition*, 31(1), 15–37.

Kahn, M. (2005) The death toll from natural disasters: The role of income, geography, and institutions. *Review of Economics and Statistics*, 87(2), 271–84.

Kamradt-Scott, A., and McInnes, C. (2012) The securitisation of pandemic influenza: Framing, security and public policy. *Global Public Health*, 7(2), 95–110.

Kuttschreuter, M., Gutteling, J., and de Hond, Maureen (2011) Framing and tone-of-voice of disaster media coverage: The aftermath of the Enschede fireworks disaster in the Netherlands. *Health, Risk and Society*, 12(2), 201–20.

Lenz, G. (2010) Understanding and curing myopic voting. Preliminary draft, Massachusetts Institute of Technology, www.princeton.edu/csdp/events/Lenz%2012092010/Lenz-12092010.pdf (accessed 28 February 2015).

McLennan, B., and Handmer, J. (2012) Reframing responsibility-sharing for bushfire risk management in Australia after Black Saturday. *Environmental Hazards*, 11(1), 1–15.

Mesquita, B., Smith, A., Siverson, R., and Morrow, J. (2003) *The Logic of Political Survival*. Cambridge, MA: MIT Press.

Morrow, J., Mesquita, B., Siverson, R., and Smith, A. (2008) Retesting selectorate theory: Separating the effects of W from other elements of democracy. *American Political Science Review*, 102(3), 393–400.

Óden, T., Ghersetti, M., and Walling, U. (2005) Tsunamins genomslag en studie av svenska mediers bevakning. *kbm's temaserie*, 13, http://rib.msb.se/Filer/pdf%5C26159.pdf (accessed 28 February 2015).

Omelicheva, M. (2011) Natural disasters: Triggers of political instability? *International Interactions*, 37: 441–65.

Pelling, M., and Dill, K. (2006) '*Natural' Disasters as Catalysts of Political Action*. ISP/NSC Briefing Paper, 06/01, www.disasterdiplomacy.org/pb/pellingdill2006.pdf (accessed 28 February 2015).

Reeves, A. (2011) Political disaster: Unilateral powers, electoral incentives, and presidential disaster declarations. *Journal of Politics*, 73(4), 1142–51.

Remmer, K. (2014) Exogenous shocks and democratic accountability: Evidence from the Caribbean. *Comparative Political Studies*, 47(8), 1158–85.

Roberts, G. (2003) 'Taken at the flood'? The German general election 2002. *Government and Opposition*, 38(1), 53–72.

Rubin, O. (2010) *Democracy and Famine*. Abingdon, Oxon: Routledge.

Rubin, O. (2015) The Danish and Swedish political dynamics in the wake of the 2004 tsunami. Paper for the 2nd International Conference on Dynamics of Disasters, Greece, July.

Rubin, O., and Rossing, T. (2012) National and local vulnerability to climate-related disasters in Latin America: The role of social asset-based adaptation. *Bulletin of Latin American Research*, 31(1), 19–35.

Sainz-Santamaria, J., and Anderson, S. (2013) The electoral politics of disaster preparedness. *Risk, Hazards and Crisis in Public Policy*, 4(4), 234–49.

Sen, A. (1999) *Development as Freedom*. New York: Knopf.

Sen, A. (2009) *The Idea of Justice*. London: Allen Lane.

SurveyUSA (2005) Approval rates for president, www.surveyusa.com/50StateTracking. html (accessed 28 February 2015).

Thieken, A., Kreibich, H., Müller, M., and Merz, B. (2007) Coping with floods: Preparedness, response and recovery of flood-affected residents in Germany in 2002. *Hydrological Sciences Journal*, 52(5), 1016–37.

UN Press Release (2004) Cuba: A model in hurricane risk management. IHA/943, www. un.org/News/Press/docs/2004/iha943.doc.htm (accessed 28 February 2015).

UN Statement (2011) President of the United Nations General Assembly on Disaster Risk Reduction, 9 Feb., www.un.org/en/ga/president/65/statements/isdr90211.shtml (accessed 28 February 2015).

Wolfers, J. (2002) *Are Voters Rational? Evidence from Gubernatorial Elections*. Stanford GSB Working Paper, 1730 http://papers.ssrn.com/sol3/papers.cfm?abstract_id=305740 (accessed 28 February 2015).

7 Legal scholarship and disasters

Kristian Cedervall Lauta

Introduction

In 2009 a horrible earthquake shook L'Aquila, Italy (pop. 73,150). The disaster caused the death of 309 people and destroyed the medieval town.[1] However, it was seven unharmed individuals that hit the global headlines in the aftermath of the disaster, commonly referred to as the L'Aquila Seven. The L'Aquila Seven had, in their capacity as publicly designated risk experts[2] – just a week before the quake – informed the inhabitants that there was no risk of a major earthquake. As a result, the L'Aquila Seven were charged with involuntary manslaughter. According to these charges, the information provided by the L'Aquila Seven was not in keeping with their actual knowledge (i.e. they were in fact aware of the risk of a major earthquake), or with the state-of-the-art seismological scientific knowledge. Thus, the Seven should have known the risks were bigger than assessed during their meeting before the disaster event.

The charges caused global upheaval, not least in the scientific community (Alexander 2014), and criticism reached new heights in 2012, when the L'Aquila Seven were convicted.[3] Even though most of the global scepticism and attention were, and are, mainly caused by a misperception of the judgement (Alemanno and Lauta 2014; Alexander 2014), the case serves as a perfect example of a shift in the relationship between law and disasters, which is the topic of this chapter.

Natural disasters permeate modern life. In the course of the last twenty years, natural disasters have affected the lives of 4.4 billion people, caused the death of 1.3 million people and left damage amounting to US$2 trillion (Picard 2014). Simultaneously, with this growth and increased visibility of disasters, our understanding of what a disaster *is* has changed significantly. Disasters have changed from being understood as acts of God and nature, to today being understood through our communities' inability to avoid them (Perry 2007). This *socialization* of our understanding of what constitutes a disaster affects how we understand, speak of and are expected to manage disasters; not just within the boundaries of the nation state, but on a global scale.

Returning to the courtroom in L'Aquila: when earthquake survivors, through the epistemological change in what a disaster *is*, understand that their economic and human losses were caused not by *something*, but by *someone*, their misfortune is turned into perceived injustice (Shklar 1990). The guilt that was formerly attributed to God, misfortune or nature is now addressed within the social system, and law is a platform for this social (re)negotiation. In simpler terms, as disasters become social, they become legal (Lauta 2014a). Accordingly, every phase of modern disaster management contains a legal aspect, and law has become an essential element in preparing for, responding to and recovering from disasters.

In the following sections of this chapter, I will provide some examples of (1) what disaster law does; (2) investigate how legal scholarship approaches the field; and (3) finally analyse Hurricane Katrina as a case study for legal scholarship. The article will accordingly touch upon both the content of the portfolio of disaster law, and the present academic approaches to it. In the concluding remarks I will touch upon the future implications for research in disaster law.

Regulating disasters: a field of disaster law

Traditionally, law has no role in the accommodation of crisis. Emergencies were understood as exceptional factual circumstances, and were therefore accommodated through exceptional legal regimes. Disaster accommodation followed a legal model we can generically refer to as the state of emergency or state of exception – a non-legal state temporarily enforced to solve the crisis at hand (see Chapter 4 by Illner and Holm in this volume for more). In this state the government, or a specially designated person (a commissarial dictator or disaster tsar), could do what was necessary, without legal constraints, unnecessary procedural delays or the risk of following legal scrutiny. In short, disasters were by definition exceptions, in fact and in law.

Coinciding with increasing expectations about societal ability to respond efficiently to major hazards, another type of disaster management emerges. This development is driven both by an epistemological shift in our understanding of disasters (from God to social system), a derived public demand, and by increasing social complexity. As our societies become increasingly complex (technologically, socially, culturally), the idea of one person (a dictator or tsar) able to orchestrate an effective response is undermined (Lauta 2011: 95ff; 2014a). In other words, the state of emergency becomes both normatively (as it is against the wishes of the affected population) and instrumentally (as it is not an effective regime) dysfunctional. Today, the state of emergency is replaced by a comprehensive body of law regarding all phases of disaster management (Farber and Faure 2010: xiii ff.) and every conceivable aspect of effective disaster prevention. Consequently, law becomes one of the main instruments to recalibrate and reinstitutionalize society's overall approach to disasters, allowing a *field* of disaster law to emerge.

In the *preparedness* or *preventive phase* of disaster management, law plays an important role in creating incentives (such as taking out suitable insurance) and enforcing preventive initiatives (such as certain building standards or zones, or by developing and updating emergency plans). Law provides a grid for political prioritizations of resources and risks. In Hawaii, houses in tsunami elevations must be built on stilts, and in Japan your real estate value it is absolutely determined by whether your house is built prior to or after the shin-taishin standard (the mandatory earthquake building code after 1981). While it is not law that dictates the explicit content of these technical standards, law is the grid for its negotiation and implementation. Law here performs the difficult task of mediating between state-of-the-art scientific knowledge and actual policy outputs (Jasanoff 1990, 2007); that is, to translate scientific knowledge, with the uncertainty and inherent limitation that follows, into systematic legal constructs with major social consequences. While this aspect has been obvious with regard to industrial risks in the last century, legislation increasingly addresses the input from scientific knowledge for natural hazards as well. Recent attempts to regulate so-called critical infrastructure serves as a perfect example of this tendency (Lazari 2014).

In the *response phase* to disasters, law distributes responsibility (who does what), delegates competences (what can they do), limits discretionary margins (how far can they go) and enforces basic rights (limiting what can be done), which are all essential features of a modern disaster response. Today, any self-respecting country in the world has specific disaster regulation, designating responsibilities, competences and relations to other spheres of regulation during disasters, though these differ in scope and efficiency (Picard 2014). A good example of the increasing need for regulation of the response phase is the development of international disaster response law (Guttry *et al.* 2012). The 2004 Indian Ocean tsunami was an eye-opener for the international community in this respect. According to one study, 372 different organizations, believing to be subject to at least four different jurisdictions, were responding to the effects of the tsunami on the ground (Comfort 2007). Accordingly, a surge of international regulation was initiated on a global scale in general (Guttry *et al.* 2012), and within regional institutions in particular (Lauta 2014a: 84ff.). While this is an ongoing process, the body of international law on disaster response has exploded over the last ten years, and must be expected to further grow in the coming years.

Thereon follows a period of *reconstruction* and *adaptation*. As systematically documented by American sociologist Thomas Birkland, in the aftermath of disasters follows legal reform; often in the narrow context of the just-experienced hazard, yet every time expanding the general legal preparedness for disasters (Birkland 1997, 2006). Law is thereby also a sphere for addressing issues of general resilience, e.g. training, community competences or the use of technology. Moreover, law is the platform from which criminal as well as economic liability can be addressed. This was famously so in L'Aquila, with similar cases having emerged in Chile, Saudi Arabia and Japan (Lauta 2014b). Even in communities traditionally averse to legal action, like the Japanese, a great number of legal actions have set the agenda for the aftermath of the triple 3-11 disaster in 2011 (Nottage 2013). Liability discussions after disasters are becoming as certain as death and taxes, and the law is presently facing a major challenge in providing legal instruments able to facilitate this discussion in a just, yet expedient, manner. Rather than taking on this entire legal field, I will in the following investigate the approaches taken by scholars when addressing this portfolio of legal norms.

Approaches to disaster law

A vast amount of literature has emerged on or is relevant to disaster law. Disasters are in legal scholarship addressed under a number of different labels such as: disaster law,[4] emergency law,[5] risk law[6] or catastrophe law.[7] The labels seem scarcely elaborated, and often overlap in scope, theoretical assumptions and methodology. Thus, the field is perhaps more convincingly organized in five different methodological approaches: the approaches to law and disasters can roughly be distilled into (1) a *doctrinal* approach, aiming to describe the disaster law portfolio or specific sections hereof pursuing a classical legal doctrinal methodology (Baum 2007; Faure and Bruggeman 2007); (2) a *critical* approach, analysing distributive aspects (risks, response or compensation) of disasters to criticize concrete political decisions or the architecture of law as such (Farber 2007; Verchick 2007, 2010); (3) a *theoretical* approach, addressing the foundations of emergency response, and in particular law's ability to accommodate crisis (Dauber 2013; Gross and Nâi Aolâain 2006; Lauta 2011); (4) an *interdisciplinary* approach, aimed at integrating different interdisciplinary aspects of disasters (Birkland 2006; Sarat and Lezaun 2009; Sarat *et al.* 2007); and finally (5) a *risk* approach, addressing legal design and law's (in)ability *a priori* to accommodate major risks (Alemanno 2010; Fischer 2007; Posner 2004).

The *doctrinal approach* aims to describe, as comprehensively as possible, present norms in force. This is by far the most prevalent approach taken by legal scholarship in general, including disaster law. Doctrinal studies aim to fill gaps or clarify contradictions in present law, or to comment on new development in case law, and its implications to legal doctrine. Often such studies aim to identify a solution to the legal problems or development coherent with the legal order and embedded legal knowledge. Consequently, doctrinal studies thereby come to criticize present interpretations or implementations of law, and in some cases to point out gaps in the present regulation, but this always occurs from an internal legal perspective, aiming to present a competing, more accurate (coherent) account of the present law.[8]

Doctrinal scholarship either addresses the portfolio of disaster law (Chen 2011; Farber *et al.* 2010); a thematic specific section thereof (Guttry *et al.* 2012); or, most often, a specific problem relevant to the portfolio (Faure 2007). Studies focusing on the latest developments in case law are especially prevalent, for instance on the so-called *L'Aquila verdict*[9] (Alemanno and Lauta 2014; Alexander 2014; Simoncini 2014); the European Court of Human Right's decision in *Budayeva and others v. Russia*[10] (Hilson 2008–9; Pedersen 2013); or the *In Re Katrina Levee Breach Litigation*[11] against the Corps of Engineers (Farber 2013; Andrews *et al.* 2007; Richards 2012).

The critical approach aims to analyse and criticize present law through a non-legal standard: such as social justice (Verchick 2004, 2007, 2012); state-of-the-art scientific input (Lauta 2014c; Verchick 2010); or economic rationales (Kunreuther and Michel-Kerjan 2007; Posner 2004). Often such studies produce insights unattainable for a pure legal analysis. However, for that very reason, they run the risk of being conceived as more *normative* (here as politically motivated) studies within legal scholarship. Rightfully, such studies quite openly pursue a particular perspective (social or environmental justice, or a particular economic model), with the advantages and disadvantages such endeavour brings about.

While the critical and the doctrinal approach seeks to influence and interact with present law, the *theoretical* approach aims to describe and understand the foundations of law. As the field has undergone a dramatic transformation over the last fifty years, a number of studies seeks to describe this development and its relation to law and society. This often takes place as legal theoretical discussions on fundamental concepts applied to concrete legal decisions relating to political philosophical considerations of state, sovereignty or law. In particular, the discussion of emergency powers for extraordinary situations is a recurring theme in the post 9/11 literature (Agamben 2005; Gross and Nâi Aolâain 2006; Sunstein 2005). This discussion takes its form as a constitutional law discussion (Yoo 2009), a political philosophical discussion (Agamben 2005) and legal theoretical discussion (Gross and Nâi Aolâain 2006). Common for these discussions are that they all fundamentally regard law's limits, and ultimately its foundations.

The *interdisciplinary* approach covers studies examining legal issues pursuing a fundamentally non-legal methodology. This includes sociological studies of legal reform (Birkland 1997, 2006); philosophical and anthropological considerations on legal responsibility (Douglas 1992; Green and Ward 2004); or economic considerations on the regulation of first-party insurance (Auerswald *et al.* 2006; Kunreuther and Michel-Kerjan 2007). While these contributions are central to studies of law and disasters, they would traditionally not be considered part of a portfolio of legal scholarship (but rather sociology, anthropology or philosophy). However, in recent years a still larger ascription to, and appreciation of, such interdisciplinary inputs to legal scholarship can be traced, not least through the inclusion of references to such works.

Finally, the *risk approach* might be best described as a subcategory in the cross-field between the interdisciplinary and theoretical approach. It does however have a number of characteristics warranting special mention. Originating from European risk sociology, the approach sets out to analyse how law deals with major risks in general. This often makes the contributions very policy-oriented, with strong emphases on regulatory design, and integration of scientific knowledge (Alemanno 2010, 2011). The approach is contrary to the bulk of literature on law and disasters not emerging from disaster studies, but from a broad cross-section of risk studies (public health-related, food safety or traffic safety just to mention a few). The approach is distinct as it is mainly anchored to European scholarship, it inscribes disaster studies in a somewhat different context (that of risks) and is predominantly policy-focused.

In the following a case study is undertaken in order to exemplify the interplay between legal scholarship and disaster law.

When the levees broke: Hurricane Katrina and legal scholarship

Katrina left America ruined. The hurricane not only entirely destroyed New Orleans and the areas around the Gulf Coast – it ripped open historical traumas, populist political prioritizations and lack of proper legal reforms (Chen 2009). A knowing nation was caught entirely unprepared. The disaster also left significant marks on American legal scholarship. The hurricane opened a flood-gate of social scientific scholarship, particularly legal scholarship. In the following, I will set out to provide some examples of the scholarly discussions on Hurricane Katrina.

'Failing to plan is planning to fail' as the American Environmental Law professor Denis Binder wisely points out (Binder 2002). Post-Katrina, changes in the planning towards major disasters took place at all levels of government in the US (federal, state, local); and scholarly discussion on the role of central actors (Cigler 2007), the environment (Verchick 2010), and the built environment (Richards 2012) inevitably followed. The disaster created a frenzied activity level in the re-establishment and recalibration of the disaster response and prevention systems, as well as forced an ongoing reconceptualizing of the disaster response system (Evacuteer 2011). Obviously, this recalibration of the city has called upon several legal scholars to partake in the debate. Scholarship on creating the right incentives for home-owners – not least through insurance schemes and zoning laws – is favoured in the field. Not only physical changes are analysed: a number of contributions on different inequality perspectives such as sex (Verchick 2007), poverty (Alexandre 2009), race (Elliott and Pais 2006) and physical condition (Bassett 2009; Lord *et al.* 2009) of the affected population, but also the criminal system, is under critical review (Garrett and Tetlow 2006). The American Law professor Robert Verchick takes on the (re)distribution of economic agency between the sexes after a disaster, examining how the job-market is naturally favourable to men, and why this necessitates a gender perspective in legal scholarship, as well as in the applicable legislation (Verchick 2007). The need for a gender lens is also convincingly accounted for in Lynn Horton's Chapter 10 of this volume.

As already mentioned, in the last ten years we have seen an explosion of case law on responsibility after disaster in general, and cases regarding compensation in particular. After Hurricane Katrina over 1 million legal claims were filed. This *juridification* of disaster in the recovery phase takes up a large proportion of the literature.[12] Methodologically, this body spans from critical encounters taking departure in a certain standard of justice (Bullard and Wright 2009; Farber 2007; Verchick 2007) to case studies of either concrete cases or applications of legal doctrines, not least the 'act of God' defence (Chocheles 2010; Kaplan 2007; Kristl 2010; Lauta 2014a: 110ff.; Mercante 2005–6). Three examples however have attracted particular interest among scholars.

First, the applicability of the so-called 'act of God' defence, a common-law doctrine resolving parties from liability, when the damages are caused by a natural, external and unforeseeable force (Lauta 2011: 192ff.). The defence is comparable to the *force majeure* doctrine, or Pufendorf's doctrine of impossibility (*impossibilium nulla est obligation*), though only applicable to natural hazards. Traditionally, the defence was one of the main liability-avoidance defences in the aftermath of a disaster, as all damages were, almost *per se*, considered acts of God. The defence is therefore particularly interesting to observe in light of the epistemological development of disaster accounted for above; since the application of the doctrine is fundamentally a test of what is considered inside and outside the realm of control of the parties. While the lack of applicability of the defence therefore came as no surprise to the disaster researcher, the legal community was surprised to see it falling short after Hurricane Katrina. In fact, as one scholar, somewhat dramatically, points out, not even the flood of Noah would qualify as an act of God (Kaplan 2007). A fairly uniform legal scholarship thereby concludes that the act of God defence is more or less inapplicable to disasters like Katrina (Chocheles 2010; Kaplan 2007; Kristl 2010; Lauta 2014a: 110ff.; Mercante 2005–6).

Second, a number of home- and business-owners from New Orleans brought action against federal authorities after Katrina.[13] In the consolidated litigation local residents sought 'compensation for damages incurred in the aftermath of Hurricane Katrina, as the alleged result of certain defalcations of the U.S. Army Corps of Engineers (Corps) with respect to maintenance and operation of the Mississippi River Gulf Outlet (MRGO) navigational channel'.[14] However, as MR-GO was constructed and maintained by the US Army Corps of Engineers, they claimed to be covered by federal immunity. The federal immunity is to be understood in the strictest sense – not even in cases where federal authorities are clearly negligent has the immunity been waived.[15] Thus, the central aspect of the case was whether or not the MRGO could be considered a 'flood control project'.[16] The judgement, finding for the Corps of Engineers upon appeal, gave rise to scholarship from both a doctrinal approach (asking, what are the consequences for present law), a critical approach (how the judgement should be evaluated from or contributes to a certain discourse), and from an interdisciplinary approach (what incentives the judgement outlines for future disaster resilience).

Third, and closely related to the above, insurance schemes are widely discussed (Abramovsky 2009; Farber and Chen 2006: 178ff.; King 2005). Pursuing both a doctrinal and an interdisciplinary approach, the accommodation of a fair, resilient or effective insurance system is central. Not least the so-called National Flood Insurance Program,[17] a federal insurance programme to provide affordable insurance to people living in flood zones, and its interplay with private insurance claims and the tort system are widely discussed after Katrina (Abramovsky 2009; Rhee 2009). Insurance payouts are obviously immensely important for future disaster resilience, and the questions that arise in this regard are therefore among the most central dilemmas in a society after disasters. That is, how do we balance the need for fast recovery vis-à-vis the need to rebuild smarter (Richards 2012), and how do we, in that regard, design a comprehensive compensation system ensuring the right incentives (Rhee 2009)? Taking the National Flood Insurance Program as an example, it is a mechanism that levels out the economic disadvantage of living in a flood zone, but leaves landowners with unmarketable houses.

Conclusion: disaster law

As disasters are increasingly understood as *social* processes, the pressure on communities to establish legal mechanisms – capable of (re)distributing responsibility, obligations and justice – increases. Law is central to the socialization of disasters; it is the instrument through which disaster management can be integrated into every institution of a given community. Today, legislation addressing the mitigation of, prevention of, response to and recovery from disasters is essential to successful disaster management.

Though still somewhat incoherent, legal scholarship on disasters has grown extensively concurrently with the increase in globally registered disasters; the socialization of disasters; and most importantly the emergence of a body of law relating to disasters. Thus, a portfolio of law and an accompanied scholarly discipline, *disaster law*, are emerging. The American law professor Jim Chen poetically writes of law among the ruins, but disaster law encompasses much more than the law arising out of the ashes of specific disaster sites. Increasingly, disaster law becomes embedded in other general fields, not least development law, climate change law and torts. While striving to contribute to an independent field of study (disaster law), it is important to underline that regulation on disasters will only be effective if integrated into every aspect of society.

In this article I have tried to exemplify how law might be relevant to the management of disasters; which types of problems legal scholarship has set out to solve; and how. It is a field in flux, and in the course of the last thirty years, a dramatic development in the body of scholarship has occurred. Yet, it is safe to assume that this development will continue. Thus, in this final short section I will offer my perspective on the future of the studies in disaster and law.

Four potential implications for future research in law and disasters

In this final section, I will suggest four potential directions for future disaster law research, one methodological, one regarding the scholarship, and two led on by changes in the field.

First and foremost, modern disaster research is interdisciplinary research – or at least research requiring an interdisciplinary attitude. Disasters are, by definition, interdisciplinary objects, and studying their legal implications requires fundamental knowledge of the affected societies, technologies and natures. This is already clear from the present body of scholarship, but in line with the overall trajectories of the global research agenda, it seems reasonable to assume that we will see even more interdisciplinary research projects with implications for, and hopefully involvement of, law and disasters.

Second, as the body of scholarship on law and disasters reaches critical mass, a more comprehensive scientific landscape will emerge; a landscape where different schools or approaches to the field become clear. This will make it easier for the new reader to navigate in the scholarship, and open the possibility of further exploring a number of understudied aspects of disaster regulation.

Third, the vertical (conflicts within jurisdictions) as well as horizontal (conflicts between jurisdictions) dimensions of jurisdictional issues in disaster response will increasingly put pressure on legal scholarship to form bridges between different (national, regional, global) jurisdictions. This need is already clear from the ongoing discussion on international disaster response law; however, the other disaster management phases will also increasingly be subject to discussion, for instance as the post-2015 framework for disaster risk reduction gets traction.

Finally, a number of new actors and technologies have entered the disaster management arena, some of them challenging traditional types and modes of regulation. Not least, increasing reliance on technology calls for innovative legal ideas – and for a critical investigation of the relationships between law, science and technology. This might be relevant for the use of drones/robots, satellite technology and social media strategies in the response phase, but also more generally for technology in protection of critical infrastructure.

Notes

1 The number varies depending on the source. The *Scientific American* reports an official death toll of 309 (Bressan 2012). David Alexander (2014) reports 308 deaths and 1,500 injured, 202 of them seriously.
2 The L'Aquila Seven belonged to the National Commission for Forecasting and Preventing Major Risks (*Commissione Nazionale dei Grandi Rischi*), a commission mandated to support the Civil Protection department with scientific data. See http://www.protezionecivile.gov.it/jcms/en/commissione_grandi_rischi.wp?request_locale=en (accessed May 2014).
3 The sentence has since been revoked for the six scientists.
4 Wells 1995; Farber and Chen 2006; Malloy 2008; Verchick 2010; Farber *et al.* 2010; Baum 2007; Lauta 2014a.
5 Gross and Aoláain 2006; Dyzenhaus 2006; Agamben 2005, Hunter 2009; Ramraj 2008.
6 Posner 2004: 322; Sunstein 2005; Alemanno 2010; Bora 1999; Fabio 1994; Woodman and Klippel 2009; Everson and Vos 2009; Fischer 2007.
7 Sarat *et al.* 2007: 165.
8 Obviously, *doctrinal studies* covers a wide range of different methodologies, but can roughly be subsumed for the purpose of this current chapter as a purely internal legal perspective.
9 Case no. 380, 22 Oct. 2012, *Victims of the earthquake v. Barberi et alii.* (members of the National Commission for Great Risks), Tribunal of L'Aquila, grounds delivered on the 29 Jan. 2013 (first degree of judgement).
10 Case of *Budayeva and others v. Russia* (Applications nos. 15339/02, 21166/02, 20058/02, 11673/02 and 15343/02).
11 *In re Katrina Canal Breaches Consolidated Litigation*, 216 W.Va. 534, 607 S.E.2d 863 (W.Va., 2004). The decision was partially changed by the Court of Appeal in decision no. 10–30249 (2012).
12 Bullard and Wright 2009; Farber 2009; Farber and Chen 2006; Hartman and Squires 2006; Kaplan 2007: 155–81; Malloy 2008; Monteith 2010.
13 *In re Katrina Canal Breaches Consolidated Litigation*, 647 F.Supp.2d 644 (E.D.La. 2009).
14 647 F.Supp.2d 644 (E.D.La. 2009) at 644.
15 See for instance *Florida East Coast Ry. Co. v. United States*, 519 F.2d 1184, 1191 (5th Cir. 1975); *Graci v. United States*, 456 F.2d 20 (5th Cir. 1971); *Parks v. United States*, 370 F.2d 92 (2d Cir. 1966); *Stover v. United States*, 332 F.2d 204 (9th Cir. 1964); *B. Amusement Co. v. United States*, 180 F.Supp. 386 (Ct. Cl. 1960).
16 See also Roper (2010) at 103. Some years before the US Supreme Court had in decision distinguished irrigation water projects from flood control, and thereby circumvented the immunity clause, see *Central Green Co. v. United States*, 531 U.S. 425 (2001). This was however not in a disaster situation.
17 Adopted by the National Flood Insurance Act of 1968 later amended by the Homeowner Flood Insurance Affordability Act of 2014 (S. 1926; 113th Congress).

References

Abramovsky, A. (2009) Insurance and the flood. In R. P. Malloy (ed.), *Law and Recovery from Disaster: Hurricane Katrina*. Burlington, VT: Ashgate, 83–103.

Agamben, G. (2005) *State of Exception*. Chicago, IL: University of Chicago Press.

Alemanno, A. (2010) From the editor's desk. *European Journal of Risk Regulation*, 1(1), iii–v.

Alemanno, A. (ed.) (2011) *Governing Disasters: The Challenges of Emergency Risk Regulation*. Cheltenham: Edward Elgar.

Alemanno, A., and Lauta, K. C. (2014) The L'Aquila Seven: Re-establishing justice after a natural disaster. *European Journal of Risk Regulation*, 2, 129–132.

Alexander, D. (2014) Communicating earthquake risk to the public: The trial of the 'L'Aquila Seven', *Natural Hazards*, 72(3), 1159–1173.

Alexandre, M. (2009) Navigating the topography of inequality post-disaster: A proposal for remedying past geographic segregation during rebuilding. In R. P. Malloy (ed.), *Law and Recovery from Disaster: Hurricane Katrina*. Burlington, VT: Ashgate.

Andrews, W. J., Levine, M. S., Petcher, R. E., and McNutt, S. W. (2007) A 'flood of uncertainty': Contractual erosion in the wake of Hurricane Katrina and the Eastern District of Louisiana's Ruling in In Re Katrina Canal Breaches Consolidated Litigation. *Tulane Law Review*, 81(5), 1277–1301.

Auerswald, P., Branscomb, L. M., La Porte, T. M., and Michel-Kerjan, E. O. (2006) *Seeds of Disaster, Roots of Response: How Private Action Can Reduce Public Vulnerability*. Cambridge: Cambridge University Press.

Bassett, D. L. (2009) Place, disasters, and disability. In R. P. Malloy (ed.), *Law and Recovery from Disaster: Hurricane Katrina*. Burlington, VT: Ashgate, 51–71.

Baum, M. L. (2007) *When Nature Strikes: Weather Disasters and the Law*. Westport, CN: Praeger Publishers, pp. xiii, 227.

Binder, D. (2002) Emergency action plans: A legal and practical blueprint 'failing to plan is planning to fail'. *University of Pittsburgh Law Review*, 63, 793–814.

Birkland, T. A. (1997) *After Disaster: Agenda Setting, Public Policy, and Focusing Events*. Washington, DC: Georgetown University Press.

Birkland, T. A. (2006) *Lessons of Disaster: Policy Change After Catastrophic Events*. Washington, DC: Georgetown University Press, pp. xviii, 216.

Bora, A. (1999) *Rechtliches Risikomanagement: Form, Funktion und Leistungsfähigkeit des Rechts in der Risikogesellschaft*. Berlin: Duncker & Humblot.

Bressan, D. (2012) April 6, 2009: The L'Aquila Earthquake. *Scientific American*, 6 Apr., http://blogs.scientificamerican.com/history-of-geology/2012/04/06/april-6-2009-the-laquila-earthquake (accessed May 2014).

Bullard, R. D., and Wright, B. (2009) *Race, Place, and Environmental Justice After Hurricane Katrina: Struggles to Reclaim, Rebuild, and Revitalize New Orleans and the Gulf Coast*. Boulder, CO: Westview Press.

Chen, J. (2009) Law among the ruins. In R. P. Malloy (ed.), *Law and Recovery from Disaster: Hurricane Katrina*. Burlington, VT: Ashgate, 1–7.

Chen, J. (2011) Modern disaster theory: Evaluating disaster law as a portfolio of legal rules. *Emory International Law Review*, 25(3).

Chocheles, C. T. (2010) No excuses: Hurricanes and the 'act of God' defence to breach of contract claims. *Louisiana Bar Journal*, 57, 380–386.

Cigler, B. A. (2007) The 'big questions' of Katrina and the 2005 great flood of New Orleans. *Public Administration Review*, 67, 64–76.

Comfort, L. K. (2007) Assymetric information processes in extreme events: The December 26, 2004 Sumatran earthquake and tsunami. In D. E. Gibbons (ed.), *Communicable Crises:*

Prevention, Response, and Recovery in the Global Arena. Charlotte, NC: Information Age Publishing, 137–168.

Dauber, M. L. (2013) *The Sympathetic State: Disaster Relief and the Origins of the American Welfare State*. Chicago, IL: University of Chicago Press.

Douglas, M. (1992) *Risk and Blame: Essays in Cultural Theory*. New York: Routledge.

Dyzenhaus, D. (2006) *The Constitution of Law: Legality in a Time of Emergency*. Cambridge and New York: Cambridge University Press, pp. xv, 250.

Elliott, J. R., and Pais, J. (2006) Race, class, and Hurricane Katrina: Social diffrences in human responses to disaster. *Social Science Research*, 35(2), 295–321.

Evacuteer (2011) *Five Years Later: Emergency Preparedness Improvements in New Orleans, Louisiana since Hurricane Katrina*. Baton Rouge, LA: Gulf Coast Center for Evacuation and Transportation Resiliency.

Everson, M., and Vos, E. (eds) (2009) *Uncertain Risks Regulated*. New York: Routledge-Cavendish.

Fabio, U. D. (1994) *Risikoentscheidungen im Rechtsstaat: Zum Wandel der Dogmatik im öffentlichen Recht, insbesondere am Beispiel der Arzneimittelüberwachung*. Tübingen: Mohr Siebeck.

Farber, D. (2007) Disaster law and inequality. Symposium for 25th anniversary of Journal of Law and Inequality.

Farber, D. (2009) Tort law in the era of climate change, Katrina, and 9/11: Exploring liability for extraordinary risks. *Valparaiso University Law Review*, 43, 1075–1130.

Farber, D. (2013) Catastrophic risk, climate change, and disaster law. *Asia Pacific Journal of Environmental Law*, 16, 37–54.

Farber, D., and Chen, J. (2006) *Disasters and the Law: Katrina and Beyond*. New York: Aspen Publishers, pp. xxii, 348.

Farber, D., and Faure, M. (eds) (2010) *Disaster Law*. Cheltenham: Edward Elgar.

Farber, D., *et al.* (2010) *Disaster Law and Policy*. 2nd edn, New York: Wolters Kluwer Law & Business, Aspen Publishers.

Faure, M. G., and Bruggeman, V. (2007) Catastrophic risks and first-party insurance. *Connecticut Insurance Law Journal*, 15(1), 1–52.

Fischer, E. (2007) *Risk Regulation and Administrative Constitutionalism*. Oxford: Hart.

Garrett, B. L., and Tetlow, T. (2006) Criminal justice collapse: The Constitution after Hurricane Katrina. *Duke Law Journal*, 56(1), 127–178.

Green, P., and Ward, T. (2004) *State Crime: Governments, Violence and Corruption*. London and Sterling, VA: Pluto Press, pp. viii, 255.

Gross, O., and Nâi Aolâain, F. (2006) *Law in Times of Crisis: Emergency Powers in Theory and Practice*. Cambridge: Cambridge University Press, pp. xxix, 481.

Guttry, A. d., Cestri, M., and Venturini, G. (eds) (2012) *International Disaster Response Law*. The Hague: T.M.C. Asser Press, Springer.

Hartman, C. W., and Squires, G. D. (2006) *There is No Such Thing as a Natural Disaster: Race, Class, and Hurricane Katrina*. New York: Routledge.

Hilson, C. (2008–9) Risk and European Convention on Human Rights: Towards a new approach. *Cambridge Yearbook of European Studies*, 11, 353–375.

Hunter, N. D. (2009) *Emergency Law: Public Health and Disaster Management*. Amsterdam: Elsevier.

Jasanoff, S. (1990) *The Fifth Branch: Science Advisers as Policymakers*. Cambridge, MA: Harvard University Press.

Jasanoff, S. (2007) *Designs on Nature: Science and Democracy in Europe and the United States*. Princeton, NJ: Princeton University Press.

Kaplan, C. P. (2007) The act of God defense: Why Hurricane Katrina and Noah's Flood don't qualify. *Review of Litigation*, 26, 155–81.

King, R. O. (2005) *Huricane Katrina: Insurance Losses and National Capacities for Financing Disaster Risk.* CRS Report for Congress. Washington, DC: Congressional Research Service.

Kristl, K. T. (2010) Diminishing the divine: Climate change and the act of God defense. *Widener Law Review,* 15, 325.

Kunreuther, H. C., and Michel-Kerjan, E. (2007) Climate change, insurability of large-scale disasters, and the emerging liability challenge. *University of Pennsylvania Law Review,* 155, 1795–1842.

Lauta, K. C. (2011) *Exceptions and Norms. The Law on Natural Disasters.* Copenhagen: University of Copenhagen.

Lauta, K. C. (2014a) *Disaster Law.* New York: Routledge.

Lauta, K. C. (2014b) New fault lines? On responsiblity and disasters. *European Journal of Risk Regulation,* 2, 137–145.

Lauta, K. C. (2014c) A drop in the ocean: Marine oil pollution preparedness and response in the Arctic. *Arctic Review on Law and Politics,* 4(2), 227–250.

Lazari, A. (2014) *European Critical Infrastructure Protection.* New York: Springer.

Lord, J. E., Waterstone, M. E., and Stein, M. A. (2009) Natural disasters and persons with disabilities. In R. P. Malloy (ed.), *Law and Recovery from Disaster: Hurricane Katrina.* Burlington, VT: Ashgate, 71–83.

Malloy, R. P. (ed.) (2008) *Law and Recovery from Disaster: Hurricane Katrina.* Burlington, VT: Ashgate Pub. Co.

Mercante, J. E. (2005–6) Hurricanes and act of God: When the best defense is a good offense. *University of San Francisco Maritime Law Journal,* 18, 3–38.

Monteith, S. (2010) Hurricane Katrina: Five years after introduction. *Journal of American Studies,* 44(3), 475–82.

Nottage, L. (2013) Japanese law after the 3-11 disasters, and ANJeL's Anniversary Conference on Asia-Pacific Disaster Management. *Journal of Japanese Law,* 34(5), 1–5.

Pedersen, O. W. (2013) Environmental risks, rights and black swans. *Environmental Law Review,* 15(1), 55–62.

Perry, R. W. (2007) What is a disaster? In H. Rodríguez, E. L. Quarantelli and R. R. Dynes (eds), *Handbook of Disaster Research.* New York: Springer, 1–16.

Picard, M. (2014) *Effective Law and Regulation for Disaster Risk Reduction: A Multi-Country Report.* Geneva: International Federation of Red Cross and Red Crescent Societies.

Posner, R. A. (2004) *Catastrophe: Risk and Response.* Oxford and New York: Oxford University Press.

Ramraj, V. (2008) *Emergencies and the Limits of Legality.* Cambridge: Cambridge University Press.

Rhee, R. J. (2009) Participation and disintermediation in a risk society. In R. P. Malloy (ed.), *Law and Recovery from Disaster: Hurricane Katrina.* Burlington, VT: Ashgate, 103–127.

Richards, E. P. (2012) The Hurricane Katrina levee breach litigation: Getting the first geoengineering liability case right. *University of Pennsylvania Law Review,* 160, 267–87.

Roper, M. (2010) Government liable for Hurricane Katrina damage. *Journal of Consumer and Commercial Law,* 13(2), 103.

Sarat, A., and Lezaun, J. (eds) (2009) *Catastrophe: Law, Politics, and the Humanitarian Impulse.* Boston, MA: University of Massachusetts Press.

Sarat, A., Douglas, L., and Umphrey, M. M. (2007) *Law and Catastrophe.* Stanford, CA: Stanford University Press.

Shklar, J. N. (1990) *The Faces of Injustice.* New Haven, CT: Yale University Press.

Simoncini, M. (2014) When science meets responsibility. *European Journal of Risk Regulation,* 2, 146–158.

Sunstein, C. R. (2005) *Law of Fear.* Cambridge: Cambridge University Press.

Verchick, R. (2004) Feminist theory and environmental justice. In R. Stein (ed.), *New Perspectives on Environmental Justice: Gender, Sexuality and Activism.* New Brunswick, NJ: Rutgers University Press, 63–78.

Verchick, R. (2007) Katrina, feminism, and environmental justice. *Cardozo Journal of Law,* 13, 791–800.

Verchick, R. (2010) *Facing Catastrophe.* Cambridge, MA: Harvard University Press.

Verchick, R. (2012) Disaster justice. *Duke Environmental Law and Policy Forum,* 23, 23–71.

Wells, C. (1995) *Negotiating Tragedy: Law and Disasters.* London: Sweet & Maxwell.

Woodman, G. R., and Klippel, D. (ed.) (2009) *Risk and the Law.* London and New York: Routledge-Cavendish.

Yoo, J. (2009) *Crisis and Command.* New York: Kaplan.

8 Natural disasters, conflict and security

Olivier Rubin

Introduction

This chapter examines the impact of natural disasters on conflict and security. The interest in conflicts should need no elaborate justification. Violent conflicts constitute the most extreme manifestation of social breakdown: nations and communities are destroyed; families and villages torn apart; and social divisions exacerbated for years to come. The long-term economic costs are substantial: it has been estimated that it takes decades for a country involved in civil war to reach the income level it would have attained in the absence of the conflict (Collier 2009). The larger social implications of conflict relate to issues of random violence, legal collapse, loss of livelihoods, rape, stigmatization and exclusion, an increased number of orphans and widows, mental traumas, physical handicaps and forced migration.

The literature contains two contrasting perspectives on the link between natural disasters and conflicts: some theoretical arguments stress the *potential of conflict* in natural disaster situations, while others emphasize the *scope for increased cooperation*. In the following, both theoretical arguments will be presented and contrasted. Ultimately, the extent to which natural disasters spur either conflict or peace is an empirical question. The 2004 Indian Ocean tsunami will be included as an example of a natural disaster with both conflictual and diplomatic dynamics. The chapter concludes by laying out some potential analytical implications.

Natural disasters and conflict

Scholars have long tried to identify the most explosive cocktail of socioeconomic factors that increase the risk of violent conflicts. In general, studies have shown the importance of history (past conflicts increase the risk of present conflicts), demography (a large population will be exposed to more conflicts and a high proportion of young males has a destabilizing effect on society), geography (neighbouring instability and conflict can spill over), developmental level (low income levels raise the likelihood of conflict), institutions (a legitimate and strong state lowers the risk of violent conflicts irrespective of regime type) (Harris *et al*. 2013; Omelicheva 2011; Dixon 2009; Collier and Hoeffler 2004). Within the frame of these socioeconomic factors, natural disasters could increase the risk of armed conflict through three channels: (1) by increasing people's incentives for engaging in conflictive behaviour; (2) by undermining state legitimacy and power; and (3) by spurring migration. These same channels could also impact (4) small-scale violence and crime. The theoretical arguments and empirical evidence underlying these channels are the focus of this chapter.

Incentives for conflict

Incentives for conflict differ according to whether the natural disaster exerts a continuous *stress* on society (slow-onset disaster such as droughts and sea-level rise) or whether it constitutes a *shock* to society (rapid-onset natural disasters such as earthquakes, flash floods and hurricanes).

The theories of stress-based incentives focus primarily on resource depletion caused by natural disasters. Natural disasters could lead to increased scarcities of food, clean water, forests, energy and land. Many studies hypothesize that such scarcities will increase competition for the remaining resources, spurring internal unrest or even border conflicts (Uexkull 2014; Harris *et al.* 2013; Council of the European Union 2008; Smith and Vivekananda 2007; Schwartz and Randall 2003; Homer-Dixon 1999). Homer-Dixon has been involved in the analysis of the link between ecological scarcities and conflict for several case studies (in Mexico, South Africa, China, India, Indonesia, Rwanda and Pakistan among others), and has identified multiple local links varying from the direct effects of rural livelihood erosion to the more indirect effects of forced urbanization and weakened local institutions (Homer-Dixon 1999, 1996, 1995).

More recent large-scale quantitative studies have corroborated the findings of these earlier case studies. Raleigh and Urdal (2007) conducted a study based on disaggregated geospatial data where fresh-water scarcity and land degradation were regressed with violent conflicts each stretching out in a 300 km radius. Considering various socioeconomic control variables and interaction terms, the authors conclude that demographic and environmental variables do indeed increase the risk of civil conflict, but that the effect is very moderate. Urdal (2008) also uses disaggregated data in his subnational analysis based on a time-series of data for twenty-seven Indian states. He finds that scarcity of productive land appears to be associated with higher risks of violent conflict, particularly in circumstances of high rural population growth and low yields. Urdal (2008: 609) therefore concludes that 'while cross-national studies have provided very little support for the resource scarcity perspective, disaggregated studies seem to capture this dynamic better. These findings support claims that environmental scarcity and conflict relationships should be studied at the local level.'

Uexkull (2014) draws on geospatial disaggregated data from Sub-Saharan Africa to investigate the link between droughts and incidents of civil conflict. While the results suggest that droughts do appear to increase the risk of civil conflicts – in particular in areas dominated by rain-fed cropland – Uexkull is careful to caution that 'a closer look at the data reveals that drought seems mostly to add fuel to already existing conflicts and tension in agricultural regions' (Uexkull 2014: 24). Slettebak (2013) has conducted disaggregated studies based on Indian data on Hindu–Muslim riots located 250 km or less from disaster areas. By comparing the distributions of Hindu–Muslim riots before and after disasters, Slettebak found that the risk of Hindu–Muslim riots on average was statistically significantly higher in the days after a natural disaster, compared to the days leading up to the disaster. One of the main conclusions reached by Dixon in his comprehensive meta-study of the general causes of civil war was that there is substantial evidence that severe environmental destruction is a danger to stability and peace (Dixon 2009: 713). Thus, while research suggests that natural disasters can influence the risk of conflicts, the effect is primarily on intrastate conflicts rather than interstate wars, as most natural disasters are mainly local phenomena that cause shifts in internal economic balances and power structures (Urdal 2008; Kahl 2006; Barnett 2003).

Taking a more historical perspective by looking back at cases where whole societies have collapsed due to natural disasters, Diamond describes how natural disasters have either spurred devastating internal conflicts (as was the case with the Easter Islands in the 1800s) or expansionist conflicts (such as with the Vikings in the 800s) (Diamond 2005). In these cases, natural disasters and ecological degradation appear to have pushed civilizations beyond the tipping-point for existence, leaving them with only one option: a violent fight for survival. In more recent times, the lengthy conflict in Darfur, Sudan, has also been partly ascribed the many periods of extreme drought, which have exacerbated ethnic and social tensions (UN 2007; UNEP 2007).

The theories of shock-based incentives emphasize sudden changes in resources and power relations. Scarcities in the wake of natural disasters are not the only trigger for violent conflict; perceptions of unfairness, inequality and neglect following a rapid-onset natural disaster make it easier to rally people into armed revolt (Barnett and Adger 2007). A sudden collapse of livelihoods due to natural disasters might be conducive to conflicts, as the opportunity costs of refraining from engaging in conflict become negligible. With livelihoods collapsed, individuals have little to lose by engaging in anti-social behaviour such as looting and fighting. Nafziger and Auvinen analysed the socioeconomic factors leading to war and state violence in developing countries, and concluded that what matters in terms of conflict is *changes* in key variables (e.g. economic decline or increasing inequality) rather than their *levels* (Nafziger and Auvinen 2002: 159–69). One of the key findings of Devlin and Hendrix's (2014) large-scale interstate war study similarly highlights the importance of changes in key variables, as they determined that long-term variability in precipitation patterns is associated with increased interstate military disputes. Gleditsch and Urdal (2002: 286) further conclude that objective deprivation seldom produces strong grievances, yet relative deprivation – where people perceive a gap between the situation they believe they deserve and the situation that they actually experience – generates a much more volatile situation. Goodhand (2003) argues that the empirical evidence suggests that the transient poor are more likely to take part in violent rioting than the chronically poor, due to two factors: relative poverty simply builds up more grievances; and the chronically poor are often the most marginalized and badly organized groups in society (Goodhand 2003: 637). These general findings are important because natural disasters can cause power relations to shift and perceptions of fairness and envy to be recalibrated according to the new situation. If this perception of injustice or neglect reaches influential social groups, the situation can quickly turn unstable and even violent (Nafziger and Auvinen 2002: 159–60). Thus, natural disasters increase the risk of conflict, not so much because they lead to a deficiency of natural resources, but because they unleash feelings of injustice, envy and powerlessness. This is also why rapid-onset natural disasters appear to increase the risk of conflict more than slow-onset disasters, and with greater certainty (Nel and Righarts 2008). According to Nel and Righarts (2008: 174), a country that experiences a rapid-onset natural disaster can be up to 50 per cent more prone to violent conflict than a country with no disaster. Rapid-onset geological disasters (volcanoes and earthquakes) appear to contain the greatest conflict potential as the extent of the disaster will often be greater than that of climatic disasters. Brancati (2007) analyses the connection between earthquakes and violent conflict through a systematic analysis of 185 countries over the period 1975–2002. The predicted probability that a country will experience conflict in a given month is 5 per cent higher if an earthquake has taken place in the same month (Brancati 2007: 729). The study concludes that the risk of conflict from earthquakes is particularly high in densely populated areas with a poor economy and a history of violence (Brancati 2007).

The dynamics above (both stress- and shock-based) are all related to grievances and to increased incentives for conflict in society. However, natural disasters also increase the opportunities for conflict by undermining the states' legitimacy and capacity (Nel and Righarts 2008).

State legitimacy

The chaotic conditions that often follow in the wake of natural disasters could be exploited by rebel groups to challenge governmental authority – an authority that might already have suffered due to inadequate disaster response. The country's infrastructure might be damaged by natural disasters and certain areas isolated, thereby limiting state reach and control. The power vacuum in the affected regions could be exploited either by local militant groups or other hostile countries seizing the moment to attack governments with low legitimacy and weak logistical capacity caused by repeated natural disasters (Barnett and Adger 2007). Countries with a widely dispersed population and mountainous terrain have, for example, a greater risk of conflict simply because of the opportunity for riot groups to operate outside the state's physical reach (Collier and Hoeffler 2004). Natural disasters can create similar opportunities in weak states in particular, by undermining the state's infrastructure, isolating areas and dispersing the population. The state might be put under financial pressure due to expenses for disaster management, falling tax revenues, and reconstruction works, as well as under military pressure, as the army is often used to distribute emergency aid and to maintain order in the disaster zone. In the wake of hurricane Katrina in 2005, for instance, more than 70,000 US soldiers were mobilized to the disaster zones (Busby 2007: 1). Natural disasters can further expose a state's weakness and undermine its legitimacy if it is unable to mobilize a satisfactory response to the disaster. One way to counter this loss of legitimacy is by framing the disaster as a *state of exception* (see Chapter 4 by Illner and Holm in this volume for more details). Still, states are much more likely to lose rather than gain legitimacy during a natural disaster, because the expectation is for the state to protect its citizens even under (or especially under) extreme conditions (Shawn *et al.* 2012).

In regards to the state's capacity and legitimacy, it appears that strong states, whether democratic or not, have a lower risk of natural disasters fostering violent conflict (Dixon 2009; Collier *et al.* 2009; Collier and Hoeffler 2004). Omelicheva (2011) finds in her quantitative cross-country study that natural disasters appear to increase instability only in cases where political institutions are already weak. The conflict potential of natural disasters in regimes that are either highly democratic or authoritarian tends to be below average (Omelicheva 2011; Dixon 2009; Hauge and Ellingsen 1998). An explanation might be that strong state capacity reduces the opportunity for conflict, while legitimacy reduces the incentives. Less established political systems or systems in transition might be short on both accounts. Carlin *et al.* (2014) show how the 2010 earthquake in the less established Chilean democracy bolstered public support for military coups and for disregarding parliamentary and judiciary procedures. In their quantitative study on political violence, Besley and Persson (2012) find that experiencing a natural disaster is positively correlated with political violence but only for countries with non-cohesive political institutions (proxied by the extent of executive constraints).

The balance of power between the state and opposing groups might shift in the wake of natural disasters. A study has found that extremes in rainfall (positive and negative deviations from the mean) during the period 1990–2009 across 6,305 districts in Africa increased the risk of various social conflicts such as riots, strikes, communal conflict and armed violence (Hendrix and Salehyan 2012). Interestingly, the only identified effect with regards to armed conflict was from an *increase* in rainfall, which the authors hypothesize could be caused by an affluence (rather than a scarcity) of essential resources, thus allowing opposing groups the 'luxury' of taking up arms against each other or the state (Hendrix and Salehyan 2012: 45).

Migration

Natural disasters could lead to migration. Some migrants may have been subject to the *pull* forces of a continuous deterioration of livelihoods due to slow-onset natural disaster – others might have been subject to *push* forces where rapid-onset natural disasters force people to migrate urgently. Generally, migrants could increase the risk of conflict if they change the religious or ethical composition in the receiving country/area; increase pressure on already scarce resources in the receiving country/affected area; harbour enemy combatants; introduce new ideologies, cultures and ideas that conflict with existing ones; use refugee camps as recruitment bases for military groups; bring anti-authoritative and rebellious values; or cause friction and chaos through their sheer scale (Reuveny 2008, 2007).

The link between natural disaster migration and conflict has found empirical support in some academic papers. Although Urdal (2005) does not find evidence of a link between migration and conflict, both Salehyan and Gleditsch (2006) and Reuveny (2008, 2007) report that migration appears to increase the risk of conflict, albeit with a moderate impact. Salehyan and Gleditsch (2006) have undertaken a comprehensive quantitative study with data on refugees and conflict going back to 1950, and conclude that the majority (73 per cent) of countries that had received high numbers of refugees from neighbouring states did not experience internal conflicts later on. Still, conflicts were more frequent when compared with countries that did not accept refugees (27 per cent compared with 12 per cent), controlling for various socioeconomic factors. However, the conflict potential of natural disaster migration might be different from that of more traditional refugees, where conflict and persecution are the driving forces behind migration. Contrary to such conflict refugees, natural disaster refugees 'do not have the same political agenda and grievances, nor do they have the same experience in organizing armed insurgencies' (Nordås and Gleditsch 2007: 632). Natural disaster migration is also much more likely to be temporary and occur within the state. It is estimated that only up to 30 per cent of the disaster migrants choose to relocate permanently, and the majority of those remain within their own borders (International Organization for Migration 2009: 273). Naturally, this could still cause friction and conflict, but intrastate and temporary migration is, *ceteris paribus*, often less socially disruptive. Reuveny's (2007) study focuses exclusively on the potential for conflict of environmental refugees by analysing thirty-eight cases where substantial cross-national refugee influxes had occurred, often as a result of a natural disaster. In half the cases, the recipient countries did experience increased conflict. It should be noted, however, that in most such studies of natural disasters (Reuveny's studies included), migration and conflict focus is on the risk of conflicts in the *recipient* country, while the potential positive effects on the conflict dynamics in the country of *origin* is often overlooked.

Natural disasters and crime

Frustration and desperation in the wake of disasters do not need to be expressed through armed conflicts, but can be articulated through a rise in crime. While armed conflicts require larger organized groups, crime is often committed on an individual basis. The extent to which disasters might lead to increased crime depends on the changes in incentives and opportunities that have previously been outlined. A study focusing on localized crime rates across Indian states following large-scale disasters found that only property crimes rose after natural disasters – but that high newspaper circulation and coverage could cancel out this increase (Roy 2010). It follows then that press coverage of large-scale disasters could translate into greater relief and consequently lower crime rates (Roy 2010: 19). Generally, it appears that most types of crime actually drop immediately following a natural disaster, only to rise again during the reconstruction phase (Varano *et al.* 2010; Zahran *et al.* 2009; Tucker 2001). This could be explained by the large military presence in the area, by the fact that survival and restitution take priority, or quite simply because higher morals prevail when disaster strikes. The level of crime does, however, quickly rise again, and if the natural disaster has resulted in a rise in inequality or feelings of unfairness, the level of crime can end up being higher than prior to the disaster (Leitner *et al.* 2011). Like other major social disruptions, natural disasters appear to increase domestic violence (Zahran *et al.* 2009; Enarson 1999). Sexual violence and harassment against women, for instance, were rampant in Sri Lanka in the aftermath of the 2004 Indian Ocean tsunami (Fisher 2010). Horton's Chapter 10 in this volume provides a more thorough discussion of gender violence in the wake of disasters.

When Hurricane Katrina hit New Orleans in August 2005, 150,000 of the city's residents were evacuated to Houston, Texas. According to a 2010 study by Varano *et al.*, this massive influx of people only led to minor increases in crime, and even more importantly these 'small but notable crime increases were as reflective of victimization of evacuees as they were of offending' (Varano *et al.* 2010: 49). Another study of the state of Louisiana found that crime rates actually declined in regions receiving the most evacuees from Katrina (Leitner *et al.* 2011). The combination of a stronger military presence, an influx of government aid and widespread pro-social behavior could help explain this decline in crime (Leitner *et al.* 2011). In the months immediately following the hurricane, New Orleans, previously one of the most violent cities in the USA, had a murder rate close to zero. The mayor announced that for the first time ever the city was free from drugs and violence. New Orleans University estimated that just over 300 murders would have been committed in New Orleans during 2005 had the hurricane not struck the city – a figure much higher than any homicide increase in the surrounding areas and cities (Nossiter 2005). Today, however, crime rates in New Orleans are back to pre-Katrina levels.

Natural disasters and conflict-resolution

While the arguments above have focused on the conflict potential of natural disasters, other theories point to the opportunities that natural disasters can carve out for increased diplomacy in an attempt to end existing conflicts (Kelman 2012, 2007, 2006; Akcinaroglu *et al.* 2011; Enia 2008; Quarantelli and Dynes 1976).

The focus on the collaborative aspect of natural disasters is at least in part justified by recent contributions questioning the existence of a strong and robust relationship between natural disasters and violent conflicts. Theisen (2008) has revisited some of the earlier scarcity and conflict literature by performing a number of sensitivity calculations. He finds many of the reported results to be rather feeble, if control variables are reconfigured or other variables accounted for. Rather than pointing to natural disasters and resource scarcity as drivers of conflict, Theisen's own quantitative analysis suggests that poverty and dysfunctional institutions are robustly related to conflict.

Slettebak and de Soysa (2010) are also critical of previous studies claiming to have uncovered a causal relationship between natural disaster and conflict. These studies, the authors argue, suffer from at least two weaknesses. The first weakness relates to an omitted variable bias: Brancati's (2007) and Nel and Righarts's (2008) studies do not take into account the population size of the countries. This could very well cause a substantial bias. Dixon notes in his previously mentioned meta-study of the causes of civil war: 'One of the most widely-recognized causes of civil war is the simple presence of more people in a state' (Dixon 2009: 701). When accounting for population size, the overall fit of the models improves, but the relationship between natural disasters and conflicts loses its significance (Slettebak and de Soysa 2010). The second weakness relates to Brancati's (2007), Besley and Persson's (2011) and Uexkull's (2014) use of proxies for *incidences* of conflicts instead of proxies for the *onsets* of conflicts. The latter proxy would be a more precise and direct measure for the causal impacts of disasters. Studies based on incidents (rather than onsets) of civil conflict might struggle with reverse causality bias as ongoing conflicts increase the risk of natural hazards turning into disasters (Theisen *et al.* 2013). Using civil conflict onsets in a cross-country dataset from 1946 to 2007, Slettebak and de Soysa (2010) find that the impact of natural disasters on the risk of intrastate conflict does not appear very robust. To the extent that natural disasters affect the risk of civil war, the effect is actually negative: natural disasters appear to lower the risk of conflict. Bergholt and Lujala's (2012) cross-country study of the onset of armed civil conflicts in the period 1980–2007 also finds no effect of natural disasters – not even indirectly, through the significant negative impact of natural disasters on income growth. Yet another study supporting the negligible effect of natural disasters looks at the conflict potential in the months after major natural disasters in the period 1950–2006 (Nelson 2010). In more than 90 per cent of the cases no conflicts occurred after the disasters. When the impact of the disaster was moderate, the countries actually appeared to have a lower risk of conflict, while countries that had experienced major disasters (≥ 5,000 fatalities) did have a higher risk of conflict (Nelson 2010: 167). Such descriptive statistics, of course, say nothing about whether major natural disasters actually caused the onset of civil and interstate wars. An extensive cross-country study examined whether the lack of water in nearly 2,000 cases caused conflict with neighbouring countries, or whether the lack of water actually increased cooperation (Wolf 2007). In two-thirds of the cases, the lack of water created interstate relationships that could best be described as cooperative, while just over a quarter of cases caused confrontational relationships without developing into full-blown military conflicts. Military conflict only occurred in 2 per cent of the cases, and they were between Israel and neighbouring countries, which suggests that there were other significant geopolitical factors involved (Wolf 2007: 260).

One reason natural disasters could have such a small – or even sometimes a negative – effect on the risk of conflict, is that disasters also generate more beneficial dynamics: they provide the opportunity to improve relations between conflicting countries or internal factions.

Slow-onset natural disasters can lead to a lack of essential resources (food, water, power, etc.) and thereby increase the state's or other conflicting groups' incentive to work together to try to conserve and effectively manage the remaining resources. Such interaction can both pre-emptively limit the risk of conflict, as well as act as a calming force on already existing conflicts. States' preference for cooperation could be explained by the fact that wars, especially interstate wars, cannot solve the basic problem (they do not create more resources), and that interstate wars constitute an expensive and dangerous strategy to increase access to resources. It therefore appears reasonable to expect that cooperation can indeed be a viable strategy in the aftermath of natural disasters. In a subnational study of Kenya, Theisen's analysis suggests that years of drought tend to have a peaceful effect on the following year, which could be 'due to the infeasibility of large scale violence in times of extreme scarcity as reconciliation, cooperation, and peace are normally sought in pastoralist societies if a drought occurs' (Theisen 2012: 93). Devlin and Hendrix's (2014) study on interstate disputes finds that dyads where both countries experience below-average precipitation rainfall are less conflict-prone. A potential explanation is that below-normal rainfall puts strains on essential resources, thereby increasing the opportunity costs of engaging in interstate conflict (Devlin and Hendrix 2014: 35).

A rapid-onset natural disaster can promote peace negotiations in existing conflicts by directly weakening the actors involved. Enemy combatants will often find themselves in remote and tough terrain where they are particularly exposed to the impact of natural disasters. A natural disaster might also provide the conflicting factions with the opportunity to resolve their disputes and work together to meet the challenges inflicted on the area (Kelman 2012, 2006). This has been termed 'disaster diplomacy' (Kelman 2012, 2007, 2006) and can be defined as the extent to which disaster-related activities, from the local level to the international level, positively affect bilateral relations between conflicting states (Kelman 2007: 289). In his many articles and books on the subject, Kelman provides several examples of disaster diplomacy, but he cautions that, although there is evidence that disaster-related activities can catalyse diplomatic activities, 'evidence does not exist that disaster-related activities can *create* diplomatic activities' (Kelman 2006: 235).

Rapprochement processes could be furthered by an international awareness and presence. Natural disasters often increase the presence of international media, NGOs and representatives from foreign governments; for a brief period the international spotlight is on the humanitarian situation in the region. Such international awareness and pressure can facilitate a peace process, and the in-country presence of multiple NGOs can play an important role in implementing various peace measures/policies as well as increasing transparency and trust. Emergency aid from rival nations, and (often graphic) information of those suffering from the disasters might also catalyse changes in societal and public attitudes in opposing countries and promote rapprochement (Akcinaroglu *et al.*

2011). However, it is important to acknowledge that humanitarian imperatives rarely dominate the diplomatic agenda for very long, and the potential impact of disaster diplomacy might be modest in many cases (Kelman 2012).

The Turkish earthquake in August 1999 is an example of the possibilities of a change in hostile attitudes. Turkish and Greek relations had been strained for decades when the Turkish earthquake left 20,000 dead and half a million Turks homeless. A study by Akcinaroglu *et al.* documents that in the six months prior to the earthquake negative newspaper coverage about the rival country was 69 per cent in Turkey and 60 per cent in Greece. However, in the six-month period after the earthquake, negative newspaper coverage had been reduced to zero in Turkey and to 13 per cent in Greece (Akcinaroglu *et al.* 2011: 265). By 2000, the level of trade between the two countries had nearly doubled, investments increased by almost 800 per cent, nine bilateral agreements were ratified and Greece acknowledged Turkey's potential for joining the EU for the first time (Akcinaroglu *et al.* 2011: 269).

Case: The 2004 Indian Ocean tsunami contained both conflict and peace dynamics

The 2004 Indian Ocean tsunami in Sri Lanka – conflict

In Sri Lanka, the 2004 Indian Ocean tsunami killed around 30,000 people, made half a million people homeless and destroyed vital infrastructure. The impact was most severe in the eastern provinces where the separatist group the Tamil Tigers fought the government for independence. Despite the fact that the Tamil Tigers were hit hard by the tsunami, they quickly organized relief to the affected Tamils – while at the same time accusing the government of ignoring the plight of the Tamils. This bolstered the organization's standing in the affected communities. The Tamil Tigers also took advantage of the high share of orphans after the tsunami, enlisting them in the organization. The violence that dissipated shortly after the tsunami returned with a vengeance in 2005, when the Tamil Tigers killed three times the amount of people they did in 2004, and assassinated the Sri Lankan Foreign Minister.

The 2004 Indian Ocean tsunami in Indonesia – peace

The same 2004 tsunami that exacerbated existing conflict in Sri Lanka had the opposite effect in Indonesia, by accelerating peace negotiations. In Indonesia the tsunami hit the northern Ache province, where over 100,000 people died and 500,000 lost their homes. The province was the hub of Gerakan Aceh Merdeka, a guerrilla organization which for thirty years had fought the Indonesian government for independence. The tsunami led to significant losses of both human life and materials for both parties in the conflict, and attracted significant international awareness. This pressure brought both parties to the negotiation table, and on 25 August 2005 a peace agreement was signed which is still upheld today.

When the same seismic event can have such different impacts on war and peace, it is clearly hard to talk generally about the extent to which natural disasters create positive or negative synergies. Walch (2014) describes how two rebel groups in Mindanao, the Philippines, went down two very different paths following the same 2012 typhoon: one group increased collaboration with the government, while the other intensified hostilities. Much depends on the relevant country's existing processes and institutions. In the Indonesian example, the tsunami occurred at the same time as the instatement of a new president, which – together with a changed leadership in Gerakan Aceh Merdeka – created a favourable negotiation environment that enabled a neutral third party (Finland) to facilitate peace negotiations.

Analytical implications and venues for future research

The literature does not point towards a deterministic (or even probabilistic) relationship between natural disasters and conflict (Kallis and Zografos 2014; Theisen *et al.* 2013; Rubin 2010). Some studies suggest that natural disasters in combination with the wrong socioeconomic factors – like any other significant exogenous shock – might destabilize societies and increase the risk of conflict. With the right mix of socioeconomic factors, on the other hand, natural disaster could be a force for conflict resolution.

Due to the difficulty of establishing a clear link between natural disasters and conflict, one suggestion would be to approach the issue of natural disasters and conflict not with deterministic causal theories but with analytical frameworks based on mobilization and security theory (in a recent article, for instance, Vivekananda *et al.* (2014) work with natural disasters in the context of human security). A security and mobilization approach would take the position that certain socioeconomic factors are in themselves merely seeding the ground for the fundamental condition for violent conflict: the mobilization of people with the purpose of challenging the state, or other dominant groups. In the words of Haldén (2007: 59): 'The most important proximate causes of conflicts may be the presence of politicians who want to exploit the situation or the absence of politicians who make conscious choices to avoid conflict by addressing socio-economic hardships resulting from natural disasters.' What often matters for conflicts are the actors' perceptions of conflict situations, rather than simple causal links between contributory factors and outcomes (Martin 2005: 335). These perceptions can easily be formed by the prevalent discourses.

Rather than arguing that natural disasters could have causal impacts on the risk of conflict, it might be fruitful to look at natural disasters as a potential tool for mobilization – in much the same way that other major societal transformations (political reforms, financial crises, etc.) might mobilize different groups for violent purposes. The conflict potential of natural disasters, therefore, relies on the prevailing discourses, narratives and symbols that emerge in the wake of the natural disaster. One such narrative is securitization; when natural disasters are securitized, it entails reserving the right to address threats using extraordinary means not necessarily confined by the rules that apply on a day-to-day basis (Wæver 2009). That way, natural disasters can be used to pursue broader security-political agendas on a national level through securitization. A state of emergency following a natural disaster gives a government increased authority, and thereby the opportunity to cement its power (see Chapter 4 by Illner and Holm for the use of state of exception). Securitization can also mean that local elites use natural disasters as a tool to mobilize parts of the population to pursue a specific agenda.

One of the greatest unknowns going forward is how states and groups would react to the fact that natural disasters, especially climate-related disasters, can to a greater degree than before be ascribed to human activity (Rubin 2010). Today, the blame for drought and flooding can, at least in part, be placed at the doorsteps of the social groups and societies emitting greenhouse gases. This represents an important break, considering the vital aspect of mobilization. It is difficult to mobilize against Mother Nature (or God) – it is easier to mobilize against someone who can be held accountable for the disasters. Kallis and Zografos (2014: 80) warn that 'framing hydro-climatic change as a national security and military concern not only diverts resources from where they are most needed, but also runs the risk of a self-fulfilling prophecy'. Droughts and famines are increasingly blamed on the effects of global warming by governments eager to avoid being held culpable. President Mugabe, for instance, has repeatedly blamed global warming for much of the food insecurity in Zimbabwe (Mugabe 2008). Eva Morales, the Bolivian President, has expressed the view that natural disasters are a result of the Western capital system and industrialization's exploitation of the planet's resources (*Newsweek* 2008). Such reasoning can, regardless of factual validity, create powerful resistance among the poor (who are the first to feel the consequences of climatic disasters) and the wealthy (who can be blamed for the climatic disasters) locally, nationally and regionally. The framing of disasters, therefore, adds an additional (and more complex) dimension to the analysis of conflict. In order to improve our understanding of the link between natural disasters and conflicts, these more discursive aspects should be included in the analytical framework alongside the well-known socioeconomic factors.

Summary

Natural disasters are not inherently to blame for wars or peace, but they can act as catalysts for both conflict and cooperation depending on the specific socioeconomic conditions. Disasters affect the opportunities and incentives for engaging in conflict behaviour. If a country is characterized by financial inequality, a weak state and a history of previous conflicts, natural disasters might spur armed conflicts and crime. In situations where there is an existing forum for peace negotiations, where combatants are exhausted and where a certain level of social capital can be traced, natural disasters might help promote peace and cooperation.

Rather than pursuing causal theories of general applicability, a fruitful analytical approach might be to examine how natural disasters are being framed and/or securitized in different contexts. The scope for conflict-based mobilization depends crucially on the particular narratives that end up being associated with the natural disaster. The facts that more and more natural disasters are perceived as man-made, and that states are increasingly expected to provide protection in dire situations, could potentially pose a threat to national and regional stability in the future.

References

Akcinaroglu, S., DiCicco, J.M., and Radziszewski, E. (2011) Avalanches and olive branches: A multimethod analysis of disasters and peacemaking in interstate rivalries. *Political Research Quarterly,* 64(2): 260–75.

Barnett, J. (2003) Security and climate change. *Global Environmental Change* 13(1): 7–17.

Barnett, J., and W.N. Adger (2007) Climate change, human security and violent conflict. *Political Geography,* 26(6): 639–55.

Bergholt, D., and Lujala, P. (2012) Climate-related natural disasters, economic growth, and armed civil conflict. *Journal of Peace Research,* 49(1), 147–62

Besley, T., and Persson, T. (2011) The logic of political violence. *Quarterly Journal of Economics,* 126, 1411–45.

Brancati, D. (2007) Political aftershocks: The impact of earthquakes on intrastate conflict. *Journal of Conflict Resolution,* 51(5): 715–43.

Busby, J. (2007) *Climate Change and National Security: An Agenda for Action.* CSR, 32. Washington, DC: Council of Foreign Relations, US, www.cfr.org/climate-change/climate-change-national-security/p14862 (accessed 28 February 2015).

Carlin, R., Love, G., and Zechmeister, E. (2014) Natural disaster and democratic legitimacy: The public opinion consequences of Chile's 2010 earthquake and tsunami. *Political Research Quarterly,* 67(1), 3–15.

Collier, P. (2009) *Wars, Guns and Votes: Democracy in Dangerous Places.* New York: HarperCollins.

Collier, P., and Hoeffler, A. (2004) Greed and grievance in civil war. *Oxford Economic Papers,* 56, 563–95.

Collier, P., Hoeffler, A., and Rohner D. (2009) Beyond greed and grievance: Feasibility and civil war. *Oxford Economic Papers,* 61: 1–27.

Council of the European Union (2008) Climate Change and International Security. Paper from the High Representative and the European Commission to the European Council, www.consilium.europa.eu/uedocs/cms_data/docs/pressdata/en/reports/99387.pdf (accessed 28 February 2015).

Devlin, C., and Hendrix, C. (2014) Trends and triggers redux: Climate change, rainfall and interstate conflict. *Political Geography,* 43, 27–39.

Diamond, J. (2005) *Collapse: How Societies Choose to Fail or Succeed.* New York: Viking Press.

Dixon, J. (2009) What causes civil wars? Integrating quantitative research findings. *International Studies Review,* 11, 707–35.

Enarson, E. (1999) Violence against women in disasters: A study of domestic violence programs in the United States and Canada. *Violence Against Women,* 5(7), 742–68.

Enia, J. (2008) Peace in its wake? The 2004 tsunami and internal conflict in Indonesia and Sri Lanka. *Journal of Public and International Affairs,* 19, 7–27.

Fisher, S. (2010) Violence against women and natural disasters: Findings from post-tsunami Sri Lanka. *Violence Against Women,* 16, 1902–18.

Gleditsch, N., and Urdal, H. (2002) Ecoviolence? Links between population growth, environmental scarcity and violent conflict in Thomas Homer-Dixon's work. *Journal of International Affairs,* 56(1), 283–302.

Goodhand, J. (2003) Enduring disorder and persistent poverty: A review of the linkages between war and chronic poverty. *World Development,* 31(3), 629–46.

Haldén, P. (2007) *The Geopolitics of Climate Change.* Stockholm: Swedish Defence Research Agency.

Harris, K., Keen, D., and Mitchell, T. (2013) When disasters and conflicts collide, ODI, www.odi.org/sites/odi.org.uk/files/odi-assets/publications-opinion-files/8228.pdf (accessed 28 February 2015).

Hauge, W., and Ellingsen, T. (1998) Beyond environmental scarcity: Causal pathways to conflict. *Journal of Peace Research,* 35(3), 299–317.

Hendrix, C., and Salehyan, I. (2012) Climate change, rainfall, and social conflict in Africa. *Journal of Peace Research,* 49(1), 35–50.

Homer-Dixon, T. (1995) *The Project on Environment, Population and Security: Research Results for Gaza, Rwanda and South Africa,* www.homerdixon.com/projects/eps/results.htm (accessed 28 February 2015).

Homer-Dixon, T. (1996) *The Project on Environment, Population and Security Research: Results for Pakistan and Mexico,* www.homerdixon.com/projects/eps/results.htm.

Homer-Dixon, T. (1999) *Environment, Scarcity, and Violence.* Princeton, NJ: Princeton University Press.

International Organization for Migration (2009) *Migration, Environment and Climate Change: Assessing the Evidence.* Geneva: IOM, http://publications.iom.int/bookstore/free/migration_and_environment.pdf (accessed 28 February 2015).

Kahl, C. (2006) *States, Scarcity, and Civil Strife in the Developing World.* Princeton, NJ: Princeton University Press.

Kallis, K., and Zografos, C. (2013) Hydro-climatic change, conflict and security. *Climatic Change,* 123, 69–82.

Kelman, I. (2006) Acting on disaster diplomacy. *Journal of International Affairs,* 59(2), 215–40.

Kelman, I. (2007) Hurricane Katrina disaster diplomacy. *Disasters,* 31(3), 288–309.

Kelman, I. (2012) *Disaster Diplomacy: How Disasters Affect Peace and Conflict.* Abingdon, Oxon: Routledge.

Leitner, M., Barnett, B., Kent, J., and Barnett, T. (2011) The impact of Hurricane Katrina on reported crimes in Louisiana: A spatial and temporal analysis. *The Professional Geographer,* 63(2), 244–61.

Martin, A. (2005) Environmental conflict between refugee and host communities. *Journal of Peace Research,* 42(3), 329–46.

Mugabe, R. (2008) Speech at General Assembly 63rd Session General Debate 25 Sept. GA/10754. www.un.org/News/Press/docs/2008/ga10754.doc.htm (accessed 28 February 2015).

Nafziger, E., and Auvinen, J. (2002) Economic development, inequality, war, and state violence. *World Development,* 30(2), 153–63.

Nel, P., and Righarts, M. (2008) Natural disasters and the risk of violent civil conflict. *International Studies Quarterly,* 52, 159–85.

Nelson, T. (2010) When disaster strikes: On the relationship between natural disaster and interstate conflict. *Global Change, Peace and Security,* 22(2), 155–74.

Newsweek (2008) The people's pugilist: Interview with Evo Morales. 22 Apr., www.newsweek.com/id/133279 (accessed 28 February 2015).

Nordås, R., and Gleditsch, N.P. (2007) Climate change and conflict. *Political Geography,* 26(6), 627–38.

Nossiter, A. (2005) Nature's crime fighter: Hurricane Katrina. *New York Times,* 11 Nov., www.nytimes.com/2005/11/10/world/americas/10iht-crime.html (accessed 28 February 2015).

Omelicheva, M. (2011) Natural disasters: Triggers of political instability? *International Interactions*, 37, 441–65.

Quarantelli, E.L., and Dynes, R. (1976) Community conflict: Its absence and presence in natural disasters. *Mass Emergencies*, 1: 139–52.

Raleigh, C., and Urdal, H. (2007) Climate change, environmental degradation and armed conflict. *Political Geography*, 26(6), 674–94.

Reuveny, R. (2007) Climate change-induced migration and violent conflict. *Political Geography*, 26(6), 656–73.

Reuveny, R. (2008) Ecomigration and violent conflict: Case studies and public policy implications. *Human Ecology*, 36(1), 1–13.

Roy, S. (2010) *The Impact of Natural Disasters on Violent Crime*. Working Paper, http://nzae.org.nz/wp-content/uploads/2011/08/Roy__The_Impact_of_Natural_Disasters_on_Violent_Crime.pdf (accessed 28 February 2015).

Rubin, O. (2010) Social perspective on the symbiotic relationship between climate change and conflict. *Social Development Issues*, 32(2), 29–41.

Salehyan, I., and Gleditsch, K. (2006) Refugees and the spread of civil war. *International Organization*, 60(2): 335–66.

Schwartz, P., and Randall, D. (2003) An abrupt climate change scenario and its implications for United States national security. Global Business Network (GBN) for the Department of Defense, www.gbn.com/articles/pdfs/Abrupt%20Climate%20Change%20February%202004.pdf (accessed 28 February 2015).

Shawn, C., Healy, A., and Werker, E. (2012) Do voters demand responsive governments? Evidence from Indian disaster relief. *Journal of Development Economics*, 97, 167–81.

Slettebak, R. (2013) Climate change, natural disasters, and post-disaster unrest in India. *India Review*, 12(4), 260–79.

Slettebak, R., and de Soysa, I. (2010) High temps, high tempers? Weather-related natural disasters and civil conflict. Draft paper for the conference on climate change and security, Trondheim, Norway, 21–24 June, http://climsec.prio.no/papers/Slettebak%20and%20de%20Soysa%20-%20Temp%20and%20Temper.pdf (accessed 28 February 2015).

Smith, D., and Vivekananda, J. (2007) *A Climate of Conflict*. International Alert, www.international-alert.org/resources/publications/climate-conflict (accessed 28 February 2015).

Tucker, E. (2001) Crime and disaster. *Business Recovery Managers Association Newsletter*, Sept., www.praetorianprotective.com/Crime_Disaster.pdf (accessed 28 February 2015).

Theisen, O. (2008) Blood and soil? Resource scarcity and internal armed conflict revisited. *Journal of Peace Research*, 6, 801–18.

Theisen, O. (2012) Climate clashes? Weather variability, land pressure, and organized violence in Kenya 1989–2004. *Journal of Peace Research*, 49(1), 81–96.

Theisen, O., Gleditsch, P., and Buhaug, H. (2013) Is climate change a driver of armed conflict? *Climatic Change*, 117, 613–25.

Uexkull, N. (2014) Sustained drought, vulnerability and civil conflict in Sub-Saharan Africa. *Political Geography*, 43, 16–26.

UN (2007) A climate culprit in Darfur speech by Ban Ki Moon, www.washingtonpost.com/wp-dyn/content/article/2007/06/15/AR2007061501857.html (accessed 28 February 2015).

UNEP (2007) *Sudan Post-Conflict Environmental Assessment*, http://postconflict.unep.ch/publications/UNEP_Sudan_synthesis_E.pdf (accessed 28 February 2015).

Urdal, H. (2005) People vs. Malthus: Population pressure, environmental degradation, and armed conflict revisited. *Journal of Peace Research*, 42(4), 417–34.

Urdal, H. (2008) Population, resources and political violence: A sub-national study of India 1956–2002. *Journal of Conflict Resolution*, 52(4), 590–617.

Varano, S., Schafer, J., Cancino, J., Decker, S., and Greenee, J. (2010) A tale of three cities: Crime and displacement after Hurricane Katrina. *Journal of Criminal Justice*, 38(1), 42–50.

Vivekananda, J., Schilling, J., and Smith, D. (2014) Climate resilience in fragile and conflict-affected societies: Concepts and approaches. *Development in Practice*, 24(4), 487–501.

Walch, C. (2014) Collaboration or obstruction? Rebel group behavior during natural disaster relief in the Philippines. *Political Geography*, 43, 40–50.

Wæver, O. (2009) Klimatruslen: En sikkerhedsteoretisk analyse. *Tidsskriftet Politik*, 12(1), 5–26.

Wolf, A. (2007) Shared waters: Conflict and cooperation. *Annual Review of Environment and Resources*, 32, 241–69.

Zahran, S., Shelley, T., Peek, L., and Brody S. (2009) Natural disasters and social order: Modeling crime outcomes in Florida. *International Journal of Mass Emergencies and Disasters*, 27(1), 26–52.

9 Analysing communication processes in the disaster cycle

Theoretical complementarities and tensions

Nina Blom Andersen

Challenges in the disaster communication research field

This chapter explores how communication processes in relation to disastrous events are understood, analysed and theorized upon. It deals with communication processes on a societal level, involving the communication between authorities, citizens and the media. The internal communication processes for organizations involved in disasters will not be the focus of this chapter.

The discipline of disaster communication is not a clearly demarcated research field. There is no consensus regarding what defines the communication research field in general, or the disaster communication research field in particular. Craig argues that '[t]he various traditions of communication theory each offer distinct ways of conceptualizing and discussing communication problems and practices. These ways derive from and appeal to certain commonplace beliefs about communication while problematizing other beliefs' (Craig 1999: 120). The communication discipline lacks a common vocabulary for understanding the different communicative processes; there is no theoretical canon; and there are no common goals related to the practices of analysing the different phases of the disaster cycle. In this chapter, I suggest a framework for dividing the research field into categories, without claiming that this particular division is conclusive. I build on Craig's recommendations of 'exploring the field' (1999: 149), with the aim of providing further discussion instead of dictating final definitions.

The overall structure of this chapter relates to the central distinction between the understanding of two overall 'territories' (Griffin 2009: 51) within the research field: (1) *communication as an intentional activity* and (2) *communication as a constitutive practice*. In this chapter three theoretical traditions will be argued to refer to the intentional territory and two traditions will be presented in relation to the constitutive territory. These five theoretical traditions will be discussed in relation to the most disastrous incident on Danish soil since the Second World War: the Seest firework warehouse fire in 2004, which led to an unexpected mass explosion.

The warehouse qualified as a high-risk plant according to the European Union Seveso II directive. A container fire caused an explosion in the warehouse where

1,200 tons of fireworks – roughly the equivalent of 300 tons of net explosives – were stored. A fire fighter was killed and several other emergency workers were injured during the response phase. A prompt and efficient evacuation in the hours before the explosion led to a notably low number of casualties, especially regarding the local inhabitants. More than ten houses burned to the ground, however, and approximately 350 houses were damaged. The case is characterized as a disaster with a sudden onset that took place in Denmark – a country with a well-functioning emergency management system, an extended social security system and a population that in general holds a high degree of trust towards authorities and the media. It will be shown that in order to analyse phases of prevention, preparedness, response and recovery involving different groups of actors, very disparate and sometimes quite conflicting theoretical approaches can be applied (Andersen 2008).

Disaster communication as intentional practice

The first three theoretical traditions to be presented can be argued, in different ways, to touch on the theoretical territory that understands communication as an intentional activity, which has an overriding understanding of a distinction between *sources* and *receivers* (Craig 1999). Since disaster communication is also a practical discipline, much research is conducted with the aim of being applied in practice. From the viewpoint of institutions, authorities, politicians, etc., communication is a practical and very central dimension of disaster planning. Communication can reach small or large groups of citizens, and this is evident in the research field. In other words, given that communicative practices take place in the life-world of people, institutions and organizations struck by or involved in disasters, much research holds an interest in improving the ways societies deal with these disasters.

Research on disaster communication processes that aim to reach individuals or groups of people with a certain intention, and that are carried out as a part of a plan or strategy, is in many ways similar to Craig's (1999) argument that some communication research traditions build on the assumption that communication is a question of cause-and-effect (Craig 1999; Griffin 2009). Three theoretical traditions can be said to refer to the theoretical territory dealing with the question of intention: *transmission and information processing*; *risk communication* and *crisis communication*.

Transmission and information processing

The first tradition related to the intentional territory is that of transmission and information processing. A warning situation is an example of communication as information transmission and processing, dealing with questions of *channels* and *sources*, though this theoretical tradition has an understanding that transmission is not a linear and simple process, but a complex one that can be difficult to predict (Craig 1999: 142).

In the Seest disaster, information was intensively disseminated and transmitted in the local area around the firework storage, regionally and nationally. The first part of the response phase took place in the time from when the warehouse caught fire in the afternoon until the entire stock of fireworks exploded, less than four hours later. During this time, the authorities used sirens, radio and police officers running from door to door in order to reach the neighbours with the message of a mandatory evacuation. The diffusion of information on the important message regarding the evacuation took place in a complex web of mediated and interpersonal communication. Not only did the authorities try to reach the neighbours, they also spread the warning and some of the residents become aware of the warning through talking to each other. A number of residents were not reached by the authorities' use of official sources, but in ways that no emergency manager would ever think of. For instance, family members called from other parts of the country, urging their loved ones to leave the area.

In a disaster cycle the response phase in particular is in many cases characterized by authorities' need to get in contact with large groups of people, reach them with a message on how to manage the situation and take appropriate action within a short period of time. Studies of how early warning systems work, how they can be designed, how technical mistakes and errors can be avoided, and how warnings are perceived among citizens, are crucial in many disasters with a rapid onset (Mileti and Sorensen 1990; Sorensen 2000).

The use of media to reach a target group to disseminate a warning is to a large degree dealt with in the research in relation to a number of traditional media, such as sirens (Simmons and Sutter 2011), radio (Perry 2007; Kupec 2008) and TV (Perry 2007). These mentioned media can all be characterized as 'one to many' media – a characteristic that stresses the top-down perspective in the transmission of information. In recent years focus has moved towards the potential of using social media in order to transmit information in a response phase. This has caused scholars to broaden their perspective to investigate how *both* citizens and authorities can use social media to gain better information faster in the response phase, in case of a disastrous event (Crowe 2012; Shankar 2008; White *et al.* 2009; Veil *et al.* 2011).

As social media are characterized by being able to diffuse information from 'many to many', an important shift can be identified in the scope of research: the prior perspective of well-defined senders and receivers is now considered to be far more complex than linear, though the idea of using some form of medium to transmit information is still central. The ongoing development in technology has impacted a research tradition that is savvy on media, and so recent research focuses on transmission between all kinds of actors, abandoning the idea of the demarcated managerial perspective (Palen *et al.* 2007, 2010; Murthy and Longwell 2013; Vultee and Vultee 2011; Houston *et al.* 2014).

Risk communication – expressions' influence on behavior

The second tradition related to the territory of intentional communication is often referred to as *risk communication*. Communication is seen as a means to reach a goal:

to make people react in an appropriate way, through motivation and influence on attitudes. This research tradition is tightly coupled to an understanding of management through communication: 'risk management and risk communication should be seen as parallel activities that complement each other' (Renn 2009: 95). A central cause–effect comprehension within this tradition argues that well-designed messages can have a positive impact on people's behaviour.

In the case of the Seest disaster, far from everyone within the residential area complied with the evacuation order, despite all the efforts to spread the warning messages. The fire was perceived very differently among the residents: some residents saw it as a potentially risky warehouse that had caused anxiety for several years, and some of them evacuated in a hurry; others did not worry and had strong faith in the authorities' abilities to deal with the fire. The warnings from the police stating that 'there is a danger of explosions', 'this is an emergency situation' and 'the fire is not under control' were perceived very differently among the residents, and many engaged in discussions of the danger of the situation with family and neighbours before they decided if they would evacuate.

The question is raised in risk communication research literature: why is it that people understand and react so differently to communication about risk and threats – not only in a response phase like the one in Seest, but also concerning questions of prevention and communication about preparedness? And the next question is: 'can we do something about this through communication?'

The research on people's perceptions of risk in relation to a potential disastrous event is inspired by research on people's general *perceptions* of a number of different risks, that originally derived from the tradition of behavioural studies (Slovic 1987; Covello *et al.* 1986). As such, some of the research on risk communication is carried out in order to understand perceptions of the risk in phases of preparedness, in order to analyse how – if at all – people prepare themselves for disastrous incidents (Manuell and Cukor 2011; Wester-Herber and Warg 2011; Burningham *et al.* 2008; Olofsson and Rashid 2011; Chatterjee and Mozumder 2014). And perception of risk in a response phase is also an object of study (Zimmerman and Sherman 2011; Rowan *et al.* 2009).

Another part of the theoretical tradition investigates whether it is possible to make people react in certain ways through means of communication: 'Communication problems … are thus thought of as situations that call for the effective manipulation of the causes of behavior in order to produce objectively defined and measured outcomes' (Craig 1999: 143). The question of how to actually construct messages that persuade citizens to take appropriate action in a phase of prevention, preparedness or response is similarly central to the work of the scholars in this tradition (Wood *et al.* 2012; Terpstra *et al.* 2009, 2014).

Crisis communication – the importance of rhetoric

The third tradition within the territory which views communication as an intentional practice is often labelled *crisis communication*, and is to a large degree linked to the recovery phase in the disaster cycle. Where the above-mentioned research on risk communication is concerned with the ways messages can persuade people to take appropriate action to protect themselves from a potential threat in a response phase, the rhetorical tradition and the work on crisis communication aim at persuading an audience about the sender's credibility and accountability in order to prevent crises of legitimacy during a response phase or in a recovery phase. Disasters are often – or almost always – followed by attempts by political leaders, private organizations, officials or authorities to put themselves in a favourable light, to avoid accusations of irresponsibility and guilt, and (re)build the public's trust in their work in order to make people in societies or communities feel safe and trustful.

After the Seest disaster, ministers, the Danish Emergency Management Agency (DEMA), the local fire and rescue service, along with the local politicians and authorities, were questioned on their responsibility for authorizing the placement of 1,200 tons of fireworks in the middle of a residential neighbourhood. They all tried to give an impression of accountability; they made attempts to show concern for the residents in the neighbourhood and displayed a strong will to avoid similar accidents, not least through the media. The authorities faced accusations (since they had permitted the storing of an extensive quantity of fireworks in the middle of a suburb), while simultaneously being broadly acknowledged positively for their incident management and protective attitude towards the residents. In the recovery phase, the municipality, the fire and rescue service, and the local police invested much energy and work in order to display care for and focus on the people affected by the disaster, though they were the ones who had approved the placement of the factory in the first place.

The crisis communication field is influenced by several theoretical traditions (Benoit 1995), but the rhetorical tradition in particular has influenced the understanding of crisis communication. The rhetorical tradition is tied to the assumption that communication is carried out with specific intent, and that the sender of a message works to persuade the receiver about a certain matter (Benoit 1995; Craig 1999). Or as stated by Springston *et al.*: 'Rhetoric is influence' (2009: 269).

Two branches of crisis communication research should be emphasized. One branch of the research deals with questions concerning appropriate communication strategies, and issues of communication style and appearance. Coombs (2012) writes about the subject matter of crisis communication that it concerns 'instructing information', 'adjusting information' and 'reputational management', and in relation to the reputational management dimension Coombs mentions a number of 'crisis response strategies' (2012: 146–154). This advice on how to approach the crisis communication task comes from a practice-based field where advice is built on knowledge of best practices (Seeger 2006). A central assumption is that crisis communication is (also) a question of training and practice. This research is characterized by writing about how senders can work appropriately with communication strategies.

Another branch of the research has a more empirical focus, dealing for instance with the analysis of crisis communication in relation to political governance after disastrous events (Boin *et al.* 2008), or how authorities work with crisis communication strategies (Gallagher *et al.* 2007). A distinct challenge analysed is how public organizations communicate with the public after a disastrous incident, in a response or a recovery phase (Olsson 2014). This brings up questions with a special importance to the disaster research field, since politicians and authorities, to a large degree, are involved in disastrous events. Similarly, it is discussed how the guidelines in the field of crisis communication can be difficult to apply, and that management through normative strategies is not always possible (Clarke *et al.* 2006; Christensen *et al.* 2013).

Disaster communication as constitutive practice

The second territory in the research field of disaster communication refers to the tradition that understands communication processes as an integrated part of everyday practices – not as an intentional activity. This territory is not connected to an understanding of senders and receivers, but instead sees disaster communication as the construction of meaning, which guides societies, communities and people in their everyday lives. In this territory one finds studies that aim at understanding meaning-making in relation to disasters, in order to get an understanding of the comprehensiveness of citizens' communication about disasters, and how they are influenced by life-world matters and structural conditions. In the following two sections, it will be shown that communication processes related to these traditions are distinct in the ways that they are often out of sight of emergency manager or others who are dealing with activities concerning the phases in the disaster cycle.

This approach is beyond the narrow focus of planned communication processes where communication is carried out with an intention, since much communication has to be understood as constitutive, either producing new meanings or reproducing existing meanings (Craig 1999). The aim of the research is to analyse communication processes on a *societal* and *collective* level, in opposition to the traditions which deal with risk and crisis communication and are more focused on how *individuals* send or receive. The processes of interest to the research can take place in local, regional, national or international contexts, and the research is often concerned with how communication either gets society back on a well-known track or aims to question the existing structure and put it under pressure. Focal points in the territory are questions of cultural patterns, structural conditions, ideology, meaning and conflicts. Two traditions can be argued to relate to the territory of research on constitutive communication processes: *life-world and meaning-making;* and *media and ideology.*

Life-world and meaning-making

As people communicate in their everyday life, they produce and reproduce meaning. This is, arguably, a dominating understanding within the tradition, and it mainly focuses on people's life-worlds and ways of making sense in the phases of the disaster cycle. A part of this meaning-making takes place through interactions with others, where 'cultural patterns and social structures' (Craig 1999: 144) are either reproduced or defined in new ways, given that everyday life and the well-known social order can often be interrupted in ways that require novel definitions, in disaster situations. It is argued in this tradition that the reason for having an interest in what is going on – on an interactional level – is that processes which take place on a micro level may impact a society's macro level and vice versa.

In the Seest disaster, much effort was made by the residents to make sense of the sudden explosions and the extensive destruction of the residential area after the authorities' operation had ended, and what was defined as the recovery phase began. First, they had to make sense of the severity of the accident and the potential of additional casualties to the one person who lost his life. Furthermore, they had to make sense of the gap between mistrust in the authorities with responsibility for keeping the residents safe and the gratitude for the same authorities' hard work during the operation. Additionally, they had to deal with a large degree of uncertainty concerning the rebuilding of the area; when they could return to their homes; and whether the insurance companies would compensate their material losses. Finally, the people struck by the disaster had an ongoing negotiation regarding which parties were the ones most affected, and a local hierarchy of affectedness was constructed in which the residents would compare the severity of their own situation with others. Learning how to display affectedness and get acknowledged for the terrible situation was part of the recovery. Several of these processes never came to the attention of the media, politicians, authorities and institutions involved.

The sense-making and communication processes in local communities struck by disastrous incidents have been the subject of a number of field studies. One of the aims of these studies is to investigate the often subtle and hidden communication processes that citizens are involved in, and the point is that, while these local communication processes are not very spectacular, they can display silent dramas. Button argues that '[i]n the wake of a disaster, victims and their families often struggle to regain control over their life and assign meaning to the event. One way to uncover this meaning making process is to examine the survivors' narrative accounts' (2006: 429). Agreements and disagreements in a community regarding what has happened, and how to carry on is illustrated by Linenthal (2001), Kroll-Smith and Couch (1990), Erikson (1976), Shrivastava (1987), Picou and Gill (2000) and Andersen (2013), to name a few.

Studies of meaning-making processes in communities are, among other things, concerned with the amplification – post-disaster – of everyday discursive constructions of who is vulnerable and who is able to take care of themselves. Fordham and Ketteridge (1998) investigate how gender stereotypes get reproduced and amplified, and Santos-Hernández (2006) shows how an already excluded and silenced group of immigrants vanish even more from the attention of the public in the aftermath of a disastrous incident. But as is the case with reproduction, production is similarly often identified, and in some cases citizens have the ability to put existing structures under pressure. Social movements and resident activism are examples of citizens engaging in processes that they wish to have influence over, since they are not content with the way things are managed in questions of prevention, preparedness, response or recovery. In these cases groups of citizens try to get in contact with companies, authorities or politicians in order to convince them of alternative perspectives of either a potential disaster or the outcome of an actual disaster (Brown 1987; Coburn 2005; Fowlkes and Miller 1987; Wynne 1992). This presents an opposite situation to the one described in the first territory.

Media and ideology

The research tradition that apprehends communication as a constitutive element in society understands the media as much more than just a channel or a resource applied by a sender in order to reach a receiver with a message, as is the case in the research tradition dealing with information processing as presented above. Where the transformation and information-processing approach to disaster communication deals with dispersion and diffusion, research that focuses on media coverage deals with the symbolic, hegemonic, ideological and powerful influence that the media have on society concerning questions related to disasters since: 'media today perform a leading role in the public constitution of disasters, conditioning how they become known, defined, responded to and politically aligned' (Pantti *et al*. 2012: 5). The argument is that the role played by the media is either good or bad, but has to be scrutinized and understood.

Disasters are uncommon on Danish soil, so the explosion of the warehouse in Seest attracted extensive media coverage. Much of this media coverage concerned the particular threat of firework storage, without paying notice to the adjacent placement of other high-risk factories. The news reports displayed how the residents were simultaneously angry and how they mistrusted the authorities' acceptance of the storing of fireworks, while also being grateful that the explosions only killed one person and injured few. Considerable coverage dealt with residents' struggles to get their insurance to cover what they believed they were entitled to. A large part of the media was also concerned with the question of the cause of the accident, and who was responsible. But just as the media are sure to be present when an incident like the one in Seest strikes, they then disappear again. New disasters occur, leaving behind residents who had counted on more help from the media to set the national agenda concerning their difficult situation.

Part of the research on media and disasters is dealing with the question of in- and exclusion processes, similar to the one presented in the meaning-making tradition above. Similarly, it is often the case that attention in the media is distributed in an uneven way, and that not everyone affected by disasters around the world gets equal attention (Pantti 2009; Daley and O'Neill 1991). The writing on the mediated in- and exclusion processes also includes questions regarding how the media can be said to have an influence on ideologies in a society related to all the phases in the disaster cycle. The argument is that media agendas contribute to questions concerning what to prevent and prepare for, and how to respond and facilitate recovery, thus some discussions and debates are kept alive in the public, while others are forgotten (Gamson and Modigliani 1989; Nohrstedt 2010).

The media do however provide a possibility to raise critique and raise questions in the public sphere pre- and post-disaster. There is a *potential* for social change, and resistance against symbolic oppression through agenda setting and media coverage can in some cases lead to political action (Pantti and Wahl-Jorgensen 2011; Brown 1987). Nevertheless, it is not guaranteed that critique will be raised and changes made (Tilt and Xiao 2010; Ewart and McLean 2014).

A distinct part of the media research is concerned with the symbolic contribution to society of journalistic practices. Riegert and Olsson argue that the media contribute in a symbolic way to the public sense-making in disasters, and that the coverage is ritual in the sense that it can be recognized again and again: 'journalism is as much about ritual and meaning-making as it is about providing information' (Riegert and Olsson 2007: 143).

Two examples of symbolic media coverage of disastrous incidents are: the coverage of the deceased in disasters in relation to bereavement and casualties, and the myths that cling to disasters. Media coverage of disasters invites spectators to engage and be involved in certain ways, and to show their compassion close up and at a distance (Chouliaraki 2006; Höijer 2004; Pantti 2009). In cases of death, the media coverage is a big part of the public grief and process of mourning (Walter *et al.* 1995), not least in cases where the audiences identify with the victims. In terms of myths, the outcomes of some of media's rituals are to some extent negative, in the sense that numerous myths are propagated, regardless of whether or not they are correct. The myths regarding people first panicking and then looting are widespread, and identified in the media coverage in a number of response phases (Tierney 2006; Constable 2008). These myths can be extremely counterproductive in some cases, given that they can make authorities handle a response phase in an undesirable way, when the mediated sense-making has mischaracterized the public's reactions (Wester 2011).

Conclusion

This chapter has focused on the legitimacy of the examined traditions (Griffin 2009: 51). The traditions appeared to complement each other in the analysis of the Danish firework disaster, regardless of the tensions and dissimilarities that exist between the territories of respectively communication as intentional and constitutive practice.

A crucial contribution from the theoretical territory of intentional disaster communication is the one that all phases of the disaster cycle can be managed, and that those responsible for managing the phases can do better. In this territory there is a search for solutions: whether concerned with the fast dissemination of life-saving information; instructions on how to take care of oneself and others; the importance of holding together a community or a society after a severe incident; or making people believe in the leaders' ability to lead. Influenced by a functionalist approach and an interest in management, the intentional territory is often concerned with establishing cause-and-effect in disaster communication.

Where the territory of intentional communication sometimes aims at planning communication in order to avoid conflicts, the constitutive communication territory, on the contrary, acknowledges the importance of conflict. The reason for this can be found in the interest in the possibility of social change, and the aim to figure out how oppressing structures on a macro level or existing cultural patterns can be challenged by media discourses, social movements, etc. Planners, managers, institutions, politicians and authorities are often viewed as antagonists against groups of people with no or little voice. Hence, the constitutive territory contributes important critical perspectives on communication processes, and some would argue that the aim of the research is to pose provocative questions and nurture critical reflection (Craig 1999). The territory on communication as constitutive practice keeps watch of the ways that influential discourses are produced and reproduced in a hegemonic sense, and rejects the view that research is able to isolate the true cause-and-effects. It is, however, regrettably rare that the findings of the research are used to encourage people with no voice to object against repressive discourses and cultural practices, considering the limited audience of academic research.

Future research

Craig (1999) argues that, while communication is a theoretical discipline, it is a practical discipline as well. Although the phases in the disaster cycle have to be understood with a theoretically critical approach, the research also has to deal with the ways in which communication is carried out – since part of the research should deal with the questions and challenges that practitioners meet when people around the world are struck by disasters. The very important question of how to establish a dialogue between the intentional and managerial approach, on the one side, and the research on the constitutive communication processes, on the other, still seems unsolved. There is a lack of dialogue between the research that concerns the *strategic use of media* on the one hand, and the understanding of the *media as a forum of displaying citizenship and dominance* on the other. Further research is needed on this matter, to investigate potential bridges between the territories and the individual traditions. If dialogue is not possible, the aim of further research could be to come up with a more extensive articulation of the tensions between the two approaches.

Significant differences can also be identified *within* the territories (between the traditions), which might also call for further research. First, the two theoretical traditions related to the constitutive territory might have a number of coinciding assumptions, although more academic work should be done in order to analyse how interactions in communities influence media practices, and not least how media discourses influence communities of people with identical experiences of one or several of the disaster phases.

Second, the risk communication and crisis communication traditions hold a common interest in understanding how individuals communicate with each other, and several attempts can be identified to merge the risk and the crisis communication traditions. The transmission and information-processing tradition differs from these in the sense that it has an interest in understanding complexities and the interaction of 'human and non-human information processing systems' (Craig 1999: 142). The technological development of social media that has appeared in recent years contributes to the questioning of the top-down approach to communication, especially in a response phase; arguing that the sources of important information can be citizens, and authorities can become receivers. This development has the potential to have an interesting impact on the research field, creating new ways of theorizing upon well-known questions within the disaster communication research field. It is not probable that it will lead to general consensus and agreement but is that an ambition to strive for?

References

Andersen, N.B. (2008) *Risici og ramthed – vedtagelser, performance og definitionsmagt*. Ph.D. diss., Roskilde: Roskilde Universitet.

Andersen, N.B. (2013) Negotiations of acknowledgement among middle class residents: An analysis of post disaster interactions and performance in a Danish context. *International Journal of Mass Emergencies and Disasters*, 31(2), 270–92.

Benoit, W.L. (1995) *Accounts, Excuses, and Apologies: A Theory of Image Restoration Strategies*. Albany, NY: State University of New York Press.

Boin, A., McConnell, A., and 't Hart, P. (2008) *Governing After Crisis: The Politics of Investigation, Accountability, and Learning*. Cambridge: Cambridge University Press.

Brown, P. (1987) Popular epidemiology: Community response to toxic waste-induced disease in Wobumn, Massachusetts. *Science, Technology, and Human Values*, 12(3), 78–85.

Burningham, K., Fielding, J., and Thrush, D. (2008) 'It'll never happen to me': Understanding public awareness of local flood risk. *Disasters*, 32(2), 216–38.

Button, G.V. (2006) Voices from the Astrodome and beyond: Counternarrative accounts of disaster. In Natural Hazards Center (ed.), *Learning from Catastrophe: Quick Response Research in the Wake of Hurricane Katrina*. Boulder, CO: Institute of Behavioral Science, University of Colorado at Boulder, 429–42.

Chatterjee, C., and Mozumder, P. (2014) Understanding household preferences for hurricane risk mitigation information: Evidence from survey responses. *Risk Analysis: An Official Publication of the Society for Risk Analysis*, 34(6), 984–96.

Chouliaraki, L. (2006) *The Spectatorship of Suffering*. London: SAGE Publications.

Christensen, T., Lægreid, P., and Rykkja, L.H. (2013) After a terrorist attack: Challenges for political and administrative leadership in Norway. *Journal of Contingencies and Crisis Management*, 21(3), 167–77.

Clarke, L., Chess, C., Holmes, R., and O'Neill, K.M. (2006) Speaking with one voice: Risk communication lessons from the US anthrax attacks. *Journal of Contingencies and Crisis Management*, 14(3), 160–9.

Coburn, J. (2005) *Street Science: Community Knowledge and Environmental Health Justice*. Cambridge, MA: MIT Press.

Constable, M. (2008) Disaster mythology: Looting in New Orleans. *Disaster Prevention and Management*, 17(4), 519–25.

Coombs, W.T. (2012) *Ongoing Crisis Communication: Planning, Managing, and Responding*. 3rd edn, Thousand Oaks, CA: SAGE Publications.

Covello, V.T., Slovic, P., and von Winterfeldt, D. (1986) Risk communication: A review of the literature. *Risk Abstracts*, 3(4), 171–82.

Craig, R.T. (1999) Communication theory as a field. *Communication Theory*, 9(2), 119–61.

Crowe, A. (2012) *Disasters 2.0: The Application of Social Media Systems for Modern Emergency Management*. Boca Raton, FL: CRC Press.

Daley, P., and O'Neill, D. (1991) 'Sad is too mild a word': Press coverage of the Exxon Valdez oil spill. *Journal of Communication*, 41(4), 42–57.

Erikson, K.T. (1976) *Everything in its Path: Destruction of Community in the Buffalo Creek Flood*. New York: A Touchstone Book. Simon & Schuster.

Ewart, J., and McLean, H. (2014) Ducking for cover in the 'blame game': News framing of the findings of two reports into the 2010–11 Queensland floods. *Disasters*, 39(1), 166–84.

Fordham, M., and Ketteridge, A. (1998) 'Men must work and women must weep': Examining gender stereotypes in disaster. In E. Enarson and B. Morrow (eds), *The Gendered Terrain of Disaster: Through Women's Eyes*. London: Praeger, 81–94.

Fowlkes, M.R., and Miller, P.Y. (1987) Chemicals and community at Love Canal. In B.B. Johnson and V.T. Covello (eds), *The Social and Cultural Construction of Risk*. Boston, MA: D. Reidel Publishing Co., 55–78.

Gallagher, A.H., Fontenot, M., and Boyle, K. (2007) Communicating during times of crises: An analysis of news releases from the federal government before, during, and after hurricanes Katrina and Rita. *Public Relations Review*, 33(2), 217–19.

Gamson, W.A., and Modigliani, A. (1989). Media discourse and public opinion on nuclear power: A constructionist approach. *American Journal of Sociology*, 95(1), 1–37.

Griffin, E. (2009) *A First Look at Communication Theory*. 7th edn, New York: McGraw-Hill.

Houston, J.B., Hawthorne, J., Perreault, M.F., Park, E.H., Hode, M.G., Halliwell, M.R., McGovern, S.E.T., Davis, R., Vaid, S., McElderry, J.A., and Griffith, S.A. (2014) Social media and disasters: A functional framework for social media use in disaster planning, response, and research. *Disasters*, 39(1), 1–22.

Höijer, B. (2004) The discourse of global compassion: The audience and media reporting of human suffering. *Media, Culture and Society*, 26(4), 513–31.

Kroll-Smith, J.S., and Couch, S.R. (1990) *The Real Disaster is Above the Ground: A Mine Fire and Social Conflicts*. Lexington, KY: University Press of Kentucky.

Kupec, R.J. (2008) Tuning in: Weather radios for those most at risk. *Journal of Emergency Management*, 6(4), 51–6.

Linenthal, E.T. (2001) *The Unfinished Bombing: Oklahoma City in American Memory*. Oxford: Oxford University Press.

Manuell, M.-E., and Cukor, J. (2011) Mother Nature versus human nature: Public compliance with evacuation and quarantine. *Disasters*, 35(2), 417–42.

Mileti, D.S., and Sorensen, J.H. (1990) *Communication of Emergency Public Warnings: A Social Science Perspective and State-of-the Art Assessment*. Oak Ridge, CA: Federal Emergency Management Agency.

Murthy, D., and Longwell, S.A. (2013) Twitter and disasters. *Information, Communication and Society*, 16(6), 837–55.

Nohrstedt, S.A. (2010). Threat society and the media. In S.A. Nohrstedt (ed.), *Communicating Risks: Towards the Threat Society?* Göteborg: NORDICOM, 17–52.

Olofsson, A., and Rashid, S. (2011) The white (male) effect and risk perception: Can equality make a difference? *Risk Analysis: An Official Publication of the Society for Risk Analysis*, 31(6), 1016–32.

Olsson, E. (2014) Crisis communication in public organisations: Dimensions of the crisis communication revisited. *Journal of Contingencies and Crisis Management*, 22(2), 113–25.

Palen, B.Y.L., Hiltz, S.R., and Liu, S.B. (2007) Online forums supporting grassroots participation. *Communications of the ACM*, 54, 50(3), 54–8.

Palen, L., Starbird, K., Vieweg, S., and Hughes, A. (2010) Twitter-based information distribution during the 2009 Red River Valley flood threat. *Bulletin of the American Society for Information Science and Technology*, 36(5), 13–18.

Pantti, M. (2009) Wave of compassion: Nationalist sentiments and cosmopolitan sensibilities in the Finnish tsunami crisis management coverage. In U. Kivikuru and L. Nord (eds), *After the Tsunami: Crisis Communication in Finland and Sweden*. Göteborg: Nordicom Göteborg University, 83–105.

Pantti, M., and Wahl-Jorgensen, K. (2011) 'Not an act of God': Anger and citizenship in press coverage of British man-made disasters. *Media, Culture and Society*, 33(1), 105–22.

Pantti, M., Wahl-Jorgensen, K., and Cottle, S. (2012) *Disasters and the Media*. New York: Peter Lang.

Perry, S.D. (2007) Tsunami warning dissemination in Mauritius. *Journal of Applied Communication Research*, 35(4), 399–417.

Picou, J.S., and Gill, D.A. (2000) The Exxon Valdez disaster as localised environmental catastrophe: Dissimilarities to risk society theory. In M.J. Cohen (ed.), *Risk in the Modern Age: Social Theory, Science and Environmental Decision-Making*. London: Macmillan Press, 143–70.

Renn, O. (2009) Risk communication: Insights and requirements for designing succesful communication programs on health and environmental hazards. In R.L. Heath and H.D. O'Hair (eds), *Handbook of Risk and Crisis Communication*. Abingdon, Oxon, and New York: Routledge, 80–98.

Riegert, K., and Olsson, E.-K. (2007) The importance of ritual in crisis journalism. *Journalism Practice*, 1(2), 143–58.

Rowan, K.E., Botan, C.H., Kreps, G.L., Samoilenko, S., and Farnsworth, K. (2009) Risk communication education for local emergency managers: Using the CAUSE model for research, education, and outreach. In R.L. Heath and H.D. O'Hair (eds), *Handbook of Risk and Crisis Communication*. New York: Routledge, 168–91.

Santos-Hernández, J.M. (2006) 'Losing everything': Undocumented Latino workers and Hurricane Katrina. In Natural Hazards Center (ed.), *Learning from Catastrophe: Quick Response Research in the Wake of Hurricane Katrina*. Boulder, CO: Institute of Behavioral Science, University of Colorado at Boulder, 131–50.

Seeger, M.W. (2006) Best practices in crisis communication: An expert panel process. *Journal of Applied Communication Research*, 34(3), 232–44.

Shankar, K. (2008) Wind, water, and wi-fi: New trends in community informatics and disaster management. *The Information Society*, 24(2), 116–20.

Shrivastava, P. (1987) Preventing industrial crises: The challenge of Bhopal. *International Journal of Mass Emergencies and Disasters*, 5(3), 199–221.

Simmons, K.M., and Sutter, D. (2011) *Economic and Societal Impacts of Tornadoes*. Boston, MA: American Meteorological Society.

Slovic, P. (1987) Perception of risk. *Science*, 236(4799), 280–5.

Sorensen, J.H. (2000) Hazard warning systems: Review of 20 years of progress. *Natural Hazards Review*, 1(2), 119–25.

Springston, J.K., Avery, E.J., and Salliot, L.M. (2009) Influence theories: Rhetorical, persuasion, and informational. In R.L. Heath and H.D. O'Hair (eds), *Handbook of Risk and Crisis Communication*. Abingdon, Oxon, and New York: Routledge, 268–84.

Terpstra, T., Lindell, M.K., and Gutteling, J.M. (2009) Does communicating (flood) risk affect (flood) risk perceptions? Results of a quasi-experimental study. *Risk Analysis*, 29(8), 1141–55.

Terpstra, T., Zaalberg, R., de Boer, J., and Botzen, W. J.W. (2014) You have been framed! How antecedents of information need mediate the effects of risk communication messages. *Risk Analysis*, 34(8), 1506–20.

Tierney, K. (2006) Metaphors matter: Disaster myths, media frames, and their consequences in Hurricane Katrina. *Annals of the American Academy of Political and Social Science*, 604(1), 57–81.

Tilt, B., and Xiao, Q. (2010) Media coverage of environmental pollution in the People's Republic of China: Responsibility, cover-up and state control. *Media, Culture and Society*, 32(2), 225–45.

Veil, S.R., Buehner, T., and Palenchar, M.J. (2011) A work-in-process literature review: Incorporating social media in risk and crisis communication. *Journal of Contingencies and Crisis Management*, 19(2), 110–22.

Vultee, F., and Vultee, D.M. (2011) What we tweet about when we tweet about disasters: The nature and sources of microblog comments during emergencies. *International Journal of Mass Emergencies and Disasters*, 29(3), 221–42.

Walter, T., Littlewood, J., and Pickering, M. (1995) Death in the news: The public invigilation of private emotion. *Sociology*, 29(4), 579–96.

Wester, M. (2011) Fight, flight or freeze: Assumed reactions of the public during a crisis. *Journal of Contingencies and Crisis Management*, 19(4), 207–14.

Wester-Herber, M., and Warg, L.-E. (2011) Gender and regional differences in risk perception: Results from implementing the Seveso II Directive in Sweden. *Journal of Risk Research*, 5(1), 69–81.

White, C., Plotnick, L., Kushma, J., Hiltz, S.R., and Turoff, M. (2009) An online social network for emergency management. *International Journal of Emergency Management*, 6(3/4), 369.

Wood, M.M., Mileti, D.S., Kano, M., Kelley, M.M., Regan, R., and Bourgue, L.B. (2012) Communicating actionable risk for terrorism and other hazards. *Risk Analysis*, 32(4), 601–15.

Wynne, B. (1992). Misunderstood misunderstanding: Social identities and public uptake of science. *Public Understanding of Science*, 1, 281–304.

Zimmerman, R., and Sherman, M.F. (2011) To leave an area after disaster: How evacuees from the WTC buildings left the WTC area following the attacks. *Risk Analysis*, 31(5), 787–804.

10 Disaster through a gender lens

A case study from Haiti

Lynn Horton

Introduction

Recent years have brought an unprecedented loss of lives and livelihoods in natural disasters that are the product of complex interactions of hazards, vulnerabilities and resilience (Anderson 1994; Manyena 2012). Social science scholarship increasingly recognizes these disasters not simply as exceptional, uncontrollable natural events, but also as closely linked to human choices and actions (Enarson and Meyreles 2004; Hyndman and de Alwis 2003; Luft 2009; Wisner *et al.* 2003). In particular, pre-existing social norms, roles and inequalities shape the degree to which individuals and groups are vulnerable to disasters, as well as their capacities and opportunities to recover. However, until recently, a gender-blind perspective dominated disaster research and practices: the male experience of disasters was taken as universally representative (Always and Smith 1998; Enarson and Phillips 2008; Fordham 1998). Gender inequalities and differences were largely overlooked, despite data showing a disproportionate number of female deaths in disasters and a hampering of women's ability to rebuild after the event (Neumeyer and Plümper 2007). Scholarly and activist work on gender and disasters laid a rich groundwork to challenge these biases.

By the early 2000s, scholars, mainstream governmental and non-governmental institutions began to apply a gender lens to disasters to focus on differential gender impacts and experiences (Enarson and Meyreles 2004). This chapter outlines the characteristics of a gender approach and discusses why such application of gender analysis is essential in theorizing, preparing for and responding to disasters. It explores how gender-based inequalities and roles shape the pre- and post-disaster experiences for both women and men. The next section examines the factors that have inhibited the meaningful implementation of gender-sensitive disaster policies, including institutional biases and inadequate incorporation of intersectionality. A case study of Haiti follows and analyses that country's 2010 earthquake from a gender perspective. It identifies how the broader socioeconomic and cultural context, which has shaped women's vulnerabilities and capacities, highlights gender weaknesses in the NGO response and recovery effort, and it suggests pathways towards greater gender equality.

Need for a gender lens

While for many decades a gender-neutral approach to disasters dominated, recent feminist scholarship has highlighted key weaknesses in this method. First, in taking men's perspectives and experiences of disasters as universally representative, women's voices and experiences are rendered largely invisible (Fordham 1998). On a theoretical level, gender-blind analysis incorporates biases in favour of existing gender relations, thus failing to identify and adequately consider social root causes. In policy terms, the method works to conceal and often reproduce gender inequalities in pre- and post-disaster periods.

In contrast, focusing on gender as a central organizing concept for analysing disaster impact, vulnerability and unequal patterns of collective recovery provides a critical theoretical underpinning to support policies for equitable, sustainable recovery (Anderson 1994; Bradshaw 2001; Enarson and Meyreles 2004). A gender lens gives space for women's voices as it incorporates 'the situated knowledge of those outside the dominant power structure, without assuming a unified identity or set of experiences' (Enarson 1998: 157). Such emphasis on women's voices and experiences serves to counteract ongoing patterns of formal and *de facto* gender exclusion in disaster preparedness, response and recovery. Gender analysis also illuminates an interlocking series of differences and inequalities that disadvantage women, embedded within the global economy, state institutions, laws and policies, households, and cultural beliefs and practices. It enables NGOs and governments to better identify gender-specific needs, and potentially address them.

More broadly, a gender analysis of disasters offers a theoretical window into invisible and naturalized social structures, processes and identities as they are destabilized and reconfigured (Bradshaw 2001; Fothergill 2003). Disasters bring physical dislocations and also disrupt gender roles, norms and ideologies. They often exaggerate gender inequality as women's vulnerabilities cascade and are magnified. Under the right conditions however, disasters open up opportunities for gender transgressions, individual and collective empowerment, and transformative structural and institutional changes towards gender equity. Applying a gendered perspective to disaster is integral in identifying not only potential vulnerabilities, but also women's unrecognized and undervalued capacities.

Gender roles and inequalities

Two key areas of focus of this theoretical approach are gender inequalities and gender socialization and roles. Factors behind gender inequalities include women's subordinate position in the global economy, their exclusion from participation in formal and informal political spaces, the gender division of labour that gives women primary responsibility for domestic labour and child care, and cultural norms and values that reinforce women's subordination and inferiority (Enarson 1998). Furthermore, on a global scale women are disproportionately poor (Anderson 1994). These inequalities intensify disaster impacts for women: economically precarious circumstances, for example, force women to live in disaster-prone zones and unsafe housing, and limit opportunities for evacuation to safety. Poverty also hinders women's ability to recover from disaster (Jones-Deweever 2008). As will be discussed further below, gender vulnerabilities cannot be considered in isolation, but rather must be linked to intersecting races/ethnicities, class, and gender identities (Finch *et al.* 2010; Fordham 1998). These factors may increase stigma faced by victims of disasters and weaken women's claims for assistance and resources.

Gender socialization and roles also influence responses and actions during and after natural disasters. Men are socialized, for example, to engage in risky behaviours and deny pain in ways that may increase their death rates (Always and Smith 1998). In contrast, women's risk during disasters is often linked to caretaking responsibilities, cultural constructs of appropriate behaviour and limitations on mobility. Women put themselves at risk of death and injury as they protect children and more vulnerable adults (Dhungel and Ojha 2012; Eklund and Tellier 2012). They may have more limited access to public spaces where information and warnings about disasters are given, while norms of female modesty may hinder women's abilities to act quickly in emergency situations. In the 2004 Indian Ocean tsunami, for example, up to 80 per cent of the deceased were women and girls, in part because many women had never been taught how to swim and therefore had more limited mobility (Oxfam 2005). Poverty may also intensify women's economic dependence following disasters, leaving them vulnerable to violence and sexual exploitation (Fisher 2010; Ruwanpura 2008).

Distinct gender roles also come to the forefront in the post-disaster phase. In the absence of state services and before the arrival of external aid, women often play critical caretaking roles (Always and Smith 1998; Juran 2012; Litt 2008). They build and draw upon informal, place-based social networks to meet the physical and emotional needs of others (Litt 2008). The loss of home can be a profound blow for women whose status, meaning and sense of purpose are centred on the domestic sphere. After disasters, women face exhausting workloads, stress and frustration at being unable to fulfil traditional gender roles, when their second shift caretaking becomes more demanding (Fothergill 2003). Women's caretaking and emotional work generally receives little institutional recognition or support, as it remains largely invisible in the eyes of society, NGOs and governments (Bradshaw 2001; Ganapati 2012). In other cases, women may be punished and stigmatized for transgressing gender norms during the crisis. In contrast, men's gendered activities in rebuilding tend to be given wider recognition and status (Always and Smith 1998). Yet receiving government or NGO assistance can be perceived by men as particularly humiliating and undermining to their identities as providers and protectors. Male desire to reassert control and gender status in the post-disaster period, combined with other stresses such as crowded housing conditions, have been linked to increased aggression, forced marriages, alcoholism and gender-based and sexual violence (Ruwanpura 2008). Gender-blind approaches to development often overlook these damaging dynamics of traditional masculinities under stress, and the gaps in men's coping capacities (UNISDR 2009).

Implementing gender-sensitive policies

Since the mid-2000s, a number of guidelines for best practice in gender-sensitive disaster policies and practices have been developed, such as the United Nations IASC Policy Statement for the Integration of a Gender Perspective in Humanitarian Assistance. The implementation of gender mainstreaming in disasters institutions, however, has often been inadequate on both a theoretical and policy level. First, institutions may mainstream gender policies in a superficial and limited manner, with little engagement with the gender differences and inequalities discussed above. Reminiscent of the Women in Development (WID) paradigm, women beneficiaries are merely added into preset institutional frameworks of disaster intervention which remain unchanged and unproblematized (Hyndman and de Alwis 2003). While institutions have perhaps focused on quantifying the gender imbalances in disaster outcomes there has been reluctance to engage with deeper root causes behind these trends (Enarson and Phillips 2008; Freudenburg *et al.* 2008).

In other cases, NGOs and governments apply gender frameworks in a formulaic manner, with limited consideration of specific historical contexts, regional geopolitics and culturally specific gender relations (Hyndman and de Alwis 2003). Such superficial engagement widely persists in the field, where gender issues are often given low priority. Gender is decoupled from survival needs as a secondary issue to be dealt with later in development projects, and the transformative potential of a gender lens is diluted (Eklund and Tellier 2012; Hyndman and de Alwis 2003).

A further obstacle in the implementation of gender-sensitive policies is patterns of embedded sexist beliefs, norms and practices in institutions. Disaster planning, response and recovery tend to draw on male-dominated and technocratic institutions and traditions, including the military, civil defence and engineering (Batlan 2008; Enarson and Phillips 2008). *De facto* patterns of gender exclusion occur not only in aid-recipient communities, but also in governmental and non-governmental organizations where women are often absent from leadership and decision-making positions (Bradshaw 2001; Krajeski and Peterson 2008; Wilson and Oyola-Yemaiel 2008). When gender equity policies are put into practice they often lack adequate staff commitment and strong managerial support (De la Puente 2011). Such biases and gender blind spots lead institutions to exclude the needs and perspectives of women. NGOs and government programmes tend to overlook female-headed households, favouring male heads of household in food distribution and access to rebuilding resources, and prioritizing male income-earning activities (Jones-Deweever 2008; Juran 2012). Post-disaster aid organizations may also reinforce traditional gender roles in ways that further burden overworked women (Enarson 1998). Rebuilding programmes, for example, may assume women have unlimited time and emotional resources and make instrumental use of women's willingness to self-sacrifice (De la Puente 2011).

Finally, a factor which has undermined the effectiveness of NGOs and governmental disaster agencies is inadequate conceptualization, representation and incorporation of women's complex identities into policies and programmes. Gender risk analysis tends to operate via homogenization and reduction of women, 'marking sexual difference on their bodies and connecting their needs to reproduction' (Cupples 2007: 156). Because initial efforts to bring a gender lens to disaster often focused on biologically linked vulnerabilities and mothering roles, they often reproduced disempowering, simplified representations of women as passive victims of natural disasters. These institutional perceptions of women as dependent and weak isolate women from planning and decision-making processes (UNISDR 2009).

Institutions often conceptualize gender relations in isolation, failing to explicitly address the multiple identities that intersect to shape women's vulnerabilities, roles, opportunities and capacities in disaster contexts. In contrast, the concept of intersectionality suggests that gender, race/ethnicity, class, nation, etc., should not be considered as separate, independent systems of difference and stratification. Rather they mutually construct one another (Hill Collins 1998; Valentine 2007). The application of intersectionality shifts the focus from simply adding up forms of disadvantage to an analysis of multiple axes of intertwined modes of subordination which are experienced in qualitatively different manners. An intersectional approach identifies a 'primary form of oppression', such as gender, and asks 'how that dimension of inequality is itself subdivided and crisscrossed with other axes of power and exclusion that are less well articulated' (Choo and Ferree 2010: 135). Likewise, intersectionality does not attempt to map fixed hierarchies of oppression onto victims, but rather examines how specific identities come to the fore and are employed by women as old gender regimes are destabilized in disasters.

Disasters and gender transformations

At its most basic level, a gender approach to disasters addresses women's survival needs, including safety from physical violence and sexual assault, housing, health care and clean water. Yet a gender approach to disasters should also move beyond basic needs to encompass a more long-term project of gender transformation (Bradshaw 2001). Disaster recovery may bring pressure to re-establish the normalcy of pre-disaster gender roles and regimes, in order to regain control. Yet the disruption disasters bring can also facilitate creative, even liberating, individual and collective processes to rework and reconfigure gender identities (Cupples 2007). This links to a focus on women's resilience and capacities, and the complex ways in which women anticipate, resist and recover from disasters.

Post-disaster gender transformations occur through several processes: foremost, the exigencies of the post-disaster period and the absence of men (who may be engaged in rebuilding and/or migration activities) open spaces for women to take on non-traditional tasks and roles that may destabilize reproduction of gender identities. They also offer opportunities to learn new skills, gain self-confidence and access to new spaces of participation in NGOs, social movements and coalitions (Always and Smith 1998; Gordon 2013). The breakdown of the home facilitates fragmentation and reconfigurations of identities. It potentially politicizes once private gendered spaces and activities. In addition, the arrival of external agents may offer women resources and engagement with new gender ideologies and practices that support reconfiguring gender relations and promoting new subjectivities.

Low-income women, who face intersecting forms of marginalization and often have in-depth local knowledge and networks, are frequently the first to mobilize at the grassroots level in the immediate aftermath of disasters. In later phases of recovery, these women are left to the side in favour of outside experts with greater formal education and professional experience (Krajeski and Peterson 2008). Opportunities for local capacity-building and the potential for more profound gender transformations are missed.

In a minority of cases, mobilization around urgent practical post-disaster gender needs deepens into more strategic calls for gender change. In response to Hurricane Katrina, for example, women organized to meet service needs, but also to advocate for women's reproductive health rights (Luft 2009). In Honduras, Hurricane Mitch's destruction and the subsequent implementation of a post-disaster land distribution plan allowed women's organizations to press for women's land rights (Casolo 2009). In the cases where post-disaster collective action has begun to address more transformative gender issues, several factors can be identified. For instance, such movements tend to build on a pre-disaster organizational and ideological base of collective action. Access to external support beyond the immediate groups of women impacted by disasters may also be critical.

The 2010 Haiti earthquake

Haiti's devastating earthquake of 12 January 2010 illustrates the importance and benefits of applying a gender lens to natural disasters. In the space of only thirty-five seconds, a shallow 7.0 earthquake brought enormous destruction, as over 200,000 Haitians were killed and 1.5 million displaced. The magnitude of the disaster brought an initial outpouring of commitments for $10 billion in foreign aid. Almost five years after the earthquake, however, recovery efforts have been limited to relatively small-scale achievements in housing and health care. Conditions for many Haitian earthquake victims remain precarious, and the post-earthquake period is littered with multiple missed opportunities (Schuller and Morales 2012). The gender analysis of the earthquake that follows illuminates long-term patterns of intersecting gender-, class-, and race-based vulnerabilities intensified after the earthquake, reasons why post-disaster aid has often been ineffective and possible pathways towards more transformative gender changes.

This case study draws on fieldwork in Haiti in 2011. It incorporates fifteen semi-structured interviews with national women's movement leaders and grassroots activists identified through snowball sampling techniques. It also draws on observations carried out at two internally displaced persons (IDP) camps. Interviews focused on the conditions of Haitian women in the post-earthquake period and women's movements more broadly, and were conducted in French or Kreyol, according to the preference of the interview participant. French-language interviews were translated by the author and Kreyol interviews by a Haitian interpreter.

Embedded Haitian inequalities

The devastating death toll and injuries from Haiti's earthquake reaffirm the observation that natural disasters are also the product of broader sociopolitical patterns of development. Haiti's lack of pre-disaster preparedness – particularly the absence of national emergency planning, poorly enforced building codes and weak healthcare and rescue services – reflect Haiti's historically high levels of poverty and inequality, foreign interventions and ineffective state institutions (Pierre-Louise 2011; Schuller and Morales 2012).

Haiti's population has long been highly stratified along class, gender and racial/ colour lines. In the late 2000s a majority of Haitians lived in extreme poverty and the country ranked 149th out of 182 countries in the UN Human Development Index. Haiti's low levels of human development are linked to the country's historical subordinate position in the global economy, neoliberal economic policies dating from the 1980s, and ongoing foreign military and economic interventions, particularly by the United States (Gros 2011). Haiti's racial hierarchies have favoured an economically and politically powerful minority of Haitians of mixed Caucasian European and African ancestry. Decades of authoritarian rule by the Duvalier regime were characterized by high levels of state repression, corruption and predatory behaviour. More recently, political polarization and conflict have centred on populist, nationalist mobilizations of the Lavalas movement of Jean-Bertrand Aristide and their opponents (Fatton 2011).

Haitian women's mobilization

Within this challenging context, Haitian women have faced additional legal, sociocultural and structural barriers. Patriarchal beliefs and practices have operated both in Haitian households and the public sphere (Faedi Duramy 2014). Almost half of Haitian urban households are headed by women, who have a relative degree of economic autonomy, but also a heavy workload responsibility for both reproductive and productive labour (Charles 1995). Women have historically been considered dependent, subordinate social and political subjects, and until 1979 Haitian married women were treated as minors by the state.

Haitian women have, however, long contested attempts to limit their participation in the public sphere: from the 1980s onwards, women mobilized not necessarily for explicitly feminist goals, but in opposition to the authoritarian Duvalier regime. Under the leadership of women who often had transnational experiences, activists fought for democratization, human rights and economic transformation, and in support of popular movements under Aristide (Charles 1995; Faedi Duramy 2014; N'Zengou-Tayo 1998). Although this activism was given little recognition, women still faced gender-targeted repression for their political activism, including the systematic use of rape. A core group of women's movements also emerged in recent years, with a focus on issues such as legal equality for women, family law and sexual violence.

In a pattern common to disasters, Haitian women played vital roles in the immediate aftermath of the earthquake. They mobilized to meet basic needs of food, water and shelter; dealt with the presence of the deceased; and looked out for the emotional well-being of children under traumatic conditions. As James (2004) notes, Haitian women's responses to hardships and disasters have often centred on cultural ideals of femininity and parenthood. In this case, the female activists interviewed describe their post-earthquake organizing activities as an extension of their gendered caretaking roles, motivated by survival needs and a broader Haitian culture of mutual support and collective work groups. The earthquake literally broke down the walls of private households and expanded women's domestic activities into the public spaces of local communities. It also opened spaces for women to engage in new types of activities, such as community leadership and advocacy work with external agencies to obtain access to aid and services.

NGOs in post-earthquake Haiti

The NGO recovery and rebuilding programmes that proliferated in the months following the earthquake were an intensification of a long-term pattern of Haiti's 'republic of NGOs'. In the 1980s, donors began to increasingly channel aid through NGOs, some 10,000 of which were operating in Haiti at the time of the earthquake (Schuller and Morales 2012).

As the years have passed, a number of criticisms have consolidated about the role and practices of governmental donors and international NGOs in the post-earthquake recovery and rebuilding process. Despite initial promises of large amounts of aid, relatively little has been accomplished (Kushner 2014). By 2014, 27,000 houses had been repaired and 7,515 new permanent houses had been built. Some 55,000 families received one-time payments of $500 to leave IDP camps (Regan and Milfort 2014). However, these efforts were clearly inadequate, as approximately 200,000 people remain living in roughly 300 IDP camps (Kushner 2014).

Criticisms have also been raised at the national level that the organization created to oversee the reconstruction process, the Interim Commission for the Reconstruction of Haiti (ICRH), was dominated by non-Haitians, and incorporated only a minimal role for civil society (Bell 2010; Farmer 2011; Fatton 2011). The hundreds of NGOs doing aid work are also seen as elitist, uncoordinated, disconnected from civil society and ethnocentric in their implementation of programmes in Haiti (Schuller and Morales 2012; Zanotti 2010).

In addition, the explosion of NGO activities in the post-disaster context undermined the already weakened Haitian state, as NGOs acted parallel to state agencies, often duplicating services (Gros 2011; Pierre-Louis 2011; Shamsie 2008).

The ICRH and some international NGOs have further promoted neoliberal economic reforms and market-centred models of development in post-earthquake Haiti – notably industrial assembly plants – that critics contend reinforce class and gender inequality in Haiti (Schuller and Morales 2012).

The Haiti earthquake also highlights the importance of identifying the ways in which women's gender identities intersect with class and racial identities. Women in the most economically precarious circumstances and who lacked extended family and support networks were the most likely to still live in IDP camps years after the earthquake. In interviews, female IDP camp residents emphasized that they had to contend with a lack of privacy and dignity, dangerous and uncomfortable weather conditions, and the risk of gender-based violence and sexual assault, and that they only remained because they had no alternative.

NGO gender mainstreaming

Many international NGOs working on Haiti's recovery have adopted gender-sensitive discourses and committed to special protections for vulnerable groups, including women (Abebe 2011). The actual implementation of such gender-sensitive policies, however, has been uneven. In practice, a number of NGOs have demonstrated a weak commitment to gender mainstreaming as seen through *de facto* exclusion of women from leadership positions; a lack of attention to issues disproportionately affecting women; weak connections with existing Haitian women's organizations; and reproduction of disempowering representations of women earthquake victims (Haiti Equality Collective 2010; Klarreich 2010).

As NGOs arrived with funds and resources in the weeks following the earthquake, the initial organizing activities of grassroots women activists and more established Haitian women's organizations were overlooked, as NGOs prioritized efficiency over gender inclusiveness (Bell 2010; Schuller 2011). *De facto* processes of gender exclusion occurred in such areas as camp leadership and food distribution. For example, in one IDP camp visited, male camp leaders openly intimidated women who attempted to speak out about conditions in the camps.

The women's limited participation in disaster recovery, decision-making and leadership has several implications. It increases the likelihood that women's needs will not be recognized or addressed, and weakens overall recovery efforts as women's knowledge, skills and capacities go underutilized. It also reinforces gender inequalities and misses opportunities for gender empowerment. In addition, the lack of NGO promotion of female camp leaders has left women vulnerable to sexual coercion to meet basic needs (Haiti Equality Collective 2010; MADRE 2012). This vulnerability to sexual assault and coercion has been further amplified, as police and United Nations Stabilization Mission in Haiti forces (MINUSTAH) fail to provide sufficient protection for women in IDP camps, particularly at night.

As mentioned earlier, the weak links between the international NGO sector and Haitian civil society has extended to women's organizations and more informal grassroots groups. Women's leaders interviewed noted that some international organizations such as Oxfam GB and UNIFEM have given important assistance and aid to their advocacy efforts. In other cases, however, international NGOs have unintentionally undermined Haitian women's organizations. For example, international NGOs have drawn away more experienced personnel with high salaries and shifted funding away from medium- to long-term gender projects towards short-term disaster relief. In interviews, women leaders state that these abrupt funding shifts destabilize women's organizations, which are often dependent on external resources to maintain basic operations (Zanotti 2010).

Contested representations

An additional issue in Haiti's earthquake recovery has been gendered and racialized representations of earthquake victims by NGOs, the news media and political elites. As discussed above, representations of women as passive victims of disasters are common. Such imagery of Haitian women predates the earthquake, and was intensified after the disaster as international NGOs competed to capture funds in a crowded aid environment. Such stereotypes are not simply external creations. Haitian women are implicated in what James (2004) terms the performance of victimhood and encoding the inequalities of *victims* and *rescuers*. In other instances, aid groups focus their interventions on Haitian child 'orphans', making women— particularly in their roles as caretakers and economic providers—disappear altogether.

If victimhood is closely tied to women's poverty, Haiti's poor, black urban communities have often been represented by the country's mixed-race, mulatto elite as violent and criminal. National and foreign media reinforce images of the country's black majority as backward, lawless and on the verge of chaos (Lundy 2011; Schuller 2007a, 2007b; Ulysse 2010). Such racialized representations have operated to stigmatize residents of IDP camps, undermined the effectiveness of institutional responses to earthquake victims and weakened victims' claims to services and resources. NGO security measures – such as fortress-like aid compounds and the hazard pay – increase the social distance between aid workers and those impacted by the disaster. Likewise, in IDP camps, MINUSTAH troops patrol in full uniform, as if in a war zone.

Women in IDP camps also face gendered stigmas. While black Haitian men are linked to criminal gang activities, women in IDP camps risk being labelled as prostitutes. On the one hand, the devastation of the earthquake, weak aid responses and camp leadership structures increase the pressure on low-income women to engage in sexual activities as a means to meet survival needs. At the same time, however, Haiti's embedded patriarchal sexual dichotomies, which place married women at one end and sex workers at the other, intensify social criticism of survival sex (N'Zengou-Tayo 1998). This association of women in IDP camps with sex work operates to delegitimize their claims to dignity, respect, assistance and services from the state and NGOs. It posits an implicit hierarchy of worthy and less worthy victims of disasters and can provide cover for state institutional unwillingness or failures in meeting women's basic needs in the recovery period.

Women activists interviewed, however, suggest multiple ways in which they appropriate and challenge these representations. They contest ways in which their knowledge, networking and contributions have been overlooked through stories of motherhood and caretaking, strength and agency. Women emphasize that they are not seeking handouts, but rather resources to further enhance their own reconstruction actions. They present their motivations as driven by conviction to help others. Their gender approach is one of cooperation over confrontation and their counternarrative emphasizes traditional discourses of the family, while also pressing forward for greater gender equality.

Post-earthquake gender mobilization

This chapter suggests that more transformative post-disaster gender processes cannot be centred only on NGOs and government agencies involved in recovery and reconstruction. Rather, we need to focus on women's capacities and embedded social networks. Along with the spontaneous grassroots women's groups that emerged following the earthquake, more established Haitian women's organizations have also been active in a series of advocacy campaigns. They seek to reshape the disaster reconstruction experience by placing gender equity issues and strategies not effectively considered in NGO/aid structures at the forefront. These women's movements have promoted gender mainstreaming with Haitian government ministries, ideological transformations, formation of women leaders as well as directed actions and services to women. Haitian women activists, often embedded in transnational networks, have organized important campaigns: for example against sexual- and gender-based violence following the earthquake (Haiti Equality Collective 2010; MADRE 2012).

Women's leaders interviewed emphasized a continuum between Haiti's long-term developmental and state failures and the actual earthquake. In contrast to the technocratic and narrow visions of some NGOs, many interviewees envision a much broader nationalist project of reconstruction and transformation led by Haitians, which includes women as full and equal participants. Unlike the non-political approach of NGOs, women's movement leaders define post-earthquake gender transformation as an inherently and necessarily political process. They contest emergency and short-term responses, preferring long-term change with strategies of education, raising awareness and coalition building. Haitian women's movements have especially focused on placing women in positions of power, and strengthening the Haitian state to incorporate cross-cutting gender issues.

Conclusion

This chapter has argued that a gender focus is essential in all phases of disaster-linked interventions; from prevention, to preparedness, response and recovery. While gender mainstreaming is now routinely incorporated into NGO- and many governmental disaster plans, it is often conceptualized in a superficial manner, as an 'add on' to existing disaster frameworks. In addition, gender-sensitive policies may not be effectively implemented because of resistance from within institutions, and the perception that gender should be addressed only after the immediate crisis has passed. In Haiti, weak institutional commitment and prioritization of efficiency over gender equity were key barriers to putting gender-sensitive policies into practice.

As the Haiti case suggests, gender-sensitive policies are necessary to recognize and effectively engage with women's vulnerabilities. These vulnerabilities in Haiti did not abruptly appear with the earthquake, but rather are linked to broader historical and cultural patterns of Haiti's subordinate position in the global economy, US economic interventions, state repression and corruption, and intersecting class and race inequalities. These broader inequalities are often intensified in post-disaster periods. The Haiti experience suggests the vital need to locate gender mainstreaming in broader policy contexts, such as neoliberal macroeconomic reforms that may undermine the impact and effectiveness of gender-sensitive policies.

This case also illustrates the importance of considering intersectionality of gender, racial/ethnic and class identities. In IDP camps, gender and class disadvantages reinforced each other in issues such as lack of physical safety and exclusion from participation in camp leadership. These conditions overall weakened women's sense of dignity and capacity to fulfil caretaking roles at the level of the family and beyond. At the same time, women's efforts to hold NGOs and their government accountable in the post-disaster period were weakened by racialized representations of black Haitians associated with violence and crime. These stereotypes were reinforced by institutions' emphasis on security over grassroots connections. These negative representations are also highly gendered. Association of women and girls in IDP camps with sex work and promiscuity has been used by political leaders and others to stigmatize female earthquake victims, justify inadequate state responses and contest women's claims to housing, land and other post-disaster services.

This chapter suggests a gender lens should identify and engage with both women's vulnerabilities and capacities. While low-income, Haitian female earthquake victims are very vulnerable, they have also shown tremendous resilience. With little to no outside support, Haitian women mobilized to meet basic needs and rebuild, shifting traditional gender tasks into more visible, politicized public settings. Drawing on histories of anti-authoritarian political and social mobilization, and transnational networks, they have launched a range of legal, political and educational campaigns (Haiti Equality Collective 2010).

Women employ more traditional gender frames such as motherhood and caretaking to lend moral weight to claims for resources and hold the NGO sector accountable, while contesting gendered and racialized stigmas, patterns of exclusion and rigid public/private divides which have silenced women. Women put forth a post-disaster rebuilding project led by Haitians that attempted to disrupt Haiti's longer-term patriarchal laws, institutions and ideologies. Yet many government agencies and international NGOs, focused on efficiency and professionalization, have given only limited status or recognition to these recovery activities.

Finally, this Haiti case study suggests several directions for future research on gender and disasters. It illustrates that addressing short-term emergency needs and transformative gender change following disasters does not always need to be a tradeoff and can potentially be mutually reinforcing. One focus of future work will be to more systematically identify the types of post-disaster conditions and interventions that most effectively bridge women's immediate post-disaster gender needs and longer-term strategic projects of gender equity. This approach would highlight opportunities that emerge when disasters disrupt gender regimes, and how these disturbances might be utilized. As suggested in this chapter, links to women's movements and an emphasis on women's capacities in informal and formal spaces appear to be promising paths. At the same time, however, greater attention will also need to be paid to the still understudied area of transformation of masculinities, in part to avoid overburdening women in processes of social change. In addition, our still-evolving understanding of intersectionality and its significance in pre- and post-disaster periods invites further research. Questions remain to be explored of how women's multiple axes of identities are reconfigured and advance and retreat in salience in the context of disasters. Likewise, we need greater understanding of the implications of intersectionality in designing and implementing disaster-related policies and interventions, and in gender-based (and other) movements that seek to both acknowledge difference and also construct coalitions with practical agendas for change.

References

Abebe, A. M. (2011) Special report—human rights in the context of disasters: The special session of the UN Human Rights Council on Haiti. *Journal of Human Rights*, 10(1), 99–111.

Always, J., and Smith, K. J. (1998) Back to normal: Gender and disaster. *Symbolic Interaction*, 21(2), 175–95.

Anderson, M. B. (1994) Understanding the disaster-development continuum: Gender analysis is the essential tool. *Focus on Gender*, 2(1), 7–10.

Batlan, F. (2008) Weathering the storm together (torn apart by race, gender, and class). *NWSA Journal*, 20(3), 163–84.

Bell, B. (2010) 'We bend, but we don't break': Fighting for a just reconstruction in Haiti. *North American Congress on Latin America (NACLA) Report on the Americas*, 43(4), 28–31.

Bradshaw, S. (2001) Reconstructing roles and relations: Women's participation in reconstruction in post-Mitch Nicaragua. *Gender and Development*, 9(3), 79–87.

Casolo, J. (2009) Gender levees: Rethinking women's land rights in northeastern Honduras. *Journal of Agrarian Change*, 9(3), 392–420.

Charles, C. (1995) Gender and politics in contemporary Haiti: The Duvalierist state, transnationalism, and the emergence of a new feminism (1980–1990). *Feminist Studies*, 21(1), 135–64.

Choo, H. Y., and Ferree, M. M. (2010) Practicing intersectionality in sociological research: A critical analysis of inclusions, interactions, and institutions in the study of inequalities. *Sociological Theory*, 28(2), 129–49.

Cupples, J. (2007) Gender and Hurricane Mitch: Reconstructing subjectivities after disaster. *Disasters*, 31(2), 155–75.

De la Puente, D. (2011) Women's leadership in camps for internally displaced people in Darfur, Western Sudan. *Community Development Journal*, 46(3), 365–77.

Dhungel, R., and Ojha, R. N. (2012) Women's empowerment for disaster risk reduction and emergency response in Nepal. *Gender and Development*, 20(2), 309–21.

Eklund, L., and Tellier, S. (2012) Gender and international crisis response: Do we have the data, and does it matter? *Disasters*, 36(4), 589–608.

Enarson, E. (1998) Through women's eyes: A gendered research agenda for disaster social science. *Disasters*, 22(2), 157–73.

Enarson, E., and Meyreles, L. (2004) International perspectives on gender and disaster: Differences and possibilities. *International Journal of Sociology and Social Policy*, 24(10/11), 49–93.

Enarson, E., and Phillips, B. D. (2008) Invitation to a new feminist disaster sociology. In B. D. Phillips and B. H. Morris (eds), *Women and Disasters: From Theory to Practice*. Bloomington, IN: Xlibris, 41–74.

Faedi Duramy, B. (2014) *Gender and Violence in Haiti: Women's Path from Victims to Agents*. New Brunswick, NJ: Rutgers University Press.

Farmer, P. (2011) *Haiti: After the Earthquake*. New York: PublicAffairs.

Fatton, R., Jr. (2011) Haiti in the aftermath of the earthquake: The politics of catastrophe. *Journal of Black Studies*, 42(2), 158–85.

Finch, C., Emrich, C. T., and Cutter, S. L. (2010) Disaster disparities and differential recovery in New Orleans. *Population and Environment*, 31(4), 179–202.

Fisher, S. (2010) Violence against women and natural disasters: Findings from post-tsunami Sri Lanka. *Violence Against Women*, 16(8), 902–18.

Fordham, M. H. (1998) Making women visible in disasters: Problematising the private domain. *Disasters*, 22(2), 126–43.

Fothergill, A. (2003) The stigma of charity: Gender, class, and disaster assistance. *Sociological Quarterly*, 44(4), 659–80.

Freudenburg, W. R., Gramling, R., and Laska, S. (2008) Organizing hazards, engineering disasters? Improving the recognition of political-economic factors in the creation of disasters. *Social Forces*, 87(2), 1015–38.

Gage, A. J. (2005) Women's experience of intimate partner violence in Haiti. *Social Science and Medicine*, 61(2), 343–64.

Ganapati, N. E. (2012) In good company: Why social capital matters for women during disaster recovery. *Public Administration Review*, 72(3), 419–27.

Gordon, L. (2013) Preserving family and community: Women's voices from the Christchurch earthquakes. *Disaster Prevention and Management*, 22(5), 415–24.

Gros, J.-G. (2011) Anatomy of a Haitian tragedy: When the fury of nature meets the debility of the state. *Journal of Black Studies*, 42(2), 131–57.

Haiti Equality Collective (2010) *Gender Shadow Report: Ensuring Haitian Women's Participation and Leadership in All Stages of National Relief and Reconstruction*, www.genderaction.org/regions/lac/Haiti/gsr.html (accessed Oct. 2014).

Hill Collins, P. (1998) It's all in the family: Intersections of gender, race, and nation. *Hypatia*, 13(3), 62–82.

Hyndman, J., and Alwis, M. d. (2003) Beyond gender: Towards a feminist analysis of humanitarianism and development in Sri Lanka. *Women's Studies Quarterly*, 31(3–4), 212–26.

Ikeda, K. (2009) How women's concerns are shaped in community-based disaster risk management in Bangladesh. *Contemporary South Asia*, 17(1), 65–78.

Irshad, H., Mumtaz, Z., and Levay, A. (2012) Long-term gendered consequences of permanent disabilities caused by the 2005 Pakistan earthquake. *Disasters*, 36(3), 452–64.

James, E. C. (2004) The political economy of 'trauma' in Haiti in the democratic era of insecurity. *Culture, Medicine and Psychiatry,* 28: 127–49.

Jones-Deweever, A. (2008). *Women in the Wake of the Storm: Examining the Post-Katrina Realities of the Women of New Orleans and the Gulf Coast.* Washington DC: Institute for Women's Policy Research.

Juran, L. (2012) The gendered nature of disasters: Women survivors in post-tsunami Tamil Nadu. *Indian Journal of Gender Studies,* 19(1), 1–29.

Klarreich, K. (2010) Haiti relief: Anger, confusion as authorities relocate homeless. *Christian Science Monitor,* 20 Apr., 1.

Krajeski, R. L., and Peterson, K. J. (2008) But she's a woman and this is a man's job: Lessons for participatory research and participatory recovery. In B. D. Phillips and B. H. Morris (eds), *Women and Disasters: From Theory to Practice.* Bloomington, IN: Xlibris, 207–16.

Kushner, J. (2014) Four years after the Haiti Earthquake, what have billions in US aid bought? http://www.globalpost.com/dispatch/news/regions/americas/haiti/140114/four-years-after-haiti-earthquake-aid-money (accessed Oct. 2014).

Litt, J. (2008) Getting out or staying put: An African American women's network in evacuation from Katrina. *Feminist Formations,* 20(3), 32–48.

Luft, R. E. (2009) Beyond disaster exceptionalism: Social movement developments in New Orleans after Hurricane Katrina. *American Quarterly,* 61(3), 499–527.

Lundy, G. (2011) The Haiti Earthquake of 2010: The politics of a natural disaster. *Journal of Black Studies,* 42(2), 127–30.

MADRE (2012) *Struggling to Survive: Sexual Exploitation of Displaced Women and Girls in Port au Prince, Haiti.* New York: MADRE, CUNY, CHRGY, Center for Gender and Refugee Studies, and KOFAVIV.

Manyena, S. B. (2012) Disaster and development paradigms: Too close for comfort? *Development Policy Review,* 30(3), 327–45.

Neumayer, E., and Plümper, T. (2007) The gendered nature of natural disasters: The impact of catastrophic events on the gender gap in life expectancy, 1981–2002. *Annals of the Association of American Geographers,* 97(3), 551–66.

N'Zengou-Tayo, M.-J. (1998) Fanm Se Poto Mitan: Haitian women, the pillar of society. *Feminist Review,* 59: 118–42.

Oxfam International (2005) *The Tsunami's Impact on Women.* Oxfam Briefing Note 30. Oxford: Oxfam International.

Pierre-Louis, F. (2011) Earthquakes, nongovernmental organizations, and governance in Haiti. *Journal of Black Studies,* 42(2), 186–202.

Regan, J., and Milfort, M. (2014) Four years after Haiti's earthquake, still waiting for a roof. http://www.ipsnews.net/2014/01/four-years-haitis-earthquake-tents-homes (accessed Oct. 2014).

Ruwanpura, K. N. (2008) Temporality of disasters: The politics of women's livelihoods after the 2004 tsunami in Sri Lanka. *Singapore Journal of Tropical Geography,* 29: 325–40.

Schuller, M. (2007a) Haiti's 200-year menage-a-trois: Globalization, the states, and civil society. *Caribbean Studies,* 35(1), 141–79.

Schuller, M. (2007b) 'They forgot about us!' Gender and Haiti's IDP Camps. Interview and translation Mark Schuller. *Meridians,* 11(1), 149–57.

Schuller, M., and Morales, P. (2012) *Tectonic Shifts: Haiti since the Earthquake.* Sterling, VA: Kumarian Press.

Shamsie, Y. (2008) Haiti: Appraising two rounds of peacebuilding using a poverty reduction lens. *Civil Wars,* 10(4), 413–30.

Ulysse, G. A. (2010) Why representations of Haiti matter more now than ever. *NACLA Report on the Americas*, 43(4), 37–41.

UNISDR (United Nations Office for Disaster Risk Reduction) (2009) *The Disaster Risk Reduction Process: A Gender Perspective. A Contribution to the 2009 ISDR Global Assessment Report on Disaster Risk Reduction—Inputs from the Gender and Disasters Network*. Geneva: UNISDR.

Valentine, G. (2007) Theorizing and researching intersectionality: A challenge for feminist geography. *The Professional Geographer*, 59(1), 10–21.

Wilson, J., and Oyola-Yemaiel, A. (2008) Professionalization and gender in local emergency management. In B. D. Phillips and B. H. Morris (eds), *Women and Disasters: From Theory to Practice*. Bloomington, IN: Xlibris, 194–206.

Wisner, B., Blaikie, P., Cannon, T., and Davis, I. (2003) *At Risk: Natural Hazards, People's Vulnerability and Disasters*. New York: Routledge.

Zanotti, L. (2010) Cacophonies of aid, failed state building and NGOs in Haiti: Setting the stage for disaster, envisioning the future. *Third World Quarterly*, 31(5), 755–71.

Part III

Organizational perspectives

11 Organizational accidents theories

Alessia Bianco Dolino and Maurizio Catino

Introduction

Among the broad range of phenomena encompassed by the disaster category, the focus of this chapter is on a specific type of event: organizational accidents. The past few decades have seen an increase in number, size and technological complexity of formal organizations. Simultaneously, the possibilities of adverse consequences for social systems as side-effects of human activities have been on the rise as well. These adverse consequences have become a crucial object of research among different disciplines. In this chapter, we focus on a specific view of organizational accidents, combining a classic sociological approach to human actions with insights from different disciplines such as organizational theory, management sciences, engineering, cognitive psychology and safety sciences.

More specifically, the attention sociologists have placed on the aetiology of organizational accidents refers to the intrinsic limits of human actions (Simon 1947, 1955, 1956; March 1994), and the side-effects emerging as unplanned and unwanted outcomes of those actions (Merton 1936, 1940, 1968; Hayek 1952). Thus, the 'dark side of organizations' (Vaughan 1999) has been framed from a sociological point of view as an unplanned and unwanted deviation from the rational and socially shared expectations about the way in which complex organizations should function. With respect to the insights coming from the various disciplines mentioned above, interest in the aetiology of organizational accidents is specifically linked to the organizational construction of those events; organizational actions and decisions, and structural characteristics, can contribute to decreasing the reliability of a system, setting up a work situation prone to errors and violations (Vaughan 1996; Reason 1997; Turner and Pidgeon 1997; Snook 2000; Hutter and Power 2005).

This chapter offers a critical review of the main contributions on organizational accident genesis from this socio-organizational point of view, and identifies the core practical implications of those contributions. More specifically, the chapter describes three theories on organizational accident aetiology: (1) the normal accident theory; (2) the organizational accident theory; and (3) the epistemic accident theory. For each theory, an illustrative empirical case is analysed. In conclusion, an analytical comparison of the three theories is discussed.

Before examining the theories in detail, some terms need to be defined in order to better identify the phenomena considered in this chapter. An accident is an unplanned and unwanted event with adverse consequences for people and/or the environment, including economic losses. Accidents should be distinguished from acts of sabotage or terrorist attacks, due to the explicit intent to provoke damage which characterizes them. In contrast, accidents are side-effects of human activities which, while pursuing other ends, unintentionally cause damage. Organizational accidents also differ from environmental disasters, such as earthquakes or floods, because of their close link with technological systems created and managed directly by humans. In addition, organizational accidents diverge from individual ones (Reason 1997): they happen to organizations rather than to individuals, they are extremely rare, but have important adverse and harmful health and environmental consequences. Their causal and contributing factors are usually multiple because of the highly complex technological systems in which they occur. Recent events, such as the *Costa Concordia* accident, which occurred near Giglio Island, Italy, on 13 January 2012; the Fukushima nuclear accident on 3 November 2011; and the Deep Water Horizon oil spill, which happened on 20 April 2010 in the Gulf of Mexico, are clear examples. Although the focus of this chapter is on organizational accidents, some of the concepts and ideas developed here are, in principle, relevant to better understanding individual accidents, as well as the broad set of phenomena embodied within the disaster category, such as environmental disasters or terrorist attacks.

Organizational accident: theories and empirical cases

Historically, we can consider the changes affecting theories on organizational accident aetiology as a shift from a 'first history' to a 'second history' approach (Table 11.1). Following the 'first history' approach, investigation of accident genesis stops once a technological and/or a human failure (errors and/or violations committed by front-line operators working closest to the system) is identified and classified as the cause of the accident. In contrast, following the 'second history' approach, the investigation does not stop once a technological failure and/or human error is identified, but aims to trace the organizational criticalities, as well as the intrinsic limits of human actions and decisions that allowed room for this failure to take place. Thus, technological failures and human errors are not seen as the ultimate cause of accidents, but as the result of a systemic exposure to failures affecting the socio-organizational context in which they occur (Turner and Pidgeon 1997; Reason 1997; Catino 2006; Woods *et al.* 2010).

The three theories analyzed here are all part of this 'second history' approach. We now examine the three theories in detail.

Normal accident theory

The normal accident theory (Perrow 1984, 1999) focuses on structural and organizational properties of organizations as crucial features explaining the

Table 11.1 Change of focus in organizational accident investigations (adapted from Reason 1997)

	Years	*Focus*	*Identified causes*	*Analyzed accidents*
First history	1960s	Technological factors	Technological component failures	Aberfan, Ibrox
	1970s	Human factors	Unsafe human actions (errors and violations)	Seveso, Tenerife, Three Mile Island
Second history	1980–2010	Organizational factors	Latent factors: e.g. time pressure, poor equipment, fatigue, training deficit and understaffing, inadequate or ambiguous procedures, fallacious control systems such as unreliable alarms, erroneous management decisions, design and construction lacunas	Chernobyl, Bhopal, Long Island, Eschede, Challenger, Linate, Überlingen, Columbia

genesis and dynamics of an organizational accident. This theory is developed by looking at complex systems such as nuclear power plants, the air transport system, chemical plants, weapon systems and marine transport.

The theory's key assumption is that humans – by definition – can fail. Thus, technological systems that are designed, built and run by human hands are intrinsically vulnerable to failure. Systems are constantly exposed to possible breakdowns: every single part of such systems can potentially work in an incorrect or unplanned manner. Consequently, safety measures such as redundancies or alarms are built in, to warn operators about possible failures or to prevent a single component failure from resulting in an accident. However, normal accident genesis is not linked to a single part's malfunctioning, but to the possible and unpreventable interaction between distinct and multiple failures, which also takes into account safety measures. Indeed, even if small, single parts fail slightly, they may interact in a way that is neither foreseeable nor conceivable, leading to the collapse of the entire system. Therefore, training, formal procedures and project specifications are not shaped in a manner that is appropriate for coping with this kind of event. Moreover, safety measures can act as part of the failure chain leading to the accident, instead of performing as an avoidance or warning. This unexpected interaction leads to catastrophic 'one-off' events linked to the structural characteristics of organizational systems. Accidents are thus normal or systemic, though extremely rare. They are unavoidable properties of highly complex systems: 'the odd term normal accident is meant to signal that, given the system characteristics, multiple and unexpected interactions of failures are inevitable. This is an expression of an integral characteristic of the system, not a statement of frequency' (Perrow 1999: 5).

The unexpected interactions of multiple single-part failures are influenced by two specific structural properties: the degree of connections and the type of interactions. *Connections* can be a tight coupling or loose coupling. Loosely coupled systems have loose links between the different parts of the system, and these parts can vary in a relatively autonomous way. In contrast, tightly coupled systems have tight connections, and each variation in one part of the system leads to an immediate variation in the others, thus an uncontrolled and rapid propagation may occur. *Interactions* can be linear or complex. On the one hand, through linear interactions (e.g. a production line), the production sequences are simply connected and easily monitored, as well as easily understandable by front-line operators. Thus, failures are easily recognized and stopped, before the occurrence of dangerous interactions. On the other hand, when interactions are complex, failures lead to unfamiliar, unforeseeable and unplanned sequences of events. These sequences are not immediately visible or understandable by a front-line operator (e.g. nuclear reaction), thus interruption of the chain of events leading to an accident becomes extremely difficult. Organizations with complex interactions and tightly coupled connections are more likely to face unexpected and unfamiliar failure interactions which lead to normal accidents.

The Three Mile Island accident: a normal accident case

The Three Mile Island nuclear accident was a partial core meltdown that took place in March 1979 in Harrisburg, Pennsylvania. It was one of the most dramatic events in the history of the nuclear industry. At 4:36 a.m. some water pumps stopped working in the second unit of the electronuclear plant. This malfunction blocked the flow of water to the steam generators, hampering the turbine and interfering with the coolant system of the reactor's core. The increase in pressure caused the opening of a relief valve, the PORV (pilot-operated relief valve), which was designed to release excessive steam into a collection tank. The PORV should have shut down after 13 seconds, having stabilized the steam and pressure levels. However, it remained open for 2 hours and 22 minutes, reducing the level of refrigerated water in the nuclear core. In addition, the indicator light in the control room, which signaled the interruption of current relating to the opening of the valve, switched off. This led the operators to believe that the valve had closed in the proper manner. During the following days, those two malfunctions (PORV and indicator light) led to a near meltdown (core fusion) and to the dispersion of radiation into the area around the plant (Perrow 1999).

According to a 'first history' perspective, the Three Mile Island accident can easily be classified as a case of technological failure affecting two components of a specific power plant: the PORV valve that remained open, and the indicator light that switched off although the valve was still open. In contrast, by looking at the event from a normal accident perspective, those technical failures are not just a technical malfunction affecting the Three Mile Island power plant, but the final trigger within a production system which facilitates, both structurally and systemically, a quick and not fully comprehensible escalation from the technical malfunctioning of one or a few components to an accident.

According to the organization typology proposed by Perrow, given the tight coupling of its connections and the complexity of its interactions, a nuclear power plant such as Three Mile Island can be considered a context which is prone to normal accidents. The tight coupling connections of the nuclear energy production system determined a rapid and uncontrolled propagation chain. Thus, a minimal variation in two parts of an extremely broad set of parts – PORV valve and indicator light – interfered with the basic stabilization processes of the nuclear core. The tight coupling connections, leading a single component's malfunction to trigger a chain reaction on the other components of the system, is related to another structural characteristic of the nuclear power plant: the presence of complex connections. Consequently, the chain reaction that the valve and the light malfunction triggered was also extremely difficult to understand for front-line operators. During the hours following the breakdown, the operators either ignored or did not understand the consequences of the opening of the PORV. This state of ambiguity, of 'not knowing exactly what is going on and what to do', lasted several days, until, due to circumstances that remain unclear, the situation gradually returned to normal. In substance, the situation was completely out of control; even after the accident the reason why the reaction stopped remained uncertain. Therefore, given the complex connections affecting the production process of a nuclear power plant, when faced with a change in a single part of the system, technicians completely lost any understanding of what was occurring within the system. In addition, the failure of a safety measure (the indicator light), set up in order to warn operators about the valve malfunction, also augmented the complexity and incomprehension of the situation, rather than producing an understandable warning which indicated a possible recovery plan. Consequently, intervention aimed at interrupting the reaction was not possible. To put it simply: if one does not know and understand what is going on, what can one do to stop it?

The normal accident theory shows how the Three Mile Island accident was embedded within the structural and systemic characteristics of the production of nuclear energy, and was, therefore, not just a technical failure. This is because single component failures within a complex interacting and tight coupling connected system can generate chain reactions on the core production process that are extremely difficult to understand and, therefore, to avoid and/or to interrupt by operators.

Organizational accident theory

The importance of looking at accident genesis and dynamics from a large organizational perspective was first emphasized by Barry Turner (1978; Turner and Pidgeon 1997). He frames accidents as the outcome of everyday organizational decision-making processes. Accidents are man-made, and follow from the interaction of social, organizational and technological processes. They are not unforeseeable events, but the result of a long 'incubation period', in which errors and dangerous events keep happening, even though they are not noticed or fully understood by the organization's management team. Turner's legacy remained undeveloped for a long period of time. However, several years later, Reason (1990, 1997, 2008) broadened Turner's work by tracing a systemic approach to human error in explaining the genesis of organizational accidents. Such a systemic approach clearly links human errors and violations to the organizational characteristics of the work context in which they occur, instead of looking at those errors and violations exclusively as forgetfulness, inattention, poor motivation and/or the negligence of people located at the sharp end of organizations. Reason's first analysis was on human contribution, but from the beginning, the focus rested on the role of organizational factors, rendering errors and violations by front-line operators possible. A key idea drives Reason's approach: even though an accident's trigger may be the action performed by a front-line operator (errors or violations), this action is induced or even produced by latent organizational factors. These factors result in a situation prone to such errors or violations (Figure 11.1). Accordingly, human errors and violations are framed as a consequence of the error traps located within the organization, rather than as an accident's cause. Thus, an accident's closest triggers become the organizational factors inducing errors and violations, rather than the errors and violations in and of themselves.

Looking at the adverse effects that latent factors can lead to, they can be classified in terms of error-inducing conditions and long-standing defense weaknesses. Examples of error-inducing conditions are: time pressure, poor equipment, fatigue, training deficits and understaffing. Examples of defence weaknesses include: inadequate or ambiguous procedures, fallacious control systems such as unreliable alarms, erroneous management decisions, and design and construction lacunas. More generally, latent factors are conditions, actions or decisions whose harmful potential persists silently over time, and becomes evident only when local factors (errors or violations) pass through the defenses of the system and contribute to an accident's occurrence. Latent factors in organizations are comparable to a pathogen organism in the human body: the more there are, the more the possibility of contracting a disease increases. Similarly, the number of

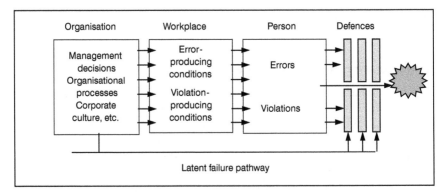

Figure 11. 1 The latent factors model (Reason 1997)

latent factors affecting an organization increases the probability of the occurrence of an error or violation leading to an accident.

The Swiss Cheese Model (Reason 1997) symbolizes the presence of a series of defenses (layers of cheese) protecting the system from dangers and threats in an organization. However, each layer has holes – the latent factors. Reason (2008: 101) states that:

> Only when a series of holes 'line up' can an accident trajectory pass through the defences to cause harm to people, assets and the environment. The holes arise from unsafe acts (usually short-lived 'windows of opportunity') and latent conditions. The latter occur because the designers, builders, managers and operators cannot foresee all possible accident scenarios. They are much more long-lasting than the gaps due to active failures and are present before an adverse event occurs.

The latent factors render the scene prone to accidents. Nevertheless, these factors are not the 'causes' of the accident, but conditions that increase the probability of an accident's occurrence. Therefore, identification and correction of the latent factors can strengthen organizational defenses, and decrease the probability that dangerous events will transpire.

The Linate accident: an organizational accident case

On 8 October 2001, at the Linate Airport, a thick fog descended and visibility decreased to between 50 and 100 meters. Shortly after 8:00 a.m., a Cessna with two pilots and two passengers on board received clearance from the control tower to leave its parking stand. The ground controller instructed the Cessna to head towards taxiway R5. The Cessna should, therefore, have taken the taxiway that loops around the aerodrome to the north, parallel to the take-off runway without crossing it. But it erroneously took taxiway R6, which reaches the main runway (Figure 11.2).

Continuing along taxiway R6, the pilots of the Cessna came to the marking 'S4' painted on the asphalt, a marking which was old and should have been removed. In communicating with the ground controller, the pilot mentioned the marking as well as the short approach to the runway consistent with taxiway R6. Both items of information could not have been mentioned by the pilot if the Cessna had been in the correct position on taxiway R5. The marking 'S4' refers to an identifier present on taxiway R6, not on taxiway R5. In addition, taxiway R5 does not lead to the main runway, but the R6 does. Nevertheless, the information was difficult for the controller to understand, because it was incompatible with his mental map of the Cessna's position. Yet the dissonant signals did not change the controller's mind-set: he was convinced that the Cessna was on the taxiway assigned to it. Shortly thereafter, when the Cessna was around 500 meters from the take-off runway, the controller – convinced that the Cessna was on taxiway R5 – cleared it to continue taxiing on the main apron (to the east of the runway). Consequently, the Cessna entered the main runway, committing what is known technically as a

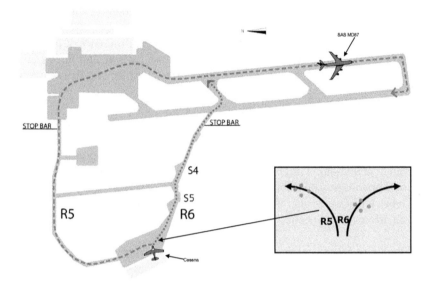

Figure 11.2 Linate Airport and the two airplanes (Catino 2010)

'runway incursion'. In the meantime, an SAS MD-87 with 110 people on board was preparing for take-off. The pilots of the two aircrafts were communicating with the tower and with their respective controllers on two different frequencies: Ground for the Cessna and Tower for the MD-87. Consequently, neither of the pilots heard the other's communications, and the two aircrafts were not visible to each other because of the fog. The MD-87 began its take-off run and collided with the Cessna, leading to the death of 118 people.

If we analyze the Linate accident from a 'first history' point of view, we can identify a series of errors and violations that made the accident possible: (1) the Cessna was not prevented from taking off, although neither of the two pilots were certified to operate the plane in conditions of low visibility (violation); (2) the Cessna crew took the wrong taxiway and entered the runway without specific clearance (error and violation); (3) there were communication failures between the tower and the Cessna pilots, as the ground controller did not realize that the Cessna was on taxiway R6 (error), and issued a clearance to taxi towards the main apron although he could not make sense of the reported S4 position.

In contrast, according to the organizational accident theory, accidents such as the Linate crash are the result not only of individual errors or violations, but of latent factors that render the organizational context in which they occur prone to those errors and violations (Catino 2010). In keeping with this perspective, we can recognize that those errors and violations were actually exacerbated by a series of organizational factors. The failures of the actors were embedded in a context characterized by numerous latent flaws and error-inducing conditions, which existed prior to the accident. Examples of those latent organizational factors are listed here. (1) The aerodrome standard did not comply with international standards (ICAO, Annex 14) as the required markings, lights and signs did not exist or were difficult to recognize, especially in low visibility conditions. Other markings were old and unknown to controllers (S4). (2) The ground radar system had been deactivated. Consequently, in poor visibility conditions the controllers had to rely on what the pilots told them. (3) The equipment for prevention of runway incursions, positioned at taxiway intersections with the runway, had been deactivated for several years. (4) The operational procedures allowed high traffic volume (large number of ground movements) in weather conditions like those evident on the day of the accident (reduced visibility), and in the absence of technical aids. (5) There was no system for reporting potentially dangerous events. As a result, the airport system was unable to learn from several previous near misses when aircrafts without clearance had erroneously entered taxiway R6.

Analysing the accident from an organizational accident theory perspective illustrates how front-line operators (Cessna pilot and Linate ground controller) had to operate in an organizational system equipped with weak defenses (e.g. no ground radar system), and which resulted in various error traps (e.g. presence of marking not in use). Generally, this analysis type shows how accidents are not the product of isolated unsafe actions, but of systemic organizational gaps. The air disaster occurred because of a concatenation of latent conditions (e.g. radar absence, unclear marking), unsafe human actions and an overwhelming assault on the defenses of the system caused by local triggers which created a trajectory of accident opportunity, resulting in the accident.

Epistemic accident theory

The epistemic accident theory (Downer 2011) is a recent development for explaining accident genesis. The theory's starting point is the 'canonical rational-philosophical model' (Collins 1992: 185) shaping engineering and technical knowledge. Following such a model, engineering knowledge is structured as a process governed by formal rules, incontrovertible premises and objectively knowable facts that are deterministically connected. Consequently, an accident's occurrence can be easily classified as an error. Such an error is by definition potentially avoidable, being the consequence of faults in the design, testing or implementation processes. More specifically, 'engineers, it is believed, work in an empirical realm of measurable facts that are knowable, binary, true or false, and ontologically distinct. So when the facts are wrong, this wrongness, and any disaster it contributes to, can be viewed as a methodological, organizational, or even moral failing: one that proper engineering discipline should have avoided' (Downer 2011: 737–8). In contrast, core insights coming from the constructivist perspective on scientific knowledge show 'that all "truths" are inescapably unproven and contingent—albeit to limited and varying degrees' (2011: 738). Consequently, 'from the perspective of the actors who define them, "true" beliefs can be *ontologically indistinguishable* from beliefs that are "false"' (2011: 739, emphasis in original).

By looking at an accident's genesis from this constructivist perspective, Downer can identify the intrinsic limits of the engineering knowledge as possible contributing factors in organizational accident genesis. Thus, organizational accidents can be seen not as occurrences 'that proper engineering discipline should have avoided' (2011: 738), but as the result of the intrinsic limits of knowledge that proper engineering discipline cannot avoid. More specifically, by looking at engineering and technical knowledge from such a constructivist approach, two qualifications emerge. First, there is 'an irreducibly social component to every "fact"' (Downer 2011: 739): technical engineering knowledge is strongly based on logical premises, tests and strict experimental methodologies; however, even in the most rigorous statements, a fundamental ambiguity persists. Thus, statements imply judgments. Second, the complexity of the real world cannot be reproduced in a closed laboratory; laboratory experiments are not able to take into account all the variables potentially affecting a technological component in the real world. In addition, the selection of relevant variables by researchers is based on assumptions and theories that are potentially weak, compared to the empirical world. Illustrating how it would be impossible to know completely and objectively the way in which technological components work in the real world, the constructivist approach highlights that: 'the idea of "failing" technologies as recognizably deviant or distinct from "functioning" technologies is an illusion of hindsight. By this view, there need be no inherent pathology to failure because there can be no perfect method of separating "flawed" from "functional" technologies (or "true" from "false" engineering beliefs)' (Downer 2011: 741).

Accidents, thus, cannot be the consequence of errors and/or of latent organizational factors, but can originate from the shared knowledge and statements upon which technological implementation is based. Essentially, the epistemic accident is a consequence of the structure of technical engineering knowledge. Thus, through the epistemic accident theory we can differentiate '*those accidents that occur because a scientific or technological assumption proves to be erroneous, even though there were reasonable and logical reasons to hold that assumption before (although not after) the event*' (Downer 2011: 752, emphasis in original).

These accidents present some properties and implications distinguishing them from the normal as well as the organizational ones. (1) Epistemic accidents are not predictable or avoidable *ex ante*. They are unforeseeable because by definition they elude any form of control, and cannot be identified before their occurrence. They question the assumptions and theories guiding a technological component's design, production and implementation. Thus, because the accident highlights new elements in contrast with such assumptions and theories, it cannot be intercepted before it occurs. They are unavoidable because their genesis is embedded in the structure of technical engineering knowledge (ambiguities leading to judgment formulation as well as distance between the real world and the laboratory). (2) Furthermore, the probability of the occurrence of epistemic accidents increases as a consequence of the introduction of new technologies – such a statement does not exclude the occurrence of an epistemic accident with technologies used over an extended period of time. However, given that well-established technology implies numerous experiments, observations, tests and ample research during operation, the probability decreases that new events breaching shared assumptions and theories will occur. (3) Finally, a learning process may follow an epistemic accident – it may retroact on the assumptions and theories, leading to a reformulation of existing paradigms. Thus, such accidents may generate knowledge improvement and learning through a reconfiguration of the previous assumptions and theories which underpinned the implementation of the technological components triggering the accident. Consequently, the occurrence of new accidents of the same kind may be interrupted, given the new knowledge developed as a result of the accident itself: 'by portraying all new technologies as "real-life experiments" with uncertain, but ultimately instructive outcomes, a constructivist understanding of failure highlights the instructive nature of accidents, as well as their inevitability' (Downer 2011: 756).

The Aloha Airlines Flight 243: an epistemic accident case

The Aloha Airline Flight 243 accident was an in-flight fuselage failure that took place on 28 April 1988, during a short flight between the Hawaiian Islands. At an altitude of 24,000 feet, an 18-foot fuselage section detached completely from the airplane, leaving the passengers exposed directly to the sky, speeding at hundreds of miles per hour. The pilots remained in control of the airplane and were able to make an emergency landing at Kahului Airport. Many of the people on board were injured, but only one person lost his life, the senior flight attendant who was sucked out of the vehicle when the fuselage separated from the aircraft.

In examining the Aloha accident from a 'first history' point of view, the official report following the formal accident investigation identified the cause of the accident as an exceptional maintenance failure. More specifically, because the process of fuselage assembly is very complex, the report concluded that the imperfect attachment of the fuselage permitted salt water to infiltrate between the metal sheets corroding them, finally inducing the fatigue crack that led to the detachment of the entire fuselage.

In contrast, from an epistemic accident theory perspective, this is just the point of departure in order to identify the intrinsic limits affecting engineering knowledge. The Aloha accident was a complete 'bolt from the blue' for the aircraft industry. The event literally 'stunned the industry' (Downer 2011: 743). More specifically, the accident indicated an unexplored development in multiple fatigue cracks to aircraft engineers: the possible and quick interaction between multiple aluminum fatigue breaks. Starting from specific assumptions and principles regarding aluminum fatigue breaks, engineers 'believed the 737's fuselage to be safe even if maintenance inspections fell spectacularly short' (Downer 2011: 742). What failed in the Aloha case was not just a fuselage, but an entire engineering paradigm, the *fail-safe* design, upon which maintenance procedures and the fatigue tolerance limits had been established. Following the fail-safe paradigm, engineers believed that the presence of multiple panels should guarantee that, in the worst case scenario, a unique panel would detach, depressurizing the cabin but preserving the integrity of the fuselage structure. In addition, for the same reason, a fatigue crack's limit of 40 inches per crack was established. This was determined according to the principle that no multiple failure cracks can grow from a level of 40 inches to a level that could lead the cracks to connect to each other in the time between two maintenance inspections. Nevertheless, the Aloha accident clearly proved such a conviction to be false. Consequently, the explanation of the Aloha accident genesis cannot be determined solely as a maintenance failure, but should also be linked to the failure of a paradigm. In fact, the paradigm, in theory and in practice, in defining maintenance programs (time between two interventions) and fixing acceptability limits (40 inches), did not consider the development and effects of multiple aluminum fatigue cracks on a 737's fuselage until the Aloha case.

An analytical comparison

As indicated previously, the three theories presented above can be located within a more general change in accident analysis (Table 11.1). All three approaches go beyond a reductive conception of accident genesis which focuses uniquely on human or technological triggers, by considering the intrinsic limits of technical engineering knowledge and the organizational and systemic factors characterizing the context in which accidents happen. If we look at the empirical cases presented above, the importance of such a change of perspective clearly emerges. For example, the Three Mile Island accident is not just a technological failure, but the possible result of the structural characteristics of a nuclear power plant (tight coupling connections and linear interactions). The Linate accident turns out to be more than just the errors of an air traffic controller and pilots, with organizational factors having contributed to those errors, as well as the weaknesses of the available safety measures in place at that time. The Aloha accident becomes something other than a fuselage maintenance error, revealing the intrinsic limits of engineering knowledge.

More generally, even if they are each extremely different, the three theories share a common approach to accident analysis. First, a systemic perspective is adopted, by which accidents are not caused by individual failures, but by the alignment of multiple contributing factors – each of which is necessary, but not sufficient, in leading to the accident's occurrence; and second, a conception is established which goes a step beyond a process of individual blame attribution. An individual blame attribution approach focuses on individual lacunas, aiming to identify front-line operators who should be held responsible for the accident's occurrence. Such an approach does not allow systemic weaknesses and organizational lacunas to be identified, thus it prevents organizations from learning. It favors the adoption of defensive behavior by front-line operators, leading to the non-reporting of problems or near misses. Moreover, it lowers circulation of relevant information, reducing learning opportunities (Vaughan 1999; Catino 2008, 2013). In contrast, the three theories presented here focus on aspects that are generally neglected by the blame attribution approach – such as the structural limits of some technological systems, the intrinsic biases affecting human knowledge and the

Table 11.2 Organizational accident genesis: an analytical comparison

Theories	*Main authors*	*Human contribution to systemic reliability*	*Implications for reliability*
Normal accident theory	Perrow (1984, 1999)	Irrelevant	Low (only structural changes)
Organizational accident theory	Turner (1978), Turner and Pidgeon (1997), Reason (1990, 1997, 2008)	Relevant	High
Epistemic accident theory	Downer (2011)	Irrelevant	Low (only ex-post)

interaction between human errors and organizational gaps that render a context prone to those errors.

Despite such common perspective on accident genesis, the three theories differ in some crucial aspects. Focusing on those differences, we propose an analytical comparison of the three theories, highlighting the practical implications of each one. More specifically, we examine two main elements differentiating the three theories: (1) the human contribution (front-line operators) to systemic reliability; (2) and the possible implications of each theory in increasing the reliability and safety of technological systems (Table 11.2).

According to the normal accident theory, human contribution to the reliability of organizations is not relevant, because accident genesis is necessarily linked to systemic and structural factors. As the analysis of the Three Mile Island accident highlights, front-line operators bear the consequences of a system that structurally prevents them from understanding and making sense of the work processes in which they operate, precluding any possibility to intervene in order to avoid and/ or limit the consequences of a failure. In contrast, according to the organizational accident theory, the human contribution to organizational reliability is extremely relevant, but linked with the need to guarantee an organizational context which contributes to front-line operators performing their task, instead of highlighting human errors and violations. As the Linate accident analysis reveals, organizational reliability is linked to the need to create the appropriate conditions to guarantee human reliability. Following the epistemic accident theory, front-line operator contributions are not specifically relevant, as an accident is seen as a consequence of the intrinsic and non-avoidable limits of techno-scientific knowledge. In fact, the Aloha accident reveals that front-line operators can promptly react to dangerous failures *when* they happen (emergency landing), but they have no possibility of avoiding or recognizing a failure *before* it happens. Consequently, the role of front-line operators is more prominent in normal accident theory than in organizational accident theory and epistemic accident theory.

With reference to the possible implications of each theory in increasing the reliability and safety of technological systems, the organizational accident theory includes models and principles that are useful in order to increase the safety, reliability and resilience of complex technological systems. The Linate case exemplifies this when identifying various organizational weaknesses that could be improved on (and actually were modified after the accident), such as the absence of a ground radar system and the confusing function of old markings. In contrast, the normal accident theory presents a more pessimistic approach: precisely because the factors relevant in organizational accident genesis refer back to the structure of organizations, it becomes extremely difficult to intervene on those factors by changing or eliminating them in order to improve the way in which complex organizations function. For example, if we look at the Three Mile Island case, the tight coupling connections characterizing a power plant represent a structural property of the system that is extremely difficult to modify.

Similarly, the epistemic accident theory does not open the door to the possibility of improving the reliability and resilience of a system by, for example, setting up safety measures that can avoid or reduce the consequences of a technical failure. Since the failure is embedded within the principles and assumptions driving the design, testing and maintenance program of a technical component, it is not possible to anticipate and limit the consequences of a technical failure before it happens. This lack of preventability renders the epistemic accident theory closer to the normal accident one. Nevertheless, the epistemic accident theory differs from the normal accident theory because of the possibility it provides to resettle a system after an accident occurs. More specifically, the accident reveals faults in the assumptions and principles adopted, thus providing the opportunity for rethinking the technical system to avoid accidents of the same type in the future. The Aloha accident opens the way for a change in the maintenance procedures, for example: once the development and propagation of multiple cracks are identified, the maintenance procedures can be redefined in order to avoid other unexpected fuselage failures from happening. Thus, the possible implications of this theory in increasing the reliability and safety of technological systems takes into account the ability of organizations to retune their activities taking the increased knowledge which emerges from the accident itself into consideration (only *ex-post*).

Conclusion

Our analysis of the different theories on organizational accident genesis and dynamics highlights how many accidents cannot be attributed exclusively to human or technological failure. In contrast, the theories underline the role of the intrinsic limits of technical engineering knowledge, and of organizational and systemic factors that make socio-technical contexts prone to an accident's occurrence. The analytical comparison of the theories illustrates how the three contributions cannot be considered general and 'all-embracing' theories. In contrast, they are specific theories allowing for a partial explanation of some aspects of organizational accident aetiology – not a complete explanation of the accident phenomenon as a whole. At the same time, a distinctive approach among the three theories emerges: some theoretical contributions envisage the possibility of improving accident prevention, while others, in referring to the radical uncertainty affecting those phenomena, consider organizational accidents as unavoidable, even if under certain specific conditions. From a theoretical point of view, the analysis shows how organizational accident studies can offer important insight, not only into understanding organizational accident aetiology, but also a broad set of objects of study such as organizational structures, decision-making processes, organizational culture and theories of knowledge.

From a practical point of view, the theories analyzed, as well as the empirical evidence coming from the study of cases of organizational accidents (Vaughan 1996; Reason 1997; Snook 2000; Catino 2010; Downer 2011), allow us to conclude the following:

- The 'human error' category runs the risk of oversimplifying the organizational accidents aetiology, focusing attention exclusively on one of the contributing factors that can lead to an accident, the final triggering one.
- The category of 'organizational error' should substitute the 'human error' one, focusing the attention on the organizational criticalities making the organizational context prone to errors and violations, despite the fact that front-line operators, being human, can by definition make mistakes.
- By increasing the number of organizational criticalities, the probability that an individual or technical failure will trigger an accident increases as well. Consequently, safety measures should target the organizational level, rather than focus solely on individual or technical ones. Safety measures exclusively targeting individual or technical levels do not change the latent underlying organizational factors that make the organizational context prone to errors and violations.
- Accidents should be considered an occasion to learn and through which to improve or change the available knowledge about the technology in use, as well as the latent organizational factors favoring human errors and violations.

In summary, by looking at accidents through different theoretical lenses, the work on organizational accidents aetiology can be considered a field of study still open to new discoveries which could favor a clearer and broader definition of this phenomenon. In addition, by looking in alternative directions for further research, we can identify approaches that go beyond the genesis of organizational accidents. For example, one of the more innovative and ambitious ones among them is the resilience engineering approach (Rasmussen 1997; Woods and Cook 2002; Hollnagel 2004; Leveson 2004; Hollnagel *et al*. 2006). Resilience engineering proposes a sort of paradigm change by identifying a new way of thinking about safety. More specifically, in resilience engineering, failures do not stand for a breakdown or malfunctioning of normal system functions, but rather represent the opposite of the adaptations necessary to cope with real-world complexity. Individuals and organizations must always adjust their performance to current conditions. Thus, success is linked to the ability of individuals and organizations to anticipate the changing shape of risk *before* damage occurs, and failure is simply the temporary or permanent absence of that.

Consequently, resilience engineering suggests a significant change in the objects of study scholars should focus on. According to resilience engineering scholars, we could learn more by looking at the millions of times in which things go right (everyday working activities), than by looking at the one time in which things go wrong – organizational accidents (Hollnagel 2009).

References

Catino, M. (2006) *Da Chernobyl a Linate. Incidenti tecnologici o errori organizzativi?* Milan: Mondadori.

Catino, M. (2008) A review of literature: Individual blame vs. organizational function logic in accident analysis. *Journal of Contingencies and Crisis Management*, 16: 53–62.

Catino, M. (2010) A multilevel model of accident analysis: The Linate disaster. In P. Alvintzi and H. Eder (eds), *Crisis Management*. New York: Nova Science Publishers, 187–210.

Catino, M. (2013) *Organizational Myopia: Problems of Rationality and Foresight in Organizations.* Cambridge: Cambridge University Press.

Collins, H. (1992) *Changing Order: Replication and Induction in Scientific Practice.* Chicago, IL: University of Chicago Press.

Downer, J. (2011) '737-Cabriolet': The limits of knowledge and the sociology of inevitable failure. *American Journal of Sociology*, 117(3): 725–62.

Hayek, F.A. (1952) *The Counter-Revolution of Science: Studies on the Abuse of Reason.* Glencoe, IL: Free Press.

Hollnagel, E. (2004) *Barriers and Accident Prevention.* Aldershot: Ashgate.

Hollnagel, E. (2009) *The ETTO Principle: Efficiency-Thoroughness Trade-Off: Why Things that Go Right Sometimes Go Wrong.* Aldershot: Ashgate.

Hollnagel, E., Woods, D.E., and Leveson, N. (eds) (2006) *Resilience Engineering: Concepts and Precepts.* Burlington, VT: Ashgate.

Hutter, B., and Power, M. (eds) (2005) *Organizational Encounters with Risk.* New York: Cambridge University Press.

Leveson, N. (2004) A new accident model for engineering safer systems. *Safety Science*, 42: 237–70.

March, J.M. (1994) *A Primer on Decision Making: How Decisions Happen.* New York: Free Press.

Merton, R.K. (1936) The unanticipated consequences of purposive social action. *American Sociological Review*, 1: 894–904.

Merton, R.K. (1940) Bureaucratic structure and personality. *Social Forces*, 17: 560–8.

Merton, R.K. (1968) *Social Structure and Social Theory.* New York: Free Press.

Perrow, C. (1984) *Normal Accidents: Living with High-Risk Technologies.* New York: Basic Books.

Perrow, C. (1999) *Normal Accidents: Living with High-Risk Technologies.* 2nd edn, New York: Basic Books.

Rasmussen, J. (1997) Risk management in a dynamic society: A modelling problem. *Safety Science*, 2/3: 183–213.

Reason, J. (1990) *Human Error.* Cambridge: Cambridge University Press.

Reason, J. (1997) *Managing the Risk of Organizational Accidents.* Aldershot: Ashgate.

Reason, J. (2008) *The Human Contribution: Unsafe Acts, Accidents and Heroic Recoveries.* Aldershot: Ashgate.

Simon, H. (1947) *Administrative Behaviour.* New York: Macmillan.

Simon, H. (1955) A behavioural model of rational choice. *Quarterly Journal of Economics*, 69: 99–118.

Simon, H. (1956) Rational choice and the structure of the environment. *Psychological Review*, 63: 129–38.

Snook, S.A. (2000) *Friendly Fire: The Accidental Shootdown of U.S. Black Hawks over Northern Iraq*. Princeton, NJ, and New York: Princeton University Press.

Turner, B.A. (1978) *Man-Made Disasters*. London: Wykeham.

Turner, B.A., and Pidgeon, N. (1997) *Man-Made Disasters*. 2nd edn, Oxford: Butterworth Heinemann.

Vaughan, D. (1996) *The Challenger Launch Decision: Risk Technology, Culture, and Deviance at NASA*. Chicago: University of Chicago Press.

Vaughan, D. (1999) The dark side of organizations: Mistake, misconduct, and disaster. *American Review of Sociology*, 25: 271–305.

Woods, D.D., and Cook, R. (2002) Nine steps to move forward from error. *Cognition, Technology and Work*, 4(2): 137–44.

Woods, D.D., Dekker, S., Cook, R., Johannesen, L., and Sarter, N. (2010) *Behind Human Error*. Aldershot: Ashgate.

12 Disasters in the sensemaking perspective

The Præstø Fjord accident

Morten Thanning Vendelø

Introduction

The sensemaking perspective first appeared in Karl Weick's book *The Social Psychology of Organizing* (1969). Since then it has continuously been developed by Karl Weick and his collaborators (see e.g. Weick *et al.* 2005), and by other organization scholars, such as Gioia and Thomas (1996), Fiol and O'Conner (2003), Maitlis and Lawrence (2007) and Rerup (2009). Since the mid-1980s there has been a growing use of the sensemaking perspective in organizational disaster research.

One of the earliest articles to examine sensemaking in the context of disasters, and 'one of the few to address how crises in organizations are enacted rather than encountered by those who work in them' (Maitlis and Sonenschein 2010: 552), is Karl Weick's seminal article from 1988, 'Enacted Sensemaking in Crisis Situations', in which he analyses the Union Carbide gas leak that occurred in Bhopal, India, in 1984 (Shrivastava 1987). Weick 'drew attention to the highly consequential role of cognition and action during crisis' (Maitlis and Sonenschein 2010: 551); a theme also pursued in his subsequent analysis of the Tenerife air disaster (Weick 1990) and the Mann Gulch disaster (Weick 1993a). More recent developments in this type of research exist in the form of Brown's (2005) analysis of the collapse of Barings Bank, Cornelissen *et al.*'s (2014) analysis of the Stockwell shooting and Vendelø and Rerup's (2009) analysis of the Pearl Jam concert accident at Roskilde Festival in 2000.

The aim of this chapter is to present the sensemaking perspective, as well as to introduce more recent theoretical developments of it, thereby showing how it can be applied in the analysis of a disaster. For the latter purpose, the chapter describes and analyses the Præstø Fjord accident, which occurred on February 11, 2011, when thirteen pupils and two teachers from Lundby Boarding School in Denmark capsized in a dragon boat[1] on Præstø Fjord, and suddenly found themselves in waters with a temperature of only 2° C. The outdoor teacher died – his body was discovered in the water fifty-three days after the accident – whereas all pupils and the accompanying teacher survived the accident. Yet, when retrieved from the water, seven of the pupils had been clinically dead for as long as two hours, and several of them will suffer from severe disabilities for the rest of their lives. Others sustained less severe physical damage, 'only' suffering from post-traumatic stress syndrome caused by the experience.

A core aim of the analysis of the accident is to produce insights about the sensemaking, which allows an innocent organizational activity to evolve and become dangerous, and in particular to explain why no attempts were made to stop the organizational activity as it unfolded. Finally, the chapter presents some directions for future disaster research, applying the sensemaking perspective.

The sensemaking perspective

The sensemaking perspective focuses on the relationship between cognition and action (Weick 1995), and is employed to explain cognitive and social mechanisms for dealing with ambiguity and uncertainty in organizations. According to Maitlis and Sonenschein (2010), sensemaking is best described as the process of social construction, which takes place when discrepant cues interrupt ongoing activity, and cause a retrospective development of plausible meanings that rationalize what people do. A core process in the development of plausible meanings is the bracketing of cues from the environment, and the interpretation of those cues based on salient frames. In sum, sensemaking is about creating an account of what is going on, by connecting cues and frames.

Sensemaking is described as an ongoing accomplishment through which people attempt to create order and make retrospective sense of the situations in which they find themselves (Weick 1993b). Sensemaking is both an individual and a social activity, and the two are not easily separated, as the cognitive process happens within the individual, but the individual always reflects his or her 'self' onto other individuals. Sensemaking is the *creation* of reality as well as the *comprehension* of reality, and thus, it is strongly linked to constructivism. Although sensemaking is a cognitive process, it is also closely linked to action, which precedes the construction of meaning, making sensemaking a retrospective activity.

The key concepts in a sensemaking analysis are: a frame, a cue and a relation, which together create meaning: 'Meaning = cue + relation + frame' (Weick 1995: 110). All three elements must be present for sensemaking to occur, regardless of the starting element. The substance of sensemaking is a frame, which summarizes past experiences such as traditions, ideologies, theories of actions or stories (Allard-Poesi 2005); a cue (e.g. a new experience, a new technology, a sudden change); and a relation between the two – as a cue or a frame alone cannot be interpreted, whereas a cue in a frame can either makes sense or not. According to Weick, 'frames tend to be past moments of socialization and cues tend to be present moments of experience. If a person can construct a relation between these two moments, meaning is created' (1995: 111).

Within the sensemaking perspective, scholars studying organizational disasters or accidents are likely to find inspiration in the concept of adaptive sensemaking (Cornelissen *et al.* 2014; Strike and Rerup in press), which refers to sensemakers' ability to first query initial frames and commitments, and subsequently mobilize alternative frames. Another recent development of interest to scholars of organizational disasters is Cornelissen *et al.*'s (2014) examination of the communicative processes through which individuals in collectives may commit themselves to possibly erroneous frames as the basis for their sensemaking, and thereby become blinded to the need for exploration of alternative framings. In a similar vein, Barton and Sutcliffe (2009) have shown how the inability to redirect ongoing actions deters organizational safety. In their study of wild-land fire management, they found that noticing early warning signs is not sufficient to drive a change in action, as the social processes of voicing concerns and actively seeking alternative perspectives are also needed to drive re-evaluation. Finally, institutional pressure and self-interest act as moderators of the process of redirecting action. Barton and Sutcliffe (2009: 1330) concluded that it is not because individuals miss cues about the need to change that they do not incorporate those cues into a new understanding of a situation, but because they are too embedded in the unfolding situation.

The Præstø Fjord accident case

Lundby Boarding School was founded in 2002, as a boarding school for 15–16-year-old pupils in their final year of secondary school.[2] The school admits up to 100 pupils every year, and has five study lines: drama, horse riding, music, outdoors and sports. The principal joined the school in August 2005, while the vice-principal has been with the school since 2002, and steps in when the principal is away. In addition, the school employs approximately ten teachers.

According to Danish law, the principal must oversee how the teachers perform their job, and at Lundby Boarding School this happens through regular evaluations of the teaching activities. In general, the principal trusts the teachers' competences, and does not micromanage, for example, by checking that the German teacher conjugates German verbs correctly. Thus, the core managerial approach applied at the school is best described as freedom under responsibility.

A core pedagogical philosophy pursued by the school is that it must encourage pupils to challenge themselves. In court, two pupils explained how the teachers often emphasized the need for participation in all activities planned for them and that, if students declined, they were sanctioned. For example, they would be penalized by being asked to run or bike a specific 8 km route. Another pupil explained that if a student did not show up for the morning runs, she or he had to cycle or run during a break in the afternoon. A fourth pupil mentioned that one would have been sanctioned for not joining the dragon boat sailing, and continued: 'once the outdoor teacher penalized me for eating one more cookie than allowed at a family meeting' (Damløv 2013d: 9:47 a.m.), 'I think it was too strict that I had to run 8 kilometers for eating one cookie more than allowed' (Damløv 2013d: 9:58 a.m.). A fifth pupil explained that they could see the teachers got annoyed when they declined to participate in an activity, 'so it was not easy to say no' (Damløv 2013d: 11:38 a.m.).

In particular, the outdoor teacher did not like pupils refusing to participate in activities. Elaborating on this, the assisting sports teacher explained that the outdoor teacher would be furious if a pupil did not want to participate in an activity at the school. A sixth pupil explained that occasionally the outdoor teacher could be very insisting: for example, during the morning runs he would sometimes push pupils to run faster, by running just behind them. In court, a former principal of the school explained: 'The outdoor teacher was a very engaged, positive person with lots of energy, but he was also a person, which I had to keep an eye on, for things not to get out of control' (Duemose 2013: 11:11 a.m.), as the outdoor teacher was seemingly not good at noticing if pupils felt unsafe when participating in outdoor activities. The former principal went on to explain that, when the outdoor teacher had planned an outdoor excursion, he had decided to take over the responsibility for the excursion and had changed the content of it, as he feared it would turn into 'a too exciting excursion': 'When I saw the plan, I became concerned that some of the pupils would not be able to complete it', he said (Duemose 2013: 11:15 a.m.).

The first pupil mentioned above, however, also described the outdoor teacher as cool, and said that he looked up to him and strived to live up to his expectations. The pupil who was sanctioned for eating one more cookie than allowed also explained that 'I had great faith in him, he was adventurous, and he liked to push boundaries' (Linddahl 2013: January 17, 9:49 a.m.). In general, the pupils felt safe when the outdoor teacher was around. 'The outdoor teacher was the type that could do everything. He was cool' (Damløv 2013e: 10:19 a.m.), one pupil said in court. When asked why everybody had strong confidence in the outdoor teacher, the accompanying teacher said it was difficult to explain to somebody who did not know him, but he was strong, cared about safety and was a very engaged person. Likewise, the principal and the vice-principal described the outdoor teacher as a competent and dedicated teacher, who was very conscientious and thorough with safety. The other teachers at the school also saw the outdoor teacher as a competent dragon boat sailor.

The organization of activities with dragon boats at Lundby Boarding School

The school acquired two dragon boats in 2006. From the beginning, the outdoor teacher – who was very enthusiastic about dragon boat sailing – held responsibility for the school's dragon boat activities, assisted by the assisting sports teacher, as he had extensive experience with elite canoeing and kayaking. Usually, the pupils sailed in the dragon boats in the school's introductory week, and again during the obligatory activity week at the beginning of September. The pupils did not receive any instructions in dragon boat sailing before they boarded the boats, but for safety reason they sailed along and close to the coast on these occasions. Apart from these two weeks the school had no regular activities with dragon boats.

The principal explained that the school regarded dragon boats as canoes, and followed the guidelines for safe kayaking and canoeing issued by the Danish Canoe and Kayak Federation. Hence, the school had not formulated its own rules for dragon boat sailing. As no written safety procedures for dragon boat sailing existed at the school, all safety measures were orally agreed upon between the outdoor teacher and the principal.[3] The principal also explained that there was a common understanding between the teachers and himself that they would not sail after October 31 and before May 1, or when the wind speed exceeded 5 m/s, and that pupils participating in dragon boat sailing should be able to swim. Yet, the accompanying teacher on the February 11 sailing knew that the pupils' swimming skills varied, and in particular, that two of the boys were especially poor swimmers. When asked in court what she did with this knowledge, she responded: 'I did not react to it, as I did not believe that we would need to swim. I had not imagined it, not even in my wildest fantasy' (Damløv 2013f: 2:02 p.m.).

The dragon boat accident on Præstø Fjord, February 11, 2011

The school planned to participate in a dragon boat regatta in Rostock, Germany, in May 2011, and the outdoor teacher and the assisting sports teacher had agreed to identify the best team for the regatta – 'but not in February' (Linddahl 2013: January 18, 2:10 p.m.), the assisting sports teacher explained in court. On Wednesday, February 9, 2011, a team from the outdoor study line sailed a 2.2 km distance, from Præstø Harbour to the mid-channel buoy in the fjord and back again, in thirty-six minutes.[4] The same distance was planned for the sailing on Friday, February 11, and the pupils were told that the aim of the sailing was to beat the time set by the team from the outdoor study line. According to the vice-principal, the pupils from the outdoor study line were positive when they returned to the school after sailing. Hence, when informed about the dragon boat sailing planned on February 11, he did not consider stopping it, as he trusted that the outdoor teacher knew what he was doing. The accompanying teacher was informed about the dragon boat sailing at 8:30 a.m. by the outdoor teacher. 'I had always felt very safe around him so I reacted by thinking "that's what we're going to do". I told him that there is some wind, but he tells me the wind blows from the West, and that it's not a problem in Præstø Fjord' (Damløv 2013f: 1:41 p.m.). Also, before they left the school, a pupil heard the accompanying teacher saying that the weather might be too rough to sail, but the outdoor teacher thought it would be alright. He assessed the weather to be better than on February 9 and told the pupils they had a good chance of beating the time set by the team from the outdoor study line.

When the dragon boat sailing was announced to the pupils on the morning of February 11, one of the girls did not want to go, and she complained to some of her fellow pupils. None of them really wanted to go either, but in the end they decided to join. In particular, one boy was not at all in favour of dragon boat sailing, and he had moved from the outdoor study line to the sports study line, as he had a very unpleasant experience with dragon boat sailing during the activity week. Yet he did not want to be sanctioned. Also, previously, the accompanying teacher had told him that he always complained, and therefore he did not complain about the planned sailing. Several of the pupils complained, saying it was too cold, and that they were freezing. One of the boys explained that it was very cold that day, and that there were ice floes on the water. 'We all complained all the way [in the bus going to the harbour] and asked if we could return [to the school]. The atmosphere was OK, but none of us wanted to go. ... The accompanying teacher and the outdoor teacher just asked us to shut up, and said it was going to be fun' (Damløv 2013d: 11:43 a.m.), one female pupil explained in court. As the group arrived at the harbour, some of the pupils joked about running away. A girl explained: 'There was no optimism, and nobody really wanted to go sailing. The outdoor teacher said that we should just do it, beat the team from the outdoor study line, and then we would go home and get some good food' (Damløv 2013d: 2:11 p.m.). Another girl was not happy when she read on the notice board that the sports study line would go sailing, because it was dark and cold: 'Actually, I did not want to go' (Damløv 2013e: 9:52 a.m.). The accompanying teacher remembered the pupils complained about going sailing, but could not remember why they complained, guessing it might have been because they thought the weather was too cold. 'Several pupils mentioned that it was cold and windy, one pupil perceived it as ordinary grumbling, and the outdoor teacher ignored it' (Danish Maritime Accident Investigation Board 2011: 11).

Before they left the school, the outdoor teacher asked the pupils to wear warm clothes and to pick a swim vest for themselves. When in the harbour, all apart from the outdoor teacher wore a swim vest. 'One of the girls asked him why he did not wear one, and he replied that they would never be so far from the coast that he could not swim to the shore' (Danish Maritime Accident Investigation Board 2011: 29).

On February 11, 2011, the wind blew with gusts up to a strong breeze (10.8–13.8 m/s) and the air temperature was 4° C. In court, a girl explained that the wind blew much stronger in the harbour than at the school, and thought, 'what do we actually do if the boat capsizes out on the water' (Linddahl 2013: January 17, 2:23 p.m.), but nobody dared to go against the outdoor teacher. When they departed from Præstø Harbour, the outdoor teacher asked one of the girls to steer the boat, but it did not go so well, and therefore, the outdoor teacher replaced her. This created an uneven distribution of weight in the boat, with approximately 15 kg to the port (the left side of the boat).

During the sailing, the waves hit one of the pupils and he found them to be fairly big. He and another boy got very wet, and it was unpleasant because of the strong wind. Also, he remembered that the outdoor teacher encouraged them to paddle faster, as they had to beat the time set two days earlier by the team from the outdoor study line. As the dragon boat advanced into the fjord, one of the girls experienced the waves getting bigger, soaking everyone: 'I thought, gosh, and my heart beat a little faster' (Damløv 2013c: 1:25 p.m.). She did not however experience things being out of control, although they did not paddle in sync. They had water on both sides of the boat, and went far out into the fjord, rather than staying close to the coast. 'I remember it seemed as if we went really far out. I can remember that because we went so far out, it was completely overwhelming to think that we had to paddle back again' (Damløv 2013c: 1:27 p.m.), the female pupil said in court. Particularly, she experienced that the wind blew stronger after they left the harbour. In fact, two of the girls remembered that the wind blew stronger out on the water: 'In the beginning we joked with one another, but as the water began to splash over the boat's gunwale, into the boat, and started knocking under the boat, then Karoline got fairly nervous, she made me nervous, and thereafter, others also became nervous', one of the girls explained (Damløv 2013d: 11:47 a.m.).

'When the dragon boat approached the mid-channel buoy from which it would return to the harbour, and where the fjord opens to the west, the forest protected it less from the wind and the waves coming from northwest. The wind got stronger, the waves higher, and the boat began to roll. Some waves felt more powerful and hit the boat hard, and water entered the boat' (Danish Maritime Accident Investigation Board 2011: 12). Twenty-two minutes after the boat left Præstø Harbour, and after sailing 1.7 km – but before reaching the mid-channel buoy – the outdoor teacher decided they should turn the boat around and return to the harbour, as the weather had got too bad. At that point it was no longer possible to beat the outdoor team's time of thirty-six minutes. The accompanying teacher also remembered that the outdoor teacher decided to return to the harbour because of bad weather. He asked the pupils to paddle faster, while he steered to port (left). First, the boat received water and wind from the front, and then from starboard (the right side of the boat). A strong wave and the wind created imbalance in the boat, which heeled to port. Instinctively, the pupils and the teachers leaned toward starboard. As the boat then heeled to starboard, this reflex repeated itself, now to port, creating further imbalance in the boat, which then capsized. When this happened, the pupils and the teachers were approximately one hour's worth of swimming away from the coast, the temperature in the water was 2° C, there was ice in some parts of the fjord, and none of the fifteen persons in the boat could feel the bottom of the site of the capsizing, as the fjord was approximately 2 metres deep there.

Immediately after the capsizing, the group panicked. In court a girl explained: 'I thought "This is simply not happening". It was hopeless. I cried and screamed, and everybody just panicked' (Damløv 2013c: 1:29 p.m.). Several pupils and the accompanying teacher remembered that the outdoor teacher looked very frightened; a girl explained: 'It changes from him being kind of superhuman to him being very, very frightened. I could see it in his eyes' (Damløv 2013d: 2:31 p.m.), and the accompanying teacher said: 'He grabs me and pulls me around the boat. He looked … fairly shocked' (Damløv 2013f: 2:16 p.m.). And then he shouts to them that they must swim to the shore.

The first person to alert the authorities was a female pupil who reached the shore after swimming for 50 minutes, and thereafter running/walking for 30 minutes, before reaching a mechanic in Præstø (Ruus and Nørgaard 2012: 8). The authorities were contacted twice more by two pupils who reached the shore 34 and 56 minutes, respectively, after the girl. The accompanying teacher and three more pupils swam to shore also, whereas the remaining seven pupils were clinically dead, as they had suffered from cardiac arrest when pulled out of the water, and had to be revived. The outdoor teacher was found dead in the water fifty-three days after the accident, and 3.5 km away from the site of the capsizing.

Making sense of the Præstø Fjord accident

Drawing on the sensemaking perspective as its theoretical basis, the present analysis focuses on how individuals comprehend reality, as well as how their actions contribute to the creation of reality. I begin by looking at the ways in which reality was framed at Lundby Boarding School, and at how the individuals involved in the accident engaged in sensemaking, as they connected frames and cues in their accounts of 'what was going on'. Then I discuss the social processes which prevented the interruption of the unfolding events, leading to the accident.

Enacted frames at Lundby Boarding School

By examining the involved individuals' and groups' framing of the school as an institution, as well as their framing of the school's dragon boat sailing activities, we can acquire insights about central aspects of the management's, the teachers' and the pupils' sensemaking, from the time when the dragon boat sailing was announced, till the boat capsized. The paragraphs below present two sets of enduring framings maintained at Lundby Boarding School.

The management and the teachers framed the school as a setting where teaching and other activities were undertaken by highly competent teachers, and where the pupils are encouraged to challenge themselves. The latter part of this framing was sustained by a culture which emphasized the pupils' obligation to participate in, for example, outdoor activities without further discussion, while the culture also acknowledged sanctions by the teachers as a necessity to maintain the pupils' focus on their obligation to take up the challenges presented to them. The framing maintained by the pupils shared the notion of the school as an institution which encouraged them to challenge themselves. Yet, it also reminded them that the teachers ruled the school, as they could sanction pupils when they refused to participate in activities. Thus, although the pupils admired some of their teachers, they also experienced a somewhat authoritarian organizational climate at the school.

When examining the framing of the school's dragon boat activities, one notes that the management, the other teachers and the pupils had great confidence in the outdoor teacher, and did not question his expertise in dragon boat sailing. In the past, there had been incidents where he went over the limit with regards to how much he challenged the pupils – but this had not affected the management's and others' belief in the outdoor teacher, as a person who knew what he was doing. The management framed the school's dragon boat activities as safe, and due to the strong confidence in the outdoor teacher's abilities, the principal did not see a need for more than an oral agreement about how the school conducted its dragon boat activities. In summation, there existed a strong commitment to the framing of the school's dragon boat activities as being in good hands.

Sensemaking during the dragon boat sailings in February 2011

As described above, the management and the other teachers often expressed confidence in the outdoor teacher's abilities as a dragon boat sailor, indicating their commitment to the framing of the school's dragon boat activities as safe, when organized by him. The sailing on February 9 did not challenge that framing: on the contrary, at least two cues, noticed during and after the sailing on February 9, confirmed it. For example, the team sailed quickly and safely to the mid-channel buoy and back again, and the vice-principal noted that the pupils participating in the sailing had a good experience and were glad when they returned to the school. Hence, the event appears to have made them frame sailing during the winter season as also being safe. Three observations from February 11 indicate this additional framing. First, the vice-principal trusted that the outdoor teacher knew what he was doing, and thus, he suspended the common understanding that dragon boat sailing could not take place between October 31 and May 1. Second, the accompanying teacher did not react on her knowledge that two of the boys who had been signed up for the sailing were not good swimmers, as she did not believe that they would need to swim. Finally, the outdoor teacher decided not to bring a telephone for the sailing, and he did not to wear a swim vest during the sailing, because, as he expressed to a pupil, they would never be so far away from the coast that he could not swim to the shore.

When the outdoor teacher announced the dragon boat sailing on February 11, as an attempt to beat the time set by the team from the outdoor study line, the accompanying teacher expressed concerns about the weather conditions to the outdoor teacher. Yet, when the outdoor teacher responded that the day's weather would not cause them any problems, she accepted this explanation immediately, as she had confidence in his judgements regarding the safety of the sailing. Hence, it appears that the accompanying teacher stopped voicing doubts about the safety of the sailing, due to her confidence in the outdoor teacher's expertise in dragon boat sailing.

After being informed of the planned sailing, several of the pupils from the sports study line complained about the weather being cold and the ice on the water, and told the teachers that they did not want to participate in the sailing. Hence, available cues suggested the pupils had some worries about the sailing, although they did not explicitly phrase them as worries about the safety. Yet, these cues fitted the teachers' framing of the pupils, as grumbling teenagers who needed to be encouraged to challenge themselves. Therefore, the teachers reacted by telling the pupils they had to go sailing, and that it would be fun. In spite of this, the pupils continued to complain while going to the harbour, as well as after arriving in the harbour – but none of them voiced concerns about dangers associated with sailing in the cold water and the windy weather, even if one of the girls speculated about what they would do if the boat capsized. Instead, several of them thought of the sanctions they would receive if they did not join, and thus, it appears that an unsafe organizational climate at the school caused them not to voice concerns about the conditions under which the sailing would take place.

Cues about the impact of the cold and windy weather were observed by the pupils as the dragon boat advanced into the fjord: the wind felt significantly stronger out on the fjord than inside the harbour; the waves began to knock under the hull; water splashed into the boat; they got wet. Some of the pupils were overwhelmed by what they experienced, but still they did not begin to voice doubts about their safety, although some of them started to get nervous. As the boat got closer to the mid-channel buoy, the outdoor teacher also observed the cues regarding the impact of the cold and windy weather, and he concluded the weather had got too bad to continue, and that they had to turn around, and return to Præstø Harbour. This, however, proved difficult, in part due to the pupils' and the accompanying teacher's limited skills in and experience with dragon boat sailing, causing the boat to capsize. After the capsizing, several of the pupils and the accompanying teacher observed a complete change in the outdoor teacher's appearance, as he went from being in control to being very frightened. Hence, it appears that he experienced a collapse of sensemaking, as his understanding of 'what is going on' had been wrong. Also, the generally accepted framing of a dragon boat sailing as safe – when organized by the outdoor teacher – had appeared as not valid in any situation.

A sensemaking explanation of the Præstø Fjord accident

In the light of the sensemaking analysis presented above and the collapse of sensemaking experienced by the outdoor teacher and others at Lundby Boarding School, it is now worth revisiting the second issue raised in the introduction: why no attempts were made to stop the organizational activity as it unfolded.

The question can only be answered by considering three factors, all of which contribute to the explanation. The first factor to consider is the strong commitment, exhibited by the management, the teachers and the pupils, to the school's framing of its dragon boat sailings as safe, when organized by the outdoor teacher. Two crucial consequences of this factor were: (a) neither the vice-principal nor the accompanying teacher doubted the safety of dragon boat sailings during the winter season when organized by the outdoor teacher – in particular, the commitment to the framing prevented them from exploring alternative frames, even if sailing with the boats during the winter season was new to the school; and (b) neither before nor during the sailing on February 11, did the pupils voice doubts about the safety of the sailing.

The second factor to consider is the pupils' fear of being sanctioned for refusing to participate in the dragon boat sailing, and thereby, what can be described as an unsafe organizational climate (Edmondson 1999). The important consequence of the unsafe organizational climate was that the pupils refrained from voicing their complaints about the sailing.

The third factor is the ease with which the outdoor teacher and the accompanying teacher dismissed the pupils complaining about the sailing as teenager grumbling – in particular, because it fitted very well with the teachers' framing of the pupils, as teenagers who needed to be encouraged to challenge themselves. Thus, the teachers did not need to seek alternative explanations of the pupils' complaining, as the school's pedagogical philosophy legitimized their rejection of the pupils' complaints.

In conclusion, the analysis of the Præstø Fjord accident shows that the interplay between three factors inhibited re-evaluation and redirection of the ongoing actions, which led to the accident. In particular, and due to various circumstances, neither the pupils, nor the accompanying teacher, nor the vice-principal, voiced doubts about the safety of sailing in February. Hence, nobody suggested the circumstances were sufficiently dangerous to call for a reconsideration of the planned sailing, and therefore, the outdoor teacher did not receive a strong signal about the need to reconsider the activity. However, from the very beginning, the outdoor teacher was highly embedded in the unfolding situation, as he wanted to identify the best possible team for participation in the upcoming dragon boat regatta in Germany, and thus, probably only a very powerful doubting or voicing of concerns would have convinced him to explore an alternative framing of the situation. Such powerful doubting or voicing of concerns did not materialize, in large part due to admiration of and respect for his expertise, as well as the pupils' fear of being sanctioned.

Future direction for disaster research employing the sensemaking perspective

This chapter has shown how the sensemaking perspective can be applied in the analysis of the unfolding of man-made disasters and organizational accidents. Although the application of the sensemaking perspective in the analysis of man-made disasters and organizational accidents is not new, unmapped territory still needs to be uncovered. As of today, we continue to have limited knowledge about the roles emotions play in relation to sensemaking during disasters, or while recovering from them. For example, it is known that disasters are associated with negative emotions, such as anxiety, which may take on the form of panic, fear and desperation (cf. Kayes 2004). Less is known about how these emotions influence the attention individuals give to cues, and whether such emotions can cause them to resort to less expansive forms of sensemaking, with limited action repertoires.

There is also a need to study how embodied experiences influence sensemaking, for example during search-and-rescue missions. There is a tendency to overlook how individuals use their bodies to make sense of the world (Maitlis and Sonenschein 2010), but it is very likely that the development of hunches about where to search for missing survivors, or practices for how to best rescue a person from for instance an entrapment in volcanic lava, are best understood by studying embodied sensemaking by search-and-rescue crew.

A third and final promising domain for disaster researchers is the phenomenon of inter-organizational sensemaking, which might be studied at the interface between, for example, off-shore and on-shore rescuing operators.

Notes

1 A dragon boat is a man-powered watercraft, traditionally made out of teak wood in the Pearl River Delta region of China's southern Guangdong Province. Dragon boats belong to a family of traditional paddled long boats found throughout Asia, Africa and the Pacific Islands. Nowadays boats are constructed for competitive purposes out of carbon fiber and other lightweight materials.

2 The main sources of empirical data presented in the chapter are two Danish television stations' (DR and TV2 ØST) live blogs from the court case, which took place almost two years after the accident, in order to determine responsibilities in relation to the accident. In addition, the accident investigation report produced by the Danish Maritime Accident Investigation Board is used here.

3 Lundby Boarding School informed the Danish Maritime Accident Investigation Board (2011: 28) that according to the oral agreement between the principal, the outdoor teacher and the assisting sports teacher, the following conditions should be observed when the dragon boats were in use:

 • All safety regulations should be respected.
 • The equipment should be in good condition.
 • The weather should be good (they had not agreed about a maximum wind speed and a minimum water temperature).
 • When needed, two teachers should participate.
 • The administration should be informed, and a list of participants should be supplied and a tour telephone should be carried along (some teachers, among these the outdoor teacher, had agreed that they could bring their own phone. For unknown reasons the outdoor teacher did not bring a telephone for the sailing on February 11).
 • Sailing should take place close to the coast (according to a common agreement, sailing should take place so close to the coast that the pupils could swim to the shore at any point in time).

4 Before Feb. 2011, the dragon boats had never been in use during the winter season, and according to the principal it had never been mentioned as an option by anyone at the school, including the outdoor teacher, who organized the sailings on February 9 and 11, 2011.

References

Allard-Poesi, F. (2005) The paradox of sensemaking in organizational analysis. *Organization*, 12(2), 169–96.

Barton, M.A., and Sutcliffe, K.M. (2009) Overcoming dysfunctional momentum: Organizational safety as a social achievement. *Human Relations*, 62(9), 1327–56.

Brown, A.D. (2005) Making sense of the collapse of Barings Bank. *Human Relations*, 58(12), 1579–1604.

Cornelissen, J.P., Mantere, S., and Vaara, E. (2014) The contraction of meaning: The combined effect of communication, emotions, and materiality on sensemaking in the Stockwell shooting. *Journal of Management Studies*, 51(5), 699–736.

Damløv, L. (2013a) Præstø-sagen dag 1: Minut for minut. January 10th, www.DR.dk. Danmarks Radio.

Damløv, L. (2013b) Præstø-sagen dag 2: Minut for minut. January 11th, www.DR.dk. Danmarks Radio.

Damløv, L. (2013c) Præstø-sagen dag 3: Minut for minut. January 15th, DR.dk. Danmarks Radio.

Damløv, L. (2013d) Præstø-sagen dag 4: Minut for minut. January 17th, DR.dk. Danmarks Radio.

Damløv, L. (2013e) Præstø-sagen dag 5: Minut for minut. January 18th, DR.dk. Danmarks Radio.

Damløv, L. (2013f) Præstø-sagen dag 6: Minut for minut. January 22nd, DR.dk. Danmarks Radio.

Danish Maritime Accident Investigation Board (2011) *Dragon Boat Capsizing, February 11th 2011.* Case no. 201102095 (in Danish).

Duemose, T. (2013) Præstø-retssagens dag 6: Minut for minut. January 22nd, DR.dk. Danmarks Radio.

Edmondson, A. (1999) Psychological safety and learning behavior in work teams. *Administrative Science Quarterly*, 44(2), 350–83.

Fiol, C.M., and O'Conner, E.J. (2003) Waking up! Mindfulness in the face of bandwagons. *Academy of Management Review*, 28(1), 54–70.

Gioia, D.A., and Thomas, J.B. (1996) Identity, image, and issue interpretation: Sensemaking during strategic change in academia. *Administrative Science Quarterly*, 41(3), 370–403.

Kayes, D.C. (2004) The 1996 Mount Everest climbing disaster: the breakdown of learning in teams. *Human Relations*, 57(10), 1263–84.

Linddahl, J. (2013) Præstø-ulykken for retten: Liveopdatering. www.tveast.dk, TV2 ØST.

Maitlis, S., and Christianson, M. (2014) Sensemaking in organizations. *Academy of Management Annals*, 8(1), 57–125.

Maitlis, S., and Lawrence, T.B. (2007). Triggers and enablers of sensegiving in organizations. *Academy of Management Journal*, 50(1), 57–84.

Maitlis, S., and Sonenschein, S. (2010) Sensemaking in crisis and change: Inspiration and insights from Weick (1988). *Journal of Management Studies*, 47(3), 551–80.

Rerup, C. (2009) Attentional triangulation: Learning from unexpected rare crises. *Organization Science*, 20(5), 876–93.

Ruus, T., and Nørgaard, M. (2012) Tilbage ved præstø Fjord et år efter ulykken: I mine mararidt drukner alle omkring mig (Back at Præstø Fjord one year after the accident: In my nightmares everyone around me drowns). *Ekstra*, 2(2), 6–15.

Shrivastava, P. (1987) *Bhopal: Anatomy of Crisis.* Cambridge, MA: Ballinger.

Strike, V.M., and Rerup, C. (in press) Mediated sensemaking. *Academy of Management Journal*, http://amj.aom.org/content/early/2015/02/09/amj.2012.0665.full.pdf+html.

Vendelø, M.T., and Rerup, C. (2009) Weak cues and attentional triangulation: The Pearl Jam concert accident at Roskilde Festival. Paper presented at the Academy of Management Meeting, August 7–11 Aug., Chicago, IL, 1–38.

Weick, K.E. (1969). *The Social Psychology of Organizing.* New York: McGraw-Hill.

Weick, K.E. (1988). Enacted sensemaking in crisis situations. *Journal of Management Studies*, 25(4), 305–17.

Weick, K.E. (1990) The vulnerable system: An analysis of the Tenerife air disaster. *Journal of Management*, 16(3), 571–93.

Weick, K.E. (1993a) The collapse of sensemaking in organizations: The Mann Gulch disaster. *Administrative Science Quarterly*, 38(4), 628–52.

Weick, K.E. (1993b) Sensemaking in organizations: Small structures with large consequences. In J.K. Murningham (ed.), *Social Psychology in Organizations: Advances in Theory and Research.* Englewood Cliffs, NJ: Prentice-Hall, 10–37.

Weick, K.E. (1995) *Sensemaking in Organizations.* Thousand Oaks, CA: Sage.

Weick, K.E., Sutcliffe, K.M., and Obstfeld, D. (2005) Organizing and the process of sensemaking. *Organization Science*, 16(4), 409–21.

13 Transboundary crises

Organization and coordination in pandemic influenza response

Erik Bækkeskov

Introduction

Globalization has more than cultural and economic consequences; new and greater risks to populations from natural and man-made disasters are emerging in its wake. Local disasters can increasingly cross borders and become global. This risk has already provided significant challenges within national polities and their systems of departments, agencies and local governments, as well as at the international level, populated by states and multinational actors.

Preparations for new influenzas with pandemic potential have received particular attention from public authorities since 2001. Pandemics are examples of the significant and growing phenomenon of transboundary crises (Ansell *et al.* 2010). Such crises are characterized by interdependence among actors (states, organizations, individuals) that are, to varying degrees, autonomous. This poses a potential challenge to coordination, particularly during response. With globalization, the rapidity of the spread of influenza is likely to be greater than in any previous period. Timely response thus comes to depend on rapid information exchanges. These factors have contributed to the development of new national and international capacities for gathering information on, and responding to, infectious disease outbreaks. Simultaneously, 'solving' influenza belongs to the domain of powerful and global epistemic communities within biomedical sciences. These develop and test solutions that are propagated at the international level, and legitimated through the scientific discourse. This leads to an expectation of uniformity in response: all humans share the same biology, so what cures (or prevents) influenza in one, does so in all. Coordination then means ensuring the use of effective interventions everywhere. Timeliness means that such interventions are applied when they are most effective.

Influenza is a familiar and widespread viral disease, particularly in the winter season. Such seasonal influenza mutates a little bit ('drifts') between the annual winter outbreaks. Much rarer is influenza with pandemic potential. Such a virus has mutated significantly ('shifted') from previously widespread influenzas. Most people have some level of immunity toward a seasonal flu because of its resemblance to previous years' outbreaks. In contrast, a large share of the population is likely to have no immunity to a pandemic flu; meaning, at worst, that a pandemic of this type brings with it high mortality rates. Coupled with the wide spread of the disease, this means death counts in the tens of millions (as in the 1918–20 Spanish Flu pandemic). However, flu pandemics can also be far less severe (as in 1957, 1968 and 2009).

Furthermore, influenza pandemics are global and simultaneous *social* events. A failure to contain or mitigate the disease in one region is likely to affect how people in other regions end up experiencing the disease (e.g. in terms of how many get it and how many are severely affected). Hence, what one government or agency does (or does not do) to respond may well affect how another can and should respond. Understanding how this global system of responders works is a vital component in improving future response efforts.

The 2009 H1N1 flu is the most recent pandemic, and was the first to test the recently developed response capacities. This chapter uses the record of this event and insights from public administration and political science to characterize the new system. It illustrates how different organizing principles (hierarchy, markets and networks) combine to create a global response which is non-uniform across national boundaries. It also illustrates how shared standards and norms (institutions) create isomorphic pressures on national polities, forming a global response which is ordered rather than chaotic.

Response is defined here to mean actions taken by single or multiple actors with the formal intention of mitigating the pandemic disease. That is, whether mitigation was achieved as effectively as it could have been and whether other real intentions were involved are beyond the scope of this chapter. The point is rather that millions of human beings and a host of organizations take actions that they would not have taken in the absence of a pandemic influenza, or in the absence of organization oriented at mitigating the pandemic. The shock of a novel pandemic disease and the presence of organizations designed to counter it are presumed to create and steer individual and collective actions.

In this chapter, I first illustrate that global pandemic response in 2009 was non-uniform in degree, but shared fundamental characteristics, across national boundaries. I then describe the emergence of the pandemic response system that yielded this response pattern. Finally, the overall response system is analysed by characterizing it in terms of how it employs different organizational principles and institutions. The system produces a pattern by centring pandemic response at the national level, while subjecting countries to common ideas and standards.

Transboundary differences and similarities in 2009 H1N1 pandemic response

The emergence of a novel H1N1 influenza in Mexico during April 2009 led national governments and international organizations to engage in various response activities. On 24 April, the Mexican government alerted the World Health Organization (WHO). Public health agencies and governments around the world mobilized their response mechanisms in the subsequent days, and on June 11, the WHO declared that H1N1 was a full ('phase 6') pandemic. Government responses continued into the subsequent winter. The record of responses to 2009 H1N1 thus offers illustrations of the extent of uniformity in contemporary, global pandemic response.

This illustration is aided by comparative methodology. In case comparisons, 'most similar systems' and 'most different systems' analyses are key methods for developing explanations of differences and similarities between cases (Przeworski and Teune 1970; Peters 1998; George and Bennett 2005). While the purpose here is illustrative, choosing cases at the extremes of systemic similarities and differences aids the categorization of pandemic response variations, in the same ways that theory development does. If differences are found despite contextual similarities, they suggest the impact of different forces. Conversely, if similarities are seen despite the wide contextual differences, they suggest the impact of similar forces.

The 2009 case showed that countries with similar conditions for vaccination policy can vary significantly in how they respond to pandemics. Figure 13.1 illustrates that similarly rich and mostly advanced democratic polities had very different policies on, and popular acceptances of, H1N1 vaccination in 2009 (O'Flanagan *et al.* 2011; Mereckiene *et al.* 2012; D.s.b. 2010; Folkenberg *et al.* 2011; Hine 2010; M.s.b. 2011; Public Health Agency of Canada 2010; RIVM 2011; Walter *et al.* 2011; CDC 2011). Vaccination is shown here because it is the critical policy in treating influenza at the population level (WHO 2005a). It is also a socially demanding intervention (Baekkeskov and Rubin 2014). National governments in these countries purchased vaccines and distributed them to health care providers. However, how many could be vaccinated depended on national policies on availability – that is, on how many vaccines the government purchased (expressed as the percentage of the national population that could receive vaccination given the government's order). In addition, even closely neighbouring populations in 2009 behaved very differently with respect to whether they accepted vaccination (uptake).

For instance, the close neighbours Denmark and Sweden purchased vaccines for 28 and 100 per cent of their populations, respectively. Subsequently, Danish authorities only offered vaccination to at-risk groups, and 6 per cent of Danes were vaccinated. Swedish authorities offered vaccination to all residents, and 60 per cent of Swedes were vaccinated. More availability did not necessarily mean more citizens vaccinated. Germany and the UK vaccinated similar percentages of their populations (8 and 10 per cent respectively) but the UK made vaccination available to its whole population, while Germany ordered vaccines for 31 per cent of its population.

The various population uptakes of vaccine (Figure 13.1 y-axis) illustrate how coordination at the level of citizens can matter to response efficacy.[1] Vaccination campaigns can work either by targeting unusually vulnerable individuals for protection, or by spreading immunity widely in a population to stop transmissions (general immunity). In order to aim for general immunity, vaccination must be offered to the general population. In countries like the UK and France, vaccination against H1N1 was offered widely in the fall of 2009. Yet 91 per cent of UK and

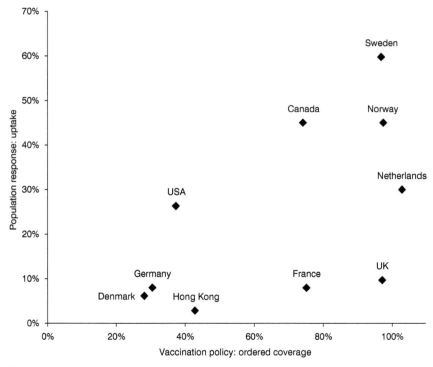

Figure 13.1 2009 vaccine availability and uptake in selected rich polities

92 per cent of French residents did not accept the offer. Hence, general immunity could not be achieved. This means that the primary national H1N1 pandemic response failed in two of Europe's most populous countries, because coordination was low at the citizen level. International variations in H1N1 responses are thus in evidence.

The 2009 response experience also showed that underlying such variations in degree can be similarities in the kinds of interventions that are used. If national responses had been truly idiosyncratic, chaos could have reigned. From an epidemiological perspective, some polities would have moved to use effective solutions, while others would have seemed to ignore efficacy. The pandemic response reality of 2009 could have been a hodge-podge of replicated efforts, initiatives that contradicted or counteracted one another, and missed opportunities. Such a chaotic state is not in evidence. Rather, national responses often shared fundamental characteristics.

Though the countries in the illustration above used different degrees of vaccination, all of them did use vaccination as a core response strategy. Such similarity in response type can be explained by shared features of the selected cases, such as national wealth (all could afford the drugs). So how similar were response strategies across very different contexts? The answer can be illustrated by comparing two cases of 'most different systems'. Figure 13.2 contrasts China

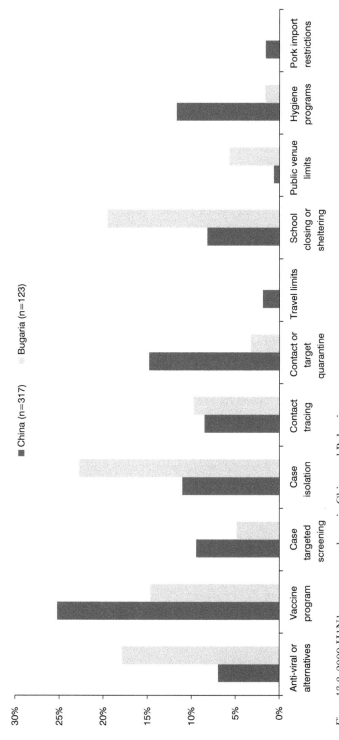

■ China (n=317)   ▓ Bugaria (n=123)

Figure 13.2 2009 H1N1 response emphases in China and Bulgaria

and Bulgaria, to illustrate the kinds of interventions that two very different polities favoured. The countries share the same influenza season (October–March). But in terms of history, size, location and culture, the countries differ markedly.

The analysis summarized in Figure 13.2 counts and categorizes mentions in national news stories of new interventions against 2009 H1N1. The two selected countries did vary in degrees. Looking at the modes, China placed most emphasis on its vaccination programme and on quarantines, while Bulgaria put most emphasis on isolation and closing schools. Reading the available news coverage shows that, for instance, China gained some notoriety in 2009 for quarantining foreign travellers in hotels for up to two weeks. In contrast, Bulgaria's main push against the pandemic occurred at the peak of spread in November, when schools were shut across the country. This confirms the pattern observed previously: different polities used different degrees of response policy.

The analysis also shows fundamental similarities between responses. It illustrates that it is possible to categorize the two national responses using a single typology of public health interventions. This is possible because few of the interventions mentioned in either country's news coverage were unique or idiosyncratic. China did use non-standard interventions, including a ban on pork product imports and encouraging uses of traditional medicine alternatives to anti-viral medications; but to the extent that news media mentions capture total effort, these arguably non-standard initiatives were marginal (they constitute at most 8.5 per cent of mentioned Chinese interventions). Hence, these very dissimilar countries were mostly relying on similar kinds of public health intervention to combat H1N1.

Given these illustrations, the 2009 H1N1 global response was non-uniform across boundaries but decidedly non-chaotic. How did this ordered variation come about? What creates response differentiation and what creates similarity? The next section begins the discussion of these issues by describing the development of the global pandemic response system that had its debut during the 2009 H1N1 pandemic.

Bioterror, bird flu and blindsiding

The development of global pandemic flu preparedness was spurred by a series of localized events with international implications. The key event that triggered political systemic attention was a bioterror attack in September 2001, one week after the infamous 9/11 events. A former US Deputy Secretary of Homeland Security has described the development in detail (Simonson 2010). Letters containing Anthrax spores were received by several members of the US Congress. Though Al-Qaeda turned out to have no hand in these mailings, the proximity of this bioterror act to 9/11 linked the issue to the larger war on terror. Several leading countries, the WHO and the European Union (EU) began in late 2001 to meet for annual discussions on bioterror response and prevention. In the second of these meetings (in 2002), *natural* biohazards were added to the agenda, alongside man-made. Among these newly recognized threats, novel influenzas were identified as particularly salient. They became parts of polities' efforts against bioterror.

The salience of the pandemic flu issue was supported by proximate experiences with two actual influenza-like (respiratory, viral) diseases. The first was the repeated emergence (in 1997 and 2003–5) of H5N1 avian influenza (bird flu) as a human disease in Hong Kong and other parts of East Asia. Though only a few people were infected and only from close contact with infected domesticated birds, the mortality rate among the hospitalized cases was an astonishing 60 per cent (WHO 2011). The 1997 H5N1 outbreak in Hong Kong had by some accounts been a significant wake-up call for the infectious diseases expert community (Lakoff 2008). But as an issue for political systems to deal with, the 2003–5 H5N1 outbreaks among people in Hong Kong and elsewhere in Asia, and in some birds populations in parts of Europe, is likely to have had a greater impact. The disease was still not communicated between humans. But the 2003–5 events showed that it spread with transported and, more critically, migratory live birds. The multiple occurrences of H5N1 in the period justified the existing bioterror-related attention to influenza by demonstrating that it could come to devastate global health.

The second disease event supporting the pandemic flu issue was the blindsiding caused by an unannounced spread of Severe Acute Respiratory Syndrome (SARS) from China's Guangdong Province (Huang 2004). Health authorities outside Guangdong were generally unprepared because of failed information flows. Chinese authorities had discovered SARS in December 2002. But official communications about the outbreak were hindered by the definition in Chinese law of public health events as state secrets.

The WHO first became aware of SARS when it hit the Vietnamese capital of Hanoi in late February 2003 (Health Canada 2003). The news spread when the organization issued a global alert on 12 March. When SARS was traced to China, its authorities had to admit that they had known, but stayed silent, about the original outbreak. Other areas affected by SARS had thus been unnecessarily blindsided. As a result, SARS came as a nasty surprise to health authorities and care providers in Hanoi, Hong Kong, Toronto, and other cities with large numbers of visitors from mainland China (Health Canada 2003).

Informed by the experiences with bird flu and SARS, the international preparedness efforts triggered by bioterror focused on transmitting information. SARS in 2003 was a direct cause of a significant change in the WHO's international reporting procedures in 2005, captured in that year's revised International Health Regulations (IHR). To comply, WHO Member State governments (including China) were obliged to and did build capacity to rapidly detect and formally report on emerging infectious disease threats. Bird flu meant that rich countries in particular scrambled to plan and materially prepare for a potentially severe pandemic. These efforts added up to a new system of pandemic preparedness and response. This system is described and characterized in the next two sections.

Organizing principles of global influenza pandemic response

> Although the 2009–2010 influenza pandemic was of low severity compared with those of the 20th century, this was the first ever opportunity for Member States to implement a 'for-real' pandemic response, drawing on plans made and planning activities undertaken in the preceding few years.
>
> (WHO 2010: 4)

Understanding how countries arrive at different degrees but similar kinds of pandemic response is aided by two perspectives. The first is a view of organizational types and levels of governance present in global pandemic response, used in this section to describe and characterize the organizing principles of the current system. The next section will add a second view, institutionalism.

Actual crises rarely fit neatly within the competencies or boundaries of a pre-existing organized entity ('t Hart *et al.* 1993). Pandemics and other multi-level and multi-jurisdictional crises offer extreme examples to show that this insight is manifest in how preparedness and responses have been organized globally since 2001. Multiple supranational and subnational jurisdictions are mobilized in pandemic response regions. Many organizations (departments, agencies, pharmaceutical providers, physicians, patients, etc.) have competences that can help make responses effective. A key issue of pandemic management becomes who, or what, is going to coordinate activities to ensure that they contribute to – and add up to – effective and timely pandemic response. At the level of ideal-type organizations, public administration theory offers three answers.

Hierarchy is the classical solution to coordination of activities between actors. It involves a designated leader that actors will follow. Leadership offers the promise of tightly coordinated actions, where each actor works in step with others, and adds what value it can, in accord with the leadership's instructions. A truly hierarchical pandemic response system could thus produce effective interventions at a global scale; much like any well-functioning hierarchical organization produces outputs.

Markets offer an alternative way to coordinate activities between actors. They rely on contracting, where buyers specify what they want from vendors and pricing is agreed. Contracting offers a potential to involve actors in pandemic response that would not otherwise take action or contribute. Buyers could thus mobilize a global response to pandemics by contracting with actors who have useful response capacities, much like markets generally bring forth goods that are in demand.

Networks offer a third mechanism for coordinating pandemic response activities. Networks are constituted of connections between independent actors. Through these, legally or morally responsible, or otherwise interested, actors might agree to voluntarily coordinate pandemic responses. They may also pool pertinent information that will help each of them to decide on actions that are compatible with what others are doing. Networks may thus create pandemic responses that vary considerably, as responders are acting on their own accord, while tending to work together and supporting each other, rather than contradicting or cancelling each other out.

Table 13.1 Sources of pandemic response leadership

Level of Governance	Formal Response Centre
International	WHO
National	Ministry of Health and public health agencies
Local	National centre OR local health dept. Health care providers
Responder hierarchies	Emergency/crisis manager, activated during response

These mechanisms contribute to pandemic response in the global system that emerged in the wake of bioterror, bird flu and blindsiding. Countries in a pandemic are interdependent (Thompson 1967; Ansell *et al.* 2010). All of them experience the event. Pandemic influenza spreads from one country to the next. Hence, the severity of the challenge in a country depends on what others have done to stop their own domestic spread. The extent to which all countries are acting to stop the disease matters to each of them.

In recognition of such interdependencies at several governance levels, public health systems have hierarchical organizations dedicated to offering guidance and creating pandemic response coordination (Table 13.1). The WHO has several formal tasks that place it in the international leadership position (defining and declaring a pandemic, providing response guidelines, managing the International Health Regulations). In each country, the national executive is formally in charge. Pandemic management responsibilities are often delegated to national health departments and related agencies. Similarly, local governments and individual organizations have formal leaderships, but often delegate to health agencies or to healthcare providers. Within organizations, there may be appointed crisis managers to head up the response.

In theory, the levels are hierarchically ordered. Each higher level of governance is putatively superior to the lower. Hence, the WHO (and in Europe, various EU agencies) 'lead' national governments. National governments lead their own administrations and local governments, and so forth. Hence, the great interdependencies of the kind of transboundary crisis that influenza pandemics exemplify have been resolved – on the drawing board – through an international hierarchy of responders.

The international character of pandemics is a particularly difficult issue to resolve through hierarchy alone, however. International relations scholars have generally recognized that policy coordination can be poor when multiple, sovereign entities make decisions in their own interest while also seeking to act collectively. At the level of making and implementing pandemic response policy, the required legal authority is national (or subnational) rather than international.

Capacity development for countering an actual pandemic disease also resides in individual countries. Among mature democracies, many national public health agencies began to develop plans for national pandemic responses in 2003 and 2004. Complying with the 2005 IHR revision also meant creating new or additional capacities for rapid outbreak detection and warning. National public health agencies have, in turn, encouraged planning by local authorities and individual healthcare providers. National agencies have also run simulations for the various designated national and local pandemic responders. Responding to a pandemic thus rests chiefly on national agencies and departments, which helps to explain why each country chooses its own mix of interventions.

This means that the putative global health hierarchy is an unreliable mechanism for coordination. The WHO and EU agencies have limited legal authority with respect to national governments. At best, national judiciaries can be used by the international organizations to force compliance with international commitments from national executives – a highly costly and time-consuming action. The organizations also suffer under information asymmetries: at the national and local levels, the 'agents' often control the information that their 'principals' need to police them. Therefore, disobedience may go unnoticed when it matters.

Networks thus offer an important organizational complement to the more visible hierarchies (Peters and Pierre 1998; Chisholm 1989; Sørensen and Torfing 2007). In global public health, a large number of networks exist between individuals and hierarchies: professionals have personal and professional networks; these can be short-lived or relatively permanent; health departments and agencies in government have formalized networks on specific issues and topics; they appoint people from their ranks to provide network 'nodes'; these people participate in meetings and generally interact with the other nodes.

Even if the WHO and national public health agencies cannot reliably command response actions, making networks meet and agree in time for an effective response to a pandemic influenza is a significant management task, and one which they are positioned to undertake. Such network 'metagovernance' lowers transaction costs and other barriers to coordination between actors by providing venues, norms and other resources (Sørensen and Torfing 2009). To the extent that the pandemic response spearheads in Table 13.1 are interacting with autonomous actors, they are probably best described as network metagovernors (Moynihan 2009). Certain agencies or departments may be assigned to this work by other network members (as facilitators, hubs, forums, secretariats, etc.). These network managers ease information flows and voluntary coordination and collaboration between network members.

Markets offer another critical complement to putative hierarchies; much response activity depends on private for-profit and non-profit organizations. Key examples are drug companies, logistics providers and private care givers and facilities. These critical responders are available to be coordinated by international, national or local authorities through contracting. A key part of spearheading pandemic response is thus to act as a purchaser in various markets, sometimes for scarce supplies, and in competition with other purchasers. For instance, international coordination of distributions of anti-viral drugs and vaccines that mitigate a flu pandemic comes about as the ultimate result of national contracting decisions. The contracts dictate when and to where producers send drugs.

Table 13.2 Multi-level system of pandemic influenza and other infectious disease response

Level of governance	Pandemic response infrastructure
International	WHO and EU hierarchies. Regular meetings and network committees. Information systems. Disease-specific and professional networks. Multinational supply chains.
National	Ministry of Health and Agencies. Pandemic committees. Horizontal and professional networks. Anti-viral stockpiles. Vaccine contracts and supply chains. Drug distribution supply chain.
Local	Local governments and agency hierarchies. Health care provider hierarchies. Emergency first responder hierarchies. Drug supply chains. Drug administration supply chains.
Responder hierarchies	Crisis management hierarchy. Expert/knowledge hierarchy. Early warning and epidemic intelligence division. Network nodes. Contractor contact points.

Some countries thus make purchases in pharmaceutical end-markets related to pandemic response. Many mature and rich democracies took material steps to prepare for medical treatment of pandemic influenza. National governments purchased and stockpiled significant quantities of anti-viral medications after the H5N1 scare of 2005. Between 2006 and 2008, several countries in North America and Europe also made contracts with pharmaceutical providers for vaccine supplies in the event of a 'phase 6' pandemic declaration by the WHO. Hence, several pharmaceutical companies were obliged to ramp up and ready development and production facilities for a rapid and large-scale vaccine roll-out to many countries in Europe and North America.

The combination of organizational forms described above at the international and national levels can aid understanding of the observed pattern of global pandemic response. A wider view of the organizing principles to include networks and markets can be shown as a 'multi-level governance system' (Table 13.2). The WHO acts as a global network metagovernor by mediating international information collection and exchange, and some planning and response coordination. At the WHO, the previously described 2005 IHR revision led to the creation of an Event Information Site which publishes postings from Member States on health events with global implications. The WHO also runs the Global Outbreak Alert and Response Network. This links Member States and aims for coordination of epidemic responses. Similarly, the EU runs an Early Warning Response System for rapid communications about disease outbreaks.

These information-sharing mechanisms are complemented by the various committees that regularly – and in emergencies – discuss international action, particularly among advanced and rich democracies. The aforementioned health security initiative meetings that began in 2001 therefore connect North America, Europe and the WHO in annual discussions. The EU instituted its own Health Security Committee in 2001, which has pandemic influenza preparedness and response as one of three foci, to be discussed in semi-annual meetings. In addition, the EU's own public health agency anchors formal networks of disease experts, and hosts regular discussions on international health threats.

The international level also includes relevant professional networks and related epistemic communities (Adler and Haas 1992). Virologists and epidemiologists share international meetings and publications. Many know each other from epidemiological training programmes and from long careers in global public health; calling up 'buddies' to get the 'scoop' (and cutting short formal reporting procedures) is not an unusual practice (PO Record 2009).

Finally, drug production and distribution is a global business. Hence, multinational pharmaceutical firms such as those mentioned previously and their supply chains and customers constitute vital markets that contribute to the pandemic response infrastructure at the international level of governance. Factories in a few locations around the world are supplied globally and, in turn, supply anti-viral drugs or influenza vaccines to the populations of many countries. Hence, countries have organizations of their own to counter the pandemic threat, but these are also more or less loosely connected through international networks, markets and theoretical hierarchies.

It is worth noting that the mix of organizations also exists at the subnational level. Actual treatment of pandemic disease is handled by healthcare providers (physicians, hospitals and dedicated facilities like vaccination centres). Unitary states (such as France and the UK) often place the bulk of decision-making about preparedness and response at the national departments and agencies. But federal systems (such as USA and Germany) and decentralized polities (such as Sweden) delegate pandemic management to regional authorities. Local governments and healthcare providers have thus been drawn into pandemic planning and exercises through delegation (a hierarchical act), and through information networks. As actors made responsible, they are formally obliged to prepare and respond. As network members, they depend on others for critical knowledge and 'good' response behaviours. National departments and agencies have pandemic response roles as network managers, in addition to hierarchical leadership and purchasing in markets.

Even within single organizations, pandemic response hierarchies can be contingent and need to adapt. The various kinds of individual responder organizations often rely on specified crisis management hierarchies. A key model used in pandemic planning is the Incident Command Structure (Moynihan 2009). This design calls for mobilizing, connecting and coordinating a variety of internal capacities and tasks that may be useful to effective response. The 2009 H1N1 pandemic experience showed that such temporary hierarchies may actually adjust during response, even formally. For instance, the US Centers for Disease Control and Prevention (CDC) began the H1N1 response by activating a response organization that emphasized operational (logistical, etc.) tasks (Ansell and Keller 2014). Epidemiological and virological experts were placed in subordinate roles. However, *knowledge* proved the crucial centrepiece of the CDC's actual H1N1 response in 2009; the formal crisis management hierarchy shifted to emphasize disease and epidemiological rather than logistical experts.

Epistemic isomorphism and institutional differentiation in global pandemic influenza response

The organizing principles used above focus on how actors in the present deliberate about problems and solutions, or choose who to follow or how to lead. This understates the place of action that follows from rules or norms rather than from full knowledge of behaviours that best serve an actor's interest or preferences. The isomorphism of shared ideas and values is particularly pronounced through the transnational force of epistemic communities (Adler and Haas 1992). The enduring and contextually differentiating forces of rules and norms are commonly studied as 'institutionalism' (DiMaggio and Powell 1983; March and Olsen 1989; Steinmo *et al.* 1992; Hall and Taylor 1996; Peters 2005).

Rules and ideas do not dictate policy choices – but they can direct them by defining the options 'in the box'. Thus, the conceptual pandemic response toolbox itself may be the substantial impact on interventions of the new global and national pandemic governance system. By identifying acceptable (scientifically defensible) ideas and qualified information, and by transmitting them through the many networks and market dealings, or 'soft' hierarchies headed by the WHO, the system can push countries and other actors to make response choices that are compatible. Sharing of ideas and information is thus likely to have made the 2009 responses more effective than results of myopic actions individually taken would have been.

A common toolbox partly exists by design. As described, the WHO and other international bodies have worked for common rules and conversations about biohazards and flu in particular since the late 1990s (cf. WHO 2005). In addition, the key sciences related to pandemic influenza are virology and epidemiology. As described, professionals in these fields are connected through transnational networks. Substantively, as in most natural sciences, international journals and meetings serve to regulate what counts as good and bad for public health (cf. Ferguson *et al.* 2006). Consequently, national or local experts who deviate from these norms are likely to lose professional status. These factors are likely to exert considerable pressures on national policy-makers and on expert groups advising them to use interventions that have been internationally defined and vetted.

However, shared rules and norms may not translate to identical actions. The international, epistemic push for uniformity confronts existing national (or even more local) rules and norms. Relevant health laws are national, and mores themselves differ between countries (Martin *et al.* 2010). These persist in ways that international negotiations and idea-sharing are unlikely to alter. For instance, civil rights make extensive uses of behavioural public health interventions – like isolation or quarantines – difficult in democracies. Similarly, different cultures have different ethical boundaries and understandings. Some countries may favour protecting the general population by isolating sick individuals, while others may prefer to immunize the general population to protect vulnerable individuals (Baldwin 2005; Vallgårda 2007). Being polite in some places and situations requires kissing those you meet (aiding flu transmission), while a wave is customary in others (hindering transmission). Limits on kissing behaviour come to matter in the former context more than in the latter.

Additional impersonal forces at the national level may also be in play to push national policy away from international uniformity. Economics is a constraint on pandemic response, with wealth and other endowments as significant international differentiators. It is expensive to buy vaccines and anti-viral medications, and not all countries can afford them for every resident. Vaccines against novel influenza can also be scarce. They take four to six months to develop and produce in large quantities with current technologies; in addition, different countries have different levels of access to such supplies due to stockpiles and contracting. Finally, shutting down people's movements to hinder transmission is costly. Weeks of inactivity in public spaces (schools and shopping venues closing), used to halt flu transmissions, is an extreme burden on any economy. Some societies, organizations or individuals may be more willing or able to bear such costs than others.

As in any distributional issue, there are also political issues in managing influenza with drugs and otherwise. For instance, drug makers and health professionals' interest groups may seek to sway policy-making, with different effects (or varying levels of success) in different polities. Politicians in charge may be engaged in simultaneous negotiations where the pandemic issue can help or hurt them. For instance, a national leadership may wish to avoid blame for pandemic response failures (Boin *et al.* 2008). Different opportunities to shield the leadership from blame could then mean international variations in response policies.

Epistemic communities that rely on transnational networks and shared norms and information mediated by the WHO and other international bodies, can help to explain why countries in 2009 seem to have shared a uniform understanding of the available means to overcoming a pandemic: these organizations and ideas created isomorphic pressures on national public health systems. But economics and national laws, ethics and politics help explain how the national organizations saddled with the bulk of the pandemic response work arrived at different uses for the interventions at their disposal: the national and local institutions create contextual conditions that responders take into account.

Conclusion: pandemic response coordination through standardization rather than centralization

The extensive preparedness for a pandemic influenza that gripped the world in the wake of bioterrorism, blindsiding by SARS and waves of avian influenza created a global system of early warning surveillance, planning and exercises. These new developments were embedded in pre-existing social contexts at national, local and organizational levels of governance. Hence, global pandemic response as it happened in 2009 was actually a product of innumerable actions taken nationally and locally.

This chapter has illustrated that national responses to the same event at the same time could be very different in what or how much was done. However, some essential similarities in the kinds of interventions that countries pursued were identified. Rather than the tight coordination that a hierarchical organization can accomplish, the global response was more than chaotic but less than coherent. It evinces a pattern of global similarities of intervention types, and local differences in degree. The pattern is a product of nationally centred responses that are drawn together by deliberate regulatory and information-sharing efforts of international health organizations and by the global epistemic community of public health professionals.

Europe offers an additional example: because of the EU and other international organizations, countries in Europe probably communicate and coordinate as well as those on any other continent. Nevertheless, ambitions for coordinated responses were greater than what was achieved in 2009. The EU and the WHO each assessed pandemic responses in their respective (overlapping) areas, and found that communication and coordination could have been better (European Commission, Health Protection Agency 2010; European Commission 2010; WHO 2010). The expressed ambition confronts the fundamental issue that nation-states are sovereign entities that tend to protect their sovereignty. The EU manages this issue every day and has inarguably increased the 'harmonization' of national policies since its creation. When variations persist, they may be irreducible beyond a point through centralized, hierarchical organization.

But the force in Europe of international efforts and epistemic ideas also shows that standardization works. Interests tend to be shared, most fundamentally, that of mitigating the disease. If there is an identifiable 'best practice' in pandemic response, then policy-makers are likely to want to use it. In democracies, they are also nearly certain to be punished in the public discourse if they do not (Boin *et al.* 2008). Epistemic communities and health agencies provide such identification and formulations. Deviation can go only so far before it becomes indefensible. Hence, in 2009, the multitude of autonomous actors chose H1N1 responses for themselves. But the isomorphic pressure from network managers, hierarchical centres and shared standards meant that a collective chaos arising from truly idiosyncratic choices is not in evidence. Epistemic standardization creates international coordination where centralization fails.

The outbreak of Ebola in Western Africa in 2014 illustrated some important limitations of a global public health event response system that is centred on pandemic influenza. As previously described, international coordination of responses has focused on information-sharing, while capacity to respond has been left to individual countries. But the Ebola outbreak showed that domestic action in highly developed healthcare systems misses the target. Capacity was missing on the ground in Africa, to treat patients and limit spread before it cascaded into a truly global problem. Ebola proved to be a fundamentally different challenge – in administrative terms – from the influenza pandemics that public health authorities had prepared for and been tested by.

Standardized understandings and information-sharing were evident in the Ebola response. The United Nations created facilities for mobilizing and coordinating efforts of many nations to provide on-site aid in the affected countries. But actual care facilities and staff to man them arrived in West Africa weeks or months after the numbers of cases of Ebola began their rapid increase. Furthermore, response effects were delayed by the absence of any pre-existing capacity to deploy treatment and epidemiology to the ground. Ebola demonstrated an unmet need – and perhaps a policy window – for rapid-response field capacity, to halt or mitigate transnational infectious diseases.

Pandemic response remains underexplored, in part because pandemics have been rare (cf. Keller *et al.* 2012). As asserted here, they are cases of transboundary crises that are extreme in scale. This means that they offer significant opportunities for more research into how different polities respond to similar crises; that is, to events that are uncertain, threatening and require rapid action from policy-makers and hands-on responders. Key frontiers include: developing theory that explains differences between polities in transboundary crisis response policy; the dynamics of related epistemic communities within each polity and at the global level; and whether international variations in pandemic flu response correspond to variations in how polities treat other diseases.

Note

1 The uptake is the percentage of the national population vaccinated, October 2009–January 2010.

References

Adler, E., and Haas, P.M. (1992) Conclusion: epistemic communities, world order, and the creation of a reflective research program. *International Organization*, 46(1), 367–90.

Ansell, C., and Keller, A. (2014) *Adapting the Incident Command Model for Knowledge-Based Crises: The Case of the Centers for Disease Control and Prevention.* Washington, DC: IBM Center for the Business of Government.

Ansell, C., Boin, A., and Keller, A. (2010) Managing transboundary crises: Identifying the building blocks of an effective response system. *Journal of Contingencies and Crisis Management*, 18(4), 195–207.

Baldwin, P. (2005) *Disease and Democracy: The Industrialized World Faces AIDS.* Berkeley and Los Angeles, CA: University of California Press.

Boin, A., McConnell, A., and 't Hart, P. (eds) (2008) *Governing After Crisis: The Politics of Investigation, Accountability, and Learning.* New York: Cambridge University Press.

Bækkeskov, E., and Rubin, O. (2014) Why pandemic response is unique: powerful experts and hands-off political leaders. *Disaster Prevention and Management*, 23(1), 81–93.

CDC (2011). *Final Estimates for 2009–10 Seasonal Influenza and Influenza A (H1N1) 2009 Monovalent Vaccination Coverage – United States, August 2009 through May, 2010,* http://www.cdc.gov/flu/fluvaxview/coverage_0910estimates.htm (accessed Oct. 2014).

Chisholm, D. (1989) *Coordination without Hierarchy: Informal Structures in Multiorganizational Systems.* Berkeley, CA: University of California Press.

D.s.b. (2010) *Ny influensa A (H1N1) 2009: Gjennomgang av erfaringene i Norge.* Oslo: Direktoratet for samfunnssikkerhet og beredskap.

DiMaggio, P.J., and Powell, W. (1983) The iron cage revisited: Institutional isomorphism and collective rationality in organizational fields. *American Sociological Review*, 48, 147–60.

European Commission (2010) *Assessment Report on EU-wide Pandemic Vaccine Strategies.* Luxembourg: European Commission.

European Commission, Health Protection Agency (2010) *Assessment Report on the EU-Wide Response to Pandemic (H1N1) 2009.* Salisbury: Health Protection Agency.

Ferguson, N.M., Cummings, D.A.T., Fraser, C., Cajka, J.C., Cooley, P.C., and Burt, R.S. (2006) Strategies for mitigating an influenza pandemic. *Nature,* 442 (26 July), 448–52.

Folkenberg, M., Callreus, T., Svanström, H., Valentiner-Branth, P., and Hviid, A. (2011) Spontaneous reporting of adverse events following immunisation against pandemic influenza in Denmark November 2009–March 2010. *Vaccine,* 29(6), 1180–4.

George, A.L., and Bennett, A. (2005) *Case Studies and Theory Development in the Social Scences.* Cambridge, MA, and London: MIT Press.

Hall, P.A., and Taylor, R.C.R. (1996) Political science and the three new institutionalisms. *Political Studies,* 44(5), 936–57.

Health Canada (2003) SARS in Canada: Anatomy of an outbreak. In: *Learning from SARS: Renewal of Public Health in Canada.* Ottawa: Public Health Agency of Canada, 23–42.

Hine, D. (2010) *The 2009 Influenza Pandemic: An Independent Review of the UK Response to the 2009 Influenza Pandemic.* London: Cabinet Office.

Huang, Y. (2004) The SARS epidemic and its aftermath in China: A political perspective. In S. Knobler, A. Mahmoud and S. Lemon (eds), *Learning from SARS: Preparing for the Next Disease Outbreak: Workshop Summary.* Washington, DC: National Academies Press, 116–36.

Lakoff, A. (2008) The generic biothreat, or, how we became unprepared. *Cultural Anthropology,* 23(3), 399–428.

M.s.b. (2011_ *Influensa A(N1N1) 2009 – utvärdering av förberedelser och hantering av pandemin.* Västerås: Edita Västra Aros.

March, J.G., and Olsen, J.P. (1989) *Rediscovering Institutions: The Organizational Basis of Politics.* New York: Free Press.

Martin, R., Conseil, A., Longstaff, A., Kodo, J., Siegert, J., Duguet, A.-M., de Faria, P.L., Haringhuizen, G., Espin, J., and Coker, R. (2010) Pandemic influenza control in Europe and the constraints resulting from incoherent public health laws. *BMC Public Health,* 10 http://www.biomedcentral.com/1471-2458/10/532.

Mereckiene, J., Cotter, S., Weber, J.T., Nicoll, A., D'Ancona, F., Lopalco, P.L., Johansen, K., Wasley, A.M., Jorgensen, P., Lévy-Bruhl, D., Giambi, C., Stefanoff, P., Dematte, L., and O'Flanagan, D. (2012) Influenza A(H1N1)PDM09 vaccination policies and coverage in Europe. *Eurosurveillance,* 17(4) [online journal] pii=20064. Available online: http://www.eurosurveillance.org/ViewArticle.aspx?ArticleId=20064.

Moynihan, D.P. (2009) The network governance of crisis response: Case studies of incident command systems. *Journal of Public Administration Research and Theory,* 19, 895–915.

O'Flanagan, D., Cotter, S., and Mereckiene, J. (2011) *Pandemic A(H1N1) 2009 Influenza Vaccination Survey: Influenza Season 2009/2010.* Bologna: Vaccine European New Integrated Collaboration Effort (VENICE).

Peters, B.G., and Pierre, J. (1998) Governance without government? Rethinking public administration. *Journal of Public Administration Research and Theory,* 8(2), 223–43.

Peters, G. (1998) *Comparative Politics: Theory and Method.* New York: New York University Press.

Peters, G. (2005) *Institutional Theory in Political Science: The 'New Institutionalism'.* 2nd edn, London and New York: Continuum.

PO Record (2009) *Participant-Observer (PO) Record for the [International Public Health Agency (IPHA)], Oct–Dec 2009.* Berkeley, CA: Emergent Networks and Distributed Sensemaking (ENDS) Project research archive.

Przeworski, A., and Teune, H. (1970) *The Logic of Comparative Social Inquiry.* New York: John Wiley.

Public Health Agency of Canada (2010) *Lessons Learned Review: Public Health Agency of Canada and Health Canada Response to the 2009 H1N1 Pandemic.* Ottawa: Public Health Agency of Canada.

RIVM (2011) *Chronological Overview of the 2009/2010 H1N1 Influenza Pandemic and the Response of the Centre for Infectious Disease Control RIVM,.* Bilthoven: National Institute for Public Health and the Environment (RIVM).

Simonson, S. (2010) Reflections on preparedness: Pandemic planning in the Bush administration. *Saint Louis University Journal of Health Law and Policy,* 4(1), 5–32.

Sørensen, E., and Torfing, J. (2007) Theoretical approaches to governance network dynamics. In E. Sørensen and J. Torfing (eds), *Theories of Democratic Network Governance.* Houndsmills: Palgrave Macmillan, 25–42.

Sørensen, E., and Torfing, J. (2009) Making governance networks effective and democratic through metagovernance. *Public Administration,* 87(2), 234–58.

Steinmo, S., Thelen, K., and Longstreth, F. (1992) *Structuring Politics: Historical Institutionalism in Comparative Analysis.* Cambridge: Cambridge University Press.

't Hart, P., Rosenthal, U., and Kouzmin, A. (1993) Crisis decision making: The centralization thesis revisited. *Administration and Society,* 25(1), 12–44.

Thompson, J.D. (1967) *Organizations in Action: Social Science Bases of Administrative Theories.* 1st edn, New York: McGraw-Hill.

Vallgårda, S. (2007) Public health policies: A Scandinavian model?. *Scandinavian Journal of Public Health,* 35(2), 205–11.

Walter, D., Böhmer, M.M., van der Heiden, M., Reiter, S., Krause, G., and Wichmann, O. (2011) Monitoring pandemic influenza A(H1N1) vaccination coverage in Germany 2009–10: Results from thirteen consecutive cross-sectional surveys. *Vaccine,* 29(23), 4008–12.

WHO (2005a) Influenza vaccines. *Weekly Epidemiological Record,* 19 Aug., 80(33), 279–87.

WHO (2005b) *WHO Global Influenza Preparedness Plan: The Role of WHO and Recommendations for National Measures Before and During Pandemics.* Geneva: World Health Organization.

WHO (2010) *Recommendations for Good Practice in Pandemic Preparedness.* Copenhagen: World Health Organization Regional Office for Europe.

WHO (2011) FAQs: H5N1 influenza, http://www.who.int/influenza/human_animal_interface/avian_influenza/h5n1_research/faqs/en (accessed Oct. 2014).

Part IV

Disaster intervention perspectives

14 Disaster financing in a developing country context

Peter Fisker, Henrik Hansen and John Rand

Introduction

The frequency and severity of disasters are on the rise, and catastrophic events have been termed one of the hallmarks of the 21st century (Michel-Kerjan 2010). In addition to human and environmental losses, disasters inflict substantial economic costs on societies that must be covered by individuals, private companies or governments. Thus, with the increasing frequency and severity of disasters, a need follows to look at ways of reducing the economic losses. Faced with the risk of disasters, individuals as well as governments essentially have two options for reducing the economic costs: *mitigation* and/or *risk financing*. On one hand, disaster mitigation helps prevent or reduce economic losses by reducing the physical vulnerability to hazards. On the other hand, disaster risk financing helps prevent and reduce the losses by reducing the financial vulnerability once the hazards have turned into catastrophic events. As long as catastrophic events cannot be eliminated completely, risk finance arrangements and institutions are needed to reduce societies' economic vulnerability and increase their resilience.

Munich Re (2014) has recorded a total of 20,700 loss events (geophysical, meteorological, hydrological and climatological) from natural disasters over the period from 1980 to 2013. The events gave rise to a total economic loss of US$4,100 billion (2013 prices) of which less than 25 per cent, US$1,000 billion, was insured in the formal insurance market. A split of the events along developed country regions (North America, Europe and Australia/Oceania) and developing country regions (Africa, Asia and South America) reveals a quite even distribution of loss events and total costs, with 48 per cent of the events occurring in the three developing country regions, giving rise to 45 per cent of the total losses. Thus, the average cost of the loss events was US$209 million in developed countries and only slightly lower, US$186 million, in developing counties. However, when it comes to insured costs, only 15 per cent of the total accrued to the developing country regions. Hence, while the insurance coverage rate (the share of insured cost to total cost) was 38 per cent in the developed countries, it was a mere 8 per cent in the less developed regions. The use of market-based insurance for disaster finance is therefore heavily skewed across developed and developing countries, in line with uses of other financial instruments.

While market-based insurance is typically seen as the best solution for transferring the risk of disaster losses, traditional insurance schemes are not necessarily the best options for individuals and governments in developing countries. The disaster risk may not be insurable, in the sense that the lowest price any insurer demands is higher than the price any buyer will give. Such discrepancies may well arise in insurance markets with high transaction costs, limited and uncertain information and low-income citizens. Acknowledging these limitations, governments and international financial institutions alike, as well as global insurance companies, have been active in developing new disaster financing instruments for citizens and governments in the developing and emerging-economy countries.

In this chapter we give examples of the available financing instruments, and assess the usefulness and actual use of these instruments. We start with a brief introduction to classical risk finance before we describe the recent developments in disaster insurance, with a focus on the instruments used in developing countries. Subsequently we describe how complex disaster risks and costs are estimated using computer-based simulation models. Unfortunately, the coverage of disaster risks in developing countries is sparse and the state of the art may not be sufficiently good for a fair pricing of the financing instruments, which is why we conclude by arguing for public support for development of better disaster simulation models, possibly funded by the international aid donor community. Our claim is that precise estimates of disaster risks and costs are a global public good.

Traditional disaster financing instruments

Encountering substantial economic uncertainty, such as the costs associated with potential disasters, individuals, private companies and governments are facing a sequence of difficult decisions involving different institutional arrangements and financing instruments. No individual or company wishes to carry the economic burden of catastrophic events on their own, so there is a natural request for sharing the cost. In the absence of perfect insurance markets, the financing solutions and instruments are often developed in tandem, and new instruments are designed by mixing existing instruments in new ways. Therefore, a good starting point is to look at some of the basic decision problems and instruments.

The economic cost of a disaster can be shared in two ways: either by spreading the cost across individuals (risk transfer), or over time (intertemporal risk spreading). Intertemporal risk spreading involves financial markets and financing instruments through saving and borrowing. The notion of precautionary saving ('saving for a rainy day') is a well-known general coping mechanism for both individuals and firms, a strategy increasingly supported by microcredit and microsavings institutions in developing countries.

In a classical risk transfer arrangement a group of people agree to share the potential cost of a random risky incident, even though not all of them will suffer a loss if the event occurs. This is a conventional insurance problem for which there are both market- and non-market instruments. The market instruments are constantly evolving: common to all of them is that they can only transfer risk if the risky event is insurable. Insurability has been analysed from many different viewpoints. Berliner (1982) outlines the actuarial conditions for insurance contracts and markets in the ideal setting; from this point of view, risky events are insurable if (1) there are a large number of loss contacts, causing the 'Law of Large Numbers' to be at work, and if (2) the losses are such that the 'Central Limit Theorem' is operating – whereby the insurer can diversify the risk away (cf. Billingsley 1995; Rumsey 2011). Among the requirements for the Central Limit Theorem we note that the maximum potential loss must be finite (and not too large). Moreover, risks should not be too correlated (so-called covariate risk) and insurers should not accept risks with a too low probability of occurrence. Finally, in this ideal setting, it is assumed that an objective loss distribution function can be estimated.

The actuarial conditions are however neither necessary, nor sufficient, for the existence of an insurance market, as has been noted by many observers and scholars. Nevertheless, the actuarial conditions provide a benchmark from which possible departures from the ideal can be analysed. Economists have noted that the economic environment must be taken into account simply because an insurance contract only exists if a seller and a buyer can agree on a price. The price setting will involve the degree of risk aversion of the buyer (his eagerness to avoid the risk of encountering the loss) and the prevalence of transaction costs, which include the cost associated with uncertain knowledge (or estimates) of the probability, and total cost of the insured event.

Non-market risk transfer instruments include informal kinship engagements and local risk-pooling arrangements (cf. Dercon 2002). Still, the most important disaster finance instrument is government support and reconstruction. Such support can be pre-specified by legal or other arrangements obligating the government to cover losses, or it can be *ad hoc*. In both cases the government must decide on its own funding of the obligation, again relying on either market or non-market instruments. Phaup and Kirschner (2010), for example, design their study around a survey of the obligations and budgeting decisions in fifteen OECD countries. For any government, non-market financing instruments involve the government budget, as it may decide to fund the costs of a disaster after it has occurred (*ex-post* financing) by lowering public expenditures or by increasing revenues (taxes).

For decades, an arrangement by which governments acted as insurers of disaster events – using non-market instruments (tax revenues) to fund the costs – was considered the optimal solution to disaster finance. The theoretical reasoning was given by Arrow and Lind (1970) who showed that, if a government (of a large country) spreads its risk over all its citizens, the expected and actual losses to each individual in the country are minimal, exactly because of the Law of Large Numbers. Moreover, the government's losses from disasters will be relatively small if the government possesses a large and diversified portfolio of independent assets, ensuring disaster funding can be invoked directly in the government budget. Thereby, the government is actually the perfect insurance company, and taxation will be the cheapest disaster insurance contract for the citizens, regardless of the prevailing financial market conditions.

In connection with today's strong interest in market-based disaster financing solutions and instruments, it is important to be specific about the Arrow-Lind result. In particular, a central part of the theorem is that the government can ignore risk because it is spreading the cost of the risky event among a very large pool of taxpayers, for whom the risk becomes insignificant. Hence, the risk is insurable in the actuarial sense; everyone ignores the risk because of the risk-spreading mechanism; and the government will never face problems of financing the loss, because of the assumption of a large and diversified portfolio of independent assets, making it the best insurance supplier simply because of its size. Further, by having the lowest transaction costs, it has the lowest total costs and the government can thereby offer the lowest price. It is important to note, as formulated by Arrow and Lind (1970), that the entity under consideration need not be a government. What is required is a total risk-sharing scheme in which the individual cost of risk bearing is negligible for all participants.

Both of the central parts of the Arrow-Lind theorem have been questioned in the context of disaster risk in developing and emerging-economy countries. Mechler and Hochrainer-Stigler (2014), among several others, question the risk-spreading capacity of governments, and argue that disasters may lead to individual costs that are non-negligible. Post-disaster financing mechanisms may for example not be easily available for developing countries (Cummins and Mahul 2009). Conventional debt financing (intertemporal, market-based risk spreading) is an option, but it is often expensive after a disaster has occurred, as the international capital markets in the immediate aftermath of a disastrous event are likely to demand significant risk premiums. Moreover, post-disaster credit with sufficiently long maturity is not likely to be available for developing countries. Domestic credit will also be an uncertain source of finance, as it is likely to be tight, due to a combination of increased withdrawals of savings and increased uncertainties of already outstanding debt (Adam 2013). Thus, inability to fully debt finance disasters creates a financing gap that may influence budget allocations away from prioritized development projects towards disaster relief, which in turn will harm the development process, thus violating the assumption in Arrow and Lind.

Several developing countries have relied on remittances and foreign aid as non-market disaster finance instruments. While the responsiveness of remittances has been positive and quick following natural catastrophic events, post-disaster foreign aid has been slower and more unreliable. Assuming that climate changes will bring worldwide increases in the frequency and intensity of losses, non-market disaster financing relying on the donor community will in all likelihood become increasingly ineffective (Cummins and Mahul 2009), emphasizing the need for governments in developing countries to look for innovative market-based disaster finance.

Linnerooth-Bayer *et al.* (2005) and Cummins and Mahul (2009) suggest that donors should use market-based insurance instruments for transferring disaster risks to the global financial markets. This would free recipient countries from depending on uncertain and volatile post-disaster assistance, and provide immediate liquidity to governments for post-disaster relief and reconstruction. This could potentially benefit both recipients and donors if such market-based instruments could be coupled with other protective measures. However, such *ex-ante* financing mechanisms are not without problems, an issue we turn to next.

New types of market-based disaster financing instruments

In this section we give three examples of relatively new insurance instruments, all centred on market-based risk transfer mechanisms. Specifically, we discuss the pros and cons of (1) government-supported catastrophe insurance programmes, (2) index-based crop and livestock insurance, and (3) catastrophe bonds. Governments, international financial institutions and the large reinsurance companies, such as Munich Re (http://www.munichre.com) and Swiss Re (http://www.swissre.com), have been important drivers in the development of these new instruments.

Government-supported catastrophe insurance programmes

Developing countries generally have inadequate private catastrophe insurance markets. As a response to this deficit, the multilateral donor community, especially the IMF and the World Bank, have looked at the possibilities of generating funding by facilitating creation of government-supported catastrophe insurance programmes. Based on an analysis of nine government-sponsored insurance programmes, the World Bank assisted Turkey in designing the Turkish Catastrophe Insurance Pool (TCIP) in 2000, in the aftermath of the 1999 earthquake. The earthquake demonstrated that large-scale disasters are associated with strong covariate risk, which has a tendency to drive up conventional insurance premiums in local insurance markets, thereby reducing coverage levels significantly, as insurance buyers find the prices to be too high. Moreover, at the time of the earthquake, the Turkish government budget was under pressure, limiting the possibilities of co-financing arrangements.

The TCIP is designed to reduce the Turkish government's fiscal exposure to future large post-disaster liabilities by gradually building up capital through insurance pool mechanisms partly funded by private contributions. Through offshore reinsurance, using external support from the World Bank, the TCIP is leveraged, such that it functions as a conventional catastrophe insurance scheme. The TCIP thereby mimics a traditional insurance pool, retaining some of the risk within the pool and reinsuring the balance in the international reinsurance market. The TCIP therefore operates as a combined risk transfer and risk financing facility and it looks as if the TCIP will continue to transfer large amounts of its risk to international reinsurance markets, where financial support from the World Bank helps to reduce the reinsurance costs until sufficient financial resources are accumulated nationally (Ozdemir and Yilmaz 2011).

Still, the catastrophe insurance pool instrument faces problems related to conventional insurance, and in order to allow risk to be sufficiently pooled, an arrangement like TCIP depends critically on the scale of the scheme. Take-up of the insurance depends on the scheme's ability to overcome the conventional moral hazard problems that so often afflict insurance markets, and although TCIP is a compulsory insurance scheme, moral hazard still prevails for this instrument. Individuals will have incentives to under-invest in disaster insurance, while local insurance companies will have incentives to cover them in the expectation that the excess cost of a new earthquake can be transferred to the state budget or foreign donors. Although recent estimates suggest that a major earthquake is expected to take place within the next thirty years in the Istanbul region with a probability of 62 per cent, as of September 2014 only around 37 per cent of the citizens in Istanbul have adopted TCIP (6.6 million insurance policies), indicating that most people are either ignoring the risk, or they are anticipating that the state will be forced to renege on its commitment and cover losses in the event of a new major earthquake (Ozdemir and Yilmaz 2011).

Index-based crop and livestock insurance

Another type of insurance, which is often linked to natural hazards, is so-called index-based insurance. The term originates from agricultural economics and describes a financial product linked to an index which is highly correlated with local yields. The index, often based on rainfall or a combination of rainfall and temperature, is typically measured at one or more weather stations and therefore effectively de-linked from the insured farmers. Along the same lines, governments who wish to insure against large-scale natural hazards could do so based on an index describing the observable and measurable features of the hazards – such as the magnitude of an earthquake, wind-speed of a hurricane or measured rainfall in relation to droughts and floods.

The most common type of index insurance in developing countries is the weather index insurance against drought risks. Payouts occur when rainfall totals during an agreed period are below an agreed threshold that can be expected to result in crop loss. An obvious advantage of the index-based insurance is the possibility of swift payout mechanisms, because time- and resource-consuming loss assessments are dismissed by design. In addition to lowering transaction costs, index-based insurance also ensures that the farmer has incentives to make the best possible farming decisions, as the use of an index eliminates the need for individual assessments, thus limiting the classical insurance problems of moral hazard and adverse selection.

Index-based weather insurance is highly developed in India, where the private sector has been the main driving force. It started in 2003 when insurances were attached to contract farmers producing groundnut or potatoes. Clarke *et al.* (2012) estimates that more than 3 million farmers had weather index insurance at either private or public insurance agencies. Farmers have reported both advantages and drawbacks from this type of insurance compared to conventional crop insurance, which covers thrice as many farmers in India. Claims are settled significantly faster than those payouts based on loss assessment. However, due to a limited number of weather stations and poor quality of weather data, the rainfall at the policy holder's farm is often different from the observed rainfall at the nearest weather station (Hellmuth *et al.* 2009). This problem is gradually being solved with the construction of automated weather stations promising to increase the number of insurance takers in coming years. An interesting aspect of weather index insurance in India is that it emerged as purely market-based, but is now largely subsidized by the government through the traditional systems of crop insurance.

Index-based insurance is not limited to weather indexes. In Mongolia, livestock herders can insure against loss of livelihoods in a simple, yet innovative manner (Hazell *et al.* 2010): every year in December there is a census of all animals; this counting of livestock has been undertaken since 1920 and provides a fairly accurate description of average mortality rates in each district. Current and historical livestock mortality rates at the district level now form the basis for an index insurance against harsh winters among herders. This way, individual herders retain their incentives to work hard to save their animals, while at the same time being insured against disastrous weather conditions that are common to their district. The structure of the insurance scheme involves several layers of risk financing. Local insurance companies take a portion of the risk, while another part is pooled with other companies. The Mongolian government reinsures and is in turn protected from the most extreme losses by the international market for reinsurance, as well as receiving a loan from the World Bank, which covers the most severe losses (Hellmuth *et al.* 2009).

The main advantage of index insurance is that it overcomes classical insurance problems by having low transaction costs, less adverse selection and reduced moral hazard. However, index-based insurance schemes also have drawbacks limiting the spread and scaling-up of the product. First of all, there is the *basis risk*. Here, basis risk refers to the difference between variation in the index and variation in the actual insured asset. The weaker the association between, for instance, a rainfall index and crop yields, the higher the basis risk. The association may be low for two reasons: losses may be caused by factors unrelated to the weather index, such as disease or insect infestation; or the rainfall at the policy holder's farm may be different from the observed rainfall at the nearest weather station. The latter can be a serious problem in places where rainfall is very localized or where weather stations are sparse, the former when losses generally do not occur because of drought.

Assuming a manageable basis risk, index insurance may still be unfeasible because insurance companies need accurate information linking the index to actual production losses in order to determine the premiums, deductibles and payouts. This typically requires extensive historical data on both productivity and weather, which is often difficult to obtain. Indeed, for infrequent catastrophic events, historical data covering thirty to forty years may not be enough for sufficiently precise estimates of risks and premiums (Barnett and Mahul 2007). Furthermore, the technical nature of index insurance means that many farmers may be reluctant to participate and pay a premium, even if the benefits would outweigh the costs.

For index insurance aimed at catastrophic events with low probability but high costs the problems are magnified. The demand is limited because individuals cannot correctly estimate the true likelihood of low probability events and – beyond some threshold – they tend to ignore the catastrophic event, effectively treating the low probability as a zero probability (Barnett *et al.* 2008). Meanwhile, suppliers are aware of the low (but non-zero) probability of massive payouts that they need to gauge based on very sparse data. In order for the index insurance to be profitable in the long run, the uncertain probability of these events must be reflected in the premium, even though the insurance buyers tend to neglect that type of risk. Thus, suppliers will charge a high price for the product, which the customers are not willing to pay because the effective assessments of risks differ, taking us back to the problem of economic insurability described above.

Catastrophe (CAT) bonds

While the index-based insurance scheme often has the government as an insurer of small-scale farmers, the idea of using both risk transfer and intertemporal risk spreading by distributing covariate risk related to natural hazards across time and space is gaining popularity among governments of countries which are highly exposed to disasters and vulnerable to their economic consequences. The Catastrophe (CAT) bond is the most popular example of such initiatives. CAT bonds are part of a broader class of financial assets known as event-linked bonds that pay off on the occurrence of a specified event. Most often payouts are based on so-called parametric insurance triggers rather than on assessed losses (like the index-based insurance), and by design CAT bonds are fully collateralized, thereby eliminating concerns about credit risk (Cummins 2008).

Obviously, the insurance trigger plays a pivotal role in the CAT bond scheme. Typical triggers are either *indemnity triggers*, where payouts are based on the size of the actual losses, or *parametric index triggers*, where payouts are based on an index not directly tied to losses. The choice of trigger is a trade-off between moral hazard and basis risk (Cummins 2008). Indemnity triggers are often favoured by insurers because they minimize basis risk, but due to moral hazard problems they require investors to have substantial knowledge of the risk exposure. Obviously, CAT bonds with indemnity triggers require more settlement time than CAT bonds with parametric index triggers, because of the length of the loss assessment processes. Parametric index triggers ensure immediate payouts and maximize the transparency of a transaction, thereby reducing moral hazard. Parametric index triggers have therefore been preferred by investors in recent years. The downside of parametric index triggers is that they expose governments to a higher degree of basis risk than indemnity triggers. This basis risk is reduced by very specific descriptions of the parametric triggers. As of September 2014 the outstanding CAT bond market was $22.9 billion (up from $13.8 billion in 2007) (www.artemis.bm). Most of the market relates to catastrophes in the US, Japan and the EU but three developing country cases may facilitate future use of CAT bond insurance instruments.

A famous and widely studied CAT bond example is that of Mexico. With the establishment of a catastrophe reserve fund (FONDEN) in 2006, Mexico became the first transition country to transfer part of its public-sector natural catastrophe risk to the international reinsurance and capital markets (Cardenas *et al.* 2007). The first initiative by the disaster relief fund was to issue a CAT bond on earthquake disasters in the Mexico City perimeter. The earthquake CAT bond trigger was defined both in terms of intensity and location of a potential future earthquake, where the bond consisted of a number of tranches of differing value, each related to the intensity and distance from the epicentre. Since then new initiatives have been taken, covering both earthquake and hurricane risks. Moreover, the latest FONDEN CAT bond ($315 million, issued in 2012) used much more detailed parametric triggers than previously. The notes pay investors a coupon of 7.5–8 per cent above the Treasury Money Market Funds. But although experiences with FONDEN have been encouraging, the private catastrophe risk market for developing/transition countries is still in its infancy.

The Malawi government has also transferred some of the financial risk associated with the country's natural hazards to the international insurance market. Being a poor, relatively small economy in an area prone to droughts, while maintaining a large rural population, a large-scale drought could prove too much of a burden for the national budget. The Malawi government has therefore signed a contract with the World Bank, specifying that low levels of aggregate national rainfall should trigger insurance payments during the growing period, such that extra liquidity is available even before the harvesting of crops. The contract links the distribution of rainfall over time and space to expected maize production, and stipulates that the government must use payouts in the event of a drought to subsidize the price of imported maize, in order to avoid potential food shortages. An interesting feature of the arrangement is that the ultimate goal is to build capacities so that future contracts can be negotiated directly between Malawi and the international insurance market, thus removing the reliance on international aid institutions such as the World Bank.

The third interesting CAT bond initiative is the regional Caribbean Catastrophe Risk Insurance Facility (CCRIF). The CCRIF was also developed under the leadership of the World Bank, where the facility acts as a financial intermediary between participating countries and the international reinsurance market. In 2014, the facility was restructured into a segregated portfolio company which now operates as a virtual company offering a broad range of disaster-related financial services. At present, the facility has sixteen member governments who join forces in issuing CAT bonds related to earthquake, hurricane and excess rainfall disasters, where the insurance coverage as in the case of Mexico relies on parametric triggers. The idea is that aggregation of individual country risks into a larger and more diversified portfolio can achieve lower costs for the reinsurance coverage. Moreover, the regional initiative could create incentives and peer pressure to help overcome internal political resistance to the purchase of insurance policies at the individual country level (Borensztein *et al.* 2009).

Despite the increasing use of CAT bond insurance, it still constitutes a tiny fraction of the total insurance market, and may continue to do so, because of underlying problems associated with market-based insurance coverage for larger natural events. Kunreuther and Pauly (2006) document how classical insurance problems such as uncertainty related to the magnitude of potential losses, highly correlated risk among the insured, moral hazard leading to excessive risk taking by the insured, and adverse selection of insured parties caused by imperfect information are problems facing all market-based insurance instruments covering developing and transition countries.

Transaction costs may also hinder future development of CAT bonds, especially in the developing/transition country setting, because the financial costs of risk-financing instruments can greatly exceed expected losses (Cardenas *et al.* 2007). This view is supported by Cavallo and Noy (2011) who state that the optimal level of insurance a country should purchase, given the cost of insurance, is still unknown. In the end it depends on the selection of alternative financing options, such as self-insurance possibilities, debt accumulation and expected support in the form of foreign aid. Furthermore, Linnerooth-Bayer *et al.* (2011) show that CAT premiums are often substantially higher than long-term actuarially fair risk premiums, indicating that governments have paid too much for disaster insurance.

Finally, the fact that CAT bonds mostly use parametric index triggers rather than indemnity triggers may be a problem in and of itself, especially if parametric triggers are becoming subject to questioning. An example is the reaction after the Japanese earthquake in 2011, where several CAT bonds did not pay out. Keogh *et al.* (2011) explain how the conditions for payment in the event of an earthquake in Tokyo were so specific that only 10 per cent of the $1.7 billion debt sold by CAT bonds was paid to insurers, because the earthquake struck 380 km northeast of Tokyo, and not in the centre.

Discussion

The presentation of specific insurance schemes shows how the core issues regarding market-based financing of disasters often end in a need to assess the information possessed by involved parties. Generally, insurance markets are most reliable when information on the likelihood of catastrophic events and their resulting damage is accurate, and when the catastrophic events (and their associated losses) are independent of each other. In particular, classical insurance mechanisms assume that natural hazards fulfil these two requirements. It is therefore implicitly assumed that sufficient data to estimate the likelihood and consequences of catastrophic events are readily available or, alternatively, that sufficiently reliable catastrophe models can be constructed.

Availability of historical data and absence of correlation between uncertain events, at some level of spatial or temporal aggregation, normally allow for the use of actuarial-based models to estimate risk. But even though international loss databases with global coverage exist for natural disasters, for example EM-DAT (www.emdat.be), NatCatSERVICE (www.munichre.com) and Sigma (www.swissre.com), there is limited information on both probabilities and costs of events, and at the same time large-scale events often involve correlated risk. Thus, besides providing information to guide the design of insurance contracts, catastrophe models are needed for insurers and risk managers to assess portfolio exposure risk, which can guide them on how much reinsurance to purchase. Reinsurers also use models to guide and validate the price and structure of reinsurance agreements, and insurance rating agencies use the modes to assess the financial strength of insurers/reinsurers who take on catastrophe risk. Finally, investors use catastrophic modelling to assess the pricing and structure of CAT bonds.

The insurance market has adopted the catastrophe models as they help to attain transparency and provide an operating plan for various types of natural hazards. As such, today, models are essential tools for insurance companies as a basis for pricing insurances according to the expected risk. But catastrophe models are very complex, and one may question the extent to which model projections can serve the insurance market appropriately in terms of precise predictions and plans for future uncertainty generated by natural hazards. Despite their complexity, catastrophe models often base predictions on historical data, and those catastrophe model projections are therefore in essence extrapolations assuming some form of regularity in the past that is useful for predicting the future – an assumption most climate change researchers would challenge as being a good representation of future natural hazard scenarios. This led a 2012 *Forbes* article to emphasize that '[c]atastrophic risk modeling is less crystal ball prognostication and more Vegas-style odds making' (Borsari 2012). Moreover, as outlined in Bouriaux and Tomas III (2014), model building is very costly for investors and these costs are likely to deter potential smaller investors, who might otherwise be willing to provide liquidity to the market.

In 2011 a Pulitzer Prize for investigative journalism was given to Paige St John of the *Herald-Tribune* for uncovering some of the flaws in catastrophe modelling, illustrating problems that may emerge if such models are trusted blindly. Paige St John argued that models suffer from the Garbage-In Garbage-Out (GIGO) syndrome, claiming that the data fed into the models is notoriously inaccurate, resulting in unreliable loss estimates (St John 2011). Historically, catastrophe models have led to widespread insurance-related underperformance, in the sense that actual losses are substantially larger than model-based estimates of losses. Even though insurers (and insurance modellers) are asked by regulators to provide historical records comparing actual losses with model predictions, very few comply. The problem of catastrophe models underestimating damages became very clear when the model-based estimated losses of Hurricane Katrina were significantly lower than actual losses, and since then scholarly papers have shown how underestimation of costs is the norm, rather than the exception (Cavallo *et al.* 2010; Hsiang and Jina 2014). According to AIR Worldwide this should not come as a big surprise, since catastrophe models are still in their infancy and are far from giving fully accurate loss estimates, especially when it comes to unprecedented low probability events. The problem is that these model errors not only misinform insurers, they will also significantly increase the costs of individual policy holders, as model uncertainty is built into the pricing mechanism of insurance. However, the insurance market is well aware of the limitations of catastrophe models, and insurers/reinsurers are continuously working on improving the models to facilitate better and more accurate insurance products in the future. Catastrophe models are not perfect, but they are better than what preceded them, while not as good as those that will follow.

Conclusion

While mitigation aims at decreasing the physical vulnerability to hazards, risk financing aims at decreasing financial vulnerability to disasters by reducing the economic losses once the hazards have materialized as catastrophic events. Thus, risk-financing instruments have the potential to assist individuals, companies and governments to cope with the sufferings of catastrophic events. Furthermore, current financial management of disaster risks in developing countries may signify the future difference between success and failure, as future post-disaster recovery may be supported or hindered by current decisions. Disaster risk can be transferred (insured) using either market-based or non-market-based instruments. For many years the prevailing theory supported a disaster financing scheme by which the government should act as an insurance company ensuring risk sharing among a large pool of taxpayers, whose decisions would not be affected by the risky disastrous events, exactly because the government would be able to compensate the involved citizens. Today, most observers have noted that the total cost of disasters for most developing countries is too large to be covered by minor variations in lump sum taxes, thereby invalidating the basis for the classical theory.

The present strategy in the World Bank and the international donor community therefore leans towards market-based insurance solutions, transferring the disaster risk to the international capital market, and several new financing instruments have been developed, utilizing public-private partnerships. The new instruments overcome some of the traditional insurance problems: specifically, by using measurable predefined triggers, such as earthquake intensity or rainfall, the costly and time-consuming investigation of claims can be avoided, whereby the transaction costs are reduced and the speed of payouts may be increased. In many cases the predefined triggers also reduce the problems of moral hazard and adverse selection, ensuring that incentives for disaster mitigation are not hampered by the insurance mechanism. However, the new instruments have drawbacks in the form of basis risk, and in the mixed experiences with the uptake of some of the new instruments. An example of this is the Turkish Catastrophe Insurance Pool, which has a surprisingly low coverage rate (37 per cent) considering the insurance is mandatory. Counter-examples of successful index insurance schemes are found in India and Mongolia.

The partnerships between the citizens and the governments of the developing countries on the one hand, and the international financial organizations (notably, but not exclusively, the World Bank) and global reinsurance companies on the other hand, may turn out to be the most important innovation. These partnerships are hopefully able to solve both the technical actuarial issues related to the insurability of disasters, by developing better catastrophe models, and at the same time the partnerships should be able to overcome the economic obstacles, making the market-based insurance instruments affordable for the poor citizens and profitable for the reinsurance companies. As such, the international donor community should probably regard catastrophe models for the developing countries as well as regional catastrophe insurance pools as global public goods.

At the global scale, a serious challenge for future marked-based insurance financing of disasters is to increase knowledge and transparency by getting better estimates of the low (and hence, largely unknown) probabilities of large-scale disasters, and by improving the simulation models such that costs of complex disaster scenarios can be moved into the realm of insurable risk.

Furthermore, as the recent disaster finance debates have mainly dealt with limitations in the capacity of governments' *ex-post* funding mechanisms, many governments and international finance institutions currently think of optimal disaster financing as providing incentives for private mitigation of potential losses, while using the risk-bearing capacity of the private insurance and capital markets to provide the best possible diversification benefits (Diebold *et al.* 2010). However, it is not obvious that this approach is always superior to the pure post-disaster financing mechanism, especially in situations where more and more events are considered unknowable, both in the true meaning of the word, and in the sense that neither the probability of the event nor the cost of the event can be precisely estimated. Hence, the best mix of market-based and non-market-based transfer of disaster risks is unknown, and more work is certainly needed.

References

Adam, C. (2013) Coping with adversity: The macroeconomic management of natural disasters. *Environmental Science and Policy*, 27(S1), S99–S111.

Arrow, K.J., and Lind, R.C. (1970) Uncertainty and the evaluation of public investment decisions. *American Economic Review*, 60(3), 364–78.

Barnett, B.J., and Mahul, O. (2007) Weather index insurance for agriculture and rural areas in lower-income countries. *American Journal of Agricultural Economics*, 89(5), 1241–7.

Barnett, B.J., Barret, C.B., and Skees, J.R. (2008) Poverty traps and index-based risk transfer products. *World Development*, 36(10), 1766–85.

Berliner, B. (1982), *Limits of Insurability of Risks*. Englewood Cliffs, NJ: Prentice-Hall.

Billingsley, P. (1995) *Probability and Measure*. 3rd edn, Chichester: John Wiley & Sons.

Borensztein, E., Cavallo, E., and Valenzuela, P. (2009) Debt sustainability under catastrophic risk: The case for government budget insurance. *Risk Management and Insurance Review*, 12(2), 273–94.

Bosari, J. (2012) Storm in a barrel. *Forbes*, http://www.forbes.com/sites/teradata/2015/02/20/storm-in-a-barrel-data-analytics-and-a-prediction-for-the-oil-industry (accessed Feb. 2015).

Bouriaux, S., and Tomas III, M.J. (2014) Why do insurance-linked exchange-traded derivatives fail? *Journal of Insurance Issues*, 37(1), 32–58.

Cardenas, V., Hochrainer, S., Mechler, R., Pflug, G., and Linnerooth-Bayer, J. (2007) Sovereign financial disaster risk management: The case of Mexico. *Environmental Hazards*, 7(1), 40–53.

Cavallo, E., and Noy, I. (2011) Natural disasters and the economy: A survey. *International Review of Environmental and Resource Economics*, 5(1), 63–102.

Cavallo, E., Powell, A., and Becerra, O. (2010) Estimating the direct economic damages of the earthquake in Haiti. *Economic Journal*, 120(546), F298–F312.

Clarke, D.J., Mahul, O., Rao, K.N., and Verma, N. (2012) *Weather Based Crop Insurance in India*. Policy Research Working Paper, 5985. Washington, DC: World Bank.

Cummins, J.D. (2008) CAT bonds and other risk-linked securities: State of the market and recent developments. *Risk Management and Insurance Review*, 11(1), 23–47.

Cummins, J.D., and Mahul, O. (2009) *Catastrophe Risk Financing in Developing Countries: Principles for Public Intervention*. Washington, DC: World Bank.

Dercon, S. (2002) Income risk, coping strategies, and safety nets. *World Bank Research Observer*, 17(2), 141–66.

Diebold, F.X., Doherty, N.A., and Herring, R.J. (eds) (2010) *The Known, the Unknown, and the Unknowable in Financial Risk Management: Measurement and Theory Advancing Practice*. Princeton, NJ: Princeton University Press.

Hazell, P., Anderson, J., Balzer, N., Clemmensen, A.H., Hess, U., and Rispoli, F. (2010) *Potential for Scale and Sustainability in Weather Index Insurance for Agriculture and Rural Livelihoods*. Rome: International Fund for Agricultural Development (IFAD) and World Food Programme (WFP).

Hellmuth M.E., Osgood D.E., Hess U., Moorhead A., and Bhojwani H. (eds) 2009. *Index Insurance and Climate Risk: Prospects for Development and Disaster Management*. Climate and Society No. 2. International Research Institute for Climate and Society (IRI), Columbia University, New York, USA.

Hsiang, S.M., and Jina, A.S. (2014) *The Causal Effect of Environmental Catastrophe on Long-Run Economic Growth: Evidence From 6,700 Cyclones*. NBER W20352. Cambridge, MA: National Bureau of Economic Research.

Keogh, B., Westbrook, J., and Suess, O (2011). The trouble with catastrophe bonds. *Bloomberg*, March 3, 2011. http://www.bloomberg.com/news/articles/2011-03-22/-hole-in-one-cat-bonds-rank-as-top-asset-eluding-japan-disaster (accessed 19 May 2015).

Kunreuther, H., and Pauly, M. (2006) Rules rather than discretion: Lessons from Hurricane Katrina. *Journal of Risk and Uncertainty*, 33(1–2), 101–16.

Linnerooth-Bayer, J., Mechler, R., and Hochrainer-Stigler, S. (2011) Insurance against losses from natural disasters in developing countries: Evidence, gaps and the way forward, *Journal of Integrated Disaster Risk Management*, 1(1), 59–81.

Linnerooth-Bayer, J., Mechler, R., and Pflug, G. (2005) Refocusing disaster aid. *Science*, 309(5737), 1044–6.

Mechler, R., and Hochrainer-Stigler, S. (2014) Revisiting Arrow-Lind: Managing sovereign disaster risk. *Journal of Natural Resources Policy Research*, 6(1), 93–100.

Michel-Kerjan, E.O. (2010) Hedging against tomorrow's catastrophes: Sustainable financial solutions to help protect against extreme events. In H. Kunreuther and M. Useem (eds), *Learning from Catastrophes: Strategies for Reaction and Response*. New York: Pearson Education, 139–55.

Munich Re (2014) *NatCatSERVICE: Geophysical Loss Events Worldwide 1980–2013*. Geo Risks Research. Munich: Münchener Rückversicherungs-Gesellschaft.

Ozdemir, O., and Yilmaz, C. (2011) Factors affecting risk mitigation revisited: The case of earthquake in Turkey. *Journal of Risk Research*, 14(1), 17–46.

Phaup, M.M., and Kirschner, C. (2010) Budgeting for disasters: Focusing on the good times. *Organization for Economic Co-operation and Development's Journal on Budgeting*, 1, 21–44.

Rumsey, D.J. (2011) *Statistics for Dummies*. 2nd edn, Chichester: John Wiley & Sons.

St John, P. (2011) Collection of Paige St John articles, http://www.pulitzer.org/works/2011-Investigative-Reporting (accessed Feb. 2015).

15 Disaster mental health

Research and implications for intervention

Silja Henderson, Peter Berliner and Peter Elsass

Introduction

On average, a disaster occurs somewhere in the world every day (Norris *et al.* 2006), and there is widespread agreement that disasters can influence the mental health of the affected population (Difede and Cukor 2009). Disaster mental health research is typically concerned with (1) uncovering the mental health effects of disasters, and (2) investigating the effectiveness of interventions for survivors. 'Understanding the psychological consequences of natural and technological disasters and terrorism – and measuring the effectiveness of postdisaster interventions – are critical tasks for contemporary researchers and practitioners' (Norris *et al.* 2006: cover).

Disaster research is motivated by a sense of urgency; researchers generally do not have the time to build complex research designs when disasters occur, and the needs of disaster survivors are often prioritized over questions of scientific rigour (Norris *et al.* 2006). Problems with infrastructure and lack of collaboration may also hinder the research process. This may be the reason that relatively few interventions studies have been carried out in the immediate context of disasters.

Despite the existence of countless guidelines and consensus-statements, much controversy surrounds the field of disaster mental health: there are disagreements on how to understand the effects of disaster; on the cross-cultural relevance of diagnoses such as post-traumatic stress disorder; and on the approaches, priorities and timing of post-disaster interventions. These disagreements are partly due to a lack of research, but mainly due to the complexity of disaster mental health, which spans over disciplines as diverse as trauma psychology, neuropsychology, epidemiology, clinical psychology, social- and community psychology and cultural psychiatry, to mention just a few.

Recent studies and reviews show an increasing awareness of community approaches, focusing on mobilizing local resources in the prevention of, immediate response to and recovery after disaster (Citraningtyas *et al.* 2010; Sphere Project 2011; Tol *et al.* 2011a). In the field of disaster intervention we increasingly meet a rights-based approach, along with a growing awareness among practitioners of the social gradient of exposure and reactions (such as traumatic stress), possibly partly fuelled by the recommendations of recent guidelines such as Sphere (2011) and IASC (Inter-Agency Standing Committee 2007) and a growing research body in the field of global mental health (Lund *et al.* 2011; WHO 2008).

In this chapter we focus on disaster mental health, particularly theoretical and research-based implications for intervention. The field of disaster mental health research is vast and impossible to cover in a single chapter, but we will visit central research, concepts and understandings within disaster mental health and intervention, and refer to further literature where meaningful. We conclude the chapter with recommendations for further research.

The field of disaster mental health

In recognition that trauma and disasters may be associated with particular types of mental health problems, the fields of disaster psychology and psychiatry (also sometimes referred to as disaster mental health) have emerged in recent years as distinct areas of study, with textbooks, journals and societies devoted to research and discussion of clinical and social issues (cf. Kirmayer *et al.* 2010; Neria *et al.* 2009; Norris *et al.* 2006; Reyes and Jacobs 2005). Disaster mental health consists of a highly diverse range of paradigms and research traditions, and this diversity has been – and continues to be – the cause of much controversy and debate, while also acting as an agent of development and progress.

Past research on mental health effects and disasters

The scholarly field of disaster mental health emerged partly from inquiries into the mental health impacts of war (Raphael and Maguire 2009), partly from research on the impact of natural disasters, and its influence on the development of psychiatric theory and practice (Kirmayer *et al.* 2010). The early work of Adler on the aftermath of the fire at the Coconut Grove nightclub illustrated the neuropsychiatric consequences for the victims (Adler 1943), and Lindemann's report on the management of acute grief brought attention to the mental health effects of disaster (Lindemann 1944). Later studies, such as that by Erikson on the Buffalo Creek flood in 1973, drew attention to the long-term effects of destruction of communal bonds and connectedness to well-being (Erikson 1976), while the detailed study by Weisaeth on the effects of a paint factory explosion and fire demonstrated the so-called dose-response effect of stressor exposures (Weisaeth 1989). These historically important case studies helped form the understanding of the different social and mental health consequences of disasters. For a more in-depth review of the history of disaster mental health research, see Raphael and Maguire (2009).

Mental health consequences of disasters

As mentioned above, a disaster occurs somewhere in the world every day, and '[e]ven more than the physical effects of disasters, the emotional effects cause long-lasting suffering, disability, and loss of income' (Ehrenreich 2001: 5). The largest extensive review to date of the empirical research on the consequences of natural disasters to mental health (Norris *et al.* 2002a, b), including data from 121 studies and 62 different natural disasters, found:

- There were specific psychological problems in 89 per cent of all samples in developing countries. PTSD was found in 81 per cent of these samples, depressive symptoms or major depressive disorder in 57 per cent and anxiety in 19 per cent of these samples.
- 24 per cent of the samples from developing countries showed an effect that could be classified as 'very severe', which meant that 50 per cent or more of the included persons showed clinically significant suffering or psychopathology at criterion level.

Studies of post-traumatic stress disorder (PTSD) shows prevalence rates ranging from 30 to 40 per cent among direct victims, 10 to 20 per cent among rescue workers and 5 to 10 per cent among the general population (Galea *et al.* 2005). As the review by Norris *et al.* (2002a, b) shows, the mental health consequences of disasters are far more diverse than PTSD, and include depression, anxiety and other psychiatric problems, as well as non-specific distress, physical complaints, interpersonal problems, chronic problems in living and deteriorating psychosocial resources (Norris *et al.* 2002a, b). Comorbidity is also very frequent.

Disasters can add to long-term suffering because they often involve many secondary stressors such as loss of homes, livelihood, social relations and community-cohesion (O'Sullivan *et al.* 2013; Difede and Cukor 2009; Norris and Elrod 2006). Both low social capital and low economic capital at the individual level have been independently associated with poor health outcomes (Ahnquist *et al.* 2012). Resilience, recovery and post-traumatic growth are some of the more positive trajectories after traumas such as disasters (cf. Bonanno and Gupta 2009), and across many trauma types, a significant proportion of the population is only minimally affected, or able to adapt to adverse experiences (Neria *et al.* 2009). However, a subgroup of survivors remain symptomatic after the experience of disasters, and at least a third of the individuals who initially develop PTSD remain symptomatic for three years or longer – which puts them at risk of secondary problems, such as alcohol or substance abuse (Kessler *et al.* 2005).

A variety of factors have been found to influence the likelihood that an individual will develop serious or lasting psychological problems in the wake of disasters: more severe exposure; being female and/or middle aged; an ethnic minority status; family strains; prior psychiatric problems; secondary stressors; and weak or deteriorating psychosocial resources. These factors have most consistently increased the likelihood of adverse outcomes (Norris and Elrod 2006; Norris *et al.* 2002b). Interactive effects between the factors have often emerged when they were tested, and it is likely that the factors interact in complex ways that the research has not yet fully captured (Norris and Elrod 2006).

Tremendous concern has also developed regarding the impact of disasters on youth (Silverman and La Greca 2002). Children and adolescents are still developing, which means that when disasters strike they hit 'moving targets', and can affect both the immediate states and the ongoing developmental transformations of the young people (Franks 2011). Though many youths adapt and rebound (Silverman and La Greca 2002), epidemiological research suggests that disasters are associated with elevated rates of psychopathology and impairment in children and adolescents (Furr *et al.* 2010; Hoven *et al.* 2009; La Greca *et al.* 1996). PTSD, other anxiety disorders and depressive disorders are the most common types of clinical problems documented in children and adolescents following disasters. However, natural disasters can also impact children's academic, social and emotional development (Silverman and La Greca 2002).

Post-traumatic stress disorder (PTSD)

PTSD is the psychiatric disorder most often studied in the aftermath of disasters, and has been found to be common across all disaster types (Neria *et al.* 2009). It is frequently a chronic condition that may persist for years, and it is highly comorbid with other psychiatric conditions. Most importantly, PTSD is associated with *poor functioning* and a *low quality of life*. Although symptoms reminiscent of PTSD have been reported following war and disaster for centuries, the actual term 'post-traumatic stress disorder' did not appear in our nosology until 1980 (Friedman *et al.* 2007). The introduction of PTSD into the Diagnostic and Statistical Manual of Mental Disorders (DSM), published by the American Psychiatric Association, launched decades of research and transformed mental health practice, but it was not without controversy, much of which continues today. Clinicians were pleased that they finally had a diagnosis that validated the symptoms of their clients, but critics claimed that PTSD was a pathologization of normal stress, that it was not a legitimate syndrome but a construct driven by feminist and veteran special interest groups. Traumatic memories were claimed to be invalid, and the PTSD diagnosis was criticized as a European/American culture-bound syndrome, with no applicability within traditional cultures (Friedman *et al.* 2007). Summerfield and others have repeatedly argued that PTSD – for the vast majority of survivors – is a pseudo-condition, a reframing of the understandable sufferings of war, and that the spread of the concept reflects a globalization of Western cultural trends of medicalization of distress, which promotes the need for psychological therapies (Bracken *et al.* 1995; Summerfield 1999). Other criticism has focused on how the PTSD diagnosis, through the lens of individual pathology, ignores collective trauma and the cultural, political and social environment from which it is extracted (Zarowsky and Pedersen 2000).

Cultural and sociopolitical understandings of trauma after disasters and war

In 1991, Eisenbruch showed how cultural traditions, values and practices influenced how Cambodian refugees in the US understood trauma, suffering and support. First, Eisenbruch's study eloquently illustrated the importance of cultural practices as a means of social coping with atrocities, and secondly, it demonstrated the limitations of the individualistic and biological focus of Western psychiatry which at times was detrimental to the rebuilding efforts of the community in question. Eisenbruch proposed the term 'cultural bereavement' to describe the experience of the uprooted group evolving from loss of social and economic structure, cultural values and identity. Bracken *et al.* (1995) have supported Eisenbruch's approach, by giving examples of how cultural and sociopolitical knowledge is crucial in helping people impacted by disaster, in their case dealing with organized violence.

In 2004, Eisenbruch *et al.* reiterated the importance of contextualizing the understanding of traumatic stress: 'traumatic events are dictated by local historical experiences as well as local cultural mediation, and … understanding local idioms of distress unlocks the local clinical symptom profile of psychological and social disorder' (2004: 129). They recommended that participatory action research should be conducted on the subject of cultural competence, and argued for a combined epidemiological and qualitative ethnographic research (2004: 129).

The critique of the concept of PTSD and trauma as an intrapersonal response in the 1990s was also fuelled by the testimony method developed during the highly violent and repressive Pinochet regime in Chile (Cienfuegos and Monelli 1983; Lira 1990). This approach argued that participation in the struggle for basic human rights (through giving testimony) was curative for people who had been traumatized by organized violence. The testimony approach was also, although differently, developed by Langer (1997) in his analyses of narratives of Holocaust survivors. In this view, trauma was seen as more than an individual reaction as it includes sociopolitical events, psychophysiological processes, a bodily and emotional experience and a narrative (Kirmayer 1996).

According to Watson *et al.* (2011), ethnocultural factors in communities after disasters have historically been underrepresented in the literature. Because individuals are embedded in a broader familial, interpersonal and social context, many experts recommend that services should be tailored to meet the needs of as many community members as possible. They refer to Norris and Alegria (2006, in Watson *et al.* 2011) for a review of the literature on ethnocultural factors following disasters. The literature confirms that one of the most crucial research questions to answer in the future is how to adapt mental health and psychosocial programmes across different cultures and communities (cf. Tol *et al.* 2011a). Examples of contextually developed programmes are presented in Berliner *et al.* (2006), Berliner and Mikkelsen (2006a) and Anckermann *et al.* (2005).

Levels of post-disaster intervention

Religious, governmental and non-governmental organizations (NGOs) have long provided aid to victims of wars, natural disasters and refugee crises. The recognition of the need to provide psychosocial support alongside survival necessities came about more recently, and to some extent reflects the horrific impacts of the genocide in Rwanda and the ethnic cleansings during the Balkan wars in the 1990s, where the grief and trauma was undeniable (Reyes 2006).

Disaster mental health   229

The Inter-Agency Standing Committee guidelines have specified the levels of care that can be addressed after disasters, in their 'pyramid-of-care' model (IASC 2007). The model resembles a triangle or pyramid, large at the bottom and narrow at the top. The pyramid is divided into horizontal layers/levels, referring to the number of people who may need a particular type of care. The bottom layer (the widest, referring to everyone) is 'basic services and security'. Interventions on this level could include advocacy, documentation of mental health impacts and influencing humanitarian actors. The next layer is 'community and family support', and represents the emergency response for a smaller number of people who are able to maintain their mental health and psychosocial well-being if they receive help in accessing key community and family supports. Useful responses in this layer include family tracing and reunification, assisted mourning and communal healing ceremonies, mass communication on constructive coping methods, supportive parenting programmes, formal and non-formal educational activities, livelihood activities and the activation of social networks (such as women's groups and youth clubs). The third layer is termed 'focused, non-specialized supports', and represents the supports necessary for the still smaller number of people who additionally require more focused individual, family or group interventions by trained and supervised workers (but who may not have had years of training in specialized care). For example, survivors of gender-based violence might need a mixture of emotional and livelihood support from community workers. This layer also includes psychological first aid (PFA) and basic mental health care by primary health care workers. Finally, the top layer, termed 'specialized services', represents the additional support required for the smallest percentage of the population whose suffering, despite the supports already mentioned, is intolerable, and who may have significant difficulties in basic daily functioning. Assistance should include psychological or psychiatric support for people with severe mental disorders (this could be survivors with severe PTSD or comorbid conditions) whenever their needs exceed the capacities of primary/general health services (IASC 2007).

An important review of mental health and psychosocial support in humanitarian settings including 160 studies, linking practice, funding and evidence for interventions, found that the five most commonly reported activities were basic counselling for individuals (39 per cent); facilitation of community support of vulnerable individuals (23 per cent); provision of child-friendly spaces (21 per cent); support of community-initiated social support (21 per cent); and basic counselling for groups and families (20 per cent) (Tol *et al.* 2011b). Tol *et al.* conclude that there is a gap between practice and research in that the most frequently implemented interventions are all placed towards the lower half of the pyramid of care, but research and debate so far have focused almost exclusively on the interventions at the top of the pyramid (i.e. specialized clinical interventions for PTSD, depression, etc.). Randomized clinical interventions have established the efficacy of exposure therapy and cognitive behaviour therapy for PTSD, but it is still unclear how well the randomized control trials (with their strict inclusion criteria) translate into the communities, where symptom patterns are much more complex (Difede and Cukor 2009). It is likewise unclear how to implement clinical interventions on a large scale in low- and middle-income countries with few mental health staff, and the public health relevance of the PTSD concept is still heavily debated. See Tol *et al.* (2011b) for a meta-analysis of the evidence of post-disaster mental health interventions.

Beyond the dichotomy of trauma-based and psychosocial interventions: research and implications for practice

The debate on the PTSD concept extends into a discussion of what characterizes appropriate mental health/psychosocial intervention. On the one hand, trauma-based approaches (the top of the pyramid of care) have been criticized for focusing too narrowly on PTSD, a concept whose cross-cultural public health value is not agreed on, and just one of many types of psychological harm that may arise after extreme stressors (Bracken *et al.* 1995; van Ommeren *et al.* 2008). One-off psychological debriefing, which was earlier a frequently implemented intervention to reduce traumatic stress, may even also be harmful (Rose *et al.* 2002). On the other hand, proponents of non-medical psychosocial approaches (toward the bottom of the pyramid of care) have been criticized for professional error in denying traumatic stress and ignoring preventable suffering (de Vries 1998; Mezey and Robbins 2001; van Ommeren *et al.* 2005). According to van Ommeren *et al.* (2005), because of the heated expressions of opinions, an impression may have been created that programme planners are faced with a choice between setting up separate, specialized, trauma-focused care; setting up separate psychosocial care programmes; or completely ignoring mental health.

Earlier evidence has pinpointed the importance of chronic or daily stressors both separately and as mediators of trauma impact (Miller and Rasmussen 2010), and research on the social determinants of health has received growing interest within disaster mental health and the wider discipline of global mental health (WHO 2008). Women, minorities, relatively poor, less formally educated people and marginalized groups are more at risk of experiencing traumatizing incidents, and their subsequent mental health suffering is more severe (Hawkins *et al.* 2014). This is one of the best documented results of trauma and disaster mental health research (Neria *et al.* 2009). Global mental health research suggests that poverty and mental disorders interact in a negative cycle in low- and middle-income countries where most disasters occur (Lund *et al.* 2011). According to the pathways of 'social causation' and 'social drift', conditions of poverty on the one hand increase the risk of mental illness, through heightened stress, social exclusion, decreased social capital, malnutrition, increased obstetric risks, violence and trauma (social causation pathway); on the other hand, people with mental illness are at increased risk of drifting into, or remaining in, poverty (social drift) through increased health expenditure, reduced productivity, stigma and loss of employment and associated earnings. The cost of mental ill-health thus sets up a vicious cycle of poverty and mental disorder (Lund *et al.* 2011; Patel and Kleinman 2003; Saraceno *et al.* 2005).

Our own small cross-sectional research study on the predictors of long-term mental health after the 2004 Indian Ocean tsunami in Sri Lanka also found socio-contextual factors to be very potent in predicting trauma and general health (Henderson 2013; Henderson and Elsass, in press). Our study analysed survey data collected by the American Red Cross in Sri Lanka nearly five years after the Indian Ocean tsunami. Through statistical analyses, we explored the predictors of mental health outcome (Impact of Event Scale-Revised (PTSD), General Health Questionnaire-12) in a sample of 404 adults with high tsunami exposure. Surprisingly, the results of the multivariate regression analysis showed that post-traumatic symptoms nearly five years after the tsunami were not predicted by the expected factors of bereavement and threat to life. Instead, post-traumatic symptoms were most strongly predicted by 'loss of income due to tsunami', as well as a number of other trauma-impact variables ('relatives/friends badly injured or missing', 'being badly injured by tsunami') which could be suspected to act as chronic stressors through lack of closure, physical disability and poverty. The regression analysis on GHQ-12 showed that general distress was predicted by age, education, language, post-traumatic symptoms and social support. The implications for long-term interventions seem to be to consider not only the effect of the past traumatic experience in itself, but also how (or if) disaster impacts may act as chronic stressors in producing current mental (ill) health (Henderson 2013; Henderson and Elsass in press). In light of their potent effect on mental health outcome, socio-contextual stressors such as loss of income and low social support should be equally valued targets for assessment and social intervention.

These conclusions are in line with those proposed by Miller and Rasmussen (2010) in their analysis of war and conflict-related trauma research. They argue that trauma-focused advocates tend to overemphasize the direct impact of war exposure on mental health, but fail to consider the contribution of stressful social and material conditions (daily stressors), and they propose a model where daily stressors partly mediate the relationship between war exposure and mental health (cf. Miller and Rasmussen 2010). This leads them to recommend an integrative, sequenced approach to intervention, very similar to that of Silove (2005), where social stressors are first addressed, and specialized interventions are then provided for individuals who are still distressed.

From a public health perspective, it is meaningful to recommend social interventions as first-line interventions, because they are generally culturally appropriate, and their implementation is not dependent on mental health staff (van Ommeren *et al.* 2008). However, to the extent that they can be delivered by non-specialized staff, and are accepted in the local cultural setting, trauma- or mental health-focused interventions may also have great impact through the social drift pathway, preventing people from drifting into poverty, stigma and exclusion. Thus it does not have to be as either/or as the controversy suggests (Miller and Rasmussen 2010; van Ommeren *et al.* 2005) – either social interventions, ignoring mental health, or trauma-focused interventions, ignoring social stressors – but rather a question of how and when.

The overall conclusion here must be that both interventions directed at mental illnesses (depression, PTSD, etc.), and interventions targeting social stressors (education, social support, income, etc.), have immense value in (1) supporting survivors of disaster and thus, in (2) breaking the vicious cycle of mental ill health and poverty – a goal on which there should be consensus, even across the diverse disciplines of disaster mental health. According to Silove (2005: 75), 'the best therapy for acute stress reactions is social', but it should be followed by services for the minority of persons who continue to suffer from severe traumatic stress reactions, and that group emerges in increasing numbers over time (Silove 2005).

Humanitarian response and recovery after disasters: participatory community-based approaches

It may not only be important to consider what *types* of post-disaster interventions to apply, but also *how* such interventions are carried out.

The newest version of the Sphere standards for humanitarian intervention (the Sphere guidelines are endorsed by more than 200 NGOs, and represent across disciplines perhaps the most widely distributed basic humanitarian aid text) has an increased focus on the *capacities* of the affected people as humanitarian actors (Sphere Project 2011). Such an approach is very much in tune with the community-based approach to disaster mental health, which perceives the disaster-affected populations as contributors and *active agents* (Magis 2010), rather than passive recipients of help or care. The community-based approach aims at building community resilience and social resilience through a participatory approach (Norris *et al.* 2006; Berliner *et al.* 2012, 2010; Anasarias and Berliner 2009). Magis describes a range of factors that are important in order to build social resilience: one of them is that the population must contribute as *active agents*, and have a high degree of confidence in the creation of welfare and security. In this way, they contribute through a common effort, sharing their knowledge and competences to achieve the common goals (Magis 2010).

Both theory and research seem to support such an approach. Along with social support/social capital, the concept of self-efficacy has been both theoretically and empirically connected to mental health (cf. Benight 2009). On the basis of their review, Batniji *et al.* state, '[t]he calls of the social science literature extend beyond the aim of "community consultation and participation", to give the community a primary role in initiating and executing any "intervention"' (Batniji *et al.* 2006: 1858). In their analysis of post-disaster community work, based on the case of Aceh in Indonesia, Citraningtyas and colleagues similarly argue that 'ethical engagement' ideally requires 'an approach beyond community involvement or … partnership, so that the community holds ownership and leadership of the processes' (Citraningtyas *et al.* 2010: 109). Citraningtyas *et al.* also refer to the influx of foreigners and financial aid as 'the second tsunami' (2010). Our own qualitative case study research into humanitarian psychosocial interventions after the 2004 Indian Ocean tsunami also suggested that understanding and building on local cultural conceptions of trauma and recovery, and providing the local disaster-affected populations an active role in the design, execution and evaluation of humanitarian psychosocial responses, was crucial to achieving the cultural appropriateness as well as effectiveness of interventions (Henderson *et al.* in press; Henderson 2013).

The Sphere standards specify the rights of affected populations to protection and humanitarian assistance in a 'people-centered humanitarian response', building on 'people's capacity and strategies to survive with dignity' (Core standard 1: 55; Sphere Project 2011). To include and build on local resources and understandings may not only be the right thing to do, from an ethical perspective, but it may also ensure the quality and effectiveness of humanitarian psychosocial interventions.

Future research

The current gap between research and practice should be reduced by prioritizing more research into the most frequently implemented psychosocial (humanitarian) interventions, such as child-friendly spaces, counselling and promotion of community supports (Tol *et al.* 2011b). Conversely, the interventions that have proven effective (such as psychological interventions for adults with PTSD and children with internalizing problems) should be made available to populations with these mental health problems. More research is needed on how to provide effective interventions in settings with few mental health personnel. Training of paraprofessional or non-formal staff may be a sensible option (van Ommeren *et al.* 2008)

A number of studies on single communities have been published (Staub *et al.* 2005; Perera 2001; Kleinman *et al.* 1997; Marsella *et al.* 1996), but there is still need for more studies based on observations and interviews, which from a non-clinical setting give knowledge on how trauma is understood and handled through the narratives of the people in the studied community (Boyden *et al.* 2006; Plummer 2001; Crossley 2000). There is a call for studies that, to a much larger extent, consider the social context, the participants' perception of their own situation and their visions for a better life. This requires a far broader approach than just meta-analyses of quantitative, evidence-based research on treatment effects.

In their development of research agenda for mental health and psychosocial support in humanitarian settings, based on the perspectives of academics, practitioners and policy-makers, Tol *et al.* (2011a) note that three of the ten most highly prioritized research questions emphasize the inclusion of perspectives from the affected people or the promotion of sensitivity to the sociocultural context. Future intervention research, whether focused on specialized clinical intervention or community-based intervention, would benefit from inquiry into the cultural acceptability and relevance of post-disaster interventions. Such an inquiry could be initiated by including a qualitative assessment in all future interventions studies of how the intervention was perceived and received in the local context, and to what extent it was felt to match local priorities. The results of these assessments should then be included in the final reporting of the study.

Furthermore, the literature calls for broadening the types of outcomes studied in both mental health effect and interventions studies (Tol *et al.* 2011b; Berliner and Mikkelsen 2006b). McFarlane and Kaplan (2012) reflect in relation to their own work that it excludes studies of interventions for other symptoms and types of impairment than PTSD, and conclude that neglect of the wider context leads to a constricted understanding of the impact of human rights violations (2012: 559).

Finally, more research is needed on how socio-contextual factors such as living conditions, poverty, education and social support can be targeted with the purpose of increasing mental health after disasters – and also how these factors could be used to reduce risk and build resilience, even before the disaster strikes.

References

Adler, A. (1943) Neuropsychiatric complications in victims of Boston's Coconut Grove disaster. *Journal of the American Medical Association*, 123, 1098–1101.

Ahnquist, J., Wamala, S.P., and Lindstrom, M. (2012) Social determinants of health? A question of social or economic capital? Interaction effects of socioeconomic factors on health outcomes. *Social Science and Medicine*, 74, 930–9.

Anasarias, E., and Berliner, P. (2009) Human rights and peacebuilding. In J.de Rivera (ed.), *Handbook of Peacebuilding*. New York: Springer, 181–96

Anckermann, S., Dominguez, M., Soto, N., Kjerulf, F., Berliner, P., and Mikkelsen, E.N. (2005) Psycho-social support to large numbers of traumatised people in post-conflict societies: An approach to community development in Guatemala. *Journal of Community and Applied Social Psychology*, 15, 136–52.

Batniji, R., van Ommeren, M., and Saraceno, B. (2006) Mental and social health in disasters: Relating qualitative social science research and the Sphere standard. *Social Science and Medicine*, 62(8),1853–64.

Benight, C.C., Cieslak, R., and Waldrep, E. (2009) Social and cognitive frameworks for understanding the mental health consequences of diasters. In Y. Neria, S. Galea, and F.H. Norris (eds), *Mental Health and Disasters*. New York. Cambridge University Press, 161–74.

Berliner, P., and Mikkelsen, E.N. (2006a) Serving the psychosocial needs of survivors of torture and organized violence. In G. Reyes and J. Jacobs (eds), *Handbook of Disaster Management*. London: Praeger Publishers, 78–99.

Berliner, P., and Mikkelsen, E.N. (2006b) Psycho-education with asylum seekers and survivors of torture. *International Journal for the Advancement of Counselling*, 28, 289–301.

Berliner, P., Anasarias, E., and de Casas Soberón, E. (2010) Religious diversity as peacebuilding: The space for peace. *Journal of Religion, Conflict, and Peace*, 4, 2–10.

Berliner, P., Larsen, L.N., and de Casas Soberón, E. (2012) Case study: Promoting community resilience with local values – Greenland's Paamiut Asasara. In M. Ungar (ed.), *The Social Ecology of Resilience*. New York: Springer, 387–99.

Berliner, P., Dominquez, M., Kjaerulf, F., and Mikkelsen, E.N. (2006) What can be learned from 'crazy' psychologists? A community approach to psychosocial support in post-conflict Guatemala. *Intervention: International Journal of Mental Health, Psychosocial Work and Couselling in Areas of Armed Conflict*, 4(1), 67–73.

Bolin, R. (1982) *Long-Term Family Recovery from Disaster*. Boulder, CO: Institute of Behavioral Science, University of Colorado.

Bonanno, G.A., and Gupta, S. (2009) Resilience after disaster. In Y. Neria, S. Galea, and F.H. Norris (eds), *Mental Health and Disasters*. Cambridge: Cambridge University Press, 145–60.

Boyden, J., Berry, J. de, Feeny, T., and Hart, J. (2006) Children affected by armed conflict in South Asia: A regional summary. In G. Reyes and G.A. Jacobs (eds), *Handbook of International Disaster Psychology*, vol. 4. Westport, CT: Praeger.

Bracken, B.J., Giller, J.E., and Summerfield, D. (1995) Psychological responses to war and atrocity: The limitations of current concepts. *Social Science and Medicine*, 40, 1073–82.

Braga, L., Fiks, J., Mari, J., and Mello, M. (2008) The importance of the concepts of disaster, catastrophe, violence, trauma and barbarism in defining posttraumatic stress disorder in clinical practice. *BMC Psychiatry*, 8, 68–76.

Chandra, A., Acosta, J., Meredith, L.S., et al. (2010) *Understanding Community Resilience in the Context of National Health Security: A Literature Review*. Santa Monica, CA: RAND Corporation.

Cienfuegos, A.J., and Monelli, C. (1983) The testimony of political repression as a therapeutic instrument. *American Journal of Orthopsychiatry*, 53, 43–51.

Citraningtyas, T., MacDonald, E., and Herrman, H. (2010) A second tsunami? The ethics of coming into communities following disaster. *Asian Bioethics Review*, 2, 108–23.

Crossley, M.L. (2000) *Narrative Psychology: Self, Trauma and the Construction of Meaning*. Buckingham: Open University Press.

Crumlish, N., and O'Rourke, K. (2010) A systematic review of treatments for post-traumatic stress disorder among refugees and asylum-seekers. *Journal of Nervous and Mental Disease*, 198, 237–51.

de Vries, F. (1998) To make a drama out of trauma is fully justified. *Lancet*, 351(9115): 1579–80.

Difede, J., and Cukor, J. (2009) Evidence-based long-term treatment of mental health consequences of disasters among adults. In Y. Neria, S. Galea, and F. Norris (eds), *Mental Health and Disasters*. New York: Cambridge University Press, 336–49.

Ehrenreich, J.H. (2001) *Coping with Disasters: A Guidebook to Psychosocial Intervention*. Old Westbury, NY: Center for Psychology and Society.

Eisenbruch, M. (1991) From posttraumatic stress disorder to cultural bereavement: Diagnosis of Southeast Asian refugees. *Social Science and Medicine*. 33(6), 673–80.

Eisenbruch, M., Jong, J.T.V.M., and Put, W. van de (2004) Bringing order out of chaos: A culturally competent approach to managing the problems of refugees and victims of organized violence. *Journal of Traumatic Stress*, 17(2), 123–33.

Erikson, K.T. (1976) Loss of communality at Buffalo Creek. *American Journal of Psychiatry*, 133, 303–5.

Franks, B.A. (2011) Moving targets: A developmental framework for understanding children's changes following disasters. *Journal of Applied Developmental Psychology*, 32, 58–69.

Friedman, M.J., Resick, P.A., and Keane, T.M. (2007) Twenty-five years of progress and challenges. In M. Friedman, T.M. Keane, and P.A. Resick (eds), *Handbook of PTSD, Science and Practice*. New York: Guilford Press, 3–18.

Furr, J.M., Comer, J.S., Edmunds, J.M., and Kendall, P.C. (2010) Disasters and youth. *Journal of Consulting and Clinical Psychology*, 78, 765–80.

Galea, S., Nandy, A., and Vlahov, D. (2005) The epidemiology of posttraumatic stress disorder after disasters. *Epidemiologic Reviews*, 27, 78–91.

Green, B.L., Friedman, M.J., de Jong, J.T.V.M., Solomon, S.D., Keane, T.M., and Fairbank, J.A., et al. (2003) *Trauma Intervention in War and Peace: Prevention, Practice, and Policy*. Amsterdam: Kluwer Academic/Plenum Press.

Hawkins, A.O., Zinzow, H.M., Amstadter, A.B., Danielsen, C.K., and Ruggiero, K.J. (2009) Factos associated withexposure and response to disasters among marginalized populations. In Y. Neria, S. Galea, and F.H. Norris (eds.), *Mental Health and Disasters*. Cambridge: Cambridge University Press, 594–610.

Henderson, S.H. (2013) Psychosocial interventions after natural disasters – an analysis of evidence and recommendations for practice. PhD thesis 2013. Faculty of Social Sciences, University of Copenahagen, Denmark.

Henderson, S.H., and Elsass, P. (in press) Predictors of trauma and distress five years after the Indian Ocean tsunami in Sri Lanka. *International Journal of Disaster Risk Reduction*.

Henderson, S.H., Elsass, P., and Berliner, P. (in press) Mental and social health in disasters: Relating the Sphere standards to post-tsunami psychosocial interventions in Asia. *Disasters*.

Hoven, C.W., Duarte, C.S., Turner, J.B., and Mandell, D.N. (2009) Child mental health in the aftermath of disaster: a review of PTSD studies. In Y. Neria, S. Galea, and F.H. Norris (eds.), *Mental Health and Disasters*. Cambridge: Cambridge University Press, 218–232.

Inter-Agency Standing Committee (2007) *IASC Guidelines on Mental Health and Psychosocial Support in Emergency Settings*. Geneva: Inter-Agency Standing Committee.

Kessler, R.C., Sonnega, A., Bromet, E., Hughes, M., and Nelson, C.B. (2005) Posttraumatic stress disorder in the National Comorbidity Survey. *Archives of General Psychiatry*, 52, 1048–60.

Kirmayer, L.J. (1996) Confusion of the senses: Implications of ethnocultural variations in somatoform and dissociative disorders for PTSD. In A.J. Marsella, M.J. Friedman, E.T. Gerrity, and R.M. Scurfield (eds), *Ethnocultural Aspects of Posttraumatic Stress Disorder*. Washington, DC: American Psychological Association, 131–63.

Kirmayer, L.J., Kienzler, H., Hamid Afana, A., and Pedersen, D. (2010) Trauma and disasters in social and cultural context. In *Principles of Social Psychiatry*. Chichester: John Wiley & Sons, 155–77.

Kleinman, A. (1987) Anthropology and psychiatry: The role of culture in cross-sectional research on illness. *British Journal of Psychiatry*, 151, 447–54.

Kleinman, A., Das, V., and Lock, M. (eds) (1997) *Social Suffering*. Berkeley, CA: University of California Press.

La Greca, A.M., Vernberg, E.M., Silverman, W.K., and Prinstein, M.J. (1996) Symptoms of posttraumatic stress in children after Hurricane Andrew: a prospective study. *Journal of Consulting and Clinical Psychology*, 64, 712–23.

Langer, L.L. (1997) The alarmed vision: Social suffering and holocaust atrocity. In A. Kleinman, V. Das, and M. Lock (eds), *Social Suffering*. Berkeley, CA: University of California Press, 47–66.

Lindemann, E. (1944) Symptomatology and management of acute grief. *American Journal of Psychiatry*, 101, 141–8.

Lira, E.K. (1990) Guerra psicológica: Intervención política de la subjectividd colectiva. In I. Martin-Baro (ed.), *Psicología social de la Guerra*. San Salvador: UCA Editores, 175–96.

Lund, C., De Silva, M., Plagerson, S., Cooper, S., Chisholm, D., Das, J., et al. (2011) Poverty and mental disorders: Breaking the cycle in low-income and middle-income countries. *Lancet*, 378(9801), 1502–14.

Magis, K. (2010) Community resilience: An indicator of social sustainability. *Society & Natural Resources*, 23(5), 401–16.

Marsella, A.J., Friedman, M.J., and Spain, E.H. (1996) Ethnocultural aspects of PTSD: An overview of issues and research directions. In A.J. Marsella et al. (eds), *Ethnocultural Aspects of Posttraumatic Stress Disorder*. Washington, DC: American Psychological Association, 105–29.

McDougal, L., and Beard, J. (2011) Revisiting Sphere: New standards of service delivery for new trends in protracted displacement. *Disasters*, 35(1), 87–101.

McFarlane, C.A., and Kaplan, I. (2012) Evidence-based psychological interventions for adult survivors of torture and trauma: A 30-year review. *Transcultural Psychiatry*, 49(3–4), 539–67.

Mezey, G., and Robbins, I. (2001) Usefulness and validity of post-traumatic stress disorder as a psychiatric category. *BMJ* 323, 561–3.

Silove, D. (2004) The global challenge of asylum. In J.P. Wilson and B. Drozdek (eds), *Broken Spirits: The Treatment of Traumatized Asylum Seekers, Refugees, War and Torture Victims*. New York: Brunner-Routledge, 13–32.

Silove, D. (2005) Round table discussion: The best immediate therapy for acute stress is social. *Bulletin of the World Health Organization*, 83, 75–6.

Silverman, W.K., and La Greca, A.M. (2002) Children experiencing disasters: Definitions, reactions, and predictors of outcomes. In A.M. La Greca, W.K. Silverman, E.M. Vernberg, and M.C. Roberts (Eds), *Helping Children Cope with Disasters And Terrorism*. Washington, DC, US: American Psychological Association, 11–33.

Sphere Project (2011) *The Sphere Project: Humanitarian Charter and Minimum Standards in Humanitarian Response*. London: Sphere Project.

Staub, E., Pearlman, A.L., Gubin, A., and Hagengimana, A. (2005) Healing, reconciliation, forgiving and the prevention of violence after genocide or mass killing: An intervention and its experimental evaluation in Rwanda. *Journal of Social and Clinical Psychology*, 24(3), 297–334.

Summerfield, D. (1999) A critique of seven assumptions behind psychological trauma programmes in war-affected areas. *Social Science and Medicine*, 48, 1449–62.

Tol, W.A., Barbui, C., Galappatti, A., Silove, D., Betancourt, T.S., Souza, R., et al. (2011b) Mental health and psychosocial support in humanitarian settings: Linking practice and research. *Lancet*, 378, 1581–91.

Tol, W.A., Patel, V., Tomlinson, M., Baingana, F., Galappatti, A., Panter-Brick, C., et al. (2011a) Research priorities for mental health and psychosocial support in humanitarian settings. *PLoS Medicine*, 8, 1–5.

Van Dyke, M., and Waldman, R. (2004) *The Sphere Project Evaluation Report*. Geneva: Sphere Project.

van Ommeren, M., Morris, J., and Saxena, S. (2008) Social and clinical interventions after conflict or other large disaster. *American Journal of Preventive Medicine*, 35, 284–6.

van Ommeren, M., Saxena, S., and Saraceno, B. (2005) Mental and social health during and after acute emergencies: Emerging consensus? *Bulletin of the World Health Organization*, 83, 71–7A.

Watson, P.J., Brymer, M.J., and Bonanno, G.A. (2011) Postdisaster psychological intervention since 9/11. *American Psychologist*, 66(6), 482–94.

Weisaeth, L. (1989) A study of behavioral responses to an industrial disaster. *Acta Psychiatrica Scandinavia*, 355, 13–24.

WHO (2008) Social determinants of health, http://www.who.int/social_determinants/en (accessed 14 December, 2014).

Zarowsky, C., and Pedersen, D. (2000) Rethinking trauma in a transnational world. *Transcultural Psychiatry*, 37, 291–3.

Epilogue

Rasmus Dahlberg, Olivier Rubin and Morten Thanning Vendelø

This volume has introduced the reader to a multiplicity of social science disciplines, all of which can facilitate the production of new insights about disasters, and thereby advance our understanding of these. In particular, it is our hope that it will inspire scholars to apply new theoretical angles when researching disasters. We acknowledge that the individual chapters provide little insight into how the presented disciplines can be combined to create novel venues for disaster analysis. The authors have contributed with their disciplinary specialist perspectives on the theme of disasters, but no attempt has been made to develop a common framework, or to integrate the various perspectives. The responsibility for this, of course, does not lie with the individual contributors – it unequivocally rests with us, the editors. Thus, in this epilogue, we propose some ways in which the various chapters, and disciplines within, can be interlinked.

In our opinion, the field of disaster research does not constitute an independent research discipline: the different disciplinary chapters cannot be distilled into one coherent academic paradigm without encroaching on the epistemological and ontological traits of the individual disciplines. How would one, for instance, integrate a post-modernistic cultural perspective with the financial perspective of index-based insurance? Both perspectives can surely inform the understanding of particular disasters, but integrating them into one coherent approach appears otiose. Another challenge is that scholars of disasters are not only intellectually diverse, but also geographically scattered. Typically, a university only employs a small handful of social scientists with an interest in disaster research, and although disaster management programmes are on the rise, they are still far and few between. For the time being, disaster research therefore only attracts little attention within the traditional disciplines. Our book should not be perceived as a call to expand the presence of disaster research within the traditional disciplines, but rather as a call to connect the small specks of disaster research within each discipline – thereby enabling disaster research to acquire enough critical mass to constitute a *multidisciplinary research community*.

An example of a multidisciplinary disaster research community was established in 2012, in collaboration between University of Copenhagen and Copenhagen Business School, in the form of Copenhagen Center for Disaster Research (COPE). A number of the contributors to this book, as well as the editors, are associated with COPE, and many of the ideas and perspectives presented in the chapters have been discussed at COPE workshops and seminars. When theologians, economists, anthropologists, microbiologists and engineers gather in order to debate disasters they rarely reach agreement, but typically they take away new inspiration, novel understandings or even plans for new cross-disciplinary collaborations. For example, in autumn 2014, a historian, a microbiologist, a disaster risk expert and a theologian, brought together by such an event, pooled their knowledge and wrote a paper presenting and debating three very different versions of resilience in disaster research at the individual, national and global level (Dahlberg *et al.* 2015).

A devil's advocate might object that there is nothing analytically distinct about disasters, which calls for the establishment of multidisciplinary research communities such as COPE. Even if disasters accentuate and magnify underlying tensions and dynamics in societies, they do not generate new dynamics that cannot be captured in existing disciplines, the critic often argues. And scholars concerned with discrete events, like earthquakes or plane crashes, are sometimes perceived as narrow-minded and short-sighted, ignoring the more complex processes and dynamics commonly captured by existing disciplines. The chapters in this book can easily be read as highly qualified responses to such accusations, as – without exception – the chapters use disasters as an *entry-point* for analysis, rather than as their analytical *end-point*. In particular, most of the presented perspectives are primed to incorporate broader societal dynamics into the analysis, and thus disasters are used as a magnifying prism that allows for a broader analysis of societal dynamics. The historical chapter by Dahlberg provides perhaps the most explicit view of disaster being a unique analytical lens that allows for a broader understanding of social practices in past societies. Rubin's chapter on conflict also situates disasters in a larger sociopolitical context, as it argues that disasters might be best considered a catalyst for pre-existing dynamics. In the gender chapter, Horton argues that disasters can bring to the forefront the unequal gender roles and gender socialization that might go unnoticed and unquestioned in everyday life. Likewise, in the chapter on communication by Andersen, and in the chapter on culture by Illner and Holm, disasters are used to inform broader issues of how myths and narratives are produced, and what these can tell us about general power relations in society. Some approaches to communication are concerned with the symbolic, hegemonic, ideological and powerful influence that media can have on society through the prism of disasters, and the cultural approach of *State of Exception* extends the analytical view beyond the immediacy of the disaster, onto the underlying structures of social and political life. Gregersen argues that theology enables the researcher to widen the scope of disaster research to include broader socioeconomic processes and expressions of the divine presence. Even when organization theory is applied to investigate specific accidents it produces analytical linkages that transcend the accident itself – both temporary ones (as in the chapter by Vendelø, where the events leading to the capsizing accident are traced several years back in time), but also ontological links (as in the chapter by

Dolino and Catino, where accidents are linked to an inherent condition in the production of scientific knowledge). Furthermore, in the chapters by Bækkeskov and by Fisker, Hansen and Rand, the authors seize the opportunity to explore different societal and political practices within coordination and financing, while the chapter by Henderson, Berliner and Elsass recommends that further research on mental health and disaster should bridge the gaps between theory and practice in an already highly multidisciplinary field.

When looking forward, one interesting question is how the disciplines contributing to the diverse field of disaster research can be joined into a disaster research community. One central question is whether the research community should consist of independent disciplinary approaches, each contributing different perspectives to the understanding of disasters, or whether the community is best served committing itself to interdisciplinary research, with the aim of generating new approaches to disaster analysis. The answer is not straightforward. Disciplinary boundaries are productive in that they demarcate shared assumptions, questions, methods and languages which facilitate the accumulation of knowledge from a shared platform; while interdisciplinary work is difficult and time-consuming. There is even a risk of diluting the research to a point where it is rejected as shallow by the disciplines the research draws upon. Hence, as individual disciplines have been continuously differentiated and refined over many years, the mixing of disciplines must be done with caution. A good allegory is the anecdote about Marilyn Monroe who allegedly once joked to Albert Einstein that they ought to have children together, as their children would surely grow up to be the most beautiful and intelligent the world had ever seen. Albert Einstein supposedly gave this some thought, but politely declined the offer: 'What if, Ms Monroe, the children inherit my looks and your brain?' Einstein's dilemma is pretty much the same facing interdisciplinary work: there is no guarantee that it will necessarily bring together the best from both disciplines, and not the worst.

Yet, in some sense, the contributors of chapters to this volume have in effect already shown the way. One of the main surprises for us, viewing the final work, is the extent to which interdisciplinary traits already thrive in the midst of clearly demarcated disciplines. Our ambition was to compile a state-of-the-art multidisciplinary book, but some of the individual chapters have strong interdisciplinary backbones. A reason for this might be that the complex and compounded nature of disasters furthers interdisciplinary research, as it is simply necessary in order to comprehend the multilevelled and multidimensional dynamics of disasters. Interdisciplinarity does not imply that the involved disciplines must carry equal weight, but that they are combined in a way that enables the participating scholars to produce other insights than if they were working within only their own discipline. The most obvious interdisciplinary venue for the production of new insights about natural disasters is the one between the natural sciences and the social sciences. Natural hazards are primarily studied in the natural sciences, while the processes through which hazards turn into disasters are primarily, though not exclusively, dealt with in

242 Dahlberg, Rubin and Vendelø

the social sciences. Effectively preventing disasters necessitates insights into both kinds of disciplines, as the complexity of disasters cannot be circumvented by concentrating exclusively on the social side of disasters *or* by understanding natural hazards.

Even within the social sciences, the chapters in this volume forcefully illustrate the vast social complexity and clear interdisciplinary streak that characterize much of the disaster research. An example is the chapter on disaster anthropology by Sørensen and Albris, in which a section on the political life of disasters describes how anthropology and political science intersect. The chapter also draws extensively on cultural research in the bibliography. In the chapter on culture, Illner and Holm introduce an approach rooted in historical analysis, and make several references to theological studies. Even the chapter on law by Lauta presents approaches which are explicitly critical and interdisciplinary, as sociological, anthropological and economical inputs are related to legal issues. In the chapter on pandemics, Bækkeskov applies insights from public administration and political science to illuminate the sorts of organization that global pandemic preparations and responses depend on. Finally, other chapters implicitly call for interdisciplinary research, but stop short of actually conducting it. The chapter on politics by Rubin, despite its strict focus on voting behaviour in times of disasters, ends up calling for inputs from other disciplines, foremost cultural and communication studies, to fully appreciate the electoral effects of disaster narratives and myths.

Of course, our publication also includes chapters that maintain focus on their own disciplinary perspective on disaster research, without interacting or overlapping with other disciplines. In the chapter on disaster communication, Andersen has her hands full accounting for the internal tensions between strands of theories, which view disaster communication as either an intentional practice or as a constitutive practice. Similarly, in the chapter on disaster financing, Fisker, Hansen and Rand present leading research on the newest financial instruments for improving disaster resilience.

When considering interdisciplinarity as an option, one also needs to consider the epistemological and ontological compatibility between the disciplines. Gender research is in and of itself an interdisciplinary field, which often draws on disciplines such as political science, anthropology and law; just as history by necessity must draw upon a variety of other disciplines, such as geography and seismology, when (re)constructing historical narratives of catastrophe. Finance, on the contrary, is a well-established positivistic discipline with limited heterogeneity in its key concepts and a strong quantitative foundation – this might make it more challenging, and perhaps less rewarding, to establish strong links with several of the other disciplines presented. Likewise, the different analytical approaches pursued within each of the disciplines also represent a substantial variation in epistemological and ontological assumptions, which thus must be taken into account when considering the formulation of interdisciplinary disaster research projects. For example, in the chapter on disaster communication, Andersen accounts for a clear rift between positivistic approaches (focusing on cause-and-effect) and post-positivistic approaches (focusing on discursive constructions of power) to communication. Also, the chapter by Illner and Holm introduces a range of cultural approaches, which differ significantly in their perceptions of cultural practices. Some approaches perceive cultural practices as expressions of concrete disaster traumas, whereas the post-modernist approaches completely deconstruct cultural images and narratives of disasters.

Our discussion has shown that disaster research is indeed a multilevelled and multidisciplinary research field. Many of the authors in this book regarded interdisciplinarity both as an option and a challenge for future disaster research. Hence, there is good reason to consider how the growth of interdisciplinary disaster research can be stimulated. One possible source of inspiration is the Changing Disasters project at the University of Copenhagen, where disaster scholars from a range of different research disciplines have gathered in three thematic clusters, and attempt to produce new interdisciplinary disaster research by focusing on: (i) *Imaginations*, addressing social, political, technical and cultural interpretations of disaster; (ii) *Interventions*, studying responses to disasters in transdisciplinary and creative ways; and (iii) *Transformations*, investigating how societies change under the influence of disasters on technical, institutional and societal levels.

Another possible source of inspiration is the newly founded Reykjavík-based Nordic Centre of Excellence on Resilience and Societal Security (NORDRESS), where disaster scholars from fifteen research institutions in the Nordic countries undertake disaster research with the aim of formulating suggestions for how to improve societal resilience in the Nordic societies, to withstand crises caused by natural hazards. Encompassing such different disciplines as geography, psychology, social work and law, the scholars participating in NORDRESS pursue multidisciplinary disaster research by structuring their research activities along thematic dimensions rather than disciplines. This way, resilience is addressed in four separate, yet connected, dimensions: (i) *Individuals*, focusing on mental and physical health effects of disasters; (ii) *Communities*, addressing risk perceptions, community coping strategies and public participation in hazard monitoring and early warning; (iii) *Infrastructures*, studying the effects of extreme weather, floods and mass movements on land, sea and air transport; and (iv) *Institutions*, analysing legislation and regulations within insurance, emergency preparedness, welfare systems and land use.

Establishing such cross-cutting thematic structures for multidisciplinary disaster research is only a necessary first step. The more challenging part is the actual tearing down of well-established disciplinary boundaries in research carried out by groups of researchers who speak very different languages. We hope that the present volume has provided important and useful insights into the language and state-of-the-art research of various disciplines. Such insights are in themselves necessary if multidisciplinary understanding among disaster scholars is to be improved, and interdisciplinary disaster research is to be facilitated. We also hope that our publication has added useful perspectives to the discussion on how to approach disaster research from a multitude of angles. We do not claim to have more than briefly addressed the much broader challenge of how to engage in interdisciplinary disaster research. Yet, we believe this book has shown that true advancements of future disaster research will require innovative approaches, combining competences across many disciplines. We encourage disaster scholars to sometimes invite a little of the chaos and uncertainty that characterizes the subject itself into the research process.

Reference

Dahlberg, R., Johannessen-Henry, C.T., Raju, E., and Tulsani, S. (2015) Resilience in disaster research: Three versions. *Civil Engineering and Environmental Systems*, 32(1–2), 44–54.

Name index

Subject index

For Product Safety Concerns and Information please contact our EU
representative GPSR@taylorandfrancis.com
Taylor & Francis Verlag GmbH, Kaufingerstraße 24, 80331 München, Germany

www.ingramcontent.com/pod-product-compliance
Ingram Content Group UK Ltd.
Pitfield, Milton Keynes, MK11 3LW, UK
UKHW052030210425
457613UK00032BA/853